Roger Paynter
August, 2021

merton: A BIOGRAPHY

merton: A BIOGRAPHY

Monica Furlong

NEW EDITION

LIGUORI
PUBLICATIONS
One Liguori Drive
Liguori, MO 63057-9999
(314) 464-2500

For Una and Leo, with love

Contents

ACKNOWLEDGEMENTS

To Canon A. M. Allchin of Canterbury, who started me re-reading Thomas Merton's writing in 1968.

To Abbot Timothy Kelly, Dom Flavian Burns, Dom James Fox, Brother Patrick Hart, and a number of the Trappist Fathers of Our Lady of Gethsemani, Kentucky, who made me very welcome, and were most patient in answering questions.

To James Laughlin, Tommie O'Callaghan, and Naomi Burton Stone, the Trustees of the Thomas Merton Legacy Trust, who both personally and in their official capacity were extremely kind and helpful.

To Dr. Robert Daggy, Curator of the Thomas Merton Studies Center, Bellarmine College, Louisville, Kentucky, for many kindnesses and much good advice.

To Robert Giroux, Gladys Marcus, Robert Lax, Dom John Eudes Bamberger, Andrew Winser, John Barber, Miguel Greenberg, Fr. John Treece, the Rector of Zion Church, Douglaston, Fr. Irenaeus Herscher, O.F.M., Dr. James Wygal.

To the Headmaster of Oakham School, Rutland, for permission to quote from *The Oakhamian*.

To the many correspondents of Merton whose letters I have been permitted to use.

To Mrs. Susan Shriver, of Chelsea Square, New York, for her hospitality and encouragement.

To Sister Madeleine and the Augustinian Sisters, of Bethanie, Highgate, London, in whose house much of the book was written.

To Mrs. Tina Milam of Louisville.

NOTE ON REFERENCES

Because many of Thomas Merton's works are cited repeatedly in text, the conventional system of notation has not been used here. Instead, all references cited in a chapter are listed at the end of that chapter, numbered consecutively in order of first appearance. Later references to a work (within the same chapter) are indicated by its original number. For example, all references to *The Seven Storey Mountain* in Chapter One are indicated by a [2].

Direct quotations (for which no reference number is given) from associates of Merton are from the author's personal interviews with them.

The acronyms TMSC and TMC appended to reference entries represent the Thomas Merton Studies Centre, Bellarmine College, Louisville, KY 40205; and the Thomas Merton Collection, St. Bonaventure's Library, St. Bonaventure's College, Olean, NY 14760. It is at these two locations that the majority of Merton's correspondence is held.

INTRODUCTION

I am among those who regard Thomas Merton's life as a victorious one, a life that, although it was cut short by accidental death when Merton was fifty-three, was lived to a rare degree of joy and fulfilment; a life that understood and revealed much about the twentieth century and, in particular, the role of religion within it.

There are other ways of looking at Merton. Some see him as a straightforward and traditional Catholic exemplar. Some emphasize his faithful and obedient monasticism, determinedly ignoring the way his views on monasticism, and on much else, changed over the years as the callow youth who entered Gethsemani in his twenties developed into the mature man whose life ended in Bangkok. Some see his final trip to the Orient as an aberration, both geographical and theological, from his stability as monk and Christian. Some feel that his patient devotion to monastic life (nearly thirty years) was itself the aberration, that the Trappists exploited and victimized him (see Edward Rice's book, *The Man in a Sycamore Tree* [1], named after an unpublished novel of Merton's with the same title), that his final trip was a desperate dash for freedom, and his death a kind of unconscious suicide. Some people, particularly in the United States, were and are disturbed by Merton's political stances in the 1960s, by his deep concern with nuclear war, and his involvement with the civil rights movement, with revolutionary factions in South America, and with those opposed to the American presence in Vietnam.

Somehow, through all these points of view, the biographer has to maintain an equilibrium, like a tightrope walker, discovering a balance and a kind of truth between all the extremes.

The starting point, for any biographer of Merton, is *The Seven Storey Mountain* [2], the autobiography he wrote a few years after entering the Abbey of Our Lady of Gethsemani near Bardstown,

Kentucky, a monastery of the Cistercians of the Strict Observance, commonly known as Trappists. In this he described an upbringing in many ways typical of the youth of Western societies in the 1930s—rootless because the old orders of society and the old sanctions of religion had broken down, apparently irretrievably. Merton, like his fellows, experimented with the ideals and panaceas of his time—communism, psychoanalysis, Lawrentian sexuality, jazz, alcohol. In the end he chose, like some other intellectuals of the 1930s, the solution of Catholicism, or rather it chose him, for he underwent a dramatic conversion while a student at Columbia.

Unlike most other Catholic intellectuals, however, he went further, taking vows as monk and priest with the Trappist Order. It is perhaps this crucial phase of his life that is most difficult to interpret and that has been most widely misunderstood. Some who have written about Merton have seen this step purely in terms of heroic self-sacrifice; some have been repelled by the extraordinary harshness of the life and have ignored the austere beauty of its medieval structure and its security for a man who, as Merton was, was orphaned early in life; some have shown a perverse interest in the masochistic elements of Trappist life; some have idealized the life, and Merton himself, into unrecognizably saintly proportions.

What has hitherto been lacking, both because of Merton's own reticence and because of the propriety of his earliest editors in the Order, has been an important key to Merton's motives as a young man in joining the Trappists rather than a more congenial Order such as the Franciscan or the Benedictine, or, as he often wished, the Carthusian or Camaldolese. The question is less baffling than it seems. Because of an event that happened in his nineteenth year at Cambridge in England, Merton suffered an excruciating sense of guilt and a conviction that a lifetime's expiation was demanded of him, and this certainly played an important part in taking him into the Trappists.

He did not, mercifully, carry this burden for the rest of his life. The enormous, and enormously painful, psychological development he went through in the 1950s, in which he struggled bravely with neurotic symptoms and disillusionment with the religious life, released him from his old self as from a prison. He moved, in the 1960s, into a naturalness, a compassion for himself and others, a concern with the wider questions that beset mankind—war, race, poverty—that seem a world away from the pious young man of the 1940s. There is continuity, however—an attractive enthusiasm and

Church Fathers but later over the whole range of modern literature and modern thought. Although he wrote some theology, Merton was less a theologian than a mystic—his deepest concern from the time of his conversion onward was the deepening of his relationship with God, and to this end he read, meditated, and conformed to the exceedingly rigid structure of Cistercian life.

As the years went by and Vatican II approached, both the Cistercian structure and Merton's own attitude to it altered somewhat. The old Rule was relaxed, and Merton, having loyally followed its discipline over so many years, became more relaxed himself in the carrying out of his vows, although he broke none of them except in the trifling, inevitable ways common to all religious. It was more that his needs had changed, that structure was no longer so important to him as solitude on the one hand and wider contacts on the other: friendships developed with writers, poets, people involved in political conflict, a Catholic woman theologian, Protestants, members of other religions, and a handful of people whom he valued mainly for their love and support—a nun; a psychiatrist in Louisville; a housewife in Louisville and her family; a photographer with a social conscience; his literary agent, Naomi Burton; an Anglican clergyman; a Dominican monk; a Benedictine monk; and one or two people he was close to in his own community. The solitude found expression in his going to live as a hermit in a cinderblock hut on a hillside about ten minutes' walk away from the Abbey, half hidden among trees and with a splendid view of the famous Kentucky "knobs," or hills, which Merton loved. He was not a hermit in the old "Desert Father" sense—he was still part of the life of the Abbey, received many visitors, answered letters, depended on his brother monks for food and drink. But the relative solitude gave him a chance to live close to nature and to the seasons and to explore his own loneliness and identity in a way that was to be very important for his religious development.

He was helped in all this not only by Christian mysticism and spirituality but also by a wide knowledge of Oriental religions, an interest that had begun superficially in his student days and been set aside in his early years at Gethsemani, but that returned later with a deep and fruitful fascination, first with Zen (partly through the influence of D T. Suzuki, whom he knew and much admired) and then with Taoism, Buddhism, and Hinduism. His understanding of these other approaches to God and religion in no way superseded or modified his understanding of the Christian religion or the Christian Fathers, but, by approaching the spiritual quest at unexpected angles, they opened up new ways of thought and new ways of experiencing that invigorated and released him (this was particularly true of Zen and Taoism, with their humour and gaiety).

For fourteen years of his life at Gethsemani, he was first Master of Students (men training for the priesthood) and then Master of Novices. Both jobs were hard work, involving the preparing of lectures that presupposed a wide and deep knowledge of the Church Fathers, of monastic history, and of the way the Rule had been and continued to be newly interpreted by each generation of monks. In the latter case, in particular, it also involved a real interest in the young monks, in their spiritual and psychological problems, and in the form of training that would help them most. The task of direction deepened Merton's psychological understanding immeasurably, throwing light on problems of his own as well as those of others.

A major problem in his own life was that of authority. In the last decade of his life in particular, he suffered under what he felt at times was an abuse of authority, yet showed what one or two friends outside regarded as an excessive submissiveness to it, a submissiveness that seemed to go beyond the required "obedience." This led at times to bitter and distressing conflict between his Abbot, Dom James Fox, and himself, a conflict he was perhaps near to resolving when Dom James retired and Dom Flavian Burns took his place as Abbot.

Dom Flavian left Merton free to go to Conferences and meetings outside the Abbey if he wished to do so and, finally, to go on the last trip to Asia, where he was to meet his death at Bangkok. By this stage of life, he was deeply involved in, and committed to, a number of important causes—ecumenism, the coming together of Eastern and Western religions, the political coming together of East and West, the struggle for peace, and a new approach to many people who had been seriously deprived—the American Indians, the migrant workers, the blacks, Mexican-Americans, and Puerto Ricans, the poor peoples of Latin America. It was as if all the years of prayer and personal struggle in the comparative isolation of the monastery had filled him with a great love and compassion, which now overflowed in a huge longing to help humanity in the agonizing effort to build a world that contained love and justice and peace.

Behind all these labours was another question, one of great

personal importance for him: What did it mean to be a monk, a contemplative, in the twentieth century? In a way his whole twenty-seven years at Gethsemani had been an attempt to find the answer to this problem, and as the years stripped away the obvious answers and the comforting illusions he felt he was left with little but his humanity. Like Dietrich Bonhoeffer in his Nazi prison, he began to see that the highest spiritual development was to be "ordinary," to be fully a man, in the way few human beings succeed in becoming so simply and naturally themselves. He began to see the monk not, as he had believed in youth, as someone special, undertaking feats of incredible ascetic heroism for the love of God, but as one who was not afraid to be simply "man," who, as he lived near to nature and his appetites, was the "measure" of what others might be if society did not distort them with greed or ambition or lust or desperate want.

In Merton, as with other ascetics in Christian history, reaching this point of simplicity coincided with a movement of self-acceptance and self-forgiveness, and perhaps too, an awareness of the feminine principle, so important within the Catholic Church and yet such a source of fear. Women, more or less excluded from his life from the time he began to think of going into a monastery, became important to him again, valued and listened to, both for themselves and for the clues they could give him about his own inner growth.

"There is no problem," he wrote when he saw the great black Shiva lingam on the shore at Mahabalipuram in Madras a few days before his death. "It is washed by the sea, and the sea is woman: it is no void, no question." [3]

Much of his struggle on the long road to becoming a contemplative had to do with the problem of identity. The hermit, or just the person who tries to explore solitude, may no longer be reassured by the affirmation of others, and may suffer deeply from the emptiness caused by loneliness, feeling that they have ceased to exist. On the far side of this emptiness, Merton believed, there is an identity scarcely dreamed, an identity to be found only in the religious search, and one that sets the contemplative free to love his or her fellow human beings.

And so his life flowed toward its end, by way of the moment of great clarity, a few days before his death in 1968 when he saw the huge reclining Buddhas of Polonnaruwa in Ceylon and felt that he had found what he was looking for; that these great holy figures, all around him like benevolent mothers and fathers, had released the love and joy in his heart that he had been seeking all his life, that he had come home, and the home was God.

Much earlier in his life, Merton had written about St. John of the Cross's description of the Unitive way, as the soul moved into detachment through the Night of the Senses, and into blindness and naked trust in the Dark Night of the soul, discovering on the journey the Prayer of Quiet and striving toward the egoless state of Union with God. By the time Merton died, he would probably have had less patience with such a schematic way of charting the labours of the soul, and it is, in any case, part of the essence of the *via negationis* (way of negation) that the soul ceases for much of the time to understand or believe or hope very much in anything except in the mysterious will that God has for it. Yet, to those who look on, Merton seems one of the very few in the twentieth century who dared to follow in the footsteps of the saints, who revealed some of their love and self-forgetfulness (as if they had found a centre outside the ego and were focused on that). It is not surprising that one of the holy men Merton visited in India recognized him at once as *rangjung Sangay* (a natural Buddha).

However, it would be to miss the point of all that Merton struggled to achieve if we were to label him "saint" and use him as a dummy to be dressed up in garments that say more about our own illusions of holiness than anything Merton himself affected or believed. I have avoided the reverential approach, have tried to see him as the normal man he was, with his fair share, perhaps more than his fair share, of human frailties. It was this base metal which, in the marvellous alchemy of the spiritual journey, became transmuted into gold.

References

1. Edward Rice. *The Man in the Sycamore Tree*. New York: Doubleday, Image Books, 1972.
2. Thomas Merton. *The Seven Storey Mountain*. New York: Harcourt Brace, 1948; London: SPCK, 1990. Also published abridged as *Elected Silence* (London: Burns, Oates, 1949).
3. Thomas Merton. *The Asian Journal of Thomas Merton*, ed. Naomi Burton, Brother Patrick Hart, and James Laughlin. New York: New Directions, 1973.

INTRODUCTION TO
NEW EDITION

In the autumn of 1978 I set off for Louisville, Kentucky, to research a biography of Thomas Merton. It was an ambition I had held ever since the late 1960s when I read an essay of Merton's called "The Cell" in the magazine *Sobornost* (later published in *Contemplation in a World of Action*). I had by then been a Christian for nearly twenty years, but I seemed to find that fewer and fewer Christian writers were talking about the world as I was experiencing it; their interests seemed too narrow, too out of touch with the terrifying political developments of the period, too ignorant of the worlds of art and literature, and the attempts of artists and writers to speak about the twentieth century.

In all of these ways I found Merton an acute and exciting writer. A fascinating irony was that, back in the 1940s and early 1950s, no one was more resolutely narrow than Merton. In *The Seven Storey Mountain* and the writing that immediately followed it, he was preposterously telling Christians not to read newspapers or listen to the radio, but rather to live in a sort of Amish seclusion. He thought they should treat the world as a place so contaminated that they should have nothing to do with it.

What I guessed as I began to read Merton's recent writing and explore his thinking was that some huge inner change had occurred in him which had released enormous energy. It was this lack of energy that I had deplored in other Christian writers, and I was intensely curious about why he was so different. Asked by the publisher Collins if there was a book I wanted to write I said promptly that I would like to write a biography of Merton.

John Howard Griffin, Merton's chosen biographer, had died before completing the work, and both Collins and I hoped for a bit that his American publisher would choose me as his successor. By underground channels I learned that as a woman, a Britisher, and an Anglican, I did not fill the bill as a potential biographer of Merton, and in fact Michael Mott got the job, and that seemed to be that. I continued with my job with the BBC that I had been on the point of giving up to write the book.

The idea, however, would not just go away. I continued to have fantasies about writing it, and to think of things I wanted to say, and on a brief vacation in America in 1977 I could not resist taking a plane down to Louisville and visiting the Thomas Merton Studies Center at Bellarmine College, where the vast majority of Merton's papers are kept. Far from feeling that my chance had been snatched from me, I had an irresistible sense that I must go ahead, and I even thought I might write rather a good book. And so in 1978, with a very much smaller advance than Collins had talked about when it looked as if I might be the official biographer, I finally set to work.

I stayed in Louisville for two long periods, going through Merton's entire correspondence (a huge task), reading lesser known articles that I had not seen before, going out to Gethsemani to interview Dom James and a number of the monks, visiting Merton's hermitage (and being photographed by Bro. Patrick Hart sitting in Merton's chair), interviewing local people who had known Merton well, and visiting places he had been to in the last few years of his life when the enclosure was less strict. Quite apart from the interest of the job I enjoyed discovering sides of America rather off the tourist track. I enjoyed watching the Fall in Kentucky, particularly at the nearby Shakertown of Pleasant Hill, and even more I enjoyed the glory of the dogwood trees in the following spring.

In December I went to New York for a symposium on Merton, and had an experience which, while somewhat comic, was potentially dangerous, when, getting out of the wrong subway in an abortive attempt to attend a service commemorating Merton's death, I managed to lose myself for more than an hour in a dark and deserted Harlem!

The book was published here in 1981 and was enthusiastically received. There was some shock about the fact that, as an undergraduate at Cambridge, Merton had fathered a child out of wedlock. A good deal later I discovered there had been some resentment in Catholic circles (by no means all) that I had depicted Merton's Abbot, Dom James Fox, in a somewhat tyrannical light. Letters came protesting that it was Dom James' duty, as the Abbot responsible for Merton's spiritual welfare, to impose discipline upon him. Naomi Burton, at a meeting in America when I was helping make a programme about Merton for the BBC, rounded angrily upon me and said that Dom James was a friend of hers, and I had hurt his feelings. Whether he was hurt, I am not sure. I hope not. Word eventually reached me from Gethsemani of his rather humorous response when he read my book. "I guess every book has to have a villain, and in this case I am it!"

However, comments did cause me to consider whether I had been unfair to Dom James, and, as part of the same process, whether I had shown too much partiality for Merton. I *am* partial to Merton—it would be dishonest to deny it—this is why I was prepared to put so much labour into writing the book. The particular axe I was grinding in writing it was exploring a personality to whom I was attracted and found deeply interesting. Not all biographers have a partiality for their subject, but I submit that one way of writing a biography involves a certain warmth for the subject, and such a warmth I had. However, this should not lead to unfairness to the subject's contemporaries, and I would feel that this showed serious unbalance in me if I had been so unfair.

Writing some years later I have slightly different perspectives on Merton from the ones I had at the time I wrote the book. I am readier to see the "prima donna" streak in him (perhaps because I have since observed it closely in other clergy), and to acknowledge how difficult this must have been at close quarters both for Dom James and for other monks. Bizarrely, this problem has continued long after Merton's death. I have not forgotten the rueful observations of Abbot Timothy Kelly, in 1978, to the effect that no one wanted to know about the life, struggles and achievements of Gethsemani in the post-Merton period, only to reimagine Merton back into his monastic setting.

I also feel a certain wryness about the whole hermit aspect of Merton's life. Certainly in the late 1960s this was a more unusual idea than it is now, but I suspect that in me, as in others, it produced an awe that I no longer quite feel. What has come to trouble me as the years have passed is the danger of self-dramatization that such a self-conscious exercise of solitude brings about (and, in fact, self-dramatization may be a risk with all kinds of monasticism). The world is, after all, full of men and women voluntarily or involuntarily living alone and making a go of it, without the kudos associated with "being a hermit." If you want to live alone in our vast, impersonal society, there is nothing easier, though you may not get the attention, the visitors, and the invitations to speak and write that Merton got. Many old ladies struggle with the secrets of surviving in solitude, and many old men go through the identity crisis that Merton depicts the apprentice-hermit undergoing, but they do not publish journals about it, and no one pats them on the back for their heroism. They know what it is to be a "marginal person" in a way that Merton could scarcely have dreamed of.

Another change in my understanding of Merton, though only slight, since writing the book, is due to increased information. Michael Mott's book *The Seven Mountains of Thomas Merton* (Sheldon Press 1984) explored a part of Merton's life of which I had heard only the faintest rumours when I was writing. Recovering from an operation in hospital, in 1966, Merton fell in love with a young nurse, who returned his affection, and for six months he struggled painfully with this relationship and his monastic vocation. The vocation won, but at great cost. I had hitherto believed that Merton's exploration of "the feminine," what Jungians would call "the anima," had been almost entirely in terms of dreams about women (and very remarkable some of these were), and friendships with women (and very remarkable some of these were too). That he was actually able to project his feelings on to a woman, to give and receive love in a way he had found so difficult as a young man, despite the powerful monastic tradition prohibiting it, moves me, and deepens my respect for him. It is worth recording what Mott makes very clear, that Dom James showed kindness and understanding of this incident, though it came in a period when there was still a good deal of conflict between the two of them.

At that particular stage of his life almost everything Merton did at Gethsemani was regarded as subversive, and I believe that Merton's subversion needs more attention than it has hitherto received. Merton was a man of considerable intelligence, ability, imagination and passion, who put himself freely (or as freely as any of us ever do anything) under the discipline of the Trappists. He did this in his late twenties with tremendous ardour, and the ardour for a long time helped him not to notice not just that he was in many ways a square peg in a round hole, but that some of the disciplines he was subjected to were unhelpful, life-denying, and had more to say about human obsession and repression than about leading a Christian life.

His reluctance to notice the root cause of his distress was extreme—so extreme that it took a number of minor nervous breakdowns and many physical symptoms before he could bring himself to consider that he might be in the wrong place—that the strenuous activism of the Trappists was antipathetic to him. He was also beginning to question many aspects of the Catholic Church. His ability to criticize was released in a desperate struggle with Dom James during the mid-1950s when Merton asked for a transfer to another order, the Carthusians or the Camaldolese; Dom James made absolutely sure, by writing secretly to Archbishop Montini, that this could not happen. It was further honed by some psychotherapeutic work he did with Dr. James Wygal, in which he learned to see further into his own psychology.

I suspect that it is impossible to be even-handed as we consider the conflict between Merton and Dom James over the possibility of his leaving. Those who believe ends justify means, or that Abbots are usually right, must see Merton as a trouble-maker, or, as Dom James described him, "a neurotic," always wanting to go where the grass is greener. Those who believe some measure of autonomy must be allowed, even to monks, some recognition of the mysteriousness of human growth, must stand aghast at Dom James' determined wire-pulling to keep Merton in the community, and must question the secret, behind-the-scenes correspondence, which blocked any chance of a transfer, and which finally disenchanted Merton with Trappist life.

Disenchanted he may have been, but he stayed, and, with minor (and one or two major) infringements, continued to show great loyalty to his vows. He lived the life with style and passion, and many of us who aspire to very different sorts of life still find him an exemplar, mainly for the courage and sense of adventure we find in him. At the time that he died the Catholic Church was digesting the huge insights and revelations of the Second Vatican Council. Since then it has again swung in the direction of conservatism, a battening down of the hatches, with the emphasis on obedience and authority, of the sort that Merton had questioned vigorously within the small world of Gethsemani. It is tempting to wonder what Merton would make of the Catholic Church if he was alive now.

Perhaps because he suffered so much over the blind requirement of "obedience" (when he was forbidden by his Order, for instance, to publish any material about peace, it being such a controversial subject, in the very year that Pope John published the admirable *Pacem in Terris*), he had already considered at length the problem of "authority" and the dangers of "obedience" for the individual. "Obedience," he noted, was the justification Eichmann had given for his role in the concentration camps. Obedience was the watchword of all totalitarian systems, the device which made people act in irresponsible and less than human ways.

Another dehumanizing device was what he called "abstract" thinking, the sort that made it possible to order canisters of gas to destroy "units"—men, women and children—in the camps. Efficiency was harnessed to lunatic ends. Taking refuge in a language drained of humanity it was possible for "decent" people to agree to, and assist, criminal acts of the greatest barbarity.

Reading accounts of the Eichmann trial and Hannah Arendt's studies of the Nazi war criminals, Merton brooded deeply on the lessons of racial genocide, and on what he thought Christians should learn from them. One lesson he took from it was the danger of "tribalism," and he immediately acted upon it. He held meetings at the hermitage with local rabbis, and with other Christian "tribes" with whom Catholics usually had nothing to do—Southern Baptists, Episcopalians and others—seeking common ground between them, putting a human face to ideas and beliefs.

He was troubled too about the tribalism of the Cold War, of the two implacable enemies—Russia and America—needing each other as objects of hate. Unlike his own early years in the monastery when nothing was told to the monks about political events—it was over a year later that they learned of the dropping of the atom bomb on Hiroshima—he made sure that the novices were fully aware of the events of their world, that their spirituality was woven deeply into the events of their time. The speech he made on the day of his death was about East–West reconciliation.

Having read extensively about Hiroshima he became, for a time, invaded by the horror of atomic war. In print he attacked American pundits like Herman Kahn who talked glibly of "rebuilding" America after a nuclear war. He was passionately involved with the issues of Civil Rights, corresponding with its leaders, and was passionately against the Vietnam war. He supported Fr. Dan

Berrigan, and the "Catonsville Nine" who burned their draft cards in protest.

He became fascinated by what Christianity had to learn from other world religions. He worked at Buddhist forms of meditation, and, on his final journey to the East, spent time with spiritual teachers from the Hindu, Jain, Muslim and Buddhist traditions, most notably with the Dalai Lama. The deepest spiritual experience of his life occurred four days before his death among the giant Buddhas of Polonnaruwa in Sri Lanka. "I don't know when in my life I have ever had such a sense of beauty and spiritual validity running together in one illumination. . . . I know and have seen what I was obscurely looking for. I don't know what else remains but I have now seen and have pierced through the surface and have got beyond the shadow and the disguise."[1]

Merton's time in the hermitage, as, to a lesser extent, his whole experience at Gethsemani, made him closely aware of the natural world, and, inevitably, of the danger to it from a society in the grip of consumerism, and with no sense of the necessary dependency of humans on the plants and creatures of their world.

Merton, in short, used his long training as a contemplative to discover new perspectives on the world, ones which the rest of us, more slowly, have been laboriously exploring since his death. In the trite phrase, he was "a man ahead of his time." He was clear-minded enough, and cared enough, and in a sense was free enough, to think through vital issues with a love and generosity towards the world which is, perhaps, the opposite of "abstract" thinking.

For him, the turning point was the moment, now famous among Merton fans, when, on a trip to Louisville, he discovered he had burst out of isolation and superiority.

At the corner of Fourth and Walnut, in the centre of the shopping district, I was suddenly overwhelmed with the realization that I loved all those people, that they were mine and I theirs, that we could not be alien to one another even though we were total strangers. It was like waking from a dream of separateness, of spurious self-isolation in a special world, the world of renunciation and supposed holiness. . . . The sense of liberation from an illusory difference was such a relief and such a joy to me that I almost laughed out loud. . . . [2]

The difficulty of living alongside other people, he noted, was to do with our fear of losing our identity, our fear that we may not have an identity at all. There is, he said, a sense in which our identities *are* illusory, and the fear that this creates tempts us to pump up a "false identity" to console ourselves for our sense of our nothingness. For Merton the only way to have a true identity was to find ourselves in God's purpose for us, as a flower or animal does, without fretting or false importance. "Each particular being, in its individuality, its concrete nature and entity, with all its own characteristics and its private qualities and its own inviolable identity, gives glory to God by being precisely what He wants it to be here and now."[3]

Another way of coming at the problem is to ask how we bear our loneliness, our sense of cut-off-ness from the world around us. Merton's paradoxicial answer to this is "enter into solitude", embrace the pain of loneliness to the point where we perceive just how illusory it is. Somehow or other, sooner or later, the Christian must voluntarily enter the desert, there to discover that far from being the place of desolation it appears, once the eye gets used to it it is full of extraordinary beauties of its own.

The desert for us, as it was for Jacob, is the place of encounter with God. It is there, says Merton, that we find God, *Qui Est*, the *I am* of the burning bush. "It is as though the Name were waiting in the desert for me, and had been preparing this meeting from eternity and in this particular place, this solitude chosen for me. . . . living in the presence of this great Name I gradually become the one He wills me to be."[4]

Merton's own desert was not in a bare sandy landscape or a city slum, but in the heart of a monastery where he felt alone and miserable, and in a cinderblock hut facing the Kentucky hills. There are as many deserts as people—the place where the meeting is prepared and where there is an opportunity to take the risk of embracing the experience of entering into solitude. It is here that there is a chance to "know God."

Merton does not underestimate the troubling, baffling effort involved in trying to reach out to God. For a start our minds are accustomed to a different kind of knowing—what Merton calls "the arrogant gaze of our investigating mind"—which does not get us very far. To know God we have to perform a sort of somersault to "become aware of ourselves as known by Him." This *is* our identity—we "possess" God in the proportion that we know ourselves to be possessed. What we thought we knew and understood about the world turns out to be fairly useless—so much junk to be jettisoned so that we can embark on the original path to which God summons us. But only as we follow the path do we discover "who we are."

In Merton's case the path led him away from the callow young man who despised "creatures" to an intense involvement with the world in all its forms. It was, in many ways, a joyous progress. What bubbles through his later letters, gazes out from the pictures of him, and sings through much of his life, is a wonderful quality of lightheartedness, as if he has seen the Great Joke. The Joke is the sense of the cosmic Dancer "playing" through us. "It is He alone that one takes seriously. But to take Him seriously is to find joy and spontaneity in everything, for everything is gift and grace."[4]

London, 1995

References

1. Thomas Merton. *The Asian Journal of Thomas Merton*, ed. Naomi Burton, Brother Patrick Hart, and James Laughlin. New York: New Directions, 1973.
2. Thomas Merton. *Conjectures of a Guilty Bystander*. New York: Doubleday, 1966.
3. Thomas Merton. *Seeds of Contemplation*. New York: New Directions, 1949; London: Greenwood Press, 1983.
4. Thomas Merton. *The Cell. Contemplation in a World of Action*. New York: Doubleday, 1971.

Part One

1

"OH SUN! OH JOLI!"

✸

Thomas Merton was born at 9.30 P.M. on January 31, 1915, at 1 Rue du 4 Septembre, at Prades, France, in the Eastern Pyrenees. He had blue eyes and reddish-brown hair (soon to turn blond) and weighed two kilos (4.4 pounds). He was registered at the *mairie* (town hall) as Tom Feverel Merton, Tom after his godfather Tom Bennett, and because Ruth Merton, his mother, disliked the name Thomas.

Ruth kept a diary of the progress of this first-born child, to be presented eventually to her mother-in-law in New Zealand. It was called "Tom's Book" and inscribed on the front page in her handwriting "To Granny with Tom's best love 1916." [1] To begin with, it records the details, so fascinating to parents and grandparents, of the baby's weight and diet, of the first time he raised his head, smiled, sat up alone, cut his first tooth, crawled, and so on. Ruth Merton emerges as a very devoted if slightly obsessional mother, feeding the baby herself until he was ten months old, well read in the latest manuals about caring for infants, and extremely conscientious about diet, hygiene, rest, and mental stimulus for her baby. Her loving observation of her little boy is often touching, and sometimes strikingly in character with the adult Merton.

From the beginning, he was a strong, active, intelligent baby, responding intently to the world around him.

He smiled for the first time in March! And could turn over in his bed, or, if we put him on his stomach he doubled up his little leg, pushed hard, and rolled over on his back. He said "aye" in many different and expressive ways, watched and talked to a flower, and hit out at a rattle swung on a string before his eyes.

May 1915. If you offered him a finger he pulled himself up, and loved doing it. When we went out he sat up against his cushions and looked about him with interest, so that old peasants remarked "Qu'il a l'air eveille!" [He notices everything!]

On the twentieth June he made a desperate effort to creep and screamed with rage that he did not succeed." [1]

(Merton read these pages many years later and against this entry wrote "Typical!!!!")

Soon baby Tom was climbing out of his cradle, pulling himself up to his feet, holding out his arms to be taken, and beginning to eat some solid food. He was not very interested in toys but loved watching other children, the river, flowers, and the fire. He was weaned, he learned his first word "Deh!" ("There!"), he was circumcised (by his godfather, the doctor Tom Bennett, who later became his guardian), and at a year old he began to walk.

In January 1916, his mother noted that he took a keen delight in books, "knowing in just which one is the picture of the Frog, the Owl or the dog and finding them for you with pleasure." Ten months later, she said that

> Tom has never cared to amuse himself with toys—except books—and has never evinced any interest in using his hands to do over and over again any simple little action such as putting a cork in a bottle. All the books I have read on child psychology presuppose that every normal child will be absorbed for a long time in such exercises. I feel inclined to say that it is an individual trait in Tom to lack this interest.
>
> He has always demanded constant change of occupation and is happiest when he is busy at something which keeps his whole body in movement such as running back and forth bringing things from one place to another. Or he will look for hours at pictures in books, recognizing all the objects he knows and sometimes pretending to read, holding the book right side up always, and moving his eyes across the printed page. [1]

Like most tiny children, he enjoyed music, dancing, and strumming on the piano, and he liked to sing to himself when he was playing "but without much tune."

"When we go out he seems conscious of everything. Sometimes he puts up his arms and cries out 'Oh sun! Oh joli!' Often it is to the birds or trees that he makes these pagan hymns of joy. Sometimes he throws himself on the ground to see the 'cunnin' little ants' (where he learned that expression, I do not know!)." [1] He also used to wave his arms at the landscape crying "Oh colour." (*Colour* was a word he used to mean landscape, his father's pictures, and all the paraphernalia of painting.)

Little Tom's energy was tremendous. Only by singing to him could his mother persuade him to the relative inactivity of being dressed and undressed. Otherwise he kicked and screamed. "It tired him less to listen to words and songs than to resist with all his might. . . . He never would be rocked, never wanted to be 'held,' and has never in his life fallen to sleep unless he was expressly put to bed for that purpose. He has fought sleep always and is rarely quiet a single moment while he is awake." [1] Like most children of around a year old, he reacted uncertainly to strangers but warmly to those he knew well. "At the mere sight of some people (women especially, as he generally liked men) he would scream in fear and anger, and we had to be very careful about letting people approach him suddenly. Others, he treated with marked rudeness and disgust, slapping them, frowning and muttering to himself. Little boys and soldiers he liked especially, and still does." [1]

The Mertons left Prades when Tom was about a year old and went to the United States to live with Ruth's parents at Douglaston, Long Island. Wartime France had become too difficult for a foreigner not in uniform. At Douglaston, Tom began to notice and enjoy other children much more.

> Here . . . there is a "crowd" of boys who play out after school and when we meet them Tom cries out with delight "Hello, Billy! Hello, Philip!" Then when he gets near them he is a bit shy but starts showing off, running around shouting, then throwing himself on the ground and kicking up his heels like a colt. . . . Before going to bed or just when he is getting up he often tells over to himself all the things which have happened. Sometimes I believe he talks about his dreams for very often when he wakes up he says Prades' names and a word or two in French, though at other times he is quite furious if I dare to talk to him in French. Once he said "Bonjour Georgette, Bonjour Germaine, Bonjour Buddha, Bonjour Victoire." Victoire is the Vignolles' cat, whose name Tom never tried to pronounce when we were in France. He also says "Madame Vignolle" now, though he called her "Olie" before we left Prades. . . . I heard him saying "Bonjour Georgette" with such delight one day that I went to see what he had found. He was standing on tip toe looking at a photograph of a girl who certainly very much resembles Georgette. [1]

Tom was still impossible to bathe or dress unless Ruth sang to him and she sang "Il était une bergère," "Pussy Cat Low," "Bye Baby Bunting," and "Au Clair de la Lune." He pretended to read and was overheard muttering, "John, John! Gwey goose gone! Fox! Den oh! Den oh!"

He loved the three dogs in the Douglaston household, Laddie, Chinner, and Teazle; enjoyed running errands and being useful, saying to himself, "That's the way" when he got things right. "He is very sure footed, very prudent and cautious and seems to have excellent control of his muscles. But he has not much patience and never bothers to do anything difficult, but flings it away in disgust, often with cries of rage." [1] Like all little children, he amused people by the freshness and directness of his observation. Thus, when his Uncle Harold played tennis, he exclaimed "Oh look at Uncle Hicky kill a fly!" [1]

But he was a thoughtful and sensitive little boy. "He already knew the wind and rain when we came here, and always holds out his hands to feel them. Lately he has taken to saying 'Monsieur Wind' and I heard him at the window saying 'What's he say, Monsieur Wind?' then answering his own question (which is a favourite game of his) by a long drawn 'Oo-oo-oo' supposed to be the voice of the wind. He has always been good at imitating sounds. Before he could talk he used to chant a peculiar little 'Dah-hou!' meant to be the church bells of Prades and *very* like them." [1]

When he reached his second birthday, Ruth noted that he weighed 30 pounds, was 34 inches tall, and had sixteen teeth, commenting that he was above average in all three respects. She wrote down his vocabulary, which amounted to some 160 words, many of them bird names.

At two years old, then, Tom was a very intelligent, very active, very well-cared-for little boy. And what of the mother who wrote so attentively about him?

Ruth Merton was the daughter of Samuel Adams Jenkins and Martha Baldwin. Sam Jenkins was born in 1862 in Bristol, Ohio, one of seven children, and rose from fairly humble beginnings to become a very successful businessman. He began by running a small stationery, news, and book shop at Zanesville, Ohio, where he had grown up and gone to school. Zane Grey, the writer of Westerns, was a native son of Zanesville, and local rumour had it that Grey had stolen his reading matter regularly from Sam Jenkins' shop. The Jenkinses left Zanesville to start another business in Philadelphia, which failed after a couple of years, but then Sam was invited to join Grosset & Dunlap, the New York publishers, and he quickly became famous for his brilliant sales schemes, a showmanship that really sold books and that included, for example, the insight that the growing movie industry, far from killing the novel, might help to sell it on an unprecedented scale. He made enough money to live comfortably even during the years of the Depression and to give a great deal of financial help to his son-in-law and his grandsons. In 1914 he and Martha built a fine house in Douglaston, Long Island, where Martha was later to care for her grandsons as well as follow her own bent, painting china.

Ruth and Harold Jenkins were born in 1887 and 1889. Ruth graduated from Bradford Academy (now Bradford College in Haverhill, Massachusetts) in 1909. In the Bradford yearbook, she is described as "cleverest," "most artistic," and having "the keenest sense of humor" and the little caption beneath her photograph (a very serious-faced girl with the high-necked blouse and upswept hair of the period) says "And still the wonder grew,/That one small head could carry all she knew." She was a talented girl who used to dance to entertain her classmates, acted in plays, and wrote well for the college journal—articles, poems, and stories.

When she left Bradford, Ruth attended the École Nationale des Arts Decoratifs in Paris, and she studied under a Canadian painter, Percyval Tudor Hart, who had a studio in Paris, for three years. She travelled a good deal on the continent and in England, and was a passionate Francophile, preferring the French language to any other and learning the art of French cooking. Later she contributed to *American Cookery* and wrote an article for the *Ladies Home Journal* about housekeeping in France. On a questionnaire sent out by her old college, she described her occupation as "interior decorator." Also, she had not given up her ambitions as a painter. Merton remembers her going out into the French countryside and painting landscapes under a large umbrella.

The grown-up Merton described his mother—guided partly by a picture as well as by recollection—as a "slight, thin, sober little person with a serious and somewhat anxious and very sensitive face." [2] Her diary, although indicating great love for her little boy, also indicates a slightly chilling detachment. Even allowing for the pride middle class parents often feel at having read the latest baby books and knowing the latest theories of child development, the emphasis on "what the scientists tell us," the comparison with what is "normal" and the curiously detached way (not evident in the extracts I have quoted) in which she notes every minute change in feeding, is perhaps a little ominous.

Toward the end of his life, Merton confessed to a very intelligent woman friend, with whom he was having a disagreement, that he found "cerebral" women diffficult; he believed this was because he had experienced his mother as "cerebral." In his autobiography, he writes somewhat bitterly of her perfectionism and of his sense that she had unrealized expectations of him. He remembered her as "worried, precise, quick, critical of me, her son. . . . It seems to me now, that Mother must have been a person full of insatiable dreams and of great ambition after perfection: perfection in art, in interior decoration, in dancing, in housekeeping, in raising children. Maybe that is why I remember her mostly as worried: since the imperfection of myself, her first son, had been a great deception. . . . I was nobody's dreamchild." [2] Ruth's high expectations seem to have taken from Merton that sense of total acceptance, that conviction of being a deeply good and satisfactory person, that children of less critical mothers enjoy, although both physically and mentally she continued to care meticulously for his development.

Merton's father, Owen, had met Ruth at Percyval Tudor Hart's studio, where he was also a student. Owen Merton was born at Christchurch, in New Zealand, in 1887. His father, Alfred James Merton, had been born at Rangiora, New Zealand: *his* father, Charles, had been the village schoolmaster at Stoke-by-Nayland in Suffolk, England, and had married the nanny of the vicar's household. Alfred was gifted as a musician and for many years was the organist and choirmaster at Christ's College, at Christchurch, New Zealand. Here Owen received part of his education, leaving early to study art at the Canterbury School of Art and going to England when he was seventeen to continue his studies. Alfred had married Gertrude Grierson, a very intelligent and gifted woman. Gertrude had been born in Cardiff in 1855 and had sailed to New Zealand when she was nine, when her father John Grierson had settled in Christchurch. She was one of the first women to attend University College, Canterbury, where she won a senior scholarship in English and German. She taught at Bingsland School in Avonside, and Christchurch West School, and eventually opened a school of her own. Gertrude loved flowers and reading and, as young Tom discovered when she visited America, was deeply pious. She lived to the age of 101.

Alfred and Gertrude encouraged Owen's artistic ambitions; his mother even arranged a show of his work in New Zealand while he was away in London. Owen became a reasonably successful artist, elected to the Royal Society of British Artists in London and eventually making a tolerable living from his work. He was in the main a watercolourist, specializing in landscapes, and he seemed to be most at home painting in hot climates—in North Africa and southern France. At one time he was on the fringes of the Stieglitz group in New York but left America before sharing their success, and in London, when he exhibited at the Leicester Galleries, his work was praised by Roger Fry.

He was, above all, an original and independent-minded man, not afraid to make his lifestyle fit his beliefs. It took courage for a New Zealander in Europe to stay out of uniform in World War I, as he did, an action that cost him friendships. "I have sifted out my real sincere friends in these three years," [3] Owen Merton wrote to an artist friend in 1917. Like most artists, he felt that art and personal relationships were what life is about, and that war, however justified, is a monstrous interruption of reality. In another wartime letter, he wrote, "We ourselves are some of the very few who are out of trouble for the time being, and we are pretty selfish to be as we are, but we are selfish on account of little Tom chiefly, and so far I do think I am worth more to Ruth and him than to the armies." [4]

The "selfishness" that made Owen Merton reluctant to go and fight as a soldier did not apply elsewhere in his life. He was profoundly aware of the kind of selfless dedication demanded of the artist, although this warred at times with the need to provide for a wife and child. Both he and Ruth had a vision of the good and simple life in which they would work with their hands, growing their own food and caring for their own animals, integrating this with the life of the artist. In a letter to a fellow artist, he tried to express this vision and the rather inchoate religious feeling that ran through it:

Sincerity gives one a clear vision, and one carries that out in work by means of *order*—and when I see a farm run well, no matter if the man's house is abominable, even if he drinks or overworks his hands or makes some other error, I find him a bit of an artist, for he is essaying to carry out some idea in work—I find this in doctors, sailors, in woodcutters and harvesters, and in everyone else. It is marked in business men (confound them). We shall never be satisfied with anyone less than Christ, however, and I think the reason is that, as Van Gogh says, he was the greatest artist we have ever had, for he dealt with men, not with colors and brushes, he *almost created men*. If our pictures do not in some measure create the men who look at them, or perhaps better *recreate* them those pictures are not much good! . . . Men like you and me *have* to paint sometime or other. I am certain it has grown to be a perfectly natural function with me. On the farm it used to make me feel absolutely sick with worry and strain till I could get to myself and go and draw for a little while. It seemed there was some essence in one's body which had to find its way out through one's fingers or not at all. [3]

Much in this passage foreshadows later attitudes of Merton's— the respect for the artist, for manual work of all kinds, the deep religious feeling, the recognition of the absolute need of artists to draw or write or express themselves as they must, the dislike of a purely commercial approach to life.

Owen Merton painted abstract pictures at a time when abstract art was in its infancy, and, like most good artists, he was profoundly self-critical, painfully exploring his psychological blocks and technical weaknesses and reaching out toward new apprehensions and resolutions. Writing to his painter friend Esmond (and attacking the painter Frank Brangwyn in the same letter), he complains of a worrying inhibition about using colour.

All this comes from a man who is at this time the poorest colourist in the world. (Why I don't exactly know.) But I have been trying to make my things more elaborate and plain to the uninitiated, and possibly in labouring over shapes and forms with a pencil, I have lost the knack of seeing where colour is vivid and where it is undercoloured. My work has been for the past eighteen months as black and triste as you ever saw. . . . I know where my own weakness lies only too well. When I sacrifice the things I cherish; such as clearness, and perfect realisation of necessary detail, I can paint a pretty bright thing, but clever sketching no longer satisfies me in the least. My weakness for the time being is that I am probably trying to fly somewhere where I have no business at all, but it is hard to sacrifice everything. By Heavens it is. [4]

Owen Merton could not afford to devote himself entirely to life as a painter; and probably his vision of "the good life" would not have allowed him to do so. In Douglaston he, and at times Ruth, served a kind of apprenticeship to farming, probably with an idea of eventually one day buying a farm of their own.

We left the place we were on last Monday, and are once more in New

York. We are going farming again up here, and I can tell you mighty glad to have made the plunge and taken to work of that kind. I could never feel easy unless I learned to earn my living properly with my hands. . . . On the farm we were on, we learnt a great deal about routine, long hours and doing a lot of work we did not know how to do, and we are now a very competent average pair of farmhands. Of course, we don't like life in this country, but anyway, some of them are fine farmers, and we are now looking for a place where we shall learn some of the most up-to-date and best modern ways of doing things. And while we are looking first, I can earn good pay, working by the day, for various farmers near my father in law's house." [3]

Soon Owen and Ruth rented a house for themselves in Flushing, Queens, about five miles away from Ruth's parents. Merton remembered it as "a small house, very old and rickety, standing among two or three high pine trees. . . . We were out in the fields in the direction of Kiljordan and Jamaica and the old Truant school. The house had four rooms, two downstairs and two upstairs, and two of the rooms were barely larger than closets." [2] Two doors away lived another painter, Bryson Burroughs.

An early memory of Merton's was of a dispute between his father and the landlord of the property, a Mr. Duggan. One evening when the Merton family were at supper, Mr. Duggan suddenly appeared in the garden, helping himself to the rhubarb that the Merton family had grown. Owen Merton rose indignantly from the table and went out to expostulate with his landlord, and young Tom, sitting at table, tried to puzzle it all out in his mind. "When Father returned I began to question him, and to endeavour to work out the morality of the situation. And I still remember it having struck me as a difficult case, with much to be said on both sides." [2]

Owen Merton continued to paint and, with the help of Buroughs, held an exhibition in Flushing, but he supported his wife and child by working as gardener and farmhand. Meanwhile Ruth was expecting another child; John Paul was born the week before Armistice Day in November 1918. Merton writes with a moving tenderness of this younger brother.

He was a child with a much serener nature than mine. . . . I remember that everyone was impressed by his constant and unruffled happiness. In the long evenings, when he was put to bed before the sun went down, instead of protesting and fighting, as I did when I had to go to bed, he would lie upstairs in his crib, and we would hear him singing a little tune. Every evening it was the same tune, very simple, very primitive; a nice little tune, very suitable for the time of day and for the season. Downstairs, we would all fall more or less silent, lulled by the singing of the child in the crib, and we would see the sunrays slanting across the fields and through the windows as the day ended. [2]

This contrast between John Paul and himself highlights Merton's sense of himself, even as a small child, as unworthy and unsatisfactory. His mother's teaching methods gave him the feeling that much was expected of him. She sent away for a progressive correspondence course, which arrived complete with blackboard and desk, and herself taught little Tom to read and write. He remembered being sent to bed early for refusing to spell *which* with an "h," "wich" seeming to him more logical. He loved the geography book and wanted to be a sailor; he was particularly fond of drawing boats, especially "ocean liners with many funnels and hundreds of portholes, and waves all around as jagged as a saw, and the air full of 'V's' for the seagulls." [2] He sent a picture of the house at Flushing and the family sitting under the trees to his grandfather at Douglaston.

He was a rather lonely child. John Paul was too small to be a companion for him, and no other children presented themselves as playmates. Like other lonely children, he invented a friend, Jack, and an imaginary dog called Doolittle, who made trouble when Tom and his mother went shopping in Flushing.

Religion did not come very much into the family's life. Merton remembers that as a child of four he heard the church bells ringing from St. George's across the fields, and catching the joyful mood of the morning he passionately wanted to go to church. Ruth Merton sometimes attended the Quaker Meeting but did not take the children with her. A year or two later, Owen Merton became the organist at the Episcopal Church in Douglaston, and Tom used to accompany him to services there, much admiring the lighted candles, and the anchor in the stained-glass windows, which he thought must have something to do with going to sea. He remembered this earliest churchgoing with pleasure. "One came out of the church with a kind of comfortable and satisfied feeling that something had been done that needed to be done." [2]

The visit of his New Zealand grandmother at about this time made a great impression on him and also caused him to learn the words of the "Our Father."

The general impression she left was one of veneration and awe—and love. She was very good and kind, and there was nothing effusive and overwhelming about her affection. . . . The clearest thing I remember about her was the way she put salt on her oatmeal at breakfast. Of this I am certain: it made a very profound impression on me. Of one other thing I am less certain, but it is in itself much more important; she taught me the Lord's Prayer. . . . Granny asked me one night if I had said my prayers, and it turned out that I did not know the "Our Father," so she taught it to me. After that I did not forget it, even though I went for years without saying it at all. [2]

Tragedy was approaching the Merton family: Ruth Merton was taken to hospital with cancer of the stomach. Tom and John Paul went to stay with their grandparents at Douglaston, and Owen played the piano every night at a movie theater to pay the hospital bills. Ruth did not see her children again after she went to the hospital, because, according to Merton, she thought scenes of morbidity should be kept from children. The little boy enjoyed the spoiling he got at his grandparents' home, played happily with the dogs and the chickens, and in the little studio where his grandmother painted china. When he did discover his impending loss, it was in a way that justified his memory of his mother as "cerebral." He was handed a letter from her, the first she had ever sent him, and alone he went out into the garden, and under the maple tree painfully worked over the letters and words until, almost like reading a message in code, he had deciphered their terrible message. "My mother was informing me, by mail, that she was about to die, and would never see me again. . . . A tremendous weight of sadness and depression settled on me. It was not the grief of a child, with pangs of sorrow and many tears. It had something of the heavy perplexity and gloom of adult grief, and was therefore all the more of a burden because it was, to that extent, unnatural." [2] Merton was six years old.

On the day Ruth Merton died, little Tom, his father, his grand-parents and his uncle went in a hired car to the hospital. The child sat in the car while the others went in, and he remembered the heavy rain and the desolate sky as he waited, and the heartbroken relatives who emerged. "When we got home to Douglaston, Father went into a room alone, and I followed him and found him weeping." [2] His grandmother too, wept, folding away locks of his mother's red hair.

A few days later Tom accompanied his relatives to his mother's funeral, again waiting in the car while the others attended the cremation service. Again the rain fell and the sky was dark. Thinking, years later, of his mother's wish for cremation, Merton found himself remembering her scrupulous tidiness and cleanliness. "I remember how she was, in the house at Flushing, with a rag tied tightly around her head to keep the dust out of her hair, cleaning and sweeping and dusting the rooms with the greatest energy and intensity of purpose; and it helps one to understand her impatience with useless and decaying flesh. That was something to be done away with, without delay. When life was finished, let the whole thing be finished, definitely, forever." [2]

The tragic early death of his mother was, in a sense, the beginning of Merton's spiritual journeying. In a literal sense it was the beginning of his travels, since from then on Owen Merton began a long search for a place in which to settle, very often taking Tom with him. But in a deeper sense, it symbolized a loss of a centre, of roots, that was to shape the rest of his life. Perhaps if his memories of Ruth had been warmer, more satisfying, he might have been able to carry a different kind of confidence into adult life. She undoubtedly loved him and cared for him to the best of her ability, but there is always a faint bitterness in his references to her; she seemed critical, pedagogic, "severe," measuring him all the time against some standard that seemed unattainable, leaving him with a sour taste of failure, and of being inadequate. "What do they think I am, anyway," he remembered thinking indignantly to himself after the spelling episode when he was sent to bed. Much later in his life he was to remark that "perhaps solitaries are made by severe mothers." [5]

References

1. Ruth Merton. "Tom's Book." Unpublished manuscript, written 1915–1916. TMSC.
2. Thomas Merton. *The Seven Storey Mountain.* New York: Harcourt Brace, 1948; London: SPCK, 1990. Also published abridged as *Elected Silence* (London: Burns & Oates, 1949).
3. Owen Merton. Letter addressed to "Dear Esmond." From Douglaston, about 1917. TMSC.
4. Owen Merton. Letter addressed to "Dear Esmond." From Prades, January 10, 1916. TMSC.
5. Thomas Merton. *The Sign of Jonas.* New York: Harcourt Brace, 1948; London: Sheldon Press, 1976.

2

THE SMELL OF
THE MIDI

For a few months after their mother's death in 1921, Merton and John Paul continued to live with their grandparents at Douglaston, and Merton attended the local school, which he remembered as "an evil-smelling gray annex on top of the hill." It was to be the first of many schools. He loved his grandparents in a quiet, undramatic way. His grandfather, "Pop," whose strange, manic bursts of energy sometimes alarmed and embarrassed his relatives, emerges from Merton's autobiography as a solid, masculine figure, part of the everyday world of commerce and commonplace enthusiasms, in a way that his own admired father was not.

Forty-five years later, Merton found himself possessed one morning by the memory of a song his grandfather used to play him on record, called "The Whistler and His Dog." For a whole day, he was possessed by its joyfulness, its idiot confidence, the confidence of people who had not known two world wars and the horrors of Auschwitz and Hiroshima. As a child, he had waited for the bark of the dog at the end, which was the bit he liked best, and he mourned the lost gaiety and innocence of Sousa's band, of the whistler and his dog so long dead. [1]

"Bonnemaman," as his grandmother was known to Merton, was a conventional, middle-class American housewife, with a rather lukewarm Protestant faith and a sentimental devotion to Douglas Fairbanks and Mary Pickford that enraged the adolescent Merton. Merton did not stay in her household long. Soon his father was off on his painting travels, first on a summer trip to Provincetown on Cape Cod. The two of them travelled overnight by boat to Fall River, then took the train over the Cape Cod Canal and through the sand dunes. The little boy remembered the Italians shooting craps on the boat, a bar of Baker's chocolate his father bought for him, and the name *Truro* as he saw it on a station sign. "I could not get it out of my mind: Truro. Truro. It was a name as lonely as the edge of the sea." [2] He got the mumps while in Provincetown, and his father read aloud to him. But most of the summer he played out-of-doors on the decks of the schooners. There was a closeness between him and his father in their mutual loss. "The only punishment I remember getting that summer was a mild reproof for refusing to eat an orange." [2]

He was returned to his grandparents for a few weeks at the end of the summer, and then he and his father were off again, this time to Bermuda. It was not a holiday resort in those days—its only claim to fame was as a British naval base. The beauty of it struck the seven-year-old Merton as he saw it first from the sea on a boat called the *Fort Victoria*. "You could already see the small white houses, made of coral, cleaner than sugar, shining in the sun, and all around us the waters paled over the shallows and became the color of emeralds, where there was sand, or lavender where there were rocks below the surface." Then, when they arrived, "Our feet padded softly in the creamy dust of the deserted road. No wind stirred the paper leaves of the banana trees, or in the oleanders. Our voices seemed loud as we spoke." [2] Already Merton did not just experience; he remembered as the writer, the poet, remembers.

Here, for the first time, the plight of the motherless child became evident. After a few weeks at a boardinghouse—"I quickly adjusted myself to the thought that this was home"—his father went off on a painting expedition, leaving the little boy alone there. Tom had started going to the local white school, where he was unhappy. "I was constantly being punished for my complete inability to grasp the principles of multiplication and division." [2] After a bit, Merton's father decided it would be better if he lived with him and took him away from school with its unresolved mathematical problems—for a while he did not go to school at all. This too had its problems, though, since a teacher from his old school occasionally bicycled past the house where they were now living. Merton used to hide when he saw her coming, in fear that she would catch sight of him and report him to the truant officer. For a time he stayed on in Bermuda with friends of his father's, while his father went to New York to hold an exhibition. Then the two of them went back to Douglaston, Tom to settle down temporarily to the normal family life of an American child, Owen Merton to go to France, his old love.

Merton wrote with unconscious pathos of the wanderings of his childhood—unconscious because, although he tried, he could not imagine any more rooted existence. He was aware of a loss but was not even quite sure what loss.

> It is almost impossible to make much sense out of the continual rearrangements of our lives and our plans from month to month in my childhood. Yet every new development came to me as a reasonable and worthy change. Sometimes I had to go to school, sometimes I did not. Sometimes Father and I were living together, sometimes I was with strangers and only saw him from time to time. People came into our lives and went out of our lives. . . . Things were always changing. I accepted it all. Why should it ever have occurred to me that nobody else lived like that? [2]

Merton never criticized his father for the mercurial changes of plan that so disrupted his early relationships and education; he recognized the dilemma of the man torn between his painting and his love for his small sons; a dilemma shaped by loneliness and the loss of the woman important to them all.

Back in Douglaston, Merton, aged eight, was beginning to sample the delights of American life. He saw movies—W. C. Fields and the beloved Doug and Mary. In that household, it would have been difficult *not* to become a movie fan. He went down to Pop's office and there read the comic books and children's adventure stories that his grandfather's firm published, until Pop had time to take him down to Child's for chicken a la king. He acquired a gang of friends with whom he built huts in the woods—the first, but by no means the last, time that Merton would enjoy being "one of the boys"—although nearly twenty years later he remembered with pain the wounding way he refused to allow his little brother to join in this heady game.

> The picture I get of my brother John Paul is this: standing in a field, about a hundred yards away from the clump of sumachs where we have built our hut, is this little perplexed five-year-old kid in short pants and a kind of leather jacket, standing quite still, with his arms hanging down at his sides, and gazing in our direction, afraid to come any nearer on account of the stones, as insulted as he was saddened, and his eyes full of indignation and sorrow. And yet he does not go away. We shout at him to get out of there, to beat it, and go home, and wing a

couple of more rocks in that direction, and he does not go away. We tell him to play in some other place. He does not move. [2]

Most grown-ups can remember taking part in such scenes as children—sometimes as victim, sometimes as oppressor. Merton, in the confessional mood in which *The Seven Storey Mountain* is written, sees his childish cruelty as part of a much larger pattern, both in himself and in the world.

> This . . . is the pattern and prototype of all sin: the deliberate and formal will to reject disinterested love for us for the purely arbitrary reason that we simply do not want it. . . . Perhaps the inner motive is that the fact of being loved disinterestedly reminds us that we all need love from others, and depend upon the charity of others to carry on our lives. And we refuse love, and reject society, in so far as it seems, in our own perverse imagination, to imply some obscure kind of humiliation. [2]

Somewhere around this time Merton picked up Pop's strongly anti-Catholic sentiments, a kind of built-in hatred and suspicion. Religion in itself did not mean very much to the boy, but the word *Catholic* had "a cold and unpleasant feeling" for him, something spooky and evil.

Owen Merton was away for a long period painting, first in the south of France, then in Algeria; a burnous came for the little boy, and a stuffed lizard. But then Owen suddenly became seriously and inexplicably ill, so ill that Bonnemaman told Tom his father was dying. At nine he had already adapted to the traumatic loss of his mother, and now he was asked to face another tragedy. "I was old enough to understand what it meant, and I was profoundly affected, filled with sorrow and with fear. Was I never to see my father again?" [2] After days of delirium, however, Owen Merton recovered, and began to work with renewed enthusiasm. Since his wife's death, he had painted with great concentration; he was at the height of his powers as a painter, and his very successful exhibition at the Leicester Galleries in London in 1925 attracted flattering critical attention.

Then he came back to America—with a beard that Tom found embarrassing—and told him that he was going to take him back to France with him. Tom was not pleased. He had settled, he had friends he liked, he liked to swim and play baseball, and he wanted to become a Boy Scout. The thought of France produced tears.

Going to France, bitterly against his will, turned out to be one of the most important experiences of Merton's life, the beginning of a deep and inexhaustible love for France and for Catholic culture that was to mould his whole life. The two of them travelled via England, journeying from Calais to Paris by train; the child woke from sleep to see Paris, which immediately appealed to him. But the experience really began to take hold of him on the express going south, into the Midi. "I discovered France. I discovered that land which is really, as far as I can tell, the one to which I do belong, if I belong to any at all, by no documentary title but by geographical birth." [2] They travelled through Aquitaine, and Merton tells it like a description of a journey in a legend. "The dusk was gathering. The country was hilly, and full of trees, yet rocky, and you knew that the uplands were bare and wild. In the valleys were castles." Finally, they descended at Montauban and made their way to a little hotel. At once Merton felt at home. "Father threw open the wooden shutters of the room, and looked out into the quiet night without stars, and said: 'Do you smell the woodsmoke in the air? That is the smell of the Midi.'" [2]

At Montauban, Merton became aware that his father had undergone some sort of religious experience during his critical illness. Always naturally religious, he now felt a great need to pray and urged his son to pray too. In addition, he felt strongly that he wanted to bring his children up himself, and was making plans for John Paul to join them when he was a bit older. Still in this religious mood, he looked over a large Protestant school as a possible place for Tom's education, but finally, not really liking either the school or Montauban, they took the train again through the wonderful hilly landscape of the Languedoc and ended at St. Antonin, named for the martyred Roman saint, St. Antoninus. It was still an almost perfect medieval town—"to walk through those streets was to be in the Middle Ages"—living, as it had done for hundreds of years, on the tannery trade, and built with a church at its heart. In retrospect, Merton felt that the whole town, with its radius of streets pointing to the church, was saying, "This is the meaning of all created things: we have been made for no other purpose than that men may use us in raising themselves to God, and in proclaiming the glory of God. . . . Oh, what a thing it is, to live in a place that is so constructed that you are forced, in spite of yourself, to be at least a virtual contemplative." [2]

Did the nine-year-old Merton ever consciously formulate such thoughts? Almost certainly not. But the sense of a contained and rooted community, and of the beauty of the landscape and of building, remained with him, and years later he traced the feelings of peace and delight that he associated with them to its source in a profound religious belief. France, in this rural setting and in this southern medieval aspect, offered a culture more ancient and satisfying than that of Doug and Mary or of W. C. Fields.

Owen Merton bought some land near St. Antonin, at the foot of a hill overlooking the valley of the Bonnette, with an old Calvary at the top of it, and a path winding through the vineyards behind it tracing the Stations of the Cross. Owen drew up his own plans for the house—a big studio downstairs, which would be the living-room, and two bedrooms upstairs. With the help of a water diviner, he found water and dug a well. He planted two poplar trees in the garden, one for Tom and one for John Paul. Then he began digging the foundations.

Meanwhile Tom had once more started school—this time at the local elementary school, where he sat, to his embarrassment, among the smallest boys, and struggled to learn French. He learned quickly, and by the following year could read and speak quite adequately in French. Father and son were warmly accepted in St. Antonin. Owen was asked to become president of the local Rugby club, and as he had been a keen Rugby player in his youth he accepted. Owen and Tom used to accompany the team on playing trips to other towns, trips keenly enjoyed by the eleven-year-old boy. The two of them also explored the Languedoc, looking for suitable places to paint. From a ruined thirteenth-century chapel that was being demolished, they took the window and door arches and stones to be part of their new house at St. Antonin. At about this time, Tom's imagination was captured by a three-volume set of books, *Le Pays de France,* full of pictures of cathedrals and abbeys and ancient towns. Here he came on pictures of La Grande Chartreuse (the monastery at the heart of Carthusian devotion), "My heart was filled with a kind of longing to breathe the air of that lonely valley and to listen to its silence." [2]

Somewhat to the distress of the Mertons, Pop announced that he was about to descend on them with the intention of "doing" France and Switzerland. He had already "done" England, or as Merton put it, "Pop had descended in force upon London, had scoured the

Shakespeare country and other parts of England—and was now preparing to cross the channel and occupy the north of France." [2] They all arranged to meet in Paris. The Mertons travelled by way of Rocamadour, stopping to see the famous Black Madonna statue. There is something slightly priggish in Merton's contrast of *père et fils*: on the one hand, French-speaking, steeped in European culture, dedicated to the good life, and the brash and colourful Pop on the other.

> At the moment that we were leaving Rocamadour, after a short visit that filled my mind with a memory of a long summer evening, with swallows flying around the wall of the old monastery up against the cliff, and around the tower of the new shrine on top of it, Pop was riding around all the chateaux of the Loire in a bus full of Americans. And as they went whizzing through Chenonceaux and Blois and Tours, Pop, who had his pockets crammed full of two- and five-sou pieces, and even francs and two-franc pieces, would dig in and scatter handfuls of coins into the streets whenever they passed a group of playing children. And the dusty wake of the bus would ring with his burst of laughter as all the kids plunged after the coins in a wild scramble. It was that way all through the valley of the Loire. [2]

They found Pop at one of the most expensive hotels in Paris, too intoxicated by the low value of the franc to know that it was beyond his means, surrounded by sixteen pieces of luggage, and, unlike the rest of his party, thoroughly enjoying himself. It is difficult for the reader not to warm to the generous and wholehearted Pop, but Tom and John Paul, after the manner of children, felt that people were laughing at him, and, by implication, at them. Bonnemaman felt "humiliated," and Owen Merton, not in the least appreciating his father-in-law's attempt to give him a lovely holiday, was superior and bored. Even remembering it as an adult, Merton identifies, rather revealingly, with his father. "The first day was not so bad for me and Father, because we were still in France. . . . But as soon as we got into Switzerland, things were different. . . . For some reason, we found it was not Father's kind of landscape . . . we found Switzerland extremely tedious. . . . As a matter of fact, the only pleasure Father got out of the whole expedition was a jazz concert he heard in Paris." [2] Poor Father. Poor Pop.

However, the embarrassment was not long lived. Eventually the party wound its way back to St. Antonin, which Pop, predictably, did not like, and then Pop and Bonnemaman and John Paul departed for Douglaston, and Tom was sent to school, to the Lycée Ingres at Montauban, wearing his new blue uniform. The first day turned out to be one of those nightmare school beginnings that mark people for life.

> Although by this time I knew French quite well, the first day in the big, gravelled yard, when I was surrounded by those fierce, cat-like little faces, dark and morose, and looked into those scores of pairs of glittering and hostile eyes, I forgot every word, and could hardly answer the furious questions that were put to me. And my stupidity only irritated them all the more. They began to kick me and to pull and twist my ears, and push me around, and shout various kinds of insults. I learned a great deal of obscenity and blasphemy in the first few days, simply by being the direct or indirect object of so much of it. [2]

Merton was not especially singled out for persecution, although his fair hair and blue eyes made him "different" and, as such, an obvious target for attack. But the school was dominated by a half-dozen bullies of fifteen or sixteen years old who filled all the younger boys with fear and with a desperate wish for their seniors' protection rather than their enmity. Reflecting that the type of boy at the school was almost identical with the type he had been so happy with at St. Antonin, Merton commented on the way the collective can control people who as individuals might be kind and good, a theme to which he returned later.

> When a couple of hundred of these southern French boys were thrown together in the prison of that Lycée, a subtle change was operated in their spirit and mentality. In fact, I noticed that when you were with them separately, outside the school, they were mild and peaceable and humane enough. But when they were all together there seemed to be some diabolical spirit of cruelty and viciousness and obscenity and blasphemy and envy and hatred that banded them together against all goodness and against one another in mockery and fierce cruelty and in vociferous, uninhibited filthiness. Contact with that wolf-pack felt very patently like contact with the mystical body of the devil: and, especially in the first days, the members of that body did not spare themselves in kicking me around without mercy. [2]

In that place, Merton was to experience a depth of grief and abandonment that was new to him, although it may well have echoed the isolation he felt at the news of his mother's death. The sheer animality and lack of conscience frightened him because, he was later to think, they reflected something tough and brutal in his own character, but he saw these traits acted out there to a degree he had not previously imagined. On occasional weekends when he returned home, he would plead with his father to take him out of his misery, but without success.

In an autobiographical novel, *My Argument with the Gestapo*, which Merton wrote in 1941, he recalled the fear, some of it specific, some nameless, that the Lycée evoked in him. Picturing a scene of interrogation with himself as the victim, he imagines the interrogator to be the *censeur*, the disciplinarian of the Lycée, of whom everyone was afraid, because of his power of inflicting punishment.

> He might ask me what I am afraid of. I am afraid of the cold walls of the corridors in the Lycée. I am afraid of the gravel in the playgrounds, and of the sickly smell of the blossoming acacias in the spring. I am afraid of getting water on my knee, because when you have water on the knee they lance your knee. I am afraid of the sound of the harsh church bells. . . . I am afraid of the rain that rained all winter so that the river flooded the suburbs . . . carrying away trees and dead cattle.
>
> He will ask me why I fear the dark room where they teach mathematics. He will ask me why I didn't believe the fierce boys when they told me that the guillotine where the murderers were beheaded was always set up behind the Lycée, and that the next morning, about the time we awoke at dawn, one might be able to hear the knife fall with a clang, behind the walls. He will ask me why I fear the little Protestant chapel built like an empty blast furnace in one of the courts—a forge where all the fires have gone out. . . . The halls of the Palais de Justice ring like the corridors of the Lycée, where the barking of the boys was sharp, like foxes' in the cold air of January mornings, and the steps of the *censeur* and the *proviseur* [principal], walking side by side on tours of inspection, fell on the stones like the ticking of a big, inexorable clock. [3]

Unprotected, orphaned in a harsh prison, Merton experienced fears both justified and ungrounded. After a while, he made friends with several of the boys; they used to go for walks together, and discuss the novels they were writing. (This exercise of simultaneous novel writing recurred when Merton was at Columbia; he and a group of friends worked on novels together during the vacations.)

At the Lycée, Merton wrote two novels, plus one unfinished one in which he shocked his French contemporaries by allowing the hero to borrow money from the heroine, an offence to the code of romance and all decent human behaviour that they unanimously condemned. So Merton altered it. He had already written an earlier novel, at St. Antonin, that he did not choose to show to his friends, because of the anti-Catholic historical plot. Not that any of them was particularly devout, but he was old enough to know that he would give offence.

The Lycée was Catholic in the sense that many of the boys came from Catholic homes, but more devout families sent their children to the Marist Fathers' school near the river. In the afterglow of his subsequent conversion, Merton felt that it must automatically have been a nicer school than his own and that the boys who went there seemed "exceptionally nice." [2]

As a nominal Protestant, he was instructed on the occasional Sundays he spent at the school by a *pasteur* who expounded the parables in a "bleak" octagonal building specially built for the purpose, the "blast furnace" that was one of the child's fears. This religious teaching did not "take" with Merton; in fact, the only sort that did, during his childhood—apart from his grandmother's teaching him the "Our Father"—was his father's deep religious conviction, emerging occasionally by precept, but more often by example. He remembered all his life a casual remark of his father's about Peter weeping bitterly when he heard the cock crow.

Merton never became happy at the school, and, as also happened later in his life in times of distress, his health began to suffer; he endured "repeated fevers." At such times his loneliness was most acute.

I remember all the nights I was ever awake, in France, when I was a child. The windows of the Lycée's Infirmary looked out over the tiled roofs of a suburb of Montauban. . . . Out there was emptiness, wood smoke, vineyards, the dark and violent night, the house of the bishop, the barracks of the African troops.

And from those barracks a fierce, outlandish Islamic bugle would blow, so that I shivered, where I lay, in my infirmary bed. I used to lie awake and listen to the sounds of the South of France outside that bare window. . . .

Later on, when the night became totally silent, I was still awake in this high, lonely infirmary room. I waited, now for the slippered, half audible approach of the night watchman along the hall outside, going his rounds. . . .

All around me, from that ward, in the infirmary, spread the Lycée in every direction in long brick wings two stories high. In these were some dormitories, part empty . . . full of iron beds where lay the peasant children of the South in their tough sleep, lean, hard, mean kids full of violence, strange humor, and rhetoric.

In the morning they would stand in the gravel yards of the Lycée in groups, in their black smocks, and taunt one another fiercely, and pull each other's ears, and twist them until they nearly wrenched them from each other's heads. [3]

A temporary reprieve was given to Merton from this prison with its bleak absence of all gentleness and tenderness. In 1926 his father had been painting at Murat, in the Auvergne, and arranged for Tom to come and spend Christmas at the house of the Privats, the couple with whom he had been boarding. The boy was at once delighted by the beauty of the place and by the kindness of the couple. They were farmers, the husband—outwardly at least—a typical peasant of the region, the wife wearing the charming traditional headdress of the Auvergne. Both deeply impressed Merton by their peacefulness and kindness. Worried about the boy's health, Owen Merton arranged that Tom should also spend his summer holidays with them, and they not only fattened him up with their excellent butter and milk but also gave him much-needed love and care, which he was to remember all his life. The memory of the Privats later prompted Merton to make a profoundly significant statement about his attitude to love:

As a child, and since then too, I have always tended to resist any kind of a possessive affection on the part of any other human being—there has always been this profound instinct to keep clear, to keep free. And only with truly supernatural people have I ever felt really at my ease, really at peace.

That was why I was glad of the love the Privats showed me, and was ready to love them in return. It did not burn you, it did not hold you, it did not try to imprison you in demonstrations, or trap your feet in the snares of its interest. [2]

Not yet twelve, Merton was baffled by the profundity of the Privats' Catholic faith. "I had never met people to whom belief was a matter of such moment." [2] On one humiliating occasion, he tried to justify Protestantism to them on the grounds that all faiths led to the same God, and received the flat denial "Mais c'est impossible". He was wounded by this conversation, and after his conversion felt it was a proper blow to his wilful Protestant pride. Another humiliation of a lesser kind around this time was inadvertently inflicted by another child staying at the house, the Privats' nephew: Merton uttered some obscenity of the kind that was routine conversation at the Lycée and perceived that the other boy was deeply shocked.

In the autumn, Merton returned to the hated Lycée Ingres. Although the house at St. Antonin was nearly completed, his father seemed to spend less and less time at home, which meant that Merton was more than ever confined to the school. Owen was away for months in Marseilles and at Cette on the Mediterranean. In the spring of 1928, he went to London to hold an exhibition. Then on one wonderful morning in May he came to the Lycée and told Tom to pack his things and come to England. He was to leave the school permanently. "I looked around me like a man that has had chains struck from his hands. How the light sang on the brick walls of the prison whose gates had just burst open before me. . . . My escape from the Lycée was, I believe, providential." He said goodbye to his friends, not bothering to hide his pleasure at his departure, and he and his father drove off together in a cab. "How lightly the cab-horse's hoofs rang out in the hard, white dirt of the street! . . . 'Liberty,' they said. 'Liberty, liberty, liberty,' all down the street." [2] The sense of relief comes through the words written so long after.

Their destination was England—18 Carlton Road, Ealing. Merton's Uncle Ben (Benjamin Pearce) was the retired headmaster of Durston House, the preparatory school next door to the house, and his Aunt Maud presided over the household. Aunt Maud made a great hit with the thirteen-year-old boy. She was old and totally unfashionable in her dress, but somehow "sprightly and charming" and like a "sensible and sensitive Victorian girl."

Merton was to go to school at Ripley Court in Surrey (where Uncle Ben's sister-in-law was headmistress), and Aunt Maud had the job of fitting the motherless boy out with the necessary grey flannel trousers, grey flannel shirts, floppy hats, and all the garments necessary for well-brought-up children of the period. They carried out this preparation at D. H. Evans and afterwards rode down busy Oxford Street on an open bus—Aunt Maud seems to have had an unerring instinct for what boys would like.

"I wonder if Tom has thought at all about his future," his aunt inquired, with a slightly excessive Victorian delicacy, and Tom made the important confession that he wanted to be a writer. Encouraged by his aunt's enthusiastic response, he went on, "I have been thinking I might write stories." His aunt pointed out, on a kind of man-to-man basis, that it was not always easy for writers to make a living, and they talked of his being a journalist, perhaps a foreign correspondent ("A knowledge of languages would be very valuable in that field"), and of other delightful possibilities all the way home to Ealing. [2]

There was to be a slightly bumpy descent to earth when they got there. Mrs. Pearce, the headmistress of Ripley Court, was awaiting them, a large and rather alarming-looking woman to Merton's eyes, whose first unnerving observation was "Does he want to be a dilettante like his father?" Aunt Maud mildly observed that they had been talking of his becoming a journalist, but this was firmly scotched by the headmistress, who said of course he must go into business and then issued further warnings about the dangers of dilettantism. [2]

So Merton was taken into Ripley Court almost at the end of the summer term. He was in the difficult situation, for a schoolboy of that period, of not knowing Latin. Again he had to study with the very youngest boys, but Ripley was a world away from the nightmare of the Lycée, and he was happy there at once. The sheer Englishness of it emerges from Merton's description. "Little box hedges along the flower-beds. Redbrick walls, fruit trees trained against them to branch like candlesticks so all the fruit will hang up against the wall in the sun. The tall elms. The ha-ha. Kedgeree for breakfast. The three pieces of dry bread on everybody's plate you had to eat up before you could take buttered bread from the plate in the middle of the table." [4]

And again, "The huge, dark green sweep of the cricket field, and the deep shadows of the elm trees where one sat waiting for one's innings, and the dining-room where we crammed ourselves with bread and butter and jam at tea-time and listened to Mr. Onslow reading aloud from the works of Sir Arthur Conan Doyle." [2] Having come late to cricket, as he had to Latin, Merton never entirely took to it, but he remembered with pride having made 32 not out for the school's Second XI. He also learned to play soccer, wearing a "prickly, woolly, black and green striped jersey."

He found the boys "red-faced" and "innocent," cushioned by their comfortable homes from the harsh realities of the world in the late 1920s. In the 1940s, when England was at war, Merton pondered on the fate of the boys he had known, remembering their names with the exactness with which we often remember the people of our youth. "All those kids at the school are probably soldiers. Clifton-Mogg who got the scholarship to Eton. And the Strobes—and Irving, and Romanoff and Lansdowne and Yates and R. G. G. M. Marsden and Percy Major who had the lead plate in his head." [4]

On Sundays they all went to the local Anglican church in Eton suits, and in the evenings they sang hymns and were read aloud to from *The Pilgrim's Progress*. Under this regular and beneficent Anglicanism, Merton began to pray with real feeling, a phase of his life that a year or two later he found embarrassing.

After a year at Ripley Court, Uncle Ben recommended Oakham as a good public school. There was no question of Merton going to one of the front-rank schools like Eton or Harrow or Winchester, because his late start in Latin made a scholarship there impossible. But a scholarship at a lesser school would leave fairly modest fees to be paid—Pop was going to pay them, in any case—so Oakham in Rutland, in the heart of the English Midlands, was chosen, and, as Aunt Maud comfortingly remarked, "I am sure you will find Oakham a very nice school." [2]

References

1. Thomas Merton. "Vow of Conversation." Unpublished journal, dated 1964–1965. TMSC.
2. Thomas Merton. *The Seven Storey Mountain*. New York: Harcourt Brace, 1948; London: SPCK, 1990. Also published abridged as *Elected Silence* (London: Burns & Oates, 1949).
3. Thomas Merton. *My Argument with the Gestapo*. New York: Doubleday, 1969. Written 1941. Originally titled "The Journal of My Escape from the Nazis." Reprinted by New Directions, 1975.
4. Thomas Merton. Unpublished journal, written 1940–1941. TMC.

3

A VERY NICE SCHOOL

Before Merton went to Oakham, in the autumn of 1929, the tragic note again sounded in his life. He had spent the Easter vacation very happily with his father in Canterbury: Owen painting, Tom exploring the Kent countryside and going to see the Chaplin movie *The Gold Rush*. In June Merton travelled into Ealing with the Ripley Court cricket team, which was to play Durston House. Merton was scorer. On the way he was informed that his father was ill, at his Aunt Maud's house, that this was why Merton had been included in the school party, and that at the tea break he was to go and see him.

Merton remembered the details of that day in the way we often remember the first omen of catastrophe—the June weather, Aunt Maud's house in the distance across the hazy field, the green door in the wall through which the boy slipped to see his father, and his father silent and ill in bed. Owen did not know what was the matter with him. Merton felt "saddened and unquiet."

At the end of term, the two of them took a train to Aberdeen to visit friends of Owen Merton's in Scotland, who had invited him to a place called Insch to convalesce. Owen stayed in his room, only coming down for meals, until gradually even that became too much for him, and on the doctor's advice he decided to return to London for treatment. As on so many occasions, he left Tom behind, to the mercy of the well-to-do household who had been glad to receive the successful painter but did not particularly want a sad and rather sulky adolescent boy.

There were ponies, and two nieces of the house a couple of years older than Tom, who spent their whole time grooming the horses, and were cold and bossy toward him. In *My Argument with the Gestapo*, Merton moves the whole painful episode from Scotland to Yorkshire, to a household called the Frobishers, but so many details tally with his autobiography that it is clearly something more than a fictional account. It was probably Merton's first encounter with an English, or Scottish, country house, and the wealth and impersonality of the household added to his loneliness and sense of strangeness, so unlike the intimacy of life with the Privats.

> The house . . . was made out of large blocks of stone and had huge windows. Dim light of the moors! In the front was a tennis lawn, and in the back, between the house and the stables, were thick rhododendrons and pine trees. . . .
>
> For morning prayers, the cook and the two maids, in their pale blue smocks and white aprons, would come sidling in at the other end of the dining room. The family knelt, with faces to the wall. . . .
>
> Then the maids went sidling silently out again, and you helped yourself from the various silver chafing dishes on the sideboard, where there would never be any ham or bacon because the Frobishers were vegetarian. . . . And I would come to breakfast with the smell of the stables still strong in my riding breeches. This was by no means criticized because the stables were part of the education that was to make a man out of an orphan. [I]

The mornings were spent furiously grooming the horses and cleaning the tack and the stables.

> When I was through with the fork, I went on working with the brush until my arm and wrist ached. I curried the warm sweet smelling flanks, until the bay pony shone like mirrors and roan like tropical wood.
>
> As we worked, a portable gramophone, set on a broken chair, ground out little nasal tunes from Gilbert and Sullivan operettas.
>
> I stood in the clean straw, brushing the side of a horse, unhappy and hungry, while the inhuman metal playfulness of the gramophone voice repeated in my ear:
>
> > To make the punishment fit the crime,
> > The punishment fit the crime.
>
> . . . Later in the day, we would ride on the stony roads or on paths through the heather. That was our reward.
>
> One learned to appreciate the ride by having to work for it, which was a good enough theory if you were crazy about riding in the first place. [I]

The young Merton was not crazy about riding, and if he clung to the nieces it was only to try to relieve his acute loneliness, in a

fatherless Scottish wasteland. Unfortunately the nieces were interested in nothing but horses. Their reading consisted entirely of
books describing methods of conducting oneself on a horse, and
their thoughts revolved exclusively around the pleasures of hunting. They rarely spoke to Tom except to tell him what he was doing
wrong, although with a wonderfully sharp satirical ear he recalls a
short speech one of the nieces made, provoked by some inquiry:
"'Riding is like good manners,' she said with a deep, rustic blush,
'after all. I mean manners is putting other people at their ease, and
riding means you consider the horse, too. After all, only a cad
would yank on a horse's mouth to pull him up: you should pull
up gradually, and also only a cad would gallop a horse down hill;
it's awfully bad for their hoofs and their hocks, and they might get
lamed for good. Besides, you ruin your own horse. Think of the
horse. You're responsible. It's like noblesse oblige.'" [1]

Their manners did not run to putting Merton at his ease. As he
became less and less interested in the hard work of grooming and
even in the "reward" of riding, they decided he was a "shirker."
Merton began to be bitterly unhappy and to long for some way to
escape from the house. He probably dramatized the extent to which
they regarded him as alien—like many adolescents he felt unap-
preciated and misunderstood—but he undoubtedly felt utterly
miserable, powerless to change a humiliating situation. "There
was a lot wrong with this orphan. Of course, he wasn't strictly
speaking English. As a matter of fact, he wasn't really British,
either: it was by no means certain you could call him a thorough
Colonial. He was showing signs of too many bad Continental traits,
a kind of French sullenness." [1]

The orphan began to sulk more and more, going off to a hiding
place to read *The Count of Monte Cristo* in French. His hostess
cornered him, on one occasion, and preached him a little sermon
on *esprit de corps*. (He had already decided in his own mind that
"Perhaps this woman is a little crazy.")

"Did you ever read *The Jungle Book* by Rudyard Kipling?"
"Yes."
"Do you remember who Mowgli was?"
"He was a boy who lived wild in the jungle, with the animals," I
said. "He lived away from people. He was wild."
The conversation was taking a wrong turn.
"Did he live alone?" she said, introducing her theme, and before I

could say anything, she answered, "No, of course not. Nobody can live alone. We all have to depend on one another. Mowgli lived with a pack of wolves. Why do you suppose the wolves and Mowgli got along together? Why?"

She paused. I had my own answer. I said:

"Because he liked the wolves and they liked him. They got along well. They were like brothers."

"First came duty," she said severely. "What duty?"

I thought a while. I couldn't remember anything about duties. I said:

"I suppose I don't remember. I just thought they liked each other."

"Duty held them together," she said, "the duty to run with the pack. The pack came first. Run with the pack. Hunt with the group. Everybody depends on everybody else. Everybody does his bit. Mowgli had his part to play too. It is like the Three Musketeers," she went on, "do you remember what kept them together?"

"They liked each other," I said.

"No," she said, "it was their motto, 'One for all and all for one,' that kept the Three Musketeers together." [I]

That painful adolescent summer contained another memory for Merton that he thinly fictionalized. Several years before at St. Antonin he had been attracted to a little girl, but had been repelled by her coquetry and his father's gentle mockery. Now he met a girl who a year or two later would be important to him, but with the gaucherie of early adolescence did not know how to manage the first awkward meeting.

He was taken with the nieces to a friend's house for tennis and tea, and there was a girl, also a niece of the household, whom he calls B.

B. was as young as I was. That made us the youngest of all the people there. We didn't play much tennis, not that we wanted any. . . . B. and I didn't get the court until everybody was tired, and it was almost dark, and time to go home anyway.

B. was a skinny, quiet girl, not pretty, with straight hair and bangs. We just sat at the edge of the tennis court, embarrassed at being the youngest of all, embarrassed at being classified together, arbitrarily, and asking one another a series of insolent questions about the schools we went to. [I]

Most of that holiday, however, Merton walked and went for bicycle rides to look at druid stone circles, and read steadily through Dumas. And Owen Merton struggled with his mysterious illness at the Middlesex Hospital in London. Then one day a peculiarly eerie and terrible thing happened that was to haunt Merton for years.

One day I was in the deserted house all by myself with Athos, Porthos, Aramis, and D'Artagnan (Athos being my favorite and . . . the one into whom I tended to project myself). The telephone rang. I thought for a while of letting it ring and not answering it, but eventually I did. It turned out to be a telegram for me.

At first I could not make out the words, as the Scotch lady in the telegraph office was pronouncing them. Then, when I did make them out, I did not believe them.

The message ran: "Entering New York harbor. All well." And it came from Father, in the hospital, in London. I tried to argue with the woman at the other end of the wire into telling me that it came from my Uncle Harold, who had been travelling in Europe that year. But she would not be argued into anything but what she saw right in front of her nose. The telegram was signed Father, and it came from London.

I hung up the receiver and the bottom dropped out of my stomach. I walked up and down in the silent and empty house. I sat down in one of the big leather chairs in the smoking room. There was nobody there. There was nobody in the whole huge house.

I sat there in the dark, unhappy room, unable to think, unable to move, with all the innumerable elements of my isolation crowding in upon me from every side: without a home, without a family, without a country, without a father. . . . And what was happening to Father, there in London? I was unable to think of it. [2]

For the second time in his fourteen years of life, he had learned of tragedy by an impersonal message that had to be painfully deciphered. This mad message from the father he admired so much was perhaps harder to take than a straightforward message of impending death.

He went to London, to see his relatives at Ealing, and was at once informed by Uncle Ben that Owen Merton had a malignant brain tumour. He went to see his father in the hospital and found him much more lucid than the telegram had suggested, but there was no hope. Owen had a lump on his forehead—it was doubtful any operation could help—and Merton realized he would become fatherless within a year or two.

It was a cruel suspense for any child of fourteen to have to live

with, and for Merton it was the background to his first term at
Oakham.

Merton's earliest memories of Oakham were of a crude, male world,
a world of fighting, eating, swearing, noise, and overcrowding. He
could hold his own quite well in this world. He remembered
learning Greek verbs, nauseating himself with potato chips and
raisin wine, pinning up on the walls pictures of actresses culled
from the New York papers and writing to his father on paper
printed with the school crest.

Oakham was a small school, set, unusually for public schools, in
the centre of a very pretty market town. The country was five
minutes' walk in any direction and it was, and remains, a beautiful
and unspoiled countryside of hills and vales, set in the heart of the
English Midlands. The boys walked in summer and skated and
tobogganed in winter, particularly in the hard winter of 1931.

Two of Merton's old Oakham friends, John Barber and Andrew
Winser, still both schoolmasters themselves, are amazed, looking
back, at how limited the curriculum was in those days and how
lacking in the cultural and artistic interests that would be taken for
granted in any comparable school nowadays. (However, Oakham
was no different in this respect from most other public schools of
the period.) The boys on the "classics side," of whom Merton was
one, learned Latin, Greek, French, and a little English and not
much else, although a new headmaster, F. C. Doherty, made his
classics students spend time each week on the "science side"
dissecting frogs or sheeps' hearts, an activity they hated. Andrew
Winser feels that until Doherty's influence began to make itself felt
in the school, the school was poor academically, and attracted
students of inferior academic ability. "Merty should never have
been there at all. He had the ability for a school like Winchester," In the sixth form, when the two of them became friends,
Winser was to become amazed at the breadth of Merton's reading
and the depth of his culture, and was particularly impressed when
he quoted bits of Italian books he was reading—the Italian self-
taught from Hugo's *Itatian Tutor*. Merton's cleverness, worldliness,
and widely travelled background impressed all his contemporaries,
who were mostly rather unsophisticated English boys from professional homes who had scarcely travelled outside their own country.
Partly because of his air of sophistication, partly because of his

enormous enthusiasm for school life, his love of rugger, and his sense of humour, Merton quite quickly became very popular in the school.

The boys slept in cubicles in big dormitories in their houses—Merton was in "School House." Once they were past the most junior levels, they did their preparation for classes in a study, and a pupil named T. F. Boys, who joined the school in the same term as Merton, remembers that he and Merton and four others shared a study when they were in the middle school. Merton started a club called the Heebul Club (the Heebul was a fabulous beast, and the club's badge was a Heebul rampant, which Merton designed), and Merton was Chief Heebul—but the club's purpose nobody now remembers.

The boys played games nearly every afternoon—Tuesdays, Thursdays, Saturdays, and Sundays were theoretically half-holidays, but on every day except Sunday they might find themselves playing games. Rugger was the game for the autumn term, athletics was for the spring term (which John Barber remembers as involving a lot of shivering and waiting around for one's turn), and cricket for the summer term. The Officers' Training Corps (OTC), an organization in which the boys drilled and practised military routines, also took up one afternoon a week.

In free time, however, the boys could eat at one of the cafés or restaurants in the town if they wanted, or go for a walk in the countryside. There was a favourite little place called Tom Froud's in Church Passage, almost adjoining the school, where the boys could buy chocolate and fruit and ice cream, and there was a bare, although much beloved, restaurant called "Joe's." Mrs. Joe made sausage rolls, fish cakes of tinned salmon, and homemade lemonade. One of Merton's contemporaries remembers that after school food Joe's was, quite simply, "heaven." You could also go to Sharp's to eat poached eggs on toast, and there were places you could buy a fizzy drink called Vimto.

A grander alternative was to go and have tea of bacon and eggs at the Crown, a simple little coaching inn, or, if you had visiting relatives with a car, to the George in Stamford. Off you went, in your Oakham boater with its black and red band, stuffing yourself against the boredom and badness of school food.

In an unpublished journal written in his twenties, Merton remembered Sunday afternoons as a particularly hungry time.

After a long walk in the country, which was the only possible occupation, the boys would return rather gloomily to school. "Hunger and no prospect of anything but that doughy, heavy bread cut in chunks: the feeling that all the joints in my legs were loose and unstable—the feeling you get from walking a long way not normally or fast but listlessly, kicking stones." [3]

But life at Oakham was not listless for Merton on the whole. In his first year or two at the school, he used to play spies, or Stalky and Co., or Bulldog Drummond with his friends in the woods around Catmose House, eating fruit and chocolate and burying the evidence, and sometimes trespassing, fearing retribution if they were caught.

A little later, he remembers, he and a boy called Douglas Highton picked up a girl they met in the woods. They sat around playing records on Merton's phonograph, too embarrassed to think of anything to say to one another, until Merton, to his later shame, made an excuse to leave them for a few moments, and did not return, meanly abandoning his friend to the strange girl.

Soon Merton's intellectual ability began to show itself at the school, and he was moved up into the Upper Fifth form, but he was not yet exempt from the routine bullying and beating that was such a feature of English public schools of the time. "We were disciplined by the constant fear of one of those pompous and ceremonious sessions of bullying, arranged with ritualistic formality, when a dozen or so culprits were summoned into one of the hollows around Brooke Hill, or up the Braunston Road, and beaten with sticks, and made to sing foolish songs and hear themselves upbraided for their moral and social defects." [2]

Merton had his share of "social defects," particularly a passion for practical joking, often of the daring kind popular in those days that involved risky climbing over rooftops to tie umbrellas to chimneys, or placing rows of chamberpots on the roofs of the new "bogs" (lavatories), or hanging towels from end to end of the quad. He also composed a song with the unsophisticated words "Do-herty, Do-herty, your feet are so dirty, we smell them miles away!" which he played on the piano at an end-of-term party, in front of Headmaster Doherty. He left out the words on this occasion, but of course the boys laughed. Even as a prefect Merton once removed all the electric light bulbs from the dormitories and was ironically put in charge of investigating the incident.

Like all public schools of the period, Oakham enforced religious observance, and the boys attended chapel twice a day. The religion of Oakham was a rather muscular kind of Anglicanism. The chaplain, who had the not very flattering nickname of "Buggy," was a Cambridge rowing Blue, and his religious classes were apt to degenerate into a demonstration of the practical points of rowing. Even in the pulpit he was likely to exhort boys about the virtues of "being British" or keeping their bowels open. His religious teaching, when he got down to it, equated Christianity with scrupulous hygiene and the ethics of an English gentleman, and on one occasion at least he went through the famous passage in Corinthians about love, substituting the word *gentleman* for *charity*. "Charity meant good-sportsmanship, cricket, the decent thing, wearing the right kind of clothes, using the proper spoon, not being a cad or a bounder." [2]

Another master used Descartes' proof for the existence of God. Merton was slightly more impressed by this than by the sportsmanlike charity of the rowing chaplain, but religion at Oakham did not touch him as it had done at Ripley Court, although he liked arguing about it. But it was "not done" to argue too vociferously about religion and was liable to invite a beating from the prefects.

Intellectually, however, Oakham began to nourish and encourage Merton. After only a year at the school, he went up into the sixth form and came under F. C. Doherty's direct influence. Doherty was young, a classics teacher, and a passionate admirer of Plato. Merton acquired an instant schoolboy dislike of Plato—the very phrase "The Good, the True, and the Beautiful" filled him with irritation, because, he later thought, of the sort of abstraction involved, a world in which, as it were, reality was all happening somewhere else rather than here, and he conceived a dislike for Socrates that lasted the rest of his life.

Yet, improbably, Doherty perceived something of Merton's individual genius, and encouraged him to go against the grain of the school and study modern languages and literature (which gave Merton the liberty to study alone a great deal, because the school had not really developed a "modern" side). Instead of making him take the School Certificate, in which Merton's mathematical ineptitude would have caused him to fail, Doherty encouraged him to take the more advanced Higher Certificate, in which he could concentrate on languages.

Merton was also developing in other ways. The school magazine *The Oakhamian* shows that Merton was captain of boxing, acted the brash American in a version of Galsworthy's play *The Little Man*, entered a relay race, helped organize a reading society, and took a vigorous part in the debating society. His views were avant-garde and must have come as a surprise to most of his contemporaries. Thus he defended socialism, "mentioning the panacea of nationalization" in one debate and spoke up for the freedom of the "Continental Sunday" in another, attacking the repressive "Victorianism" of the English Sunday. More daringly, he proposed the motion "that the English Public School system is out of date": "T. F. Merton proposed the motion, putting forward somewhat sophisticated views on co-education which were ill received by the house. J. G. Cutts opposed, denying the possibility of discipline or *esprit de corps* in a co-educational school. . . . The motion was lost by 3 votes to 31." [4]

Contemporaries of Merton's remember how natural and uninhibited he was on all matters to do with sexuality, enthusiastically heterosexual in his interests (as evidenced by his pinups) in a single-sex world where undercurrents of homosexuality were more usual. Andrew Winser remembers an occasion, deeply shocking in those prewar days, when a mother visited the school, took a fancy to one of the boys, who reciprocated her feelings, and she asked Merton if he knew of anywhere they could go to be together. "We were all staggered, absolutely staggered, but Merton wasn't. He just thought it *funny*, terribly, hilariously, ridiculously funny."

Merton later remembered the pain of his nascent sexual longings in a world that seemed to him to have been shaped in its attitudes by the woman-hating Plato. "There were no girls anywhere except some skinny pimply town girls, and only a fool wanted to go out with them, they were so ugly. And besides, you might get expelled." [3] Merton enjoyed the world of "the boys," the swearing, bawdy, crude world of school, the secret smoking and drinking under haystacks, but he later realized that the absence of girls had meant an absence of love in his life and that this was more serious than the absence of sexual expression.

"One of the things I wanted to be was in love, and at Oakham there was nobody to be in love with. But the problem was greater than that too: it amounted to the whole problem of what I was living for." [3]

Like many another frustrated adolescent Merton consoled himself as well as he could by falling in love with movie stars—Clara Bow, Anita Page, Jean Harlow, Joan and Constance Bennett, Madeleine Carroll, and, in particular, Greta Garbo. Boys were not allowed to visit the Oakham cinema, but the older ones, greatly daring, occasionally surreptitiously did so.

Merton worked off a lot of energy playing rugby, where he threw himself fearlessly into the scrum and showed his usual boundless enthusiasm. In an article on "team characters" in the year 1932–33, Merton is described as "A first class forward who improved every match: very keen and always fit: very fair hooker with a good turn of speed: defence excellent." [4]

His enthusiasm did not extend either to the Scouts, from which he resigned at an early age, or to the OTC, in which he never rose beyond the rank of lance corporal. Andrew Winser has the impression that Merton regarded the OTC, rather like the sexual exploits of the boy's mother, as "a great joke," and found life altogether too short for military efficiency and spit-and-polish. On the other hand, if it came to a competition against another house or school, as it often did, "he would have been loyal," and done his best.

Merton's chief glory at school came with his editorship of the school magazine, *The Oakhamian*, which he took on in 1931. The change in it is quite extraordinary, with witty drawings and poems contributed by Merton (a world away from the usual sober lino cuts and photographs of School House or Chapel) and gossip, editorials, and articles that, even when not signed by him, have the unmistakable touch of his wit and vitality. There are poems in Chaucerian English, mock translations of Latin, and a spoof of a school story, called "The New Boy Who Won Through."

Inevitably, Merton wrote a great deal of the material, much of it with a cosmopolitan flavour. In an article called "The City Without a Soul," Merton describes New York, dwelling particularly lovingly on the "speakeasies" [4] He also describes Strasbourg Cathedral, a funny incident on a French train, and, with unconscious tragedy, the German presidential elections of April 1932, which Merton had witnessed. The piece is called "Wahlt Hitler" and reads, "The Hitlerites, working each for all and all for each, zealously pursued an hysterical campaign. There were posters showing Hitler at every stage in his career, from the cradle upwards. The charming studies of Little Adolf in swaddling clothes and later playing marbles were by no means the least interesting. . . . The most active part of the campaign, however, was carried out by some anonymous fanatics who devoted their leisure hours to painting notices, more or less offensive, in public places. The streets of certain German towns have been teeming with Hitlerites in the early hours of the morning, slinking from house to house with pails of whitewash. One even painted a swastika on every hundred meter post for several kilometers along a frequented highroad. . . . With election day, excitement reached its climax. Even in the most primitive villages some Hitlerite was stunned with a brick, or some Hindenburger half slain with a pitchfork." [4] The schoolboy Merton recognized the violence and hysteria of what he saw, if not its import.

His first holidays from Oakham Merton spent either with his beloved Aunt Maud at Ealing, or with Aunt Gwyn—Gwyneth Trier, his father's sister. Writing to Aunt Gwyn from Gethsemani two years before his death (they had lost touch for many years but were writing regularly to one another by then), he remembered what fun Christmas had been with her at Windsor and at a place called Fairlawn. "The place I liked best of all, when we were together, was Rye. Such a heavenly little town. I remember it with awe, as though it were enchanted." [5]

In 1930, Pop came over to England with Bonnemaman and John Paul. Chastened by the Depression, like everyone else, he yet retained his old generosity. He put up at the Crown Hotel in Oakham, and there he took the fifteen-year-old Merton aside and explained the family finances to him. To the end of his life, Merton always claimed to find business incomprehensible, and others testified to his inability or unwillingness to wrestle with financial and commercial facts, but on this occasion he was so awed at being accorded adult status and moved by Pop's trust in him, that he laboured to take it in. Shaken by the economic crisis, Pop had arranged to use the money he had intended to leave the two boys in his will for an insurance annuity scheme; this would pay them a regular sum each year to finance them through school and university and even through a possible spell of unemployment afterward. This fine and loving gesture guaranteed them a period of financial security, whatever other kinds of insecurity might threaten them.

Having astounded his grandson with this bombshell, Pop then surprised him still further by the gift of a pipe. Merton had already been surreptitiously smoking a pipe for some time—mainly for the pleasure of breaking the school rules—but was gratified by this recognition of his maturity, indicative of a sensitivity in Pop (who was not a smoker himself) for which his grandson rarely gave him credit.

In the summer holidays of 1930, the whole family—in-laws, Tom, and John Paul—went to visit Owen Merton in hospital. During his first year at school, Merton had scarcely seen his father, who had undergone operations that had done nothing to aid recovery. As soon as Tom saw him again, and perceived the gigantic swelling on his head, the swollen face, the dazed eyes, he knew Owen could not live long. "The sorrow of his great help-lessness suddenly fell upon me like a mountain. I was crushed by it. The tears sprang to my eyes. . . . I hid my face in the blanket and cried. And poor Father wept, too. The others stood by. It was excruciatingly sad. We were completely helpless. There was noth-ing any one could do. . . . What could I make of so much suffering? There was no way for me, or for anyone else in the family, to get anything out of it. It was a raw wound for which there was no adequate relief. You had to take it, like an animal." [2]

The family continued to visit the sick man throughout that summer holiday, and Merton one day discovered the bed covered in little drawings on blue notepaper—pictures of tiny, irate Byzantine-looking saints with beards and great halos. It began dimly to occur to Merton that perhaps his father, the only one of them in the family with any deep religious faith, might be getting something from this terrible experience that he had not imagined, that far from simply "taking it" like an animal, he might be using it as a way to reach God, perfecting and transforming his soul in the process. But it would be a long time yet before he could really grasp such an idea.

Owen Merton lingered on through another Christmas, and when Tom had been back at school a week after the holidays, the headmaster sent for him one morning and gave him a telegram telling him his father was dead. Merton suffered depression for a while, but what was perhaps worse than the depression, or at the root of it, was the feeling that he could make nothing of the fact of his father's death. His father had been a large and generous soul, talented, loving, full of courage and goodness. And he had died a cruel and wretchedly long-drawn-out death that had brought anguish to everyone around him.

After the death of Owen Merton, Tom Bennett, Merton's god-father and an old New Zealand friend of his father's, became his guardian, and Merton began to spend school holidays at the Bennetts' London flat, in Harley Street, from which Dr. Bennett went every day to his work at the Middlesex Hospital.

Tom and his wife Iris, a petite and elegant Frenchwoman, lived with style and sophistication and with a knowledge of all that was most new and exciting in European culture; for the young Merton, visiting them could not have been more different from the cosiness of previous holidays with his aunts. Living in the centre of London was exciting, too. His days at Harley Street began with the French maid bringing him breakfast in bed—coffee and rolls and fried eggs. He would lie luxuriously in bed reading Evelyn Waugh, then bathe and dress and saunter forth, in trousers that had been pressed and shoes that had been cleaned for him, to the Times Book Club, or a museum, or for a walk in the park, or, more often, to a record shop called Levy's in Regent Street, where he would spend hours listening to jazz and perhaps come home with one of the records, which he would play to an amused Tom and Iris. He was a devotee of Louis Armstrong, Duke Ellington, King Oliver, and others, and played the "St. Louis Blues" himself (rather badly, he says) on the piano.

At meals with Tom and Iris, he suffered from a painful sense of his own adolescent awkwardness and crudity. "We would have lunch in the dining-room, sitting at the little table that always seemed to me so small and delicate that I was afraid to move for fear the whole thing would collapse and the pretty French dishes would smash on the floor and scatter the French food on the waxed floorboards. Everything in that flat was small and delicate. . . . Everything in their flat was in proportion to their own stature and delicacy and precision and neatness and wit." [2]

Perhaps there was more aggression than he knew in his attitude to this friendly and fashionable couple that caused Merton to be so fearful of smashing things and doing damage. The flat was "full of objects I was afraid to break and, on the whole, I was scared to walk too heavily for fear I might suddenly go through the floor." [2]

The boy could not fully trust these foster parents he had acquired, nor feel that they had wholly accepted him. Yet he was full of a hero-worshipping admiration of Tom Bennett and his worldliness, and hung on his words and his opinions as years before he had hung on the words of his father. From Tom and Iris, Merton learned about D. H. Lawrence and Joyce, Hemingway, Gide, Céline's *Voyage au Bout de la Nuit*. (He had already discovered Eliot at school.) They went to Paris together and looked at the paintings of Chagall, and Merton was shown Réné Clair movies and the Eisenstein films. Privately (the Bennetts did not share these tastes) Merton was also beginning to enjoy Braque and Picasso and the Marx Brothers.

Perhaps even more significant than educating Merton in the arts, the Bennetts indicated a new attitude to life, a kind of wry detachment from the conventional world that felt excitingly naughty but fun to do. "From the first moment when I discovered that one was not only allowed to make fun of English middle-class notions and ideals but encouraged to do so in that little bright drawing-room, where we balanced coffee-cups on our knees, I was very happy. I soon developed a habit of wholesale and glib detraction of all the people with whom I did not agree or whose taste and ideas offended me." [2]

In *My Argument with the Gestapo*, Tom and Iris appear as Uncle Rafe and Aunt Melissa, and Merton's feelings of adolescent worship (with the underlying sense of insecurity—the lighthearted mockery could, after all, turn against him) emerge even more strongly.

One evening we are having supper in the Monseigneur, to hear Douglas Byng. The place is garish and stupid, and the large table next to us fills with people who do not look especially awkward to me, but Uncle Rafe says:

"They are in town from the suburbs, and in a minute they will all order consommé madrilène. People from the suburbs always order consommé madrilène as soon as they see it on the menu."

Immediately, from amid the murmur of voices, I can hear the words "Consommé madrilène," spoken with a little complacency. I am filled with astonishment and admiration. . . . I also respected Uncle Rafe because he mocked the House of Windsor. . . . I once argued with him for a few minutes that Ravel's *Bolero* was not phony, but soon saw he was right. The next time I heard Ravel's *Bolero*, I knew it was phony.

Supposing I made a list of the things that I heard of, first of all, from Uncle Rafe? It would be very long.

It would be made up of the names of books of painters, of cities, of kinds of wine, of curious facts about the people in the world, about races and about languages and about writing. Only from my father did I learn what would make a longer list than that of the things I first heard of from Uncle Rafe. [1]

Uncle Rafe—Tom Bennett—was a father figure, a tutor in the ways of the world, an intellectual model against which the adolescent could measure himself. He represented a wonderful release from the safe, aunt-flavoured English world of monarchy, the Empire, horses, and hearty philistinism, giving space for Merton's mind and senses to grow, as, in its more formal way, Oakham was also doing. Yet with their sophistication and subtlety, Tom and Iris overlooked the directness with which Merton responded to what he read. The morals of D. H. Lawrence, of Gide, or Joyce were not for them models to be emulated, but ways of understanding the world and its behaviour with a certain tolerance and breadth of vision. What did not occur to them, what eventually led Merton to a sense of betrayal by them, and to a rupture between him and them, was that the boy took his favorite authors' writings about morals, and in particular about sexual morals, as a prescription of the way to live.

Then, and in the three years before he left England for good, Merton was exploring London and his emotions about England, and they were disquieting ones. His earliest impressions of England, under the ægis of the aunts, had been of neatness, cleanness and prettiness, a world of cricket and Empire, of King George V and Queen Mary, of Boots' library books, and Lyons tea shops, and muscular Anglicanism and Daniel Neal's clothes for children, and digestive biscuits, a world of middle-class comfort and decency and an almost dotty devotion to animals, particularly horses and dogs. The teenage Merton was, not unusually, in revolt against all these things and against the pleasant, but rather complacent, values they represented. He was feeling outward from this insular little world, to a bigger world, of which the prophets were D. H. Lawrence, Hemingway, and Picasso.

As he began to explore London by himself, and to move away from the safe havens of Ealing and Rye, he began to feel horror at the poverty and decadence that underlay the pin-neat, Gilbert and

Sullivan facade, to detect a brutality that frightened him and a terrible desolation that touched his own deepest wounds.

"The first city [the safe, comfortable London of his childhood] vanished when I walked the streets of the second at night, when I learned to listen to the gaiety of the taxi-drivers turn to ashes, and hear the walls of houses echoing, from street to street, the harlot's curse, and the dead good humor of the crippled beggars who lie to amuse the rich, and the servile obscenity of the songs they whisper at the corner of bars. . . . The second city . . . was as terrible as no music at all, as dark as chaos, as inescapable as Fear." [1]

Adult feelings and an adult body brought experiences that destroyed the comfortable innocence of the child. He speaks painfully of "the laugh of fear and derision that used to yawn in my entrails when the whores called out to me in the old days." The untroubled world of D. H. Evans and riding down Oxford Street on the open buses had given way to something ominous, the more so because he did not know quite what threats lay behind the cheating facade of London.

> The fast discreet silences of the city were all false.
> The huge discretion of the fog was hiding everything and was hiding too much.
> The whores in ermine marched out of the doorways, in the dark. . . .
> Then suddenly you began to suspect, inside the reticent houses, long, inarticulate insanities. Then suddenly you wondered what perversions you might read if you knew how to interpret the windows. [1]

As he got to know London better and discovered its slums, its pitiful beggars, its crankiness (as revealed in the soap-box speakers at Hyde Park Corner), his distaste for it grew. Before he finally left England altogether, it would grow into a loathing that eventually spilled out in the bitterness and spleen of *My Argument with the Gestapo*. [1] It became for him a symbol of self-satisfied wealth stifling the cries of the poor. No doubt even as an adolescent Merton must have known that other European cities (Paris and Rome, both of which he had visited) equally camouflaged and ignored the hidden sores of poverty, but it was perhaps the complacency of that prewar Britain, and particularly of the educated classes, that alienated him. Looking at the outcasts of that society—the sad entertainers of theatre queues, the organ grinders, the beggars, the tramps, the unemployed—he knew, or feared, his orphaned self to

be one of them. He knew himself not to be one of the elect—"Men in
bowlers and dark suits . . . with their rolled-up umbrellas. Men full
of propriety, calm and proud, neat and noble." [1]

Maybe it was because of this disquieting new awareness of
London that he began to read Blake. Not understanding him, he
still fell in love with his poetry, and he remembered a grey day in
spring when he walked alone on Brooke Hill near his school and
concentrated totally on what Blake was trying to say. "It was a
long, bare hog-back of a hill, with a few lone trees along the top,
and it commanded a big sweeping view of the Vale of Catmos, with
the town of Oakham lying in the midst of it, gathered around the
grey sharp church spire. I sat on a stile on the hill top, and
contemplated the wide vale."

What slowly came to the youth on the stile was a sense of Blake's
great faith and love and goodness, and the unerring way, for all his
craziness, he found his way through the minefields of the Enlightenment on the one hand, and through the pharisaism and terror of
sexuality that had marked so much orthodox Christianity, on the
other. In a world of falsity and dangerous ambiguity, Blake seemed
a trustworthy guide, prophet, and guru. He planted seeds in the
boy's mind that a few years later would grow and blossom. "I have
to acknowledge my own debt to him, and the truth which may
appear curious to some, although it is really not so: that through
Blake I would one day come, in a round-about way, to the only true
Church, and to the One Living God, through His Son, Jesus
Christ." [2]

In the summer of 1931, Pop and Bonnemamam invited Merton
over to Long Island for the vacation. He had himself a new suit
made and set off on the ten-day boat journey with some reading for
the Cambridge Scholarship examination and a determination to
find a girl to fall in love with. He was to write later of the unreal
passions felt by adolescent boys locked up in a single-sex school for
nine months of the year—they harboured falsely romantic views of
womankind and a consequent male longing for heroics, for feats of
daring and tests of chivalry. The Californian woman whom he met
on the boat (it did not occur to him until nearly the end of the
journey that she was twice his age) bore out that observation. He
fell in love with her so sentimentally, abjectly, and miserably that
even ten years later he recalled it with a deep, squirming shame and

with nothing but contempt for his sixteen year-old self. "To my dazzled eyes she immediately became the heroine of every novel and I all but flung myself face down on the deck at her feet. She could have put a collar on my neck and led me around from that time forth on the end of a chain. Instead of that I spent my days telling . . . all about my ideals and ambitions and she in turn attempted to teach me how to play bridge." [2] Part of the misery of it all was that on one level he could see that she was not very intelligent, not really "his type" at all; all the same, on the last night on board he declared his undying love for her and was gently, but firmly, told to grow up. He took a photograph of her the next morning that, perhaps not surprisingly, came out blurred.

His relatives, eagerly waiting for him on the dock, found him morose and difficult, and it was not an easy visit. On the return journey, there were no love affairs, but there were a number of American college girls going to school in France with whom he played jazz, and flirted, and got drunk, and argued about communism, which was beginning to attract him. He had bought a "gangster suit" in America with padded shoulders and a grey hat that he pulled down over one eye: he arrived back at Oakham several days late for the beginning of term, altogether a somewhat older, if not wiser, boy than the one who had left it at the end of the summer term.

Merton was now a house prefect of a section of the school called Hodge Wing. He had a big study to himself with wicker armchairs filled with cushions; he hung Impressionists and pictures of Venus on the walls and filled the bookshelf with modern novels and political pamphlets, including the *Communist Manifesto*. He was working hard at languages and beginning the wide and insatiable reading of modern literature that would continue for the rest of his life—Aldous Huxley, André Gide, John Dos Passos, Theodore Dreiser, Jules Romains, Ernest Hemingway, D. H. Lawrence. Philosophy, too, had begun to fascinate him.

At Easter, on a lone walking tour in Germany, he concentrated on trying, as he put it, to "figure out Spinoza." He knew Germany a little, from two study vacations spent with a professor at Strasbourg, but now he set off alone, with some courage for a seventeen-year-old whose spoken German was not particularly good, up the

Rhine Valley. He felt it a romantic expedition—a nineteenth-century gesture.

He took the Higher School Certificate in June, in French and Latin. Thirty years later, he remembered a precious moment of that summer, a moment precipitated by his Latin studies.

> One June morning before the exams I got up very early and walked out into the hills, taking Vergil along, and wandered with the Georgics along the ridge of Brooke Hill and the rather imaginary golf-course that was up there among the old pre-Roman British forts, marked by grassy mounds and dikes. Then I came down across the Uppingham Road, by the little village of Egleton, and ended up sitting on a fallen tree trunk over a brook behind Catmose House. There I read (for the fifteenth time) these lines:

> > Felix qui potuit rerum cognoscere causas
> > Atque metus omnes, et inexorabile fatum
> > Subjecit pedibus, strepitumque Acherontis avari.*

> . . . . For me the lines retain an inexhaustible beauty. . . . To have learned such lines as these and many others is to have entered into a kind of communion with the inner strength of the civilization to which I belong, and whatever may be the roar of Acheron . . . this inner strength is, in itself, indestructible.

References

1. Thomas Merton. *My Argument with the Gestapo*. New York: Doubleday, 1969. Written 1941. Originally titled "The Journal of My Escape from the Nazis." Reprinted by New Directions, 1975.
2. Thomas Merton. *The Seven Storey Mountain*. New York: Harcourt Brace, 1948; London: SPCK, 1990. Also published abridged as *Elected Silence* (London: Burns & Oates, 1949).
3. Thomas Merton. Unpublished journal. Written 1940–1941. TMC.
4. *The Oakhamian* 46 (1931); 47 (1932); 48 (1933). Oakham School, Oakham.
5. Thomas Merton. Letter to Aunt Gwyn (Gwyneth Trier). December 20, 1966.
6. Thomas Merton. *Conjectures of a Guilty Bystander*. New York: Doubleday, 1966.

* "Fortunate is he who can see into the meaning of things, and thus crush all fear and inexorable fate under foot, and ignore the hungry roar of Acheron."

4

DAMP AND FETID MISTS

In the summer holiday of 1932, Merton spent two months with Pop, Bonnemaman, and John Paul at a hotel in Bournemouth, that seaside bastion of all the decent English virtues. Not surprisingly, the avant-garde teenager with communist leanings felt rebellious, and expressed his rebellion by neglecting his relatives and pursuing a girl he met on the beach. It was a rather glum and quarrelsome love affair, and, still pining from it, Merton went off to camp by himself in the New Forest. He was a bit unnerved by the loneliness of the camp site, the food he cooked over a campfire upset his stomach, and he was doubtful about the safety of the local stream as drinking water, so he moved to an inn at Beaulieu, coolly admiring the broken arches of the medieval Cistercian Abbey and waiting to get a letter from his girlfriend at a local post office.

In September, Merton moved on to stay with Andrew Winser, whose father was rector of Brooke, on the Isle of Wight. It was a warm and friendly family—the Winser parents enjoyed drawing out their children's friends, and Andrew and his two younger sisters simply enjoyed Merton as a good companion. But Andrew, much as he liked Merton, found him at times a bit intense and un-English. He remembers that, when the two boys went for a walk on the downs together, Merton theatrically flung himself down on the ground and grabbed handfuls of grass with the cry "The earth—I love the earth!" It was not the kind of thing an Englishman would do.

Merton accompanied the family to matins every Sunday, and one Sunday read the lesson, chosen by himself, the parable about the men who built their houses respectively on the sand and the rock. His rendering showed a particular relish at the fate of the house built on sand, and he used dramatic intensity over the line "And it fell! And great was the fall thereof!" And Andrew again felt faintly embarrassed for his friend.

Damnation must have been somewhat on Merton's mind on that
visit, because in Andrew's bedroom at the Rectory he painted, at
Andrew's invitation, an epic mural of the Fall of Lucifer. God's boot
was apparent up in the right-hand corner, and tumbling down to
the flames of Hell were a bookmaker, a rakish undergraduate, and
other unrepentant characters. Merton spent much of his holiday
working on this picture, and it was admired by the rest of the
family, particularly by Andrew's sister Ann. Ann was only thirteen,
but she made an impression, partly perhaps because Merton had no
sisters of his own and knew no little girls, but also for other reasons.
Ann appears as Anne in *My Argument with the Gestapo*. "I respected
[her] a lot, although she was nothing but a little girl and never said
anything much or was of any account at all." [1] Twenty-five years
after writing that, Merton found himself remembering her again.
What he remembered was Ann's quietness. He had not been in love
with her—she had been too young for that—and yet he had never
forgotten her, and had an odd feeling that if life had turned out
only a little differently he might have married her. She symbolized
the kind of quiet and gentle woman whom he had never found in
life, and whose absence, he felt, had left a permanent incomplete-
ness within him. [2]

In *My Argument with the Gestapo*, Merton links that holiday in
Brooke with another stage in his emotional growing-up. He
describes going to "the pictures" with the Winser family, himself
and Ann very seriously discussing the film they were about to see, and
then, on the way out of the cinema, "I saw . . . a group of people
coming out of another door, and in the midst of them a girl with
pretty eyes and white skirt, still slim, but a lot changed: it was B." [1]

B. remembered Merton from the tennis party, and a few days
later he and the Winser children were invited to a fancy dress party
at the house of B.'s host, a local admiral. Andrew went as a friar,
Ann as an eighteenth-century shepherdess, and Merton, clad in
sombrero and boots, as a South American horse thief. (Andrew
felt Merton looked a bit raffish.) B. was a gypsy.

"I asked her to dance. She came away from the group, and we
started across the floor together immediately aware that neither of
us was a good dancer. Twice she tripped lightly against the toe of
my shoe. I made a couple of jokes about costumes." [1]

After that the party did not go too well. Lots of guests seemed to
be wearing sombreros, so Merton took his off, feeling silly and

childish; now "I looked like nothing more than a person with riding breeches on." But when the moment came to go home he was seized with a sudden longing to find B. again before it was too late. "B. was standing by the window all alone. I paused for a moment and looked at her to make sure.

"Yes, she was bored to death.

"Then I knew that I loved her more than the whole world, and we began to dance." [1]

Possibly on that holiday, possibly on an earlier one, Andrew Winser visited Harley Street to have a meal with Merton. Tom and Iris were away, and their dinner was served by the maid. Andrew was aware, then and at other times, how different Merton's circumstances seemed from his own and from that of other boys he knew. Merton struck him as "a bit of a loner."

Merton had passed his Higher School Certificate, and in December he and Andrew Winser sat the scholarship examination at Cambridge. They learned from *The Times* a few days later that Merton had won an exhibition at Clare and Winser at St. Catherine's. A few weeks later Merton was bound for Italy, but first he celebrated his eighteenth birthday.

> It is my eighteenth birthday. There is a little sun. I ride back in the bus from Dulwich, where Uncle Rafe sent me to see a man who would tell me where to find rooms in Italy. . . .
>
> Look, I still carry . . . the wallet Uncle Rafe gave me for a present. It was the best wallet I ever saw, from Finlay's, in Bond Street.
>
> On my eighteenth birthday, this wallet is new, and smells fine, and is full of tickets to Italy.
>
> The evening of the day I am eighteen, we have dinner at the Café Royal, we see a film, we go to the Café Anglais, maybe we have some champagne. . . . The next day, I take the boat train. [1]

It was a moment of hope and happiness in Merton's life; approved by the admired Tom, he set off on his adult journey. He began his grand tour by exploring the South of France on foot, and within a month, to his embarrassment, he ran out of money and had to wire to Tom for more. The money arrived accompanied by "sharp reproofs." "Tom . . . took occasion of my impracticality to call attention to most of my other faults as well, and I was very humiliated." [3]

He went to Genoa, where he was miserable, with a huge boil on his elbow, and to Florence where he stayed with a sculptor with whom he shared a passion for Greta Garbo. Eventually he arrived in Rome, still wretched from the boil; by now he also had an abscessed tooth that gave him an excruciating toothache. The tooth was removed and as he recovered, he began slowly to explore Rome. Gradually he lost interest in the relics of Imperial Rome and discovered a taste for the churches—for the shrines and altars and mosaics and frescoes. "And thus . . . I became a pilgrim," a pilgrim who, rather to his surprise, found himself turning to the Gospels to learn more of the Christian background.

He was, of course, alone, as so often in his life, and the ancient shrines he was visiting daily, with their powerful Christian symbols, acted strongly on his imagination. One night he had a profoundly religious experience, not exactly a conversion experience, but something rather like what the Puritans used to call "conviction of sin," an acute awareness of himself in the light of divine grace. Not surprisingly perhaps, it was linked with mourning for his lost father.

> I was in my room. It was night. The light was on. Suddenly it seemed to me that Father, who had now been dead more than a year, was there with me. The sense of his presence was as vivid and as real and as startling as if he had touched my arm or spoken to me. The whole thing passed in a flash, but in that flash, instantly, I was overwhelmed with a sudden and profound insight into the misery and corruption of my own soul, and I was pierced deeply with a light that made me realize something of the condition I was in, and I was filled with horror at what I saw, and my whole being rose up in revolt against what was within me, and my soul desired escape and liberation and freedom from all this with an intensity and an urgency unlike anything I had ever known before. And now I think for the first time in my whole life I really began to pray . . . praying out of the very roots of my life and of my being, and praying to the God I had never known, to reach down towards me out of His darkness. . . . There were a lot of tears connected with this, and they did me good. [3]

The next day Merton climbed the Aventine, went into Santa Sabina, took holy water at the door and knelt down and prayed, something he had never done on his previous visits to churches. It took courage to do this, because he felt painfully self-conscious about others seeing him at prayer, but he went away feeling "reborn" and full of joy. For the rest of his time in Rome, he tasted the happiness of this experience. One afternoon he visited the Trappist monastery at Tre Fontane, and fleetingly the idea occurred to him, as it occurs to many visiting a monastery, "I should like to become a Trappist monk." "Is there any man," Merton asks pertinently in his autobiography, "who has ever gone through a whole lifetime without dressing himself up, in his fancy, in the habit of a monk and enclosing himself in a cell where he sits magnificent in heroic austerity and solitude, while all the young ladies who hitherto were cool to his affections in the world come and beat on the gates of the monastery crying "Come out, come out!" [3] As always Merton is touchingly truthful about his fantasies. On the way back from that visit to Tre Fontane, he happened to meet a student he knew accompanied by his mother to whom, still enjoying his fantasy, he confided that he would like to become a monk. He was rather taken aback by the extreme horror with which she greeted this declaration.

He still had six months or so to fill in before he went up to Cambridge, so to begin with he went back to America, to his grandparents at Douglaston. The religious fervour was still on him, although beginning to cool, and he read the Bible rather surreptitiously and tried to pray, but was embarrassed because he shared his room with his uncle. He went to the Zion Church with his grandparents and decided he detested it, and he tried the Quakers at Flushing (where his mother had once gone to Meeting), but was put off by the silliness of some of the speakers, whose commonplaces offended his arrogant youthfulness.

With his habitual adventurousness, he got himself a job as a barker at a pornographic sideshow at the World's Fair in Chicago. For a day or two, he found this fun, but then discovered that it was difficult to extract his earnings from his employer and that anyway he found the sexual crudity of the spectators more offensive than he had expected.

So he took off again, this time for New York, where he spent the rest of the summer staying with the painter Reginald Marsh at his studio on 14th Street. Marsh, who had been a friend of his father's, gratified some large, vulgar, almost Hogarthian appetite in Merton.

Together they went to burlesque shows, the theatres, "stinking of
sweat and cheap cigars," and to Union Square, and to Coney Island,
and Marsh "looked out at the world through the simple and
disinterested and uncritical eyes of the artist, taking everything
as he found it." [3] It was a kind of love, and for an eighteen-year-
old an exciting introduction to the world; Marsh, like Bennett, was
another substitute father and thus deeply influential. Regretfully
Merton dragged himself away from this warm world and back
across the Atlantic to "the pale green downs of England" and
"the dark, sinister atmosphere of Cambridge." [3]

In the early 1930s, Cambridge undergraduates were drawn almost
entirely from the upper and professional middle classes, and the
place was pervaded by a kind of "gentlemanly" ethos that made
Merton feel crude and "colonial." Because of his travels, his wide
experience of the world, and his independence, he was far more
mature than most eighteen-year-olds: he was uninhibited about
women and about sexuality in a way unusual among Englishmen
of his generation who were nearly all educated in single-sex schools.
He had a kind of blatant enthusiasm and curiosity about life foreign
at any time to the English temperament but particularly strange to
the "gentlemanly" Cambridge of the 1930s, for which a cool and
understated elegance was the ideal. Merton, in fact, had more of
Pop's rumbustious vitality than he ever cared to own, or know, and,
as he says, "I was breaking my neck to get everything out of life
that you think you can get out of it when you are eighteen." [3]
    Merton's old school friends are unanimous in thinking that a
very great change came over him as soon as he went up to Cambridge. They use phrases like "he went right off the rails," was like
a "ship without an anchor," he "mucked in with the wrong set," he
took up "wenching and drinking," and "debauchery is not too
strong a word." He certainly drank a great deal with a very hearty
crowd who frequented the Lion (the "Leo," they called it) and the
Red Cow, and was gated for drinking on several occasions. He also
ran up bills that he could not afford to pay, threw a brick through a
shop window, got arrested for riding on the running-board of a car,
cut lectures, and climbed in and out of his own and other colleges
at night and helped various girls to do the same. More convention-
ally, he read Dante with Professor Bullough, drew cartoons for the
undergraduate magazine *Granta* and wrote poetry for magazines

that would not publish it, hung Impressionists and some of Marsh's etchings on the walls of his room, went to a number of plays, entered a public amateur competition for playing the drums, and rowed in the Clare fourth boat.

He was always in a scrape of some kind. Two of his friends remember waiting for him at his rooms at 71 Bridge Street. Merton arrived dripping wet from having fallen out of a punt into the river and went into his bedroom to change, leaving the door ajar. The others made so much noise singing and playing the piano that the landlord came roaring up from downstairs to complain. Seeing a strip of bare flesh through the crack in the door, he shouted (to the delight of his audience), "Don't think I don't know, Merton. You've got a girl in there!"

Merton's girls, somewhat to the dismay of his old school friends, were often shop girls, or girls "not of our class," although there were also one or two from other colleges. He remembered going out for a while with one popularly known as the "Freshman's Delight." Looking back from his fiftieth birthday, what he regretted most about his youth was his lack of love, the selfishness he had shown toward girls, covering his shyness and his longing for love with a dismissive glibness. Some of the girls had really loved him, but he could never accept or believe it. He recalled with sadness his unkindness to various girls—two called Joan and Sylvia he remembered particularly—and regretted the way he had tried to live up to an illusion of the person he ought to be, instead of simply trying to be himself. [2]

Although Merton did little work, at the end of the year he got a second-class degree in the first part of the Modern Languages Tripos examination (in French and Italian). Andrew Winser remembers meeting him coming away from one of the examinations. "'How did you get on, Merty?'

" 'Well, I was dying for a cigarette so I didn't wait till the end.'"

Into one brief year he had packed an extraordinary amount of experience, good and bad, he had lived with tremendous energy, and a certain sort of style. (Andrew remembers a very unconventional taste in dress including a velvet-lined cloak). At least some of it must have been fun. Why is it then that later Merton always wrote of Cambridge with such pain, as of an episode in his life he would prefer to forget?

There are three experiences that are the key to this pain. One is an event that he mentioned several times and that obviously had a great hold on his imagination at the time. One day at Clare a man, whom he only knew slightly, hanged himself in the showers. Because Merton was not closely involved with him, he did not feel guilt, but any suicide is threatening to others, and for Merton it seemed to strip away the feverish energy and the determined "having a good time," which was such a feature of his under-graduate life and to expose a terrible despair that he had been trying to ignore. Suicide was to occur again later in his student life and each time it would distress him deeply, however little he knew the person concerned.

The second experience concerned a girl, one of the girls "not of our class." One day Merton came to Andrew Winser and told him that he had "got a girl into trouble"; he was deeply distressed by this. Later he was to mention this to friends at Columbia. The girl eventually bore his son, but both mother and son were killed, according to Ed Rice, during the London air raids. [4]

The third experience concerned Merton's guardian, Tom Bennett. In spring 1933, he sent for Merton and asked him for some explanation of his conduct. This was not unreasonable; indeed, it was necessary, because Merton was about to become involved in legal action over the pregnancy, but what seems cruel, because the boy was already very shaken and distressed, was the way the interview was set up. Merton was summoned to London, kept hanging around for a very long time in the waiting room of Bennett's consulting office, and then "interviewed," or, more accurately, interrogated. Merton remembers mumbling some-thing about "not wanting to hurt others" which sounded ludicrous as soon as it was said. "The thing that made me suffer was that he asked me very bluntly and coldly for an explanation of my conduct and left me to writhe. For as soon as I was placed in the position of having to give some kind of positive explanation or defense of so much stupidity and unpleasantness, as if to justify myself by making it seem possible for a rational creature to live that way, the whole bitterness and emptiness of it became very evident to me, and my tongue would hardly function." [3]

Merton's orphaned state had never stood him in worse stead, for while his own parents, if they had been alive, might have demurred at his youthful rakishness and demanded an explanation, it is unlikely that they would have set up the inquiry in quite so painful and magisterial a way or with so little feeling for his youth and sensitivity. In fact, of course, Bennett's attack seemed particularly unjust because Merton was, however naïvely, attempting to follow the pattern of being "the man of the world" that he believed Bennett had indicated to him, following the sexual mores of writers such as Hemingway and Lawrence, whom Bennett admired.

In a letter written to the Baroness de Hueck (Catherine Doherty) in 1941 Merton referred obliquely to the incident, and said that "lawyers were involved." [5] Cambridge legal records reveal no mention of any legal action concerning Merton or his guardian, so unless an affiliation order was filed in some other part of England, the probable outcome was that the girl's family and Bennett settled out of court, making financial settlements for mother and child.

At the end of the academic year, Merton sailed for New York. He was expecting to return the following October and had chosen rooms in Clare. He did not say goodbye to his friends. He did not see Tom and Iris again, although he had promised to do so. Once Merton had arrived in Douglaston, Bennett sent him a letter saying that his academic achievement was not good enough for the Diplomatic Service and suggesting he would do better to stay in America; Merton seized on this suggestion with immediate enthusiasm. Tom Bennett clearly wished to be rid of an embarrassing encumbrance; in America, Merton would be his grandparents' concern more than his guardian's, and far away from the girl whose disgrace he had caused. But for Merton, despite his relief at getting away from what he called "the damp and fetid mists" of Cambridge, the decision left the sour taste of unredeemed failure and disgrace, a miserable inheritance at nineteen. He had longed for love but had found instead how easy it is to father an unwanted child. He had no further contact with the girl or her child, and because of this was deeply troubled by guilt. It was common enough then for a "gentleman" to father a child by a "lower-class" girl and then disown her, but perhaps tragic that Bennett encouraged Merton in this. A cloud seemed to have spread over his life, a cloud that he associated particularly with England.

Perhaps Merton was right to sense in that prewar England, with its rigid conventions and class consciousness, a deadness that stifled everyone it touched. But it is also clear that Cambridge and London, where he spent his holidays, were darkened by his own lowering depression and by the painful awkwardness of his

experiments in being a "man of the world," experiments that left
him sadder and lonelier than he had been to start with and that
made his identity seem ever more uncertain and elusive. Like many
of us, he projected his feelings on the landscape around him. "In
how many strange rooms in London have I awakened and lain in
bed, sometimes loving the smell of tea on the stairs, sometimes
loving the sound of water running into a bath, or the sight of
Christmas fogs: but how much oftener have I awakened to hate the
blackness of the days, the wet wind stirring the sooty curtains, the
voices of foreigners on the stairs, and the sound of water weeping in
the confinement of the air shafts on which my window opened." [1]

Both the description and the feelings are reminiscent of T. S.
Eliot, another exiled American struggling with despair. Unlike
Eliot, Merton passionately wanted to be a participant in life, not
the fastidious observer. Part of him longed to be the man of action,
the Hemingway man with his women, liquor, fights, and his easy
knowledge of the world, and he had the courage and the nervous
vitality for it. Another part, desperately vulnerable, wanted but was
afraid of tenderness, kindness, love, some real authenticity of
feeling, and was nauseated by the squalor of the ways in which
humans seek for this. An inviolable innocence remained, even in his
despairing attempts to become part of "the world."

References

1. Thomas Merton. *My Argument with the Gestapo*. New York: Doubleday,
   1969. Written 1941. Originally titled "The Journal of My Escape
   from the Nazis." Reprinted by New Directions, 1975.
2. Thomas Merton. "Vow of Conversation." Unpublished journal, dated
   1964–1965. TMSC.
3. Thomas Merton. *The Seven Storey Mountain*. New York: Harcourt Brace,
   1948; London: SPCK, 1990. Also published abridged as *Elected Silence*
   (London: Burns & Oates, 1949).
4. Edward Rice. *The Man in the Sycamore Tree*. New York: Doubleday,
   Image Books, 1972.
5. Thomas Merton. Letter to Catherine Doherty (Baroness de Hueck).
   October 6, 1941.

Part Two

5

THAT CENTRE WHO
IS EVERYWHERE

❦

Merton was obliged to return to England to make immigration arrangements to stay in the United States, so that it was November before he finally left England for good. He therefore missed the fall term and enrolled at Columbia in the winter of 1935. Columbia, on the upper West Side of New York, on the edge of Harlem, has an exciting big-city atmosphere about it. It is no isolated academic retreat, but is very much part of the bustling world around it. Merton called it a "big, sooty factory" and noted approvingly that instead of wearing the fancy scarves and blazers and caps and gowns that had been part of the Cambridge way of life, most of the students were indistinguishable from the city workers who moved around them. It felt poorer, and somehow much more real than Cambridge, and almost at once he felt at home there. Some of the shame and self-disgust at his own failures fell away, and he felt a new sense of resolution and hope.

Almost at once he came under the spell of Mark Van Doren, an influence and friendship that was to be important to him for the rest of his life. In one class Van Doren was teaching eighteenth-century English literature to about twelve students. Merton was impressed that his teacher deeply loved the literature he talked about, that he did not feel a fashionable obligation to turn it into politics or sociology or "case-histories in psychoanalysis," or to show off his own cleverness or wit or charm. "Mark would come into the room and, without any fuss, would start talking about whatever was to be talked about. Most of the time he asked questions. His questions were very good, and if you tried to answer them intelligently, you found yourself saying excellent things that you did not know you knew, and that you had not, in fact, known before. . . . His classes were literally 'education'—they brought things out of you, they made your mind produce its own explicit ideas." [1]

How much did the gifted teacher whom Merton himself was later to become, owe to this fine example? Certainly Merton's teaching method, as demonstrated in several hundred tapes of his lectures, used a clear, straightforward style—he talked about "whatever was to be talked about"—and also showed a deep interest and love in what he discussed, and thought that what mattered was for students to ask the right questions. Merton suggests a different debt he owed to Van Doren—"The influence of Mark's sober and sincere intellect, and his manner of dealing with his subject with perfect honesty and objectivity and without evasions, was remotely preparing my mind to receive the good seed of scholastic philosophy." [1] Mark, he felt, "looked directly for the quiddities of things, and sought being and substance under the covering of accident and appearances. And for him poetry was, indeed, a virtue of the practical intellect, and not simply a vague spilling of emotions, wasting the soul and perfecting none of our essential powers." [1]

Merton had not yet arrived at scholastic philosophy, however. Before he did so, he had first to tread a path very familiar among intellectuals in the 1930s. Walking the snow-covered deck on the boat out from England, he had brooded on his self-centred life, at the mercy, as he felt, of his own appetites. Searching for some ideal that would lift him out of the morass, he thought that dialectical materialism might be the answer. Communism might be, he hoped, "an open door out of my spiritual jail." At Columbia, with his usual readiness for action, he tried to put this hope into practice.

There were many communists at Columbia at the time—not perhaps quite as many as the Hearst papers made out, but a number of the brighter students had embraced the cause, and some of the faculty. There were fights and mass meetings and demonstrations, and the inevitable fascist element at Columbia used to emulate the example of Europe and turn firehoses on the communists, so the political scene was lively, if not particularly rational. Ready to act on his principles, as always, Merton put on placards and walked up and down Amsterdam Avenue as a "sandwich man," accusing Italy of aggression against Ethiopia.

Like the students at Oxford who were, at the same time, vowing that in the event of war they would not fight for "king and country," because they felt all war was wrong, the students at Columbia stoutly proclaimed in a massive demonstration in the gym that they would not fight under any circumstances. (The solemn pledge was broken by students on both sides of the Atlantic when the Spanish Civil War broke out and there was the opportunity to fight for the communist cause.)

Long before the Spanish Civil War, however, Merton's infatuation with communism had begun to fade. He had made speeches, sold literature, demonstrated, struck and attended communist parties. At one such party, he signed on as a member of the Young Communist League, taking the party name Frank Swift. His satirical mind could not help relishing the fact that the party was held in the fashionable apartment of a girl whose well-to-do parents were away for the weekend, as later he could not help being amused by a discussion at a Young Communist League about a comrade who could not come to meetings because his father would not let him. Confronted by the human actuality of revolutionary idealism, his sense of the absurd seemed to get in the way and soon after signing on his ardour failed.

Merton was living out at Douglaston with Pop and Bonnemaman and coming in to 116th Street each day on the train. When the first summer vacation came, Merton and John Paul spent it swimming and playing jazz records and perpetually, endlessly, going to the movies. Merton claims that he saw nearly every movie between 1934 and 1937. It was an addiction that he hated but could not stop, for, while he loved a few of the great stars (Chaplin, W. C. Fields, and Harpo Marx) and could get sentimental from time to time about some of the women (Joan Bennett, Merle Oberon, Lillian Harvey, and Greta Garbo), he and his brother had developed a wickedly sophisticated response to the sillier aspects of movie romance. "We were almost always in danger of being thrown out of the theater for our uproarious laughter at scenes that were supposed to be most affecting, tender and appealing to the finer elements in the human soul—the tears of Jackie Cooper, the brave smile of Alice Faye behind the bars of a jail." [1]

In the fall of 1935, John Paul went off to Cornell and Merton back to Columbia. "October," as he remarks, "is a fine and dangerous season in America. It is dry and cool and the land is wild with red and gold and crimson, and all the lassitudes of August have seeped out of your blood, and you are full of ambition. It is a wonderful time to begin anything at all. You go to college, and every course in the catalogue looks wonderful." [1]

For Merton, with his natural enthusiasm for life and his bound-less energy, life began to open up delightfully in the way it had failed to do at Cambridge. He took courses in Spanish and German and French Renaissance literature. He pledged one of the frater-nities, undergoing the traditional week of torture and humiliations (eating gigantic quantities of bread and milk was one of the ordeals), and then received his enamel pin. He began to go roaring off in the evenings with his fraternity brothers to deafening speak-easies on 52nd Street, where he sometimes stayed until it was too late to catch the last train home.

He had another try at rowing but decided that was beyond him and took to cross-country running instead, going at the training with so much enthusiasm that he got blisters all over the soles of his feet and could not even walk.

He plunged into the exciting world of student publications, all operating noisily and aggressively up on the fourth floor of John Jay Hall, where the whole place was, enjoyably, "constantly seething with the exchange of insults from office to offfice." He began to draw cartoons for *Jester* and write for *Spectator*, the *Columbia Review*, and the college yearbook, which he eventually edited. Gradually he acquired friends who were to last him the rest of his life—Bob Giroux, who was editing the *Review*, although he did not become a close friend until much later; Ad Reinhardt; Ed Rice; Robert Lax; and others. In addition to all this feverish activity, he also, like most American students, took paid jobs—in his case working as an interpreter at the Rockefeller Center, tutoring rich Jewish children in Latin, and drawing advertising cartoons to publicize paper cups.

Photographs of Merton in his Columbia days show him looking like a breezy man-about-town, watch chain over waistcoat, hat on the back of his head; but the look is belied by his touching youthfulness and by a sensitivity about the expression even when it is one of self-mockery. And there was something about the fair hair, the blue eyes, the pale Anglo-Saxon complexion that added a kind of unwanted innocence to his appearance. Ed Rice remembers his first impression of him as a "noisy bastard" as Merton played jazz on a piano, knocking hell out of it. "I have," Merton remarked modestly, "ruined more than one piano by this method." [11

There were still some disturbing currents moving under the surface of his life despite his enthusiasm and his growing confi-dence. He smoked very heavily, thirty or forty cigarettes a day, and drank a good deal, and the intense activity may in itself have been a kind of drug. He was filled with an obscure distress that John Paul, in his freshman year at Cornell, had begun to lead a rakish life as bad as his own at Cambridge, running up large debts that he could not pay yet not really enjoying himself, trapped in a kind of adolescent depression from which he could not escape. Then yet another man known to Merton committed suicide—this time it was a fraternity brother called Fred who drowned himself in a local canal.

At odd moments, a shame and self-disgust and a sense of the wrongness of his life overwhelmed Merton. He remembered being overcome by this feeling when, having taken the last possible train home to Flushing, he hung around the bus station there in the early hours of the morning waiting for the first bus to Douglaston. There he saw the workers setting off to work: "men healthy and awake and quiet, with their eyes clear, and some rational purpose before them." [1]

In the autumn of Merton's second year at Columbia, Pop, having felt ill in the morning, died quite suddenly one afternoon. In the last year love had grown between the old man and the young one, and Merton grieved, quite openly and unaffectedly, going into the old man's room and, rather to his own surprise, falling to his knees and spontaneously praying beside the dead body. At once Bonnemaman began to fail in health, falling and breaking her arm, becoming very ill. She recovered but then finally died the following summer. When Bonnemaman lay very ill, Merton once again found himself praying, "You Who made her, let her go on living," not really noticing that he was beginning to talk to a God he did not believe existed. [1]

But there had been too many deaths in Merton's young life, and Pop and Bonnemaman, from when he was six years old or so, had spelled the only domestic security he knew. To his own bewilderment, although not altogether surprisingly, he began to move toward a physical and psychological collapse. To begin with, he collapsed at a cross-country run; he "simply fell down" as he put it "and lay on the ground" feeling dreadfully ill. Then he had a terrifying attack of vertigo on the Long Island train when, filled with nausea and shaking with fear, he became afraid he might fall beneath the wheels. This was the beginning of a neurotic disturbance that was to trouble him for nearly a year—"the year in which I would be all the time getting dizzy, and in which I learned to fear the Long Island Railroad as if it were some kind of a monster, and to shrink from New York as if it were the wide-open mouth of some burning Aztec God." [1] It was a good many years, nearly twenty, before Merton began to understand the nature of such psychological disturbances or at least the kind of refusal and blindness they represented in his own life. As it was, he simply suffered the consequences. Then, as throughout his life, the consequences were partly physical.

After the collapse on the Long Island train, he felt so ill that he took a room in a hotel just for the day and asked for the house physician to examine him. The doctor listened to his heart and took his blood pressure and told him he was overstimulated and that he needed to rest. He lay in the room in the hotel sufficiently frightened to try to follow the doctor's advice, but the pounding of the blood in his head made it impossible to sleep. He felt dizzy whenever he tried to stand, and afraid of the open window and the abyss beneath it, but eventually he got up and struggled back to Long Island, wondering if he had a nervous breakdown. The collapse turned into gastritis with a suspected ulcer, and he became passionately interested in diets and in his own health.

Unconsciously, or half-consciously, he was seeking a solution for the dizzying emptiness of his life. He had signed up for a course at Columbia in medieval French literature, and as a result was being drawn gently back into the medieval Catholic atmosphere of which he had caught a glimpse in his boyhood at St. Antonin. When he saw a copy of *The Spirit of Medieval Philosophy*, by Etienne Gilson, in Scribner's on Fifth Avenue, he went in and bought it. He felt exasperated when in the Long Island train he opened it and discovered the *imprimatur*, the official declaration of the Catholic Church that there was no doctrinal objection to the book, but in spite of his disgust he persisted with the book and it effected a remarkable revolution in his understanding. His Protestant relatives had left him with a feeling that Catholicism was sinister and that it imposed dogmas, like chains, on people's minds. But, reading Gilson, he seemed to soar into a great, wide landscape the existence of which he had never suspected. What seized his imagination (and it may be that this reveals him as a natural mystic) was the concept of *aseitas*.

In this one word, which can be applied to God alone, and which expresses His most characteristic attribute, I discovered an entirely new concept of God—a concept which showed me at once that the belief of Catholics was by no means the vague and rather superstitious hangover from an unscientific age that I had believed it to be. On the contrary, here was a notion of God that was at the same time deep, precise, simple and accurate and, what is more, charged with implications which I could not even begin to appreciate. . . . *Aseitas*—simply means the power of a being to exist absolutely in virtue of itself, not as caused by itself, but as requiring no cause, no other justification for its existence except that its very nature is to exist. There can be only one such Being: That is God. And to say that God exists *a se*, of and by and by reason of Himself, is merely to say that God is Being Itself. *Ego sum qui sum* ["I am who I am"]. And this means that God must enjoy "complete independence not only as regards everything outside but also as regards everything within Himself."

This notion made such a profound impression on me that I made a pencil note at the top of the page: "Aseity of God—God is being *per se*." [1]

This, and other statements of Gilson, provided Merton with a concept of God that made intellectual sense to him; he realized that part of the trouble hitherto was that the God whom the Christians worshipped had seemed such a ragbag of impossible ideas that his mind simply could not take hold of him. Now there seemed to be a way forward, a fairly tenuous and uncertain way, but a way.

Merton began to experience a wish to go to church, and picked the Zion Episcopalian church where his father had once played the organ. He went with more humility than he had gone there in the past, but, with its liberal doubts about many of the traditional doctrines of the Church it lacked precisely the intellectual clarity and perhaps the dogmatic certainty that he craved so much at that time.

More decisive for his development was the group of friends to which Merton belonged at Columbia, some of whom were to be close to him for the rest of his life. Years later, in the unpublished journal he wrote at the end of his life, he was to say that he at last "got it together" in his senior year and that he did so was due very largely to the quality of love, humour, and intellectual companionship he found with his Columbia friends. It was as if he found a true family and would never be quite so lonely again. Mark Van Doren was a key figure in this circle of friends, not quite one of them, but a beneficent father figure who helped to make it possible. Merton

says that what bound them all together was a "common respect for
Mark's sanity and wisdom."

At the beginning of Merton's junior year, he enrolled for a history
course and arrived in what he thought was the right classroom to
find it full of old friends from *Jester*. They were, it turned out,
waiting for Mark Van Doren to come and lecture on Shakespeare.
On an impulse, Merton decided to stay, and the Shakespeare course
turned out to be "the best course I ever had at college." In that
difficult year, when Merton was wrestling with his dizziness and his
neurotic terror of the train and his suspected ulcer, "We were
talking about the deepest springs of human desire and hope and
fear. . . . This class was one of the few things that could persuade me
to get on the train and go to Columbia at all. It was, that year, my
only health, until I came across and read the Gilson book." [1]

One of the other students in that class was Robert Lax, perhaps
to become the closest friend Merton ever had. "Taller than them all,
and more serious, with a long face, like a horse, and a great mane of
black hair on top of it, Bob Lax meditated on some incomprehensible woe." [1] Lax shared some of Merton's own confusion and
misery, and unexpectedly, a similar hidden terror: "the abyss that
walked around in front of our feet . . . and kept making us dizzy
and afraid of trains and high places." [1]

Lax was a Jew, with an instinctive spirituality and a natural
affinity for contemplatives. He had "a mind full of tremendous and
subtle intuitions, and every day he found less and less to say about
them, and resigned himself to being inarticulate. In his hesitations,
though without embarrassment or nervousness at all, he would
often curl his long legs all around a chair, in seven different
ways, while he was trying to find a word with which to begin." [1]

Lax and Seymour Freedgood shared a room in one of the dormitories where they lived in a state of chaos under the gaze of a picture
of a Hindu holy man whom Lax admired. Seymour was loved by the
others for his suavity and for a wonderful talent for lying that kept
his friends both confused and amused. For instance, Seymour and his
wife Nancy owned a dog that Merton was told to call Prince.
Certainly the dog answered to the name of Prince, and it was only
later that Seymour confided that its real name was Rex. Months later,
Merton observed that the family actually called the animal Bunky.

It was Seymour who introduced Merton to a Hindu monk,
Bramachari and suitably primed Merton with any number of lies

about his ability to levitate and walk on water. The monk turned out to have qualities that affected Merton far more—a total simplicity of life, a gentleness and kindness, a capacity for sudden bursts of merry laughter at the oddity of American life, and an undogmatic approach to his own belief, about which he rarely talked. Above all, he was a man profoundly centred on God. To Merton's astonishment, Bramachari urged him to read St. Augustine's *Confessions* and Thomas à Kempis' *The Imitation of Christ*.

In addition to Lax and Seymour, there were Ed Rice, the most talented draftsman on *Jester*; Bob Gibney, who in a pained, sarcastic way was searching for some religious faith; and Bob Gerdy, who was interested in scholastic philosophy. All of them toyed with the idea of becoming Catholics, except Ed Rice, who had been one from childhood. But somehow they did not do so, perhaps because, like Bob Gerdy, they were all waiting for a "sign," some kind of jolt from God that would make their duty clear.

Influenced by Aldous Huxley's *End and Means*, however, as well as by Bramachari, they became very fascinated by Oriental mysticism. Merton remembered not only the sense of peace with which he had sat and read about Oriental religion in the empty house at Douglaston but also how he totally failed to grasp its principles. All that he really got out of it at the time was a technique of relaxation that helped his sleeplessness. At the time of writing *The Seven Storey Mountain*, he wrote with Catholic superiority of Oriental mysticism in words that he must later have lived to regret.

> Ultimately, I suppose all Oriental mysticism can be reduced to techniques that do the same thing (i.e., achieve relaxation), but in a far more subtle and advanced fashion: and if that is true, it is not mysticism at all. It remains purely in the natural order. That does not make it evil, *per se*, according to Christian standards: but it does not make it good, in relation to the supernatural. It is simply more or less useless, except when it is mixed up with elements that are strictly diabolical: and then of course these dreams and annihilations are designed to wipe out all vital moral activity, while leaving the personality in control of some nefarious principle, either of his own, or from outside himself. [1]

Merton received his bachelor's degree in 1938 and enrolled in the graduate school of English. He began work on a master's thesis on "Nature and Art in William Blake." [2] He had acquired a kind

of horror of the world that made him doubtful of his old ambition,
so long ago confided to Aunt Maud, of wanting to be a newspaper
man, although he still had ambitions as a novelist. For the time
being, however, he wanted to be a university teacher.

That summer of 1938, which ended in three of them, Lax and
Merton and a girl called Dona Eaton collectively writing a novel
that Lax needed to complete for a novel-writing course (collectively
they got "B-minus" for it), Merton and his friends went for a
holiday to Olean, in upper New York State. It was beautiful
countryside with high hills, and white farmhouses and red barns,
and Lax's sister Gladys, usually known to them as Gladio, and her
husband, had a cottage there. On that first visit, Merton only stayed
a week, being anxious to get back to New York and to a girl on
Long Island he was in love with. During that week Lax took
Merton to St. Bonaventure's, a college run by Franciscans, but
the visit was not a success. Merton refused to get out of the car.
"I don't know what was the matter. . . . Too many crosses. Too
many holy statues. Too much quiet and cheerfulness. Too much
pious optimism. It made me very uncomfortable." [1]

In the autumn of 1938, Merton left his relatives' house at
Douglaston and rented a room on 114th Street behind the Columbia Library for $7.50 a week. He was working hard on his thesis, and
the discipline of the work and the passionate interest he felt in the
relation of art to religion centred him and deepened his spiritual
awareness. His method in his thesis was to use the aesthetic ideas of
St. Thomas Aquinas (as interpreted by Jacques Maritain) as a
touchstone by which to test Blake's thought. It is not difficult to
see Merton's own spiritual conflict appearing through his comments
about Blake: "Blake is a religious artist and as such he wants the
world to be not beautiful and appealing to him, but intelligible";
"Blake always deals with the fall into a violent, tragic conflict of
ideas, and the subsequent regeneration into spiritual and intellectual
harmony. This is the drama which mystics understand to underlay
the whole of human life"; and "Children and saints [quoting Henry
Adams] can believe two contrary things at the same time." [2]

Blake's credo, with its understanding of the need to sacrifice the
ego, made a great impression on him: "Whatever natural glory a
man has is so much taken from his spiritual glory. I wish to do
nothing for profit, I wish to live for art. I want nothing whatever, I
am quite happy."

What Blake and Maritain between them taught Merton (probably with the help of the author of the *Imitation of Christ*), was that art is part of a mystical and contemplative understanding of the world, that man's passions must be transfigured by love if men are not to prey cruelly on one another, and that men should seek the state of "virtue" in which that transformation has taken place or is in the process of taking place. It came to Merton that, child of his age that he was, he had tried to interpret life in terms of sociological and economic laws, but that these separated from faith and charity became yet another form of imprisonment. In personal relationships, too, the purely natural approach advocated by some of the writers Merton most admired lost sight of the transforming processes of love. "I, who had always been anti-naturalistic in art, had been a pure naturalist in the moral order. No wonder my soul was sick and torn apart: but now the bleeding wound was drawn together by the notion of Christian virtue, ordered to the union of the soul with God." [1]

This new understanding changed Merton on a very deep level. With his usual passionate enthusiasm, he had only to perceive this great truth to want to dedicate his life to God and to achieve the heights of mystical marriage, a fact he later remembered with a certain wryness. "I was already dreaming of mystical union when I did not even keep the simplest rudiments of the moral law." [1] He smoked enormous quantities of cigarettes; "got plastered," as he says, fairly regularly; and pursued girls with his usual vigour and enthusiasm. The difference now, perhaps, was that as he got drunk he talked more and more about mysticism to his friends. He felt a growing desire to pray and began to do so fairly regularly.

He was in the habit of travelling out to Long Island each Sunday to see a girl but took it into his head one Sunday that he would rather stay in New York and go to Mass. It was, he notes, the first time he had ever spent a sober Sunday in New York, and he was surprised at the quietness of the city. It was a sunny day, and he walked to 121st Street and went to the 11 A.M. Mass at Corpus Christi, that pretty and pleasing church on the edge of Harlem that to this day has a reputation for a deep social concern and priests with radical ideas. It was a Low Mass: the church was crowded, and he was impressed at the naturalness and unselfconsciousness of the congregation, in sharp contrast to his own shyness and awkwardness. (He was embarrassed that he had not genuflected before sitting down and convinced that this omission had marked him out as an outsider.) He listened with attention to the sermon, which was about the incarnation, but then took fright before the liturgy reached its height and hurried out into the street, hastily genuflecting on the wrong knee as he did so. Despite his awkwardness and embarrassment he was filled with joy, and went to eat breakfast at Child's Restaurant on 111th Street in a daze of happiness.

While Merton moved toward Catholicism, reading Hopkins and Joyce (for the perverse reason that he so loved the Catholic atmosphere), and toyed with an attractive picture of himself as a Jesuit, the world was moving toward war. The Munich crisis filled Merton, who had all his parents' horror of war, with a kind of terror, and his private spiritual crisis was accentuated by a deep depression at the prospect of war and his own part in it. Chamberlain came back from Munich and the threat of war rolled away for a little, but there was that in Merton's own life that could no longer be postponed. One night when he was reading of Hopkins' correspondence with Newman about becoming a Catholic, the desire to take a similar step himself became irresistible.

"'What are you waiting for?' said the voice within me. . . . 'Why are you sitting there? It is useless to hesitate any longer. Why don't you get up and go?'" He walked about restlessly, trying to argue himself out of it.

> Suddenly, I could bear it no longer. I put down the book, and got into my raincoat, and started down the stairs. I went out into the street. I crossed over and went along by the gray wooden fence, towards Broadway, in the light rain.
>
> And then everything inside me began to sing. . . . I had nine blocks to walk. Then I turned the corner of 121st Street, and the brick church and presbytery were before me. I stood in the doorway and rang the bell and waited. When the maid opened the door, I said:
>
> "May I see Father Ford, please?"
>
> "But Father Ford is out." . . .
>
> The maid closed the door. I stepped back into the street. And then I saw Father Ford coming around the corner from Broadway. . . . I went to meet him and said:
>
> "Father, may I speak to you about something?"
>
> "Yes," he said, looking up, surprised. "Yes, sure, come into the house."
>
> We sat in the little parlor by the door. And I said: "Father, I want to become a Catholic." [1]

On November 16, 1938, Merton was baptized into the Catholic Church and took his first Communion. His friends Lax, Freedgood, and Gerdy came too (all Jews, as it happened), and Ed Rice was his godfather. In response to the priest's ritual question about what he sought, he said, "Faith," and in reply to the question about what faith meant to him he said, "Eternal life." He renounced the devil and all his works and made the three Credos affirming his belief in the Trinity. The act of exorcism made him feel like the man in the Bible who was possessed by Legion. The priest breathed into his face: "Thomas, receive the good Spirit through this breathing, and receive the Blessing of God. Peace be with thee." He was signed with the cross, had the salt of wisdom put on his tongue and water on his head. Then he made his confession, painfully, as he says, pulling out his sins like teeth.

The priest said the prayers that precede Holy Communion. "'Behold the Lamb of God: behold Him Who taketh away the sins of the world.' And my First Communion began to come towards me, down the steps. . . . I left the altar rail and went back to the pew where the others were kneeling like four shadows, four unrealities, and I hid my face in my hands." [1]

It had taken Merton a long while to move toward this decisive step, which was to change his whole life. After years of searching in many different places, he had found a home in the Church, and the weeks when he was getting ready to be received were some of the happiest he had known. He had attended instruction twice a week and hungrily seized on what he was taught. "I was never bored. I never missed an instruction, even when it cost me the sacrifice of some of my old amusements and attractions, which had such a strong hold over me." [1] He attended a parish mission at Corpus Christi, and, hearing a sermon on hell, tried with his habitual impulsiveness to get Father Moore to speed the date of his baptism. The priest had laughed and said that November would do well enough. Somewhere at the back of Merton's mind was already a longing to become a priest, one he did not dare mention to anyone as yet.

He did, however, form the important acquaintance with Dan Walsh that was to last him the rest of his life. Dan Walsh was a visiting professor, a layman, who came to Columbia from the Sacred Heart College in Manhattanville twice a week to lecture on St. Thomas Aquinas and Duns Scotus. Lax and Gerdy had both spoken warmly of his skills as a teacher, and for religious reasons rather

than for academic ones Merton had signed on for his course in the
graduate school of philosophy. Walsh, according to Merton, had
something of the quality of the prize-fighter about him—he was
stocky and square-jawed and tough, yet gentle and good and
smiling, and he talked "with the most childlike delight and
cherubic simplicity about the *Summa Theologica*." Merton discussed
his thesis with him and mentioned his approaching baptism.
Perhaps sensing his puritanism, the harsh self-criticism, but also
the passionate response to grace, Walsh said that Merton struck
him as Augustinian. Not having read Augustine at the time, and
knowing that Walsh was a Thomist, Merton might not have been
sure whether to take it as a compliment except for his sense of
Walsh's enormous and rare generosity in intellectual and spiritual
matters, a generosity that transcended schools and divisions and
held fast to the central Catholic truths.

And so the step was taken and Merton's life given a new and
irrevocable direction. Dante and Gilson, Blake and Maritain, Joyce
and Hopkins, and, more obscurely, Bramachari and Owen Merton
and the Privats had all played a part, and somewhere at the heart of
it all was the medieval beauty of St. Antonin, the ancient town
with the church at its centre that had given the small boy a glimpse
of a lost Catholic France. "Now I had entered into the everlasting
movement of that gravitation which is the very life and spirit of
God: God's own gravitation towards the depths of His own infinite
nature, His goodness without end. And God, that center Who is
everywhere, and whose circumference is nowhere, finding me. . . .
And He called out to me from His own immense depths." [1]

References

1. Thomas Merton. *The Seven Storey Mountain*. New York: Harcourt Brace,
   1948; London: SPCK, 1990. Also published abridged as *Elected Silence*
   (London: Burns & Oates, 1949).
2. Thomas Merton. "Nature and Art in William Blake: An Essay in
   Interpretation." Unpublished master's thesis, Columbia University,
   1939. Also at TMC.

6

OUR LADY OF COBRE

What sort of Catholic was Thomas Merton in the ardour of his conversion? Looking back on those early days from his first rigorous years with the Trappists, he thought he had been rather lukewarm about it, but by most people's standards he was devoutly pious. He went to Mass quite often on weekdays as well as Sundays, and went to confession and Communion usually once a week or at least once a fortnight. He gradually learned to say the rosary and to find his way around the missal, he did a good deal of spiritual reading, and sometimes he visited churches in the afternoons and "did" the Stations of the Cross.

There were still wild parties with terrible hangovers—at one such he remembered flinging a can of pineapple juice at a street light. And there were still affairs with girls.

At the end of January 1939, he took his M.A. exams and then went off on holiday to Bermuda, in search of the haunts where his father had painted and he himself had lived part of his childhood. He had a good time there. "I met a lot of people who liked to ride around all night in a carriage singing 'Someone's in the kitchen with Dinah—strumming on the old banjo.' The weather was so good that I came back to New York brown and full of health, with my pockets full of snapshots of the strangers with whom I had been dancing and sailing in yachts." [1]

It was a good moment in his life. He was beginning work on his Ph.D. dissertation—on Gerard Manley Hopkins—with the help of a scholarship. He was teaching some university extension courses in English in the evenings. He found himself a rather nicer apartment than the one behind Columbia. It was at 35 Perry Street, in Greenwich Village—not then the expensive and fashionable quarter it has now become, but still a haunt for artists, writers, and refugees. He used to sit out on the balcony in the sun, drinking Coca Cola, letting his legs hang down through the holes in the slats of the floor and watching the liners pass the west end of Perry Street. He had his own telephone at Perry Street, where he had long, zany conversations with Lax at the expense of Lax's employer. He went to Mass at the church of Our Lady of Guadeloupe on 14th Street, a lovely little Mexican church full of statues and paintings and alight with candles, and visited St. Veronica's Catholic Library on Eighth Avenue, and ate many meals at the little German bakery next door.

He spent most of his mornings trying to be a writer. He was already doing some reviews for the Sunday book section of the *New York Times* and the *Herald Tribune*. More excitingly, he was beginning to write poetry. It came slowly and laboriously and had to do with his having become a Catholic; he had not been able to write poetry before then, despite one or two painful attempts. In 1938 and 1939, his voice was still rough and unpractised—he did not really develop as a poet until 1940—but from the time of his baptism onward he was writing poems, sometimes in a rough Skeltonic style, sometimes copying Marvell or Crashaw, working away in rhymed iambic tetrameters, walking around the docks near his apartment trying desperately to get some words down on paper. Then he would go home, type the poem out, and mail it "in the mailbox at the corner of Perry Street just before you got to Seventh Avenue." His description of his struggles to achieve those early poems are the first hint in his writing of the contemplative in Merton, of the man who was not only fiercely active, but was capable of passivity, of receiving something given. "I would go out on the chicken dock trying to work out four lines of verse in my head, and sit in the sun. And after I had looked at the fireboats and the old empty barges and the other loafers and the Stevens Institute on its bluff across the river in Hoboken, I would write the poem down on a piece of scrap paper." [1]

His friends, particularly Lax, continued to be very important to Merton. Lax had not yet followed him into the Catholic Church, as he was eventually to do, but he had an integrity and a depth of spiritual understanding that deeply influenced Merton and made him ashamed of his own fierce and self-centred ambition to be a successful writer; Lax had a kind of Oriental indifference to the "fruits" of what he did.

One day as they were walking down Sixth Avenue together, Lax said to Merton that the only worthwhile ambition was to be a saint and that all you had to do to eventually become one was to want it badly enough. Merton told Mark Van Doren about the conversation:

" 'Lax is going around saying that all a man needs to be a saint is to want to be one.'

" 'Of course,' said Mark." [1]

Merton felt rather crushed by the clarity of his non-Catholic friends. "All these people were much better Christians than I. They understood God better than I. What was I doing? Why was I so slow, so mixed up, still, so uncertain in my directions and so insecure?" [1] In order to find out, he began reading St. John of the Cross, but the clarity of the saint left him even more dazzled, less able to see the way forward.

There was a good social life with his old Columbia friends, and it was not unusual for three or four to end up sleeping on sofas and chairs and on the floor in the tiny apartment at Perry Street after a night out. They had a kind of collective friendship with some girls who worked in a show at the Center Theater; they would pick them up at the stage door and go and drink in Dillon's Bar or listen to jazz at a place called Nick's in Sheridan Square.

In June, Merton and Lax and Rice took off for Olean and the cottage that belonged to Benjy Marcus and Lax's sister Gladys (Gladio). There was one big living room with a stone fireplace, and a number of bedrooms upstairs, and a big porch with a view over the valley where Merton liked to sit in the evening and play the drums (Cuban bongos). They lived on baked beans, hamburgers, and junk food.

The three of them were writing novels—Merton's an interminable autobiographical story that was successively called "Straits of Dover," "The Night Before the Battle," and "The Labyrinth." [2] They also drank a good deal at Lippert's Bar down the road, picked up girls from the local tuberculosis sanitarium, and grew beards. (Merton secretly thought his made him look like Shakespeare.) The Marcuses owned Olean House, a hotel in Olean, and when the boys appeared there with their partly grown beards and their generally disheveled appearance, a friend of Benjy Marcus advised him to keep them away for the sake of business. Benjy and Gladio, however, enjoyed their company enough to take the risk. "I think they were really the first hippies," Gladys Marcus says now.

Rice kept a journal in which he noted that "we are eating waffles for breakfast (which comes at noon), waffles for lunch, which is in the evening. Merton makes hamburgers soaked in scotch. They are so bad (we are eating outdoors) that he takes them all and throws them over the roof of the house one after another like baseballs and tries to throw the peas after them singly. . . . Not liking the food but hungry all the time . . . we are potted, absolutely potted all summer." [3] There was also a lot of jazz on records—Bessie Smith, Louis Armstrong, King Oliver, Bud Freeman, Jess Stacey, Bix, Teschmacher, Pops Foster.

It was a male paradise of jokes, horseplay, and fun with the boys, but Merton at least, and probably the others, caught a glimpse of something else, something that was to be important for Merton. "I think we all had a sort of feeling that we could be hermits upon that hill: but the trouble was that none of us really knew how and I, who was in a way the most articulate, as well as the least sensible . . . still had the strongest urges to go down into the valleys and see what was on at the movies, or play the slot machines, or drink beer." [1] One night they went to a carnival and let a confidence man of whom they all were thoroughly suspicious, clean them out of every cent they had.

Merton did at least read St. Augustine's *Confessions* lying outside the cottage in the grass, and also parts of the *Summa*. He was reaching out toward a different kind of life, but for the moment the youthful craziness was still strong. He remembers them having to park the car in the drive because they were too drunk to drive it into the garage.

> We opened the doors of the car and rolled out and lay on the grass, looking blindly up into the stars while the earth rolled and pitched beneath us like a foundering ship. The last thing I remember about that night was that Rice and I eventually got up and walked into the house, and found Lax sitting in one of the chairs in the living-room talking aloud, and uttering a lot of careful and well-thought-out statements directed to a pile of dirty clothes, bundled up and ready for the laundry, which somebody had left in another armchair on the other side of the room. [1]

Apart from fantasizing about hermitages, Merton got something else from that summer that was to be important to his future. Lax once again took him to St. Bonaventure's, and this time he did not run away, but stayed to talk to the librarian Fr. Irenaeus, who gave them free access to the library. "I did not know," says Merton, "that I had discovered a place where I was going to find out something about happiness." [1]

That happy summer ended, and Merton went back to New York

toward the end of August full of plans to sell his novel and achieve fame. He even prayed earnestly about it. In addition to prayer, he also took the step of finding an agent, Curtis Brown, at whose office he made the acquaintance of Naomi Burton, recently arrived there from England. They had drinks together at the Roosevelt Bar, and her first memories of Merton and of a relationship that was to be important for both of them was of "straight yellow hair, a boyish face." He showed her "The Labyrinth," and she duly sent it out to publishers, including Robert Giroux, who had recently begun work with Harcourt Brace. The young editors at the publishing houses loved it—it was about a young man and his struggles with the world—but everyone turned it down. "It lacked resolution," Robert Giroux remembers.

In one of the versions of this novel, the "Straits of Dover," Aunt Maud appeared and, as always, is described by Merton with deep love. "She appeared to be old, tall, thin, straight, white-haired: but you knew that her sixty-five years were some kind of playful fiction and that she was really young and beautiful all the time. She wore great silly old fashioned hats, and plain grey and brown dresses, but there are very few women in the world more beautiful than she was. I don't think she ever did anything except for someone else." [2]

In any case, the world was absorbed in more desperate matters. At Olean they had not bothered with newspapers and radio and had missed the terrible tension that was seizing New York as the war in Europe appeared ever more likely. Over the weekend on which England declared war on Germany, Merton was spending Labor Day with a girlfriend, Jinny Burton, in Richmond, Virginia. It was meant to be a lighthearted weekend, with the Burton family sailing their boat in the regatta, but the news of war and of the sinking of the *Athenia* filled everyone's minds, and Merton developed a raging toothache, due to an impacted wisdom tooth, and a few days later went to have his jaw operated on and stitched.

Now that war had actually come, some of the tension seemed to evaporate. London was not being bombed, and, except in Poland, nothing very much seemed to be happening.

In the middle of a night with his friends, or rather when they were all sitting on the floor having breakfast at Perry Street after a wild night, the thought suddenly came to Merton "I am going to be a priest." [1] He did not know why this idea had come to him, but it left a feeling of peace and clarity in his mind. He put the idea to Bob Gibney: "You know, I think I ought to go and enter a monastery and become a priest." [1] Gibney received the idea without much interest or surprise, no doubt thinking it was one of Merton's sudden enthusiasms. The idea continued to seethe inside, and, when everyone had gone home except Peggy Wells, Merton tried again. It was afternoon by then, and the two of them sat and looked at the river, and then Merton walked her to the subway, once again reiterating "under the elevated drive over Tenth Avenue" that he meant to go to a monastery and become a priest. Peggy was as polite and baffled by the news as Gibney had been.

He went to St. Veronica's and tried to find a book about religious orders, but the only one he could find was one about Jesuits, which he took to the bakery to read. On the way home, he went to the St. Francis Xavier Church on 16th Street. A novena service was in progress; as he gazed at the host in the monstrance Merton knew that the moment of decision was on him and that his life hung on what he decided now. He felt that Christ was asking him if he would consent to become a priest, and, well knowing the abyss over which he was tumbling, he replied "Yes, I want to be a priest, with all my heart I want it. If it is Your Will, make me a priest—make me a priest." [1]

As wholeheartedly as he had once followed what he believed to be the bohemian life, Merton now changed his lifestyle. He gave up smoking—no mean task for a man accustomed to over forty cigarettes a day—as well as heavy drinking, and began to avoid girls. When classes began again at Columbia, Dan Walsh told him that he had believed all along that Merton had a vocation to the priesthood. In the men's bar at the Biltmore, the two of them sat and discussed possible orders he might join. Merton was put off the Dominicans by a French book that described them sleeping in a common dormitory, and off the Benedictines by the fear of ending up as a schoolmaster, and off the Jesuits because they seemed altogether too busy and worldly. The Franciscan ideal appealed to him, partly because of the lack of systems and routine and partly because of the joy at the heart of the ideal of poverty. Dan talked with most enthusiasm of the Trappists, the Cistercians of the Strict Observance, having made a retreat at the Abbey of Our Lady of Gethsemani, in Kentucky, but Merton was appalled by the descriptions of the fasting and the silence, and the vegetarian diet. "In my heart, there was a kind of mixture of exhilaration at the thought of such generosity, and depression because it seemed such a drastic and cruel and excessive rejection of the rights of nature." [1] In the end, Dan gave him an introduction to someone at the Franciscan house on 31st Street.

Merton was warmly received there, questioned about his vocation, and told that he might make an application to be received the following August. With typical impatience, Merton demurred and asked if he might not be admitted sooner, but the Franciscans took in novices once annually and were doubtful about changing their system. All the same, the interview had given his life meaning and purpose, and he settled happily into his changed life.

He now went to Mass every day, and he bought a copy of *The Spiritual Exercises of St. Ignatius*. Without any instruction from anyone he proceeded to go through it, an hour at a time, sitting crosslegged on the floor at Perry Street.

Aside from the *Spiritual Exercises*, he was occupied teaching university extension classes in the evening and rewriting his novel in the mornings. Earlier that year, he had begun a journal, which was the beginning of a lifetime's habit of keeping journals, all of them wonderful mixtures of jokes, comments, reflections, and confessions. Merton's journal complained of a late spring—"Who seen any robins?," noted Cicero's advice about it being important to stamp your foot during a speech, but did not take this advice when he spoke, very nervously, at the Columbia Writers' Club. He was in love with two girls called Pat Hickman and Doris Raleigh ("early Fall in between being in love with them was a fine space"), and then a nurse really took his fancy: "I met Wilma Reardon and I guess from now on she will be one of my favorite girls to meet for she is very pretty and nice." [4]

He went to the beach when he could afford it, discovered that he loathed Wagner, paid several visits to the Cuban Village at the World's Fair with Gibney. He was fascinated by the dancers Antonio and Marquita: "Marquita is small and very lovely and neat, and I love her very much. We make them come and have a drink with us, and Marquita asked for 'Some Tom Collins, please.' She walks very straight and smiles fine and talks in pretty Spanish and not much English at all." [4]

He complained about the noise of Perry Street. "The Perry Street kids are fine kids but all the same I wish that little bastard would put away the bugle that he does not know how to play." [4]

Parts of this journal were later edited by Merton to make *A Secular Journal* [5], and although parts of it were still funny and lighthearted, the edited version emerged as much more portentously concerned with religion, with the constant mention of girls cut out. The edited *Secular Journal* begins with a discussion of Blake and then of Dante's *Paradiso*, and then moves on, in a flavour very reminiscent of Merton's mature writing, to look at a legal case brought by the highway department in Connecticut about some beavers who had thoughtlessly built a dam that flooded the roads. Merton was on the side of the beavers.

If Merton wrote as an ecologist ahead of his time he also, most remarkably for the date (March 1940), showed an awareness of the plight of Latin America that compels admiration. Lying in bed looking at guidebooks about Cuba and Latin America (while he recovered from his jaw operation) he ran across a writer of guide books who had an insulting way of referring to the poorer Mexicans collectively as "Mex," and then going on, from the lofty moral standpoint of Dives in the Gospels rejecting the poverty stricken Lazarus, to sneer at their precarious morals and to advocate a firm line in dealing with them. "The average Mex beggar is a chrysalis usually ready to develop into a full fledged thief," and "Children are taught to beg from infancy, and though one pities the bedraggled and poor clad mites, it should be constantly borne in mind that money given them goes directly into the hands of shiftless parents who as promptly spend it for drink." [5] No doubt Dives had some such excuse for not helping Lazarus. Merton's concern for the poor was deep and sincere. Remarkably for someone who all his life (except perhaps in the early Long Island days) had never gone short of money, and who had enjoyed a privileged education, he felt a natural and unselfconscious identification with the poor, as if he himself were one of them.

In Lent Merton suddenly developed appendicitis and went into hospital. That stay in hospital, and the convalescence with his uncle and aunt at Douglaston (Uncle Harold had inherited Pop's house), gave him time for spiritual reading and prayer, which continued to nourish his rich dream of the priesthood and of joining a religious order. Finally, he went off to Cuba for a recuperative holiday.

Cuba filled him with joy, with his special sort of passionate interest and enthusiasm for life about him. He loved the colour and the sunshine and the noise, and the great, dark interiors of the churches on Sundays and holy days filled with "beautiful eyes and faces, beautiful gestures, people full of joy and kindness and grace." He carried away precious images of his visit. One was of his room in

Havana, a cheap hotel room in which the bed frequently collapsed. His bedroom window looked out at the big church of Nuestra Señora del Carmen; waking up in the mornings, he would lie and look at the great statue of the Virgin, reflected in the mirror of his wardrobe.

The other important image or images came in the form of a poem, the first good one he believed himself to have written. It was inspired by the black Virgin of Cobre, La Caridad, and it is full of the particular joy of Merton resurrected from dissipation and illness.

> The white girls lift their heads like trees,
> The black girls go
> Reflected like flamingoes in the street.
>
> The white girls sing as shrill as water,
> The black girls talk as quiet as clay.
>
> The white girls open their arms like clouds,
> The black girls close their eyes like wings:
> Angels bow down like bells,
> Angels look up like toys,
>
> Because the heavenly stars
> Stand in a ring:
> And all the pieces of the mosaic, earth,
> Get up and fly away like birds. [6]

He sent the poem to Mark Van Doren with a letter:

Dear Mark,

Here is a poem I wrote. Cobre is a place in the mountains of Cuba near Santiago and the Virgin of Cobre is miraculous. I am in S. now. It is a fine place with a fine harbor and a lot of mountains around it but very hot so tomorrow I expect to start back to Havana.

When I get back to America I hope to go into a monastery to be a Franciscan. Back in October and November some angels told me it would be a good thing. My novitiate begins in August. Will you be in Connecticut in May, June or July and if so may I come up and see you? I suppose I will run out of money and come back to America in about two weeks. Please give my regards to Mrs. vd.

Sincerely,
Tom Merton [7]

Another poem came from Cobre, a description in conga rhythm, of an exotic religious procession full of colour and life.

Drums of the early evening wake
The mountains full of ore, and the canebrake.
Up at Cobre tall tambores call
One who rings gangarias with a nail,
One with feathers for sleeves,
One whose arms are birds,
One with a mouth full of great fires
And lights instead of words.

Five angels beating bongos,
Seven saints ringing their bells,
Wear coats made out of paper money
And shoes made out of shells.
They clatter like a box of nickels,
Holding candletowers, on fire:
They whirl these as solemn as wise men,
Paper temples in the air. [8]

If he had visited Havana and the other cities of Cuba only a year or
two before, his time would have been spent in the bars and "dives,"
but now the joy of his newfound belief made everything different.
"At every turn, I found my way into great, cool dark churches, some
of them with splendid altars shining with carved retables [upright
paintings or carvings] or rich with mahogany and silver: and
wonderful red gardens of flame flowered before the saints or the
Blessed Sacrament." [1] More wonderful to Merton than the architecture and the altars and the processions and the lights was the sense
of the presence of the Virgin, represented in innumerable statues.
Belatedly he decided his visit was a pilgrimage to Our Lady of
Cobre. Her beneficent presence bestowed a peace and richness on
him that he had lost many years before, and for the first time in years
he felt not alone, but like a favoured son. "I was living like a prince in
that island, like a spiritual millionaire." He was steeped in attending
Masses, and saying rosaries and doing the Stations of the Cross, and
reading spiritual books. Heaven seemed very close to him.

In May 1940, Merton was back in New York, longing for August
and the Franciscan novitiate. In June, France fell. Merton, Lax, and
Rice went off to Olean again for the summer. The entry in *The
Secular Journal* for June 16, 1940, reads "The French have been
driven south to the Loire. Lax, Rice and Gibney have gone to the
lake, and I am sitting by myself in the middle of the driveway

outside the cottage, looking at the woods. . . . Here it is very quiet and sunny. In front of me there is a bush covered with pale white blossoms that do not smell of anything much. Somewhere under some thorns and weeds a cricket sings drily. Everything is quiet and sunny and good." [5] A long way from the hell-raising Merton of yesteryear. Yet the violence of the world came between Merton and his contemplative peace. Dramatically he imagined a man coming out of the woods in front of him, aiming a gun at him and shooting him dead. More seriously, he was wrestling with the knowledge of war, with his own inner bafflement that there are people in the world who want war, usually because they want something other people have—possessions, colonies, *Lebensraum*. His own response to this was to make no claims on the world; it seemed "desperately important to be voluntarily poor, to get rid of all possessions this instant." He was also praying for peace, with a self-conscious piety that unconsciously reveals his own self-drama-tization. "Of course, all Catholics should be praying every minute for peace. I hope we are. It is astounding how little we really pray. . . . If a person prays an hour a day, it seems tremendous: he begins to think himself a monster of asceticism." [1]

The cottage at Olean became impossibly crowded. Seymour and his wife, Ad Reinhardt, Gibney and Gerdy, Peggy Wells and Nancy Flagg and other girls joined the original four. Merton used to go out and sit on the fence of the driveway to get enough peace and quiet to say the rosary. The kitchen was full of unwashed dishes and cockroaches, the cottage intolerably full of people. "There is always someone eating, someone shitting, someone sleeping, someone cooking, someone typing, drawing, chopping wood, rattling dishes, pouring coffee," wrote Ed Rice. [2] The food was terrible, and in July, when the weather turned wet and it was bitterly cold, the bedrooms were damp and smelled of damp sheets and blankets. There were cockroaches in the kitchen and fleas in the rest of the house. But despite discomforts the friends were still youthful and lighthearted, enjoying the absurdity of life and of one another. "Ed Rice has been reading, in a pamphlet that had once belonged with an album of tangos, that many people had broken their legs doing the tango." [3] One night Merton talked to them at length in his sleep and laughed wildly; they monitored this performance.

At one point, Merton escaped from the cottage for a couple of weeks to St. Bonaventure's. He scrubbed floors, and washed dishes and worked in the garden, but there was plenty of time to read (he sat in the library and read St. Thomas) and to go to Mass, and to dream of his coming life as a Franciscan. He listened eagerly to discussion of what the life would be like and closely observed the Franciscans around him. He gathered that the first year was the hardest part, but that after that he might expect a life of teaching and writing, probably in a place as beautiful as St. Bonaventure's. Even poverty did not involve too much hardship; there were kindly Catholic families around who loved entertaining the brothers in their homes. The life of prayer seemed full of attraction, and after the racketing life of the last years chastity seemed a welcome idea. "I had suffered so much tribulation and unrest on their account [the pleasures of the flesh] that I rejoiced in the prospect of peace, in a life protected from the heat and anguish of passion by the vow of chastity. . . . I imagined in my stupid inexperience, that the fight against concupiscence had already been won." [1]

He thought romantically that he would like to be known as Frater John Spaniard, and when he got back to Olean he timidly tried the idea out on his friends. Seymour took to it at once—it reminded him of Torquemada and the Spanish Inquisition. At the cottage, they were all arguing about what they would do when conscription arrived. Their minds were full of problems of conscience, about whether the war was justified or not, but Merton, rather smugly, let all this heartsearching wash over him. *He* would be safely in his monastery. He was already receiving lists of the things he would need to take with him to the monastery, including an item that would certainly have surprised St. Francis—"one umbrella." The romantic dream had taken over completely. "The list made me happy. I read it over and over. I began to feel the same pleased excitement that used to glow in the pit of my stomach when I was about to start out for camp in the summer, or go to a new school." [1]

And then, quite suddenly, the dream faded; the bubble of religious bliss in which he had been living for the last six months burst. Whether he had been living beyond his spiritual means—too much prayer, too many masses, too much pious reading—and had neglected his other needs, is not clear. Certainly he became aware that there was something false, something willed, some kind of playacting, about the whole situation in which he found himself. He realized what he had not chosen to realize before, that the

Merton whom the Franciscans had provisionally accepted was a kind of pseudo Merton. They knew nothing of the boy who had fathered a child, of the man who had repeatedly seduced women and who had led a rakish life. They had been presented with the new, Catholic, Merton, and had accepted him as that.

Theoretically, Merton was not bound to rub the Franciscans' noses in the sins and failures of his past life. They had not invited such confidences, and the sexual and other sins had been confessed and absolved at Merton's first confession. So why tell them now? Perhaps it was overscrupulousness, perhaps it was an unconscious awareness that the earlier "sinful" Merton was a very important part of the adult man, who could not, and would not, just be swept out of sight as something undesirable. It *was* part of Merton, and either he would be accepted whole, or not at all.

With his usual impulsiveness, he at once set off for New York to tell the Franciscans "the worst" and see what happened. He recalled an agonizing insight evoked by a scene he witnessed from the train: "We were slowing down, and the first houses of the village were beginning to file past on the road beside the track. A boy who had been swimming in the river came running up a path through the long grass, from the face of the thunderstorm that was just about to break. His mother was calling to him from the porch of one of the houses.

"I became vaguely aware of my own homelessness.

"When we had gone around the bend and I could see the stone tower of the seminary on the hilltop among the trees, I thought: 'I will never live in you; it is finished.'" [1]

The boy who had lost his mother belonged nowhere. He had thought for a little while that he did, had rejoiced in the wonderful hope that he had once again found a home. But it had been a trick of fate.

All the same, he confided the story of his past to the Franciscan father who had at first admitted him, hoping a little that his own doubts and fears might be waved aside. But a serious view was taken of his misdemeanours, and a few days later he was advised to withdraw his application.

As he left the monastery in an agony of mind, shut out forever, as he thought, from the priesthood, a terrible thing happened. On an impulse, he went into a Capuchin church and knelt to make his confession, mainly because he was desperate for someone to talk to. Distraught as Merton was, the priest got the whole story wrong and thought he was a novice who had been expelled, which made him unsympathetic. Merton began to weep helplessly and became incoherent with anguish. "So the priest, probably judging that I was some emotional and unstable and stupid character, began to tell me in very strong terms that I certainly did not belong in the monastery, still less the priesthood and, in fact, gave me to understand that I was simply wasting his time and the Sacrament of Penance by indulging my self-pity in his confessional.

"When I came out of that ordeal, I was completely broken in pieces. I could not keep back the tears, which ran down between the fingers of the hands in which I concealed my face." [1]

Despite his desperate attempts to please her, Mother Church had rejected him resoundingly. "The only thing I knew, besides my own tremendous misery, was that I must no longer consider that I had a vocation to the cloister." [1]

The bitter rejection he had endured stripped away, at least for the time being, the romanticism and the playacting. Beneath the poetry of a friar's brown habit and sandals and the dramatic renunciation of living in a cloister, he discovered a true and genuine longing that had little to do with romance. He still very much wanted to lead a life of dedication to God; indeed, he not only wanted to but knew that he must, if he was not to destroy himself with his appetites, as had nearly happened in the past. "There could be no more question of living just like everybody else in the world. There could be no more compromises with the life that tried, at every turn, to feed me poison. I had to turn my back on these things." [1] There was, perhaps, an arrogance in those sentences, a sense of his own "specialness" and a failure to realize that he had himself turned the gifts of the world to poison. But the last sentence is probably accurate. The world had become destructive for him, as alcohol is destructive to the alcoholic. Yet what to do when the cloister had rejected him?

He hit on a solution that needed a good deal of humility and a great deal of self-discipline. If he couldn't be a religious, he could at least live like one. He would join the Third Order of Franciscans; work, if he could, at a Catholic college; and say the office daily, exactly as if he were a priest or monk. He bought a set of breviaries, and with a good deal of difficulty, and some help from Fr. Irenaeus, he learned his way around them.

The euphoria that had sustained him so happily earlier in the year was gone now. In that painful August that should have seen him setting off for the novitiate with his umbrella and the other items on his list, he divided his time between Douglaston and Olean, having to answer the painful questions about his lost vocation. It was a brutally hard experience and utterly lonely. There was no one with whom to share the pain and the grief. "I was starting again to make a long and arduous climb, alone; and from what seemed to be a great depth." [1] His old passions returned in unabated force. "It seemed that every step I took carried me painfully forward under a burden of desires that almost crushed me with the monotony of their threat, the intimate, searching familiarity of their ever-present disgust. . . . I no longer dignified what I was trying to do by the name of a vocation. All I knew was that I wanted grace, and that I needed prayer, and that I was helpless without God. [1]

Apart from these spiritual consolations, what helped most was getting a job teaching English at St. Bonaventure's. They gave him a room in the dormitory on the second floor, with a window that looked out over Five Mile Valley, and he moved in with his typewriter and his books and the portable phonograph he had used since his Oakham days. They paid him $45 a month plus his room and board.

As the days went on, he found a kind of peace in his new existence. There were still times when an Augustinian war seemed to be waging within him between the old attractions of the world and his newfound way of life, but the calm, structured life of the college suited him. He enjoyed teaching, and became fond of many of his students. He was learning how to read the breviary, saying it on the train up from Olean to New York or wandering around out of doors. When the snow came that winter, he continued, "even though the cold bit down into the roots of my fingernails as I held the open Breviary in my hands." [1]

He had entirely purged himself now of nicotine and alcohol and had given up his old love-hate occupation, the movies. On a visit to New York in the Christmas vacation of 1940, he confined himself austerely to work in the Columbia library and to meeting a few friends. When Rice and Gibney took him to visit two pretty and flirtatious girls at Northport, he seemed awkward and embarrassed, and a little superior to ordinary human preoccupations. "They had me figured for a priest, at which I scarcely know whether to be delighted or annoyed—to be a priest is in my eyes a good thing, but in the eyes of two little dames wanting to play around, a bad thing." [5] He saw his sacrifices not just as a way of avoiding future trouble, or as penitence for his past sins, but as a continuing penance for the sins of the world, now tearing itself terribly apart in Europe.

Daily he read in the newspapers about the destruction of London and other British cities in the blitz, and he felt that so much horror required drastic remedies, and that by it our whole civilization was condemned.

He deplored, half-seriously, half-humorously, the kind of salesman's ethic that seemed to underlie much American life and that did so little justice to the real needs of a human being. He came across the sentence "Mr. Edison's motto is 'If you hustle while you wait you will succeed'" and poured sarcasm on it: "If you are forced to stand in one place for a few minutes, at least do not stand still. Turn somersaults, cartwheels, handsprings. . . . While waiting for that big appointment, ceaselessly climb up and down all over the furniture of the outer office. . . . They will never forget you." [5]

Merton's scorn for the naiveté of the Edisons of this world (a naiveté masquerading as common sense) was a scorn in the end directed at himself. He had much of Pop Jenkins in his makeup, much hustle, much naive enthusiasm for schemes that might not solve world problems but that seemed exciting and worthwhile at the time. He had been for years a man who had the greatest difficulty in sitting still; Mr. Edison touched on a sore nerve.

References

1. Thomas Merton. *The Seven Storey Mountain*. New York: Harcourt Brace, 1948; London: SPCK, 1990. Also published abridged as *Elected Silence* (London: Burns & Oates, 1949).
2. Thomas Merton. "Straits of Dover." Unpublished fragment, also called "The Night Before the Battle" and "The Labyrinth." TMC.
3. Edward Rice. *The Man in the Sycamore Tree*. New York: Doubleday, Image Books, 1972.
4. Thomas Merton. Unpublished journal. Written 1940–1941. TMC.
5. Thomas Merton. *The Secular Journal of Thomas Merton*. New York: Farrar, Straus, 1959; London: Sheldon Press, 1977.
6. Thomas Merton. *Thirty Poems*. New York: New Directions, 1944.
7. Thomas Merton. Letter to Mark Van Doren. May 1960. TMSC.
8. Thomas Merton. *Early Poems*. New York: New Directions, 1944.

7

THE COURT OF THE QUEEN OF HEAVEN

෴

In January 1941, Merton was twenty-six. He was later to describe this as the most momentous year of his life. The pain of his rejection by the Franciscans had not entirely crushed him, and with his usual vitality he was again entertaining fantasies of joining a religious order. In February, he asked himself in the light-hearted form he often adopted in his journal,

"Q. . . . The plan you once entertained this time last year, of entering a monastery: how does it look now?
"A. The same. But I think I'd be a Trappist.
"Q. Now you're joking!
"A. You think so?" [1]

Never one to let the grass grow under his feet, he planned to spend Holy Week and Easter at the Trappist monastery in Kentucky that Dan Walsh had told him about. "As soon as I thought about it, I saw that this was the only choice. That was where I needed to go. Something had opened out, inside me, in the last months, some-thing that required, demanded at least a week in that silence, in that austerity, praying together with the monks in their cold choir. And my heart expanded with anticipation and happiness." [2]

Meanwhile he continued with his hopes of becoming a novelist. The novel he had written two summers before at Olean, "The Labyrinth," had now been rejected by Macmillan, Viking, Knopf, Harcourt Brace, *Modern Age, Atlantic Monthly*, and McBride. He was waiting to hear what Carrick and Evens thought of it. "So many bad books get printed, why can't *my* bad book get printed?" he rather touchingly inquired of his journal. [1] He also had another novel, "The Man in the Sycamore Tree," going the round of publishers. (Rice later took this title for his biography of Merton.) A fragment of this novel still exists; it is a story about a man, Jim Mariner, who lives in an apocalyptic world and is afflicted with a sense of "plague." How to free himself of it is the dilemma of the book:

> He felt that it took nothing less simple than a pure act of volition to liberate himself from everything that now filled him with despair and that he could clean himself of the plague by merely wanting to.
>
> One other time, he had held the intuition up before him and tried to estimate only some sort of aesthetic, or literary, or dramatic possibilities it held. But it had to be different, more than an apprehension that gave some delight to the intellect. You could not escape the plague by knowing that it was possible but only by actively wanting to: only by an *act*. [3]

So the hero is nerving himself for some sort of leap. What does he see as an heroic act? The only hero Mariner can see on his horizon is the priest because, paradoxically, he has nothing. He alone is exempt from the crippling hunger that is destroying Mariner. "Mariner could not imagine any sum of money big enough to make him anything but a beggar. . . . It was the same for everybody else, except the priest. He was the only one who was rich, who had anything. They came to him, ragged, hungry, thirsty. He could give them something to cover their nakedness, and give them to drink." [3]

But, Mariner broods, the cost of becoming a priest is great, and he adds up the sum just of some of the smaller things he would have to renounce. "He would never go dancing again, and there would be no more parties, and he would never bang on a drum again to the noise of Riley's crazy trumpet. There would be no more congas and no more Bajan songs. He would never be able to hitch hike, if he felt like it, to California, or move wherever he pleased, or walk his way to Mexico, or Brazil, or Peru." [3] The priest, as Merton saw him then, had to mould himself into a straitjacket of conformity, into which jazz and free travel would not fit.

While he waited for the verdict on his novels, he was working on another, entitled "The Journal of My Escape from the Nazis." This, the only one of his novels to survive, was eventually published by Doubleday (as *My Argument with the Gestapo* [4]) in 1969 and later by New Directions. It is a fascinating book, often brilliantly written in a rather Joycean style, and deeply interesting to those interested in Merton. It does not really work as a novel, being uneasily poised between fiction and autobiography, having neither the unity of the first nor the simple factual basis of the second.

The novel is about a young man, Thomas James Merton (the name that Merton adopted for himself thereafter), who is in London during the Blitz. He meets an old girlfriend, "B.," now in uniform, and a cosmopolitan older woman, Madame Gongora, and many people and places from his past life come into the story— the family who made him so miserable in Scotland, Tom and Iris (as Uncle Rafe and Aunt Melissa), Andrew Winser (as Andrews) and his sister, Oakham, the Lycée Ingres, and Clare. But all the incidents are shot through with a terrible sense of menace, and a desperate sense of disintegration—an inner disintegration of which a shattered London is only the outward symbol. The menace lies partly in Merton's feelings about England and London—his horror of the slums and poverty, the beggars and harlots whom he felt lay hidden behind the trim musical comedy facade of Buckingham Palace and the Tower and Cambridge and Boots' library. But part of the menace, the Nazi part, lies in a paranoid nightmare that recurs throughout the book. The young hero is perpetually interrogated by officials who appear by turns to be Nazis, or American security men, or British agents who have been to Cambridge, or Russians. All of them disapprove of him, suspect him of dark plots, resent his refusal to adopt any nationality save that of a "native of *casa* [home]," of a land which the hero has lost but is trying to get back to.

It is a profoundly unhappy book. Merton, we feel, is going desperately over his past life, recalling incident after incident and trying to see what meaning it has, where he went wrong, how he lost *casa* and became a stranger and sojourner on the face of the earth.

One of the most moving passages concerns B. She comes and goes throughout the book as the true love he loses and finds again, but then there is a scene where they feel that love is defeated by the squalor and cruelty and lust and falsity of war.

They spend a day together and "for once, B. is not in uniform, but wears a dress. She is something like herself, the way she stood with folded arms in the crowded green interior of Queen's Hall when we went to some promenade concerts; the way she leaned her elbows on the tablecloth at Pagani's, and smoked; the way she sat curled up in a chair looking at *Vogue*. Her hair hangs down to her shoulders." [4]

They walk together in Kensington Gardens, and it is a beautiful summer day, but they know themselves followed by a detective. B. feels that the war has made a lie of all love. There was once love between her and Merton, but now it is all too difficult, he has to go away, and all they can hope for, perhaps the only genuine form of love left when sexual love has become so corrupted, is friendship. The despair for the future, for private love as opposed to public corruption, foreshadows Orwell's *1984*.

Who is B.? Probably a composite figure of the girls Merton feels he truly loved, beginning with the girl he met at the tennis party and including Ann Winser, and ending with Ginny Burton, of whom he wrote at the end of his life, "When I came to the monastery, Ginny Burton remained as the symbol of the girl I ought to have fallen in love with but didn't and she remains the image of one I really did love, with a love of companionship and not of passion." [5] Robert Lax remembers Ginny Burton as "really cute, a dark-haired, dark-eyed Barnard girl, very funny: she wanted to be a stage comedienne, like Imogen Coca, whom she loved." Lax, Merton, and Gibney once spent Christmas together at the Burton home in Virginia, and it was a while after that that she and Merton got really close, were, as Lax puts it "drinking companions all over the Village." Lax thinks she had not got round to thinking of marriage—a stage career was her only ambition.

Merton had high hopes of publishing "The Journal of My Escape from the Nazis," but Naomi Burton could not be whole-heartedly enthusiastic about it. At a time when many journalists were filing firsthand reports about what life was like in wartime Britain, she could not imagine that many people were going to want to read an imaginary account of it. Worse, Merton revealed a hostility to Britain and to British values that was at odds with the official American attitude, and that would cause deep offence on both sides of the Atlantic.

There is, in fact, something odd and a bit disturbing about Merton's contempt for people who were enduring the misery of nightly bombing with fortitude and cheerfulness. He had perhaps endured too much of the nauseating propaganda about brave little Britain standing alone, and, rather as with the old Alice Faye films that he and John Paul used to mock, he could not resist knocking the sentimentality. Incensed as he was, he puts words into the mouth of the characters that it would never have occurred to anyone involved to use at the time.

"An old man comes up to me: 'What nationality are you?' he says. 'You are not English. Where do you come from, to see us

English people in our silent, incomprehensible courage? What do the people in your country think of our resistance? Do they know how brave we are? Do they understand our bravery?"' [4]

Naomi Burton had only recently come to work in America from Britain, and she sensed the "wrongness" of this mood, and the hopelessness of, as she put it, "trying to buck contemporary public opinion." The book was not offered extensively to publishers.

Perhaps Merton really felt at this stage that there was little to choose between the Allies and the Nazis, that all were wicked warmongers equally steeped in the morass of human sin, and that who did what to whom was in a sense immaterial. He seems to show no awareness at this stage of the racial persecution and the depth of physical and mental cruelty of which Nazism was guilty; he still had a kind of amazed incomprehension that any individual or any country was prepared to engage in war.

He did not think of himself as a pacifist—he thought war was legitimate in self-defence, and, although he was not quite certain, he thought it "probable" that in this case the Allies really were defending themselves. However, the bombing and killing of civilians seemed to him to be mortal sin, so that he felt it right to fill in his draft papers asking to be considered as a noncombatant objector. He was prepared to do anything helpful to the Allied cause, particularly of a medical kind, "so long as I did not have to drop bombs on open cities, or shoot at other men."

"After all," he says, perhaps rather smugly, "I might be able to turn an evil situation into a source of much good. In the medical corps—I would not be spared any of the dangers that fell upon other men, and at the same time I would be able to help them, to perform works of mercy, and to overcome evil with good." [2]

If this seems a naive way of talking of an evil that could be responsible for Auschwitz or the agony of the Warsaw ghetto, many other people on the Allied side were equally ignorant of the crimes Nazism was perpetrating, and no one in England or America was fully aware of all of them. Merton was working on the principle, as he was to do all his life, of trying to make his practice match his beliefs. He still hoped and believed that in such a war it was possible for a man to keep his hands clean.

There was a wonderful weekend with Lax and Gibney and Seymour in New York, followed by a St. Patrick's Day celebration—Merton wore a shamrock about which Mark Van Doren remarked "That is the greenest shamrock I have ever seen." Then Merton went down to Olean for a draft board medical where it was bitterly cold, "standing around in your skin passing from doctor to doctor. The room was full of tongue-tied doctors and tongue-tied, naked farmboys." [1] The doctors gave him a Wassermann test, looked at his teeth, and expressed concern that he didn't have enough of them. He would probably be rated 1-B. After that, they felt it would be a waste of time to do much more investigation. As he was leaving, one of the doctors handed him a folder intended for future soldiers; Merton discovered that it was full of advice about venereal disease and contraception.

He returned to St. Bonaventure's with a poem about April he had written in that idyllic weekend in New York, one of the few entirely lyrical poems he ever wrote:

> Though jealous March, in marble skies
> Prisoned our April Saturdays,
> This air is full of courtesies.
>
> The walls, that wept with arrowy rain,
> Turn a new presence to the sun.
> Flowers and friendly days are in.
>
> The bended lanes are loud with cries,
> And are become our Italies,
> And bring sweet songs and strawberries. [6]

Poems filled his mind during that year at St. Bonaventure's. He said the hills "milked them out of him."

There were still three weeks left before his retreat with the Trappists at Easter. Impatient as ever, he took down the Catholic Encyclopedia and learned that Trappists were Cistercians. Even more moving than the Trappists were the Carthusians and the hermitages of the Camaldolese.

> What I saw on those pages pierced me to the heart like a knife.
> What wonderful happiness there was, then, in the world! There were still men on this miserable, noisy, cruel earth, who tasted the marvelous joy of silence and solitude, who dwelt in forgotten mountain cells, in secluded monasteries, where the news and desires and appetites and conflicts of the world no longer reached them.
> They were free of the burden of the flesh's tyranny, and their clear vision, clean of the world's smoke and of its bitter sting, were raised to

heaven and penetrated into the deeps of heaven's infinite and healing light.

They were poor, they had nothing, and therefore they were free and possessed everything, and everything they touched struck off something of the fire of divinity . . . everything around them was simple and primitive and poor, because they were the least and the last of men, they had made themselves outcasts, seeking outside the walls of the world, Christ poor and rejected of men.

Above all, they had found Christ. [2]

It was a romantic vision of the hermit, yet one to which, in an important sense, Merton was to remain true to the end of his life. At the time he was so excited by it that he slapped the book shut and could not resist saying to the first friar he met, "I am going to a Trappist monastery to make a retreat for Holy Week." It seemed to Merton that the friar was made uneasy by the thought of the severity of the Trappists.

" 'Don't let them change you!' he replied.

"I said: 'It would be a good thing if they did change me.' " [2]

The week before Easter, Merton made the long train journey to Gethsemani, remembering the details of it later in the rapt way a man may remember the first miraculous meeting with the girl he loves. He travelled via Cincinnati and Louisville and Bardstown, and at length arrived late at night on Palm Sunday evening, when all the brothers were in bed. The steeple shone silver in the moonlight, and the wooded hills seemed to him a barrier against the world, preserving the silence of this hidden place. He was shown to his room by a brother who asked him pointedly if he had come to stay ("Oh no!" Merton replied quickly), and he was up at four o'clock, after the night office, when many Masses were being celebrated at the little altars all round the church. It seemed to him that the hard and sacrificial life lived by the Trappists was being offered up on all those altars on behalf of the agonized world, and he imagined Christ speaking to him about what he was seeing. "These men are dying for Me. These monks are killing themselves for Me: and for you, for the world." [2] He continued to attend the offices throughout the day, almost intoxicated by what he found in the church.

"Now the church was full of light, and the monks stood in their stalls and bowed like white seas at the ends of the psalms. . . . The whole earth came to life and bounded with new fruitfulness and significance in the joy of their simple and beautiful chanting." [2]

Simplicity and beauty marked all that the Trappists did, and, deeply moved by what he saw, spiritually, aesthetically, and humanly touched to the core, Merton had a sense of homecoming, of having found something he had searched for. In his enthusiasm, he turned his own excitement and joy at the discovery into a more questionable generalization:

> The eloquence of this liturgy was even more tremendous: and what it said was one, simple, cogent, tremendous truth: the church, the court of the Queen of Heaven, is the real capital of the country in which we are living. This is the center of all the vitality that is in America. This is the cause and reason why the nation is holding together. These men, hidden in the anonymity of their choir and their white cowls, are doing for their land what no army, no congress, no president could ever do as such: they are winning for it the grace and protection and the friendship of God. [2]

The Trappists represented power to Merton, a power all the greater for being clothed in humility and penance, and for having none of the vulgar ornaments of the world.

But throughout Holy Week he watched the ceremonies that described the absence of earthly power—the washing of the feet of seventy old men, the long hours of chanting before, on Good Friday, the church was left empty with its altars stripped and its tabernacle wide open and empty. Throughout, he was questioning, questioning—must he take the advice of the Franciscans and the cruel rebuff of the Capuchin friar as the final answer? Might he yet become a Trappist? Much that he had read attracted him to the Carthusians—something lonelier than this community life seemed to be his real *attrait*—but the war made it impossible to get to La Grande Chartreuse, and probably they would reject him as the Franciscans had done. He might have asked advice of one of the Trappists, but the pain of his experience in the confessional at the Capuchin church was still so strong that he dared not risk repeating the experience, and so he struggled alone with what felt like a vocation. One of the postulants, he noticed, who had been wearing secular clothes when Merton arrived, had suddenly assumed the white robe and could no longer be picked out from the rest. "The waters had closed over his head, and he was submerged in the community. He was lost. The world would hear of him no more. He was drowned to our society and become a Cistercian." [2]

Merton's imagination still played with the idea of being a Franciscan, but he felt it was some lack of generosity in himself that made him have doubts about being a Trappist. It was the thought of giving everything, even to the point of giving himself to a life that might not be altogether congenial, that in a way made the Trappist life attractive. He feared the claustrophobia of the enclosed life, yet because he feared it so much, it seemed that he must make that particular offering. He had been told that no request made at the fourteenth Station of the Cross was ever refused, and before he left Gethsemani, he did the Stations, asking, at the last, for a vocation to the Trappists.

When he went home from that retreat, Merton suffered a kind of homesickness for Gethsemani, trying to remember the tune they had used for *Salve Regina*, picturing himself there as a Trappist. But he could not bring himself to talk to anyone about his possible vocation, and he went on giving his courses at St. Bonaventure's, and writing, and leading his life of prayer. Robert Giroux ran into him one day by chance in Scribner's bookstore. Merton had just come from the *New Yorker* and mentioned that they wanted him to write a piece about Gethsemani.

"Gethsemani?" said Giroux. "What's that?"

"Oh, it's a Trappist monastery in Kentucky. I went there recently."

Giroux had had no idea of Merton's interest either in Catholicism or the Trappists, and said that he was glad he was going to write the article.

"I'm not. I couldn't possibly do that."

Giroux thought it very strange that any aspiring writer would turn down an invitation from the *New Yorker*, and this was his first inkling of Merton's feelings about religion.

Merton's thinking underwent another development when he met the Baroness de Hueck. The baroness was a Russian refugee who had found herself alone in New York after the revolution and kept herself by working in a laundry. Her own experience of poverty had given her a deep sympathy for the poor. Her greatest concern was for the misery of the blacks in Harlem; she had taken a room in a tenement there, determined to share their lot, and had gradually built up an organization called Friendship House, with clothing and recreation rooms and a library, so that together the black poor might work toward a better life. Friendship House, on 135th Street, had become a symbol of Christian caring, a symbol deriving from the baroness's own courage and faith. She was a forthright lady, and when she came to speak about Harlem at a summer school at St. Bonaventure's Merton was both delighted and impressed. "She put her fist on her hip and made a slow gesture with the fist of her other hand and said 'Baloney!' in the middle of the speech and knocked all the religious off their chairs." [2]

The baroness seemed to spell out for Merton a practical, poverty-centred religion that he had hoped to find among the Franciscans. But Franciscan life at St. Bonaventure's seemed too safe, too comfortable, too socially respectable—the baroness, however, with her fierce courage, seemed to indicate a path of caring that appealed at once to Merton's idealism. "[She] made good, simple, unhysterical gestures, very natural, and had a strong, sure voice: and best of all she used the word "martyrdom" without embarrass-ment, not like something crazy and "imprudent" and abstract in some old book." [2]

Merton at once asked the baroness if he might come and help at Friendship House, and within a few days he was down there helping to sort dresses and shoes, watching a play put on by the children, playing the piano to keep the children amused. For a few weeks of that summer vacation, he was there every evening, singing Compline with the helpers last thing at night, entering fully into the joys and pains of Harlem. He writes with passion of the Harlem he found, a passion that was later to move Eldridge Cleaver in prison when he read Merton's autobiography:

> Here in this huge, dark, steaming slum, hundreds of thousands of Negroes are herded together like cattle, most of them with nothing to eat and nothing to do. All the senses and imagination and sensibilities and emotions and sorrows and desires and hopes and ideas of a race with vivid feelings and deep emotional reactions are forced in upon themselves, bound inward by an iron ring of frustration: the prejudice that hems them in with its four insurmountable walls. In this huge cauldron, inestimable natural gifts, wisdom, love, music, science, poetry are stamped down and left to boil with the dregs of an elementally corrupted nature, and thousands upon thousands of souls are destroyed by vice and misery and degradation, obliterated, wiped out, washed from the register of the living, dehumanized.

What has not been devoured, in your dark furnace, Harlem, by marihuana, by gin, by insanity, hysteria, syphilis? [2]

Inevitably, Merton saw the tragedy of Harlem as an indictment of the white culture that had brought it about and lived off it.

Friendship House, however, showed him another side of Harlem, the vitality and humour and holiness of the black people; he was particularly impressed by the face of an old woman who, it was claimed, had visions of the Virgin. In October, he wrote a five-page letter to the baroness, thanking her first for letting him be part of Friendship House for a bit, and raising other issues. "First, thanks very much for letting me stand around . . . for a couple of weeks of evenings: I hope I can do that more often. I liked most of all the clothing room, but wasn't there much. I think the cubs [a children's club] are certainly very smart fine kids, and think about them a lot, all the time." [7]

Now that term had started again at St. Bonaventure's, Merton told the baroness, he was reading, studying, meditating, and doing a little writing. What he was trying most of all to work out was something about lay vocations, and his own vocation in particular. He wondered a lot about how political a Catholic should be; he thought anything more than "a sort of academic, polite and rather reserved" interest a waste of time. He thought Catholics should get on with the job of feeding the hungry and clothing the naked, on the one hand, and with saving their souls, on the other. "When you get down to it, Catholic Action means not voting for anybody but going out and being a saint, not writing editorials in magazines, even, but first of all, being a saint." [7] What had put him off the direct kind of involvement in politics was what he saw as the corruption of Catholic political parties in some European countries, or some Catholic leaders.

Where it (the problem) comes in with me is, trying to explain guys like Franco, or some of the medieval Popes, in whom Catholic Action (or what they imagined to be that) got totally submerged in a completely materialistic and political struggle between certain social and political groups. . . . If a Catholic gets into a position of power in a country where the political atmosphere is made up of struggles between a lot of religious and frankly selfish minorities, how can he ever do anything at all except by compromising with religious principles, or, worse than that, fooling himself that he is leading a crusade, and then turning the country upside down in the name of religion, the way Franco did. [7]

Yet his convert's idealism was still very evident: "On the other hand, I believe there is only one free and just state in the world, and that is the Vatican City: but that is less a state than a glorified monastery." [7]

He is quite clear about rejecting the "political solution."

> The first thing to do is to feed the poor and save the souls of men, and in this sense feeding the poor means feeding them not by law (which doesn't do a damn bit of good), but first of all at the cost of our own appetites, and with our own hands, and for the love of God! . . . Only when the majority of the people in this country return to the love of God will it make any real sense for us to get hot about politics. . . . It seems to me that saving souls, and, of course, our own souls first (because that is the only case where selfishness is not a sin) is a long way ahead of economics, and art, and politics, and the European war. [7]

He went on to wonder about how he must work all this out as a writer. He could write for fame and success, and to show his own cleverness, and how much smarter he was than those who disagree with his arguments. Or he could write, as he put it, "simply for God," a writing that came out of the middle of himself and might happen to be what other people want to read.

He summed up what he had concluded and thrust it down before the baroness: "If I can only make myself little enough to gain graces to work out my sanctification, enough to keep out of hell and make up for everything unpleasant, in time, and on top of that write a lot in the second way and none at all in the first way, the lay vocation, as far as I'm concerned, presents no further problems, because I trust God will put in my way ten million occasions for doing acts of charity and if I am smart maybe I can catch seventeen of them, in a lifetime, before they get past my big dumb face." [7]

It is clear that his meeting with the baroness, and the example of her work, had stirred him to the roots, and that he felt an almost adolescent need to pour out his religious ideas at length to this older woman. Beneath the fascination with his own problems was a deep longing to discover how to give himself to what he believed, how to live a life of love that makes a difference to the suffering of the poor. He did not yet see the root of his own identification with the poor, the inner neediness that was unconsciously displaced on to *their* neediness.

Meanwhile, Merton made another Trappist retreat, this time at Our Lady of the Valley, Rhode Island. He enjoyed it, but found none of the wonder of his Easter visit to Gethsemani. He was now considering whether he should join the baroness at Friendship House. He saw himself as the rich young man who was hampered from coming to Christ by his great possessions, and he considered giving everything he had, both in the sense of working full-time in Harlem, which did not altogether appeal to him, and of giving what was left of his grandfather's money to Friendship House.

The baroness anticipated the first.

"Well, Tom, when are you coming to Harlem for good?" she asked him. Merton hedged, saying he did not see how he could write at Harlem. The baroness, speaking of his letters, also asked, "Tom, are you thinking of becoming a priest?" "Her words turned the knife in that old wound. But I said: 'Oh no, I have no vocation to the priesthood.'" [2] After that conversation, he told the principal of St. Bonaventure's that he would be leaving at Christmas, as he would be going to Harlem in January. And he sent the baroness a cheque for the rest of his grandfather's money.

The correspondence between them grew deeper and more intense. The conversation in October had lingered in his mind; he felt she had seen through him with loving understanding and had cut through his generalizations about religion with important questions about his vocation. At last he uncovered to her his most secret longing and touched on his secret wound. "The priest business is something I am supposed to be all through and done with. I nearly entered the Franciscans. There was a very good reason why I didn't . . . so that settles that vocation." [8] St. Bonaventure's, he said, was always only a temporary resting place, a place of quiet and order where he was glad to be for a bit, but to which he felt no commitment. So there was no reason that he should not come to Friendship House, although he was simply and straightforwardly scared of Harlem. "My body is terrifically afraid. Afraid of bedbugs. Afraid of exchanging this nice healthy mountain for a slum full of pestilences. Afraid of being cold and hungry. Afraid of losing all the nice consolations, the quiet and good and fruitful kind of prayer that is possible here. Afraid I may never write anything decent again Afraid of being beaten up. Etc." [8] He was ready to come, but full of doubt about the rightness of the move, and felt he must warn her. "Wait until I get to Harlem and get scared by my first cold in the head or the first five nights I can't sleep, and watch me start trying to do things my way instead of God's, and start worrying about myself!" [8]

There is another, much more painful, thing about which he must warn her.

> I don't know if you are concerned about the past of people who come to work for you. I am bringing this up because it might possibly be important. I got in some trouble once which I don't particularly want to tell anybody about. If you absolutely want to know, I will tell you, but otherwise I can say in good conscience that I don't believe, myself, that it would disqualify me from working in Friendship House, or bring any scandal to be connected with FH in any way, or reflect on you or anybody else, but once I did get in some trouble, enough for it to be an impediment to my becoming a *priest*. I repeat, to the best of my knowledge it does not in any way affect my fitness to work at Friendship House. On the other hand, it is something that definitely demands a whole life of penance and absolute self sacrifice: so that if I thought the Trappists would take me I think I would want to go to them. But I have to do penance, and if Harlem won't have me, then where may I turn?
>
> If I had never mentioned this, I am sure it would never have come up in any other way, and I am sure it could not possibly be dragged up out of the past, because it remains only something between me and God and the other persons involved, with whom I have unfortunately lost all contact: or so it seems. Maybe it would have been better to have ignored the whole thing.
>
> However, it came up and spoiled my last "vocation," and I don't want to leave anything in the background to spoil this one. I assure you that it is something which, if the President of the college knew, I don't think he would fire me for. I just got a sudden attack of scruples, maybe, when I brought it up.
>
> But if you have any doubts at all, say so, and I will tell you the whole story, in which I am no white-haired hero, no model of self-sacrifice or of holiness either.
>
> The general burden of this letter is to let you know that, in me, you are getting no bargain, and I feel I should especially tell you this, because you have done me an inestimably great honor . . . in asking me to come to FH, even before I got around to asking it myself. I believe that, since with God all things are possible, with His help I can some day be a Saint, if I pray without ceasing and

give myself totally to Him. In all this, I depend on a miracle: but His grace is always a miracle. Apart from that miracle, however, there is the present fact that I am not only a Saint but just a weak, proud, self-centered little guy, interested in writing, who wants to belong to God, and who, incidentally, was once in a scandal that can be called public, since it involved lawyers. So that's the dirt. Never forget me in your prayers.

Yours in Christ: Tom [8]

The incident at Cambridge had left a deep mark—eight years after it happened, Merton felt the only way to live with it was to devote his life to expiation. He had no contact with the girl nor with the small boy living in England, but the awareness of the huge consequences of his own appetites had made him fearful and ashamed, and the rejection by the Franciscans and the harshness of the Capuchin confessor had touched a very sore place.

His life continued for a while on several levels. He planned to go to Harlem, and informed the head of the English department at St. Bonaventure's that that was what he intended to do. But also his imagination began more and more insistently to revolve around the idea of being a Trappist and becoming a priest in that order. The very fears the idea aroused—some of the same fears he had outlined to the baroness, physical discomfort and ill health, made the idea all the more attractive. He wanted to give *everything*, in one supreme gesture of abandonment and self-sacrifice.

Alongside these heroic dreams ran his old ambition to be a writer; pursuing that ambition, in November he lunched with Mark Van Doren at the Columbia Faculty Club. Mark had just read "The Journal of My Escape from the Nazis" and had suggestions to make about publishers. But the meeting turned out to be important for another reason. They were collecting their coats from the cloakroom when Mark asked, "What about your idea of being a priest? Did you ever take that up again?" Merton shrugged painfully. "'You know,' he [Mark] said, 'I talked about that to someone who knows what it is all about, and he said that the fact you had let it all drop, when you were told you had no vocation, might really be a sign that you had one.' " [2]

Merton was deeply moved by this loving insight from a man not himself a Catholic, but whose wisdom and integrity he so deeply trusted. The deep and gentle penetration of his pain seemed to release something inside him, an awareness that whatever anybody said he really believed in his own vocation to be a priest, and he confided to Mark "If I ever entered any monastery, it would be to become a Trappist." [2]

About a week later, he was aware of a sudden appalling conviction: "The time has come for me to go and be a Trappist." [2] He could think of nothing else. He went out into the grounds of St. Bonaventure's in a kind of agony, and before the little shrine to St. Thérèse of Lisieux he prayed desperately for help, pledging himself to be her monk if she would help him to the monastery. Suddenly it was as if he heard the great bell of Gethsemani tolling through the night, as he put it, "calling me home."

He went at once to speak to one of the Franciscans, Father Philotheus, telling him of his longings, his fears, the old drawbacks that had made it all seem impossible, and as he spoke he realized how he had exaggerated his fears, how there was really no reason that he should not become monk and priest when his vocation to do so was so strong. Father Philotheus asked only one question: "Are you sure you want to be a *Trappist?*"

And Merton replied simply, "I want to give God everything." In the tear-stained entry in his journal five days before he entered Gethsemani, he prays that he may renounce everything and belong entirely to the Lord. And he beseeches the Little Flower to pray for him. [9]

The next thing was to write to Gethsemani asking if he might come and make a retreat at Christmas, trying to hint that he really wanted to come as a postulant. He was scared to ask straight out if they would have him, so fearful was he of rejection.

While he waited to go on the retreat, he received another call from the draft board. They were lowering their conditions of admission and wanted to see him again. He persuaded them to defer his medical examination until he had a chance to try his vocation at Gethsemani. On the day that he received this news, the Japanese attacked Pearl Harbor and America was at war. Fearful that this would wreck his chances of becoming a monk, Merton decided he could wait no longer. He packed up most of his clothes and sent them off to Friendship House, gave away many of his books to Fr. Irenaeus and St. Bonaventure's library, burned his novels, sent his poems and *The Secular Journal* to Mark Van Doren for safekeeping, wrote letters to some of his closest friends, and was ready to set off. Apart from a box of books he was taking with him to Gethsemani, all his possessions fitted into one suitcase.

Robert Giroux remembers the telephone call from Mark Van Doren that announced this momentous news. "He's lost to us forever. We'll never hear from him again."

Naomi Burton, who heard the news from Robert Lax, had a more robust response. " 'Oh God,' I said. 'He'll never write again.' What hurt was the sheer wicked *waste*." [10]

References

1. Thomas Merton. *The Secular Journal of Thomas Merton*. New York: Farrar, Straus, 1959; London: Sheldon Press, 1977.
2. Thomas Merton. *The Seven Storey Mountain*. New York: Harcourt Brace, 1948; London: SPCK, 1990. Also published abridged as *Elected Silence* (London: Burns & Oates, 1949).
3. Thomas Merton. "The Man in the Sycamore Tree." Unpublished novel. TMSC.
4. Thomas Merton. *My Argument with the Gestapo*. New York: Doubleday, 1969. Written 1941. Originally titled "The Journal of My Escape from the Nazis." Reprinted by New Directions, 1975.
5. Thomas Merton. "Vow of Conversation." Unpublished journal, dated 1964–1965. TMSC.
6. Thomas Merton. *Early Poems*. New York: New Directions, 1944.
7. Thomas Merton. Letter to Catherine Doherty (Baroness de Hueck). October 6, 1941. TMSC.
8. Thomas Merton. Letter to Catherine Doherty (Baroness de Hueck). November 10, 1941. TMSC.
9. Thomas Merton. Unpublished journal. Written 1940-1941. TMC.
10. Naomi Burton. *More than Sentinels*. New York: Doubleday, 1964.

Part Three

8

AMONG THE SHINING VINEYARDS

❦

It was bitterly cold at Gethsemani—even the great church, where so many hours were spent in prayer, was unheated. Merton had immediately confessed his wish to become a novice, but he was given a room in the guest house while they decided whether to accept him or not. It was relatively warm in the guest house, but with his usual passionate thoroughness Merton opened the window and sat in his room without a coat, with the result that almost at once he developed a shattering cold. There were two other would-be postulants beside himself.

The world in which he found himself was a thousand years away in time from twentieth-century America. Its inhabitants wore medieval clothes, ate a medieval diet, and followed a set of religious observances that had remained more or less unchanged since the Middle Ages (although De Rancé in the seventeenth century had deepened the Cistercian austerity and introduced an element of self-punishment lacking before. The name "Trappist" is derived from "La Grande Trappe" where De Rancé had carried out his "reform," and Gethsemani, like all Trappist houses, followed in this strict and penitential tradition).

The medieval Cistercian tradition was one of simplicity in all things—architecture, ritual, and way of life. Following the earlier Benedictine rule, they believed in a life devoted to prayer and manual work—a life lived in common with other monks. Unlike the Benedictines, however, they lived a life of silence, communicating only by sign language (except when talking to superiors), they ate and drank very sparingly, and their use of the night office meant getting up at two in the morning to pray, going down to the church (they slept fully clothed), and spending the rest of the night in prayer, meditation, or reading. They were also enclosed on a fairly strict basis, more or less confined to the house and the immediate environs and only able to go further with permission. The purpose of the silence, meagre diet, confinement, and prayer was, of course, that monks should be set free from other distractions and therefore able to concentrate on the contemplation of God.

The way of life could not have been further from that of the average American of the 1940s, something that immediately made it attractive to Merton. The very hardships of the life meant that the men lived very close to nature, as their ancestors had done—they saw the sun rise and often went to bed as it set. They knew cold and heat, real hunger and the satisfaction of hunger, the joy and weariness of manual work. In a life shorn of other sensual delights, they often became acutely aware of birds, flowers, trees, the sky, and the stars. Weather became important in a way it can never be to those who are buffered by heating in winter and air-conditioning in summer.

Merton threw himself into the life with the joyous enthusiasm of one who has at last found what he is looking for. For a day or two, he was kept at the guest house, working at polishing floors with another applicant, being visited by the Master of Novices from time to time for conversations intended to probe the sincerity of his intention. In one of these conversations, with real fear, he unloaded what he calls "the big shadowy burden" on his conscience, and the pain it had caused him in thinking it made a vocation to the priesthood impossible. The Master of Novices promised to discuss this with the Father Abbot, but Merton did not get the impression he was disturbed by it. While he waited for the verdict on whether he was accepted, he wrote a farewell poem for Mark Van Doren and Robert Lax, and when the glad news came he wrote to Mark Van Doren, "I have been tentatively accepted and will enter the community within the next few days. I still don't know what about all those books I sent you but will let you know. Possibly I might ask you to send the handwritten notebooks down sometime—and the poems. As to *Journal of My Escape from the Nazis*, and all rights connected with it—I make you a present of it. Pray for me. Tom Merton." [1]

He was told to collect his things and enter the enclosure, and as he followed the Novice Master he made a gesture that later he remembered with a mixture of amusement and embarrassment, as typical of "the old Thomas Merton who had gone around showing off all over two different continents." He saw a line of local farmers waiting downstairs to go to Confession, and whispered dramatically to one of them "Pray for me." The old man nodded solemnly. [2]

Merton was taken to see the Abbot, Dom Frederic Dunne. Dom Frederic was a man of tremendous vitality and zeal, young-looking for his age (he was about seventy), as most of the monks of Gethsemani were, and are. He was made Abbot in 1935 and between then and his death in 1948 he undertook a tremendous building programme—a dam, artificial lake, cellars, a new novitiate wing, new farm buildings, a garage, and a fireproof horse barn. He also installed electric light, a house telephone, and a fire-fighting system, and had made plans for a future heating system. Under his rule, the numbers at Gethsemani rose from 70 to 160, and two "daughter" houses were founded, at Georgia in 1944 and Utah in 1947.

He was also noted for the austerity with which he interpreted the already austere Trappist Rule, and although details are often trivial— for example, he instituted "barley coffee" as the habitual drink of the monks in place of real coffee—in practice it meant that the monks of Gethsemani had a poorer diet and a harder life than, say, some of the French Trappists of the period, who were allowed wine to drink (the Rule permitted "the drink of the country") and were given more general latitude in the interpretation of the Rule. Contemporary monks at Gethsemani who remember the old regimes under Dom Frederic and his successor Dom James suggest that American enthusiasm and activism, acting on an already austere way of life, produced a hardship unprecedented elsewhere in the Trappist houses.

It was to this austere, but kindly, Abbot that Merton was taken. He gave Merton and his companion a little advice about their future lives in the Community, they both kissed his ring, and then they went to hand over to the Treasurer their few valuables—fountain pens, and watches and loose cash, and they signed documents about their willingness to undertake manual labour without payment.

Then they moved on into the enclosure (Merton liked the smell of baking bread that pervaded the place) and went to the tailor's shop to be measured for robes. They were shown the novitiate chapel, and then the washroom, full of novices, where an ex-Marine was appointed as Merton's guardian.

I was in a building [wrote Merton] with huge thick walls, some painted green, some white and most of them with edifying signs and sentiments painted on them. "If any man thinks himself to be a religious, not bridling his tongue, that man's religion is vain." And so on. I never quite discovered the value of those signs, because for my own part as soon as I had read them once I never noticed them again. . . . What was important was not the thick, unheated walls, but the things that went on within them.

The house was full of people, men hidden in white cowls and brown capes, some with beards, the lay brothers, others with no beards but monastic crowns. There were young men and old men, and the old ones were in the minority. At a rough guess, with all the novices we have in the house now I think the average age cannot be much over thirty. [2]

Merton felt at home at once in the novitiate. There was youth and enthusiasm and a good deal of humour, or at least such humour as can be expressed in a Community that dispenses almost entirely with speech. The traditional method of Cistercian communication was by signs. "The religious shall have no communication with each other, either by word of mouth or by writing. When they have anything useful to communicate, they do so by signs. Noises with the mouth, although inarticulate, and useless signs are expressly forbidden. The choir religious speak ordinarily to two persons only, the first Superior and the Prior . . . . The novices can speak to the first Superior and to their Father Master." [3]

It was, therefore, imperative for novices to learn the signs quickly. They inherited a language of surprising complexity and subtlety, one that sometimes proclaimed its medieval roots in revealing ways. Using mostly the right hand and in particular the forefinger, the monks had over 400 signs, which covered mainly everyday objects, words for food and for work, and clothes, and signs of liturgical or theological significance—vessel, breviary, office, and so on; God (a triangle with the thumbs and forefingers raised up); and the Holy Ghost (sign of God and Wing). Some of the signs have a simple and delightful poetry about them. For "fast," the instruction was "Press the lips together with the thumb and forefinger." For "cat," you made the sign for "animal," "curving the finger and moving it at the end if the nose," but in addition "pulled at the moustache." For "morning," you touched the under eyelid, and for night you put the thumb and forefinger over the eyes. For "candle," you combined signs of "bee" (for beeswax) and "light."

Some of the signs frankly proclaimed their ancient origins. For "lavatory" or "toilet," the sign indicated "shame house." For "devil," one described a wing, "placing the end of the thumb on the corner of the mouth, spreading out the hand and moving it whilst striking the head in several places with the tip of the finger."

Despite the stricture on "useless signs," a large vocabulary of joke signs also crept into use, and much ingenuity was exercised in inventing new signs, something at which Merton was reputed to be particularly talented. There were signs of cheerful insult ("Drop dead" and "Get lost"), and there were witty combinations of existing signs ("past," "your," "eyes," and "milk" for "pasteurised milk"). There were humorous indications of nationality: an Englishman was represented by a snobbish raising of the nose with a forefinger, a Frenchman by the twirling of imaginary moustachios, and an Irishman (and there were always Irishmen at Gethsemani) by a stroking of the cheek that meant "green."

In addition to the new form of language, Merton had to get used to the diet and the method of eating it. Writing a few years later about the Trappistine Mother Berchmans and her early days in a Trappist house, he described the Trappist table—water jug, wooden spoon, fork, knife, an earthenware mug, an enamelled plate, a napkin folded and disposed over the mug, and other implements. [4] After the Trappist had eaten—soup, bread, vegetables, an apple—the custom was to wash the knife, fork, and spoon in the drinking water, dry them on the napkin, empty the mug into the soup bowl, and dry *it* on the napkin, leaving everything in its original place on the table. Merton imagines the Trappistine feeling repugnance at this (a fair indication that he did so himself)—"one of those trivial crosses that God in his favor gives to Trappists as a special favor." It was a diet largely lacking in protein—no meat, eggs, or cheese, except for brothers in the infirmary. Nor was the food well cooked. Merton mentions the Trappistine food as "often completely tasteless," and again this seems to be an echo of his own experience. Robert Giroux and James Laughlin, who visited Gethsemani regularly a few years later, remember even the food in the guest house being almost uneatable.

Within a few days of his arrival, Merton was given his oblate's habit—white canvas drawers ("It took me a few minutes to figure out the complications of the fifteenth-century underwear," he wrote [2], a white robe and scapular, a white cloth band around the waist and a white cloak about his shoulders, all the upper garments made of wool. One of the trials of Cistercian life as he, and others, discovered, was wearing the same heavy underclothes in both winter and summer. They changed into denim robes for work. The ample woollen robes worn in the church and cloister were comforting in winter. They were beautiful garments. Merton wrote of the white cowl that was given after first vows as "the garment of contemplation that envelops and encloses the body in its ample folds like the cloud that protected the children of Israel in their escape through the desert." [4] It did not only protect, however.

Wearing a light-weight cowl of cotton flannel, the Cistercian retired to sleep in his dormitory, removing only his shoes and, if permission was given because of the heat, his cowl. "In the dormitory," as it says in the *Regulations*, "the couches are separated by partitions, and the entrance to each cell is closed by a curtain only; the name of the religious and his number are written above. The couch is composed of a straw mattress stitched through, covered with a serge cloth and laid on boards; a bolster of straw; and one or more blankets according to need. The only furniture in the cell consists of a crucifix, a holy water stoup, one or two pious pictures, and a few pegs. Nothing can be added without permission. . . . No one is allowed to go to the dormitory without necessity, much less to take rest there without permission. [3]

The only other place in the monastery apart from his bed, which a monk might, so to speak, call his own (in fact, he was obliged always to speak of "our" bed, "our" shoes) was in the scriptorium, where he was allowed a box in which to keep a notebook, a few books, and a letter or two. Merton printed the words "Frater Maria Ludovicus" (the Abbot had decided his name in religion was to be Louis, pronounced "Lewis" in the community), on the front of it. It contained some poems he had written, a volume of St. John of the Cross, Gilson's *Mystical Theology of St. Bernard*, and letters from Mark Van Doren, Robert Lax, and his brother John Paul.

There was not, in these early years in the monastery, much time for writing. Gethsemani maintained a large farm with plantations of trees, fields of corn and alfalfa, and its own livestock, and the novices worked hard in the fields hoeing, cutting, stacking, and threshing.

Most of the rest of the day was taken up in prayer in the big church, with its many altars and statues. The monks would rise at 2 A.M. for the night office, mental prayer, Angelus, and private masses, said simultaneously at the side altars. Then they would meditate or read until Prime at 5.30 A.M. There was Tierce, High Mass, and Sext at 7.45; None, Examen of Conscience, and Angelus at 11; Vespers and mental prayer at 4.30; Lecture (pious reading), Compline, Salve, and Angelus at 6.10 before retiring to bed at 7 P.M. There were slight variations on this on feast days, Sundays and in summer months, but this was the basic structure of the monk's day, and into it were fitted meals, work, and a very limited amount of free time.

Every other detail of his life was no less structured, the most minute particulars of conduct being laid down in the *Regulations*. The way he drank—"both hands holding the cup"; the way he comported himself—"The religious ought always to observe the greatest modesty, walking without haste and without turning the head . . . except in church, we always keep the hands in the sleeves of the cowl. If we are in scapular, we keep the hands hidden under the scapular, above the girdle, or in the sleeves of the robe. If one of the hands is occupied, we keep the other under the scapular, above the girdle." The way the monk warmed himself in "the calefactory," the one warm room in the house: "We may take off our shoes to warm ourselves, but not our socks; we take care not to burn our garments." The way he greets his superiors: "When we meet the Reverend Father Abbot, we stop and uncover, and turning towards him, make a profound bow." The way he asked permission to leave a gathering ("We do not ask this permission for a bleeding of the nose or for vomiting"). And, finally, the careful and elaborate respect shown to all superiors and senior monks. [3]

The way he looked after his growth of beard, and his tonsure, usually called "a crown," was also specified. "The beard is shaved every week. The Superior may, however, in certain cases, permit the religious to shave more often. The crowns are renewed once a month. . . . The Reverend Father Abbot assigns the duty of shaving to those of the choir religious or lay brethren whom he considers to be the best qualified for this work. Each one lathers himself. A crown of hair about three-quarters of an inch in width all the way round is left around the head." [3]

A regular feature of life at Gethsemani, as at most monastic houses of the period, was the Chapter of Faults. Its frequency depended on the wishes of the Abbot, but it was within the regulations to hold it every day except Sundays and holy days. At the invitation of the Abbot, monks came forward, bowed low, and accused themselves of faults in carrying out the Rule. Others also were invited to "proclaim" the faults of the individual with the words "I proclaim Father X" and going on to state the faults he had noticed. "It is to be regarded as a fault to excuse oneself . . . even though we are not guilty." [3]

The Superior imposed penances for faults, varying from light to grave. For a light fault, the monk might take his meals after the rest of the Community and be deprived of any duty in choir. At each office, he would prostrate himself on the presbytery step. Or he might have to accuse himself in the refectory, or read some relevant portion of a pious book aloud, or say a prayer, perhaps with his arms extended in the form of a cross. Or he might eat at a small stool in the middle of the refectory instead of at table; or be instructed to prostrate himself at the door of the refectory, so that everyone who entered had to step over him; or have to kiss the feet of the whole Community, bowing to them two at a time between the exertion. Graver faults might mean a monk being deprived of part or the whole of his regular habit, or receiving the "discipline" in Chapter. (The discipline was a small whip usually used in private. Each monk was given one, which he kept in his cell and with which he scourged his shoulders regularly. Only very occasionally would it be used publicly in Chapter.)

All these practices had been common in medieval times and had been hallowed by unbroken tradition since. The total stylization of the punishment of faults in a sense robbed it of some of the pain—everyone partook of the experience and always in the same way—yet it was without doubt humiliating and intended to be so. Writing of Mother Berchmans, Merton describes with feeling the postulant "who would fall on her knees and accuse herself of dissipation, or read, in a loud clear voice, St. Benedict's ninth and tenth degrees of humility concerning monks who talk too much or laugh too much." "The rule is careful to demand of novices," he says, "that they be zealous for humiliations." [4]

It is difficult, looking at this life from outside, at the harshnesses and the deprivation—of food, of sleep, of privacy, of speech, of sexual satisfaction, of entertainment, of freedom to move and meet people outside the monastery—to imagine what the positive satisfactions were. Part of its appeal was undoubtedly its very bareness; deprived of so much that others take for granted, men often lived an intense inner life within the great space and silence left to them. "It was," says Dom John Eudes Bamberger, a contemporary of Merton's at Gethsemani in the 1960s and now Abbot of the Genesee, "a wonderful life if you could stand it."

There was a real beauty in the medieval structuring of the days; in the ancient rituals and practices; the great poetic liturgies of Christmas, Lent, and Easter; in the procession of saints' days. Merton wrote well of the astonishing impact of Easter after the bareness and fasting of Lent, the kind of total experience that no one easily forgets, but which few people experience nowadays with such intensity.

> Finally the long liturgy of penance came to its climax in Holy Week, with the terrible cry of the Lamentations once more echoing in the dark choir of the Abbey Church, followed by the four hours thunder of the Good Friday Psalter in the Chapter Room, and the hush of the monks going about the cloisters in bare feet, and the long sad chant that accompanies the adoration of the Cross.
> What a relief it was to hear the bells once more on Holy Saturday, what a relief to wake up from the sleep of death with a triple "alleluia." Easter, that year, was as late as it could possibly be, and there were enough flowers to fill the church with the intoxicating smell of the Kentucky spring—a wild and rich and heady smell of flowers, sweet and full. We came from our light, five hours' sleep into a church that was full of warm night air and swimming in this rich luxury of odors, and soon began that Easter invitatory that is nothing short of gorgeous in its exultation.
> How mighty they are, those hymns and those antiphons of the Easter office! Gregorian chant that should, by rights, be monotonous, because it has absolutely none of the tricks of modern music, is full of a variety infinitely rich because it is subtle and spiritual and deep . . . . Those Easter "alleluias," without leaving the narrow range prescribed by the eight Gregorian modes, have discovered color and warmth and meaning and gladness that no other music possesses. [2]

Merton's words make a particular paradox clear—that by abstaining from sensual experience we do not kill our senses but sharpen them to a point of much greater intensity. The Cistercian observance, as to a lesser extent all religious observance, aimed not at ultimately denying the senses but at focusing them anew—on the love and contemplation of God. With this end in view, the man or woman whose imagination has been caught by the idea of the love of God resents the minor pains and frustrations no more than a man in love objects to the smaller inconveniences of his state. The physical hardships in any case fall into the background of life—the body becomes adjusted fairly quickly to a hard board or a rather monotonous diet—and the man or woman who joins a religious community, convinced that this well-trodden path is the royal road

to loving God, is not usually disposed, at least at first, to argue and
rebel over the details.

Merton later remembered the two years of his novitiate as
physically very hard but mentally very happy years. There were a
number of reasons why they should have been happy. He had made
the leap for which he had been nerving himself for several years;
now that particular agony of uncertainty was over, and he had only
to give himself to the life, which he did with his habitual whole-
heartedness and enthusiasm. The life was, at least in its early stages,
and at least to the eye of a writer, an intensely interesting one. A
man who entered it had stepped out of the twentieth century and
back into the eleventh. The huge, unending, unchanging work of
the liturgy, the clothes, the reading—St. Augustine, St. Gregory,
St. Ambrose, William of St. Thierry—the prescribed performance
of actions, permissions, and penances, with almost every moment of
the day accounted for, the signs and the silence, all built a new and
almost unimaginable structure in a man's life, a structure rigid but
spacious. The puzzled undergraduate who, a few years earlier, had
scarcely known which way to turn between ambition and intellectual excitement, aesthetic pleasures and women, drink and the
movies, found all the tormenting variety and opportunity of his
old pursuits cut away from him at a single blow. He no longer had
choice, or at least very little, and the firm structure felt supportive
and consoling. It also began to feel like home, a deeply consoling
experience to a man who had not really belonged anywhere since he
was six years old; enclosure and stability were the antithesis of the
wandering that had taken up so much of his young life. At twenty-
six, he had come to rest, and he rested with a delight that is very
evident in *The Seven Storey Mountain*.

There was perhaps another reason for his satisfaction with
Gethsemani, a satisfaction made up of a blend of pleasure and
pain. Merton came to the monastery, as we know, with a strong
sense of the need for personal penance, to expiate the sins of his past
life—one sin in particular—and there was much in the structuring
and outlook of Gethsemani for that wish to feed on. The Cistercians, even more than most monastic orders, had a strong call to
penance, to offering up their painful and sacrificial lives as some
kind of atonement for the wickedness of the world. Most of their
austerities were directed to this end. On this already severe mould,
the fanatical reformer De Rancé had placed his imprint. "The

cloister is a prison in which everybody is held as guilty (before God) whether he has lost his innocence or not," [5] he wrote, and "Monastic congregations are bodies of men reckoned as criminals, men considered, by reason of their very state, as public penitents and who no longer have any claim on the goodness of God until they have made satisfaction to His justice by chastisements worthy of their sins." [5] La Trappe became famous for the "stinging reproaches, words of fire, public humiliation, and everything that could possibly contribute to their abasement" [5] to which the monks were obliged to submit.

Did Gethsemani in the 1940s still hold De Rancé's views on the forming of monks? No, for while never entirely repudiating their reformer, the Trappists had tacitly recognized the extremism of De Rancé and the impossibility and undesirability of living at the kind of pitch that La Trappe had, in its day, represented. All the same, the note of severity, of punishment and self-punishment, was still there, and in the 1940s, at least in provincial America, there was no warning voice to speak of the psychological dangers of an enthusiastic response to humiliation and pain. In this Merton, for all his reading, was no more sophisticated than the rest and he writes warmly of the humiliations of the Trappistine heroine and notes with pleasure the proud response of the Novice Master when he uttered a passing, and recurring wish, that he had entered the Carthusians.

"You wouldn't get the penance there that we have here." [2]

It is possible to make too much of the masochism that peeps out from such monastic utterances. If you believe, as Merton and his fellows did, that your willed suffering may really diminish the agony of the world (this idea of "substitution" is not a central or necessary part of orthodox Christian belief, but many Christians do believe it), then the idea of penance may have little or nothing to do with the sexual satisfaction of masochism. The question is, were other mechanisms at work in the physical suffering, the humiliations, both public and private, and the elaborate apparatus of "obedience"?

The novice Merton had a simple explanation for the kind of life he had chosen to lead.

The monastery is a school—a school in which we learn from God how to be happy. Our happiness consists in sharing the happiness of God, the perfection of His unlimited freedom, the perfection of His love. . . . The beginning of love is truth, and before He will give us His love, God must cleanse our souls of the lies that are in them. And the most effective way of detaching us from ourselves is to make us detest ourselves as we have made ourselves by sin, in order that we may love Him reflected in our souls as He has re-made them by His love.

That is the meaning of the contemplative life, and the sense of all the apparently meaningless little rules and observances and fasts and obediences and penances and humiliations and labors that go to make up the routine of existence in a contemplative monastery: they all serve to remind us of what we are and Who God is—that we may get sick of the sight of ourselves and turn to Him: and in the end, we will find Him in ourselves, in our own purified natures which have become the mirror of His tremendous Goodness and of His endless love. [2]

There is something moving about the ardour of these lines, if we accept that the way to healing is by self-detestation. The deprivation of many normal appetites—food, sleep, sex, and communication with others—do in a sense remind a man of "what he is," in the sense that appetites denied often become much more obtrusive. But the whole spiritual technique seems to beg the question of why people should detest themselves for appetites that they cannot help, that are, in fact, essential to their survival. Instead of simply accepting what they are and making the best they can of it, they do something much more dramatic, which is to turn the whole of their lives into a battlefield, with their will at war with their senses, and it is certainly this approach that most Christian monasticism has attempted. It forces the soul in one of two difficult directions; if the senses cannot be overcome by the will—and because the body has certain specific needs they only can be overcome up to a certain point—then there is shame and guilt and continued self punishment; if the senses *can* be overcome by the will, then there is pride, which again is a sin, and so once again the battle for "goodness" has been lost. The person who is split between their senses and their will is in a "no win" situation.

Many of Merton's early comments about monastic life have this split quality, which emerges in a peculiar kind of falsity. There are two Mertons—the one who craves, or is supposed to crave, luxury and comfort, and the one who wants to prevent this, feeling that spiritually it will not be good for him. Thus when he gets flu in Lent, the "wicked" Merton is delighted, thinking of having peace and solitude and a chance to think and pray in quiet. Not terribly wicked, one might think, but he says, "I was fully convinced that I was going to indulge all the selfish appetites that I did not yet know how to recognize as selfish because they appeared as spiritual in their new disguise. All my bad habits, disinfected, it is true, of formal sin, had sneaked into the monastery with me and had received the religious vesture along with me; spiritual gluttony, spiritual sensuality, spiritual pride." [2] So even in the monastery there can be no place of rest, no sense of his own worthiness. Longings, too, are dramatized out of existence. Tiredness, a need to be alone to rest and to recuperate from infection—simple and normal enough human states in themselves—are blown up into major "sins."

Perhaps it is this sense that nothing is quite what it used to be outside, but is now given some other name, that is what makes some of this writing ring hollow. Writing of the day when the Reverend Father sent for him when he was working in the fields to tell him that his brother John Paul had arrived to visit him (a long-anticipated event) he describes how, by the time he had changed his clothes and got to the Reverend Father's room, the old man had forgotten he was coming. When Father Louis knocked respectfully on the door, "he [the Abbot] flashed the 'Please Wait' sign that is worked from a button at his desk, and so there was nothing for it but sit down and wait, which I did, for the next half hour. Finally Reverend Father discovered that I was there, and sent for my brother." [2]

All the normal human responses—resentment of inefficiency and discourtesy in others, irritation, and impatience—are inappropriate here in the context of obedience. There seems a slavish pleasure in "so there was nothing for it but sit down and wait." The needlessness of the delay—assuming it was not staged as a kind of "training" for the novice—is superficially used by him as an exercise in patience; underlying it, perhaps, is a pleasure in being passive in the hands of a superior.

John Paul's visit was a momentous one, not only because visits were allowed only four times a year but also because John Paul, who was now trained as a bombardier with the Royal Canadian Air Force, was shortly to be sent to Europe. When he arrived, he asked, not altogether unexpectedly, to be instructed as a Catholic, and with the connivance of Merton's superiors he was given several days of intensive instruction by Merton himself and then baptized at a local church.

Merton had a tragic memory of his departure. "I went to see him off at the Gate. . . . A visitor gave him a ride to Bardstown. As the car was turning around to start down the avenue, John Paul turned around and waved, and it was only then that his expression showed some possibility that he might be realizing, as I did, that we would never see each other on earth again." [2]

John Paul was sent to England, and met and married a girl there, Margaret Evans. The following April he went on a bombing mission to Mannheim, and the plane crashed in the North Sea. With his companions, he survived in a rubber dinghy. "He was very badly hurt: maybe his neck was broken. He lay in the bottom of the dinghy in delirium. He was terribly thirsty. He kept asking for water. But they didn't have any. . . . It did not last too long. He had three hours of it, and then he died." [2]

Once again Merton had had to face the painful death of a member of his close family circle; his loneliness, and the insecurity of human love, had been reinforced once more. Now none of his immediate family remained. He wrote movingly of his loss, in a poem reminiscent of classical epitaphs for young men lost in battle, yet with the distinctive Christian note of linking young John Paul's death to that of the young Christ, and hoping that his own agony and deprivation might mitigate his brother's suffering and loss.

Sweet brother, if I do not sleep
My eyes are flowers for your tomb;
And if I cannot eat my bread,
My fasts shall live like willows where you died.
If in the heat I find no water for my thirst,
My thirst shall turn to springs for you, poor traveller.

Where, in what desolate and smokey country,
Lies your poor body, lost and dead?
And in what landscape of disaster
Has your unhappy spirit lost its road?

Come, in my labor find a resting place
And in my sorrows lay your head,
Or rather take my life and blood
And buy yourself a better bed—
Or take my breath and take my death
And buy yourself a better rest.

When all the men of war are shot
And flags have fallen into dust,
Your cross and mine shall tell men still
Christ died on each, for both of us.

For in the wreckage of your April Christ lies slain,
And Christ weeps in the ruins of my spring:
The money of Whose tears shall fall
Into your weak and friendless hand,
And buy you back to your own land:
The silence of Whose tears shall fall
Like bells upon your alien tomb.
Hear them and come: they call you home. [6]

At Christmas of the year of John Paul's death—1943—Merton was performing some minor ritual in the sanctuary of the church when he found himself unexpectedly looking into the eyes of Robert Lax. Lax had come not only to spend Christmas with the Trappists, but to tell Merton that he himself had just been baptized a Catholic. "'You were a Jew and now you are a Catholic,' Bob Gibney had remarked at the news. 'Why don't you black your face? Then you will be all the three things Southerners hate most.'" [2]

From Lax, Merton learned news of the rest of his friends. Bob Gerdy had also become a Catholic. Seymour was in the army in India. Rice, Lax, and Gibney were making a success of journalism; the girls, either in journalism or on the stage.

Lax's arrival, or the news of his friends, revived the latent writer in Merton, and when Lax returned to New York he carried a collection of Merton's poems for Mark Van Doren to see, later to be published by New Directions in 1944 under the title *Thirty Poems*. [6] Some of the poems dated back to St. Bonaventure's, and about half had been written in odd moments since Merton had entered the novitiate. Just sorting the poems and choosing them was a strange experience. It was like "editing the work of a stranger, a dead poet, someone who had been forgotten."

Yet the poet had never really died. In his earliest days at Gethsemani, Merton found that the time after the night office was a wonderful time to write. "After two or three hours of prayer your mind is saturated in peace and the richness of the liturgy. The dawn is breaking outside the cold windows. If it is warm, the birds are already beginning to sing. Whole blocks of imagery seem to crystallize out as it were naturally in the silence and the peace, and the lines almost write themselves." [2]

It was explained to the novice that, although his superiors had no objection to his writing poetry, he could not do it then, as that was the time set aside for the study of Scripture and the Psalms. "I found that this was even better than writing poems," Merton says loyally, but it is the first conflict that has arisen between the needs of the writer and the needs of the monk; the monk won.

In fact there was little time between the long hours of the liturgy and the heavy manual work in the fields to write at all. "The succession of our offices, and all the feasts and seasons of the liturgical year, and the various times of sowing and planting and harvesting, and, in general, all the varied and closely integrated harmony of natural and supernatural cycles that go to make up the Cistercian year tend to fill a man's life to such overflowing satiety that there is usually no time, no desire for writing."

Usually, perhaps—but Merton's desire to write did not die, and he continued to produce a small but steady stream of poems: at Christmas, one or two in January, one at the Purification, and one more in Lent. Then summer came and he was quite simply too busy, and too tired by the long hours of hard work under the hot Kentucky sun. There is much joy in his earliest Gethsemani poems—much about love, about light, about children, about the Virgin Mary

> And when my Mother, pretty as a church,
> Takes Me upon her lap, I laugh with love. [6]

as if a new security, a new safety, a new sense of home and of belonging has come into Merton's life. A few of the poems are unashamedly imitations of the style of St. John of the Cross; for example,

> O sweet escape! O smiling flight!
> O what bright secret breaks our jails of flesh?
> For we are fled, among the shining vineyards,
> And ride our praises in the hills of wheat,
> To find our hero, in His tents of light!
> O sweet escape! O smiling flight! [6]

Only one poem, "The Vine," reveals some of the desolation and fear of the old Merton, the orphaned child intolerably stressed with fear:

> When wind and winter turn our vineyard
> To a bitter Calvary,
> What hands come out and crucify us
> Like the innocent vine?

How long will starlight weep as sharp as thorns
In the night of our desolate life?
How long will moonlight fear to free the naked prisoner?
Or is there no deliverer?

A mob of winds, on Holy Thursday, come like murderers
And batter the walls of our locked and terrified souls.
Our doors are down, and our defense is done.
Good Friday's rains, in Roman order,
March, with sharpest lances, up our vineyard hill.

More dreadful than St. Peter's cry
When he was being swallowed in the sea,
Cries out our anguish: "Oh! We are abandoned!"
When in our life we see the ruined vine
Cut open by the cruel spring,
Ploughed by the furious season! [6]

In the final verse of the poem, there is a resolution when April comes, and the vine flowers like the tree of Calvary, but something of the cold and hunger of Lent at Gethsemani has come through, and temporarily at least for the ardent novice "the doors are down."

References

1. Thomas Merton. Letter to Mark Van Doren. St. Lucy's Day, 1941. TMSC.
2. Thomas Merton. *The Seven Storey Mountain*. New York: Harcourt Brace, 1948; London: SPCK, 1990. Also published abridged as *Elected Silence* (London: Burns & Oates, 1949).
3. *Regulations of the Order of Cistercians of the Strict Observance*. Dublin: General Chapter of the Order of Cistercians of the Strict Observance, 1926.
4. Thomas Merton. *Exile Ends in Glory*. Milwaukee: Bruce, 1948.
5. Armand-Jean le Bouthillier de Rancé. *De la Sainteté et des Devoirs de la Vie Monastique*. Paris, 1846.
6. Thomas Merton. *Thirty Poems*. New York: New Directions, 1944.

9

THE PRISON OF SELFHOOD

The Abbey of Gethsemani lies in wild, lonely countryside. There is a long, straight road running through the heart of it, along which, for a good many years, the youth of the district have liked to "hot rod," but that apart the landscape is unspoiled and quiet, except for the occasional day, or evening, when the ground shakes underfoot with the throbbing of the guns at Fort Knox. The landscape is bounded by the "Kentucky knobs," the strange, volcano-shaped hills that change colour during the day through many shades of green and violet and blue. There are woods, often laced with creepers; valleys, locally known as "hollers," near the Abbey; and wide fields and ponds; a marvellous abundance of birds and animals and flowers, enormous butterflies in plenty, and big crickets and katydids. Despite all this abundance, the local farmers have, until recent times, been poor, struggling desperately for a living, some of the poorest of them building illicit stills, and making and drinking the dangerous local moonshine. In the 1940s the Abbey was much involved in the social problems of the local communities, and it was to them that local farmers who were down on their luck, or needed to borrow farm implements, would turn for help.

In such spare time as he had, Merton had a certain amount of freedom to explore the countryside. In the immediate neighbourhood of the Abbey were about fifty acres of land surrounded by a wall, which represented the official enclosure. Many monks never went beyond this, but Merton had the habit of walking in the woods, presumably with permission, and drew immense pleasure from this limited freedom. There was not much contact with local people, although he met an occasional farmer on his walks.

There were not many other freedoms. The routine of manual work for five or six hours a day that obtained then, and about five hours of prayer in church, was gruelling. The Kentucky summer is hot and humid, and the working conditions in the barns as the monks brought in the harvest were extremely exacting, as sweat and prickly heat and insects took their toll. The noise of the crickets and the heat in the monastery made the heavily clad monks feel as if they were in "a gigantic frying pan standing over a fire," and in choir the flies could be torture: "you have to bite your lip to keep your resolution about never swatting them, as they crawl over your forehead and into your eyes while you are trying to sing." [1] In the winter, cold inflicted equal suffering—the water was frozen in the dormitories and the monks wrote, studied, and prayed in virtually unheated rooms.

Food was not adequate either in quantity or quality, for such an exacting life, and the fasts were very strict indeed. Merton writes painfully of his wobbling knees as he worked, on an empty Lenten stomach, wielding a sledgehammer. Probably because of his quickness of mind and his love of change and variety, the most painful aspect of the life for Merton was the long, slow hours in choir, a torment he was to mention ruefully many times in the course of his writing. Revealingly, in writing about Mother Berchmans, the Trappistine, he describes her "worst trial" as "the liturgical life, the divine office, choir, the psalms." [2] It is unlikely that either Mother Berchmans or most of his fellow monks felt as strongly about this as Merton did—the liturgical life was so central a part of Trappist life that many would not have chosen it, or continued in it, if they had hated it as much as Merton did. It seemed to represent a fundamental reservation he had about life as a Cistercian.

Silence he never complained about, but other monks mention the peculiar difficulties it imposed on the Trappist. It made real friendship within the monastery impossible, and, because ideas, feelings, moods, could not be shared with others in conversation, there was a very real loneliness. This threw the monk back on himself, and, because this ultimately became defeating, on God, and in the silence the monk either acquired a sense of deep relationship with God that could sustain him in his isolation, or he failed and went back to "the world." This particular crisis—the crisis of identity—did not seem to reach Merton at this stage of his monastic life, but several years later. At this stage, he still brought an all-embracing enthusiasm to the life that seemed almost not to notice the incidental pains and inconveniences in the joy of commitment and self-dedication.

"If you ever receive a letter," he was to write a few years later, with a kind of schoolboy enthusiasm, "or see a document signed by someone who puts the letters OCSO after his name (Order of the Cistercians of the Strict Observance) you can tell yourself he is someone who has found out the meaning of life." [1]

He undoubtedly found great joy in the graceful medieval ordering of his life, and in the sheer physical beauty of the place daily unfolding around him. But did this claim to have found out the meaning of life—to have resolved all his earlier problems—truly represent his feelings in his novitiate or were there doubts that he was repressing? Writing many years later, he thought back to those earliest years and admitted that there had been difficulties, although difficulties of which he had allowed himself to become aware only very gradually and over a long period of years.

"Do you, perhaps, imagine that the monastic life is romantic? It is not. It is terribly prosaic. We who live it are more aware than others that the ideal and the real are very far apart. . . . Perhaps we must confess, that some of us came here with a kind of secret, romantic enthusiasm in our hearts; and that we are angry because it is all shot." [3]

For Merton, the discovery that it was not possible to live the whole of his life on a high, romantic plane came not at first by resentment of the hardships, or by a longing for freedom, or by disappointment in his fellow monks, but by the sad little discovery that, despite the outward change in his way of life, inwardly he had not changed at all. The writer who had followed him into the cloister, rather against his will, could not die, could not let him be a monk in peace, but was full of ideas that kept his imagination in a ferment. "He generates books," says Merton of this alter ego, "in the silence that ought to be sweet with the infinitely productive darkness of contemplation." [1] The willed identity, that of the recollected monk, was being usurped by another identity that arose unbidden. "One of us," he remarked ominously, "has got to die." [1]

The irony of it was that it was not Merton's superiors but Merton himself who was convinced that the writer needed to die. At this stage, Dom Frederic and the Father Master were tolerant of Merton's wish to write poetry, although like all who are not writers they could not guess how much time is needed in apparent trifling and vegetation for the writer to produce anything worth-while, nor perhaps what fundamental harm it does to a natural writer not to have time to write. But it was the exhausting schedule that made concentrated writing impossible, not the attitude of those who were training Merton in the monastic life.

Partly, no doubt, because of this inner conflict, and partly because of exhaustion from hard manual work, poor food, and inadequate sleep (and Merton's contemporaries remember him at this stage of his life as inclined to augment the given hardships rather than try to minimize them), toward the end of his novitiate Merton's health began to decline rather seriously. Tuberculosis was feared; *collapse* was not too strong a word.

Merton's superiors had the sense and compassion to see that something was wrong, and he was relieved of much of the harder manual work and set to making French translations. At the time, he was also studying philosophy and theology as part of his preparation for the priesthood, so his life had begun to move away from the more vigorous outdoor life toward the intellectual life he was used to, with much more emphasis on reading and writing, although he continued to enjoy manual labour for the rest of his life.

Merton had discussed his need to write with his superiors at the time of his physical breakdown. Intellectual work was not fully within the Cistercian tradition. De Rancé, in particular, had railed against it—it seemed to have a sophistication, a physical ease, and a mental enjoyment about it that sorted ill with his ideas about how a monk should feel. But the extraordinary boom the Trappists were enjoying in the immediate postwar years, with three new monas-teries being founded, others planned, and the existing houses like Gethsemani packed to bursting point, meant that there was a huge public curiosity about Cistercian life and Cistercian history, one that needed to be satisfied by print. So that when Merton, obviously in physical and mental distress about the loss of his vocation as a writer, confided in his superiors about his need to write, it not surprisingly occurred to them that they might get him to write "edifying" books suitable to place in the hands of those hungry for the Cistercian approach to spirituality.

First, however, came Merton's first, or "simple," vows, which he made on the Feast of St. Joseph, 1944. The first vows are the vows of "temporary profession." The novice has learned the liturgical and other customs of the house, and now, if all has gone well with him, he is ready to embark on the monastic life proper, although not yet ready to take his final vows, to become fully "professed." Those who were already professed voted for him, in a simple and graceful ceremony. At a Chapter from which postulants, novices, and those in temporary vows were dismissed, the Father Prior moved round the group of Fathers giving each two balls, a white one and a black one. In the middle of the room was a "vessel" to receive the balls, and each Father would move to it in turn, placing in it a white ball or a black ball, according to whether or not he thought the novice should be received into temporary vows, carefully hiding the colour of the ball with the sleeve of the cowl, so that his vote might be secret. In Merton's case, the election was in favour.

Before taking temporary vows, a novice made a retreat of eight days, during which he thought about the motives that had led him into the religious life—"the grace which led him to the desert," as the *Spiritual Directory* puts it. "Far from allowing his ideal to be lowered by experience, he ought rather to show an ever-increasing esteem and fidelity towards it, so that if, when receiving the habit, he only aimed at becoming an edifying monk, he forms on the eve of his profession the irrevocable resolution to become a saint." [3]

At this point in the religious life, the novice gives away whatever property he may have left, and writes out a long, formal profession in Latin promising stability, "conversion of manners" (i.e., a conformity of his whole personality to the ideals of the religious life), and obedience to the Abbot. This schedule is read and signed by the monk in Chapter, obedience to the Abbot is separately sworn to, and then the novice is clothed with the black scapular, leather girdle, and the great white cowl of the Cistercians. A year or two later, Merton was to write, of Mother Berchmans at this point in her life, words that applied equally to himself: "She became in truth and in fact, a Cistercian, a contemplative, and as she knelt in the middle of the choir after being clothed in this lovely vesture, and tried to raise up her hands in the immense, ungainly sleeves, she could reflect that this very ungainliness, which made any but the simplest activities all but impossible was the symbol of her contemplation, which made her, by her sacrifice, useless and alien to the works of this world, and fit only for the liberty and rest of the pure love of God." [2]

While preparing for his temporary vows, Merton had composed a poem to St. Agnes, the child martyr; it is written in the tradition

J. B. Chautard's *The Soul of the Apostolate* from the French [11], and a translation of texts by St. Bernard of Clairvaux from the Latin [12].

The two biographies are bravely and spiritedly done, with a desperate attempt to inject life and originality into the milk-and-water tradition of hagiography (and, as already pointed out, the account of Mother Berchmans throws interesting light on Merton's own experiences as a novice) yet there is something depressed and depressing about them. The former reviewer for the *New York Herald Tribune*, with his immense reading in several languages, seems ill at ease in this tiny world, like a giant in a doll's house. Putting these propagandist exercises beside the wide, imaginative scope of his poems written at the same time, we feel embarrassed for Merton, as he was later to feel embarrassed for himself. Looking back at this time later, when collecting material for *A Thomas Merton Reader*, he said, "At first the writing was very bad. Two books were written which are not represented here [*Exile Ends in Glory* and *What Are These Wounds?*] although they were unfortunately published." [3] At the time, they seemed part of the price to be paid by an obedient Trappist monk.

Not for long, however. Zealous for humiliations Merton may have been at this period, but he knew good writing from bad, the authentic from the inauthentic, and if he must write, and his superiors thought he should, then it must be something at once more personal, more original, and generally of better quality than this raking over of past Cistercian glories. Merton was nothing if not a man of immense intellectual vitality and originality, and he began— surely with doubts—to try out a distinct Trappist voice of his own.

The crucial year was 1946. In this year he began writing his autobiography, *The Seven Storey Mountain* and also began a journal, much in the old tradition of the journals he had kept at Columbia and at St. Bonaventure's, which was eventually to be published as *The Sign of Jonas* [14]. In 1947 he wrote an original and striking book of spirituality *Seeds of Contemplation* [15], in which we hear Merton's voice as a teacher of spirituality for the first time, and this was followed in 1948 by *The Waters of Siloe* (published in England as *Waters of Silence* [3]), less original than the other three, and more in the tradition of Cistercian lip service, but more courageous, more confident and more genuinely questioning than his earlier works. He still occasionally slipped back into the old propagandist tone of voice—it was years before he became quite sure that his commitment did not demand this of him—but the new writer had been born, and like all good writers he listened to the inner voice and not to the voice of others' expectations.

With its careful retracing of the pathways that had led him to his present life, *The Seven Storey Mountain* (of which more in the next chapter), seemed to release Merton as a writer in a way that his earlier attempts at writing novels had been unable to do. It began the torrent of books and articles that was to flow from Merton's pen for the next twenty-four years.

At the same time, he was working again in a way he had used and enjoyed in the past—keeping a journal. The published extracts begin on December 10, 1946. "It is five years since I came to the monastery. It is the same kind of day, overcast. But now it is raining. I wish I knew how to be grateful to God and to Our Lady for bringing me here.

"There was a long interval after afternoon work. It was good to be in the big quiet church. The church is dark, these winter afternoons." [14]

The entry for December 13th is a pregnant one. "Yesterday, although it is Advent and we are not supposed to receive any letters at all, Dom Frederic gave me a letter from Naomi Burton of Curtis Brown Ltd. I had sent her the manuscript of *Seven Storey Mountain*. [14]

The journal continues in a wonderfully vivid and readable style, evoking small but precious moments in his daily life. We see him praying quietly in the church in the afternoons, listening to the sound of the rain on the roof as he did so. Working out of doors, spreading manure, rooting out brambles and cedar stumps, felling trees (nearly cutting off his legs with the axe), making hay, picking apples. He continued in his studies for the priesthood, taking an examination in moral theology, preaching sermons that were criticized by his fellow scholastics. "I was praised for 'avoiding [my] usual heavy philosophy.' Another said I was in general 'too scholastic.' I was blamed for giving a lecture rather than a sermon. That was true. In fact, I felt myself sliding into the embarrassing mannerisms of a ham radio announcer. This embarrassed me very much, but I could not seem to pull myself together." [14] He took part in the rituals of Trappist life, lighting much too large a fire in the censer when he was thurifer. He enjoyed the visits of monks from Europe, particularly French monks with whom he often had a

chance to talk because he acted as interpreter. He also enjoyed the
first visit by James Laughlin of New Directions, who published his
poetry, and found himself enormously stimulated by hours of talk
about books, writers, and the world of publishing. He was perhaps
more bothered than he cared to admit by Laughlin's lack of formal
religion, but he felt Laughlin was "looking for God," although he
seemed doubtful about Laughlin's enthusiasms for D. H. Lawrence
and Henry Miller.

He wrote of summer torments. "Prickly heat. Red lumps all over
your neck and shoulders. Everything clammy. Paenitentiam agite! It is
better than a hairshirt." And of November chill. "Today it rains, and I
put on a winter shirt before the Night Office. . . . The other winter
clothes have not been given out yet." [14] He wrote of how fasting is
not so bad in hot summer weather, and also, rather charmingly, of
pleasure in eating. "Here I come with blackberry seeds in my
teeth. . . . It is nice, sitting in the refectory, dipping a chunk of
bread into a dish of blackberry juice and listening to the silence." [14]

For the first time, and only very gradually, we now begin to note
in Merton the keen pleasure in natural life that was to be so
important to him later on. Both *The Seven Storey Mountain* and his
earlier writings show little awareness of the natural world, but now,
as if the processes of contemplation and the indigences of Trappist
life have opened his eyes, he begins to note, here and there, the
dogwood bloom, the prettiness of a hickory tree, catbirds singing
"with crazy versatility," the heavy smell of honeysuckle, the stare of
a buzzard, and the hills turning "red and brown and copper" in the
clear weather of the autumn. And, as if this new and heightened
awareness of the world about him extends to his brethren, he begins
to note with compassion the failing of the older men, the frailties
and illnesses with which they bravely contend.

There were problems with his life, some of which, no doubt, he
dwelt painfully on with the sudden onset of insomnia. "On and off
since Easter," he wrote on April 28, 1947, "I have been playing a
new game called insomnia. It goes like this: You lie down in your
dormitory cell and listen to first one monk and then another monk
begin to snore, without, however, going to sleep yourself. Then you
count the quarter hours by the tower clock and console yourself
with an exact knowledge of the amount of sleep you are missing.
The fun does not really begin until you get up at 2 A.M. and try to

keep awake in choir. All day long you wander around the monastery bumping into the walls." [14]

There were two conflicts in his life just then. One concerned the
still-vexed question of his writing. All his superiors and his friends
urged him to be a writer, but he could not write without taking on
too much—some of it pouring from his overactive mind, some of it
imposed by superiors, who wanted to make good use of his talents.
At about the time that he complained of insomnia, he said, "Today
I got two new jobs. Father Abbot gave me the notes that Father
Alberic was working on, for the revised edition of his history of the
Order. Then I am to write a new postulant's guide. That means I
have no less than twelve jobs in various stages of completion." [14]

He had no proper place to work on all this material although
later in 1947 he was allowed to work in a vault where the archives
were kept—his typewriter had broken down from old age, and he
had to borrow the typewriter of another writer monk, who was
liable to want to use it himself at any moment.

It was not so much the physical difficulties of writing that he
worried about, however, as the fact that all these schemes and ideas
filled his mind so full with anxiety and excitement that he could
not concentrate on prayer—and it was for prayer that he had come
to the monastery. Already he was beginning to ask deeper questions
about the work he found himself doing and about the underlying
structure of "obedience."

"Just because a cross is a cross, does it follow that it is the cross
God intends for you?

"Just because a job is a nuisance, is it therefore good for you?

"Is it an act of virtue for a contemplative to sit down and let
himself be snowed under by activities?

"Does the fact that all this is obedience make it really pleasing to
God? I wonder. I do not ask these questions in a spirit of rebellion.
I would really like to know the answers." [14]

Merton had already spent much time with his superiors discussing
his worries about his intense activity in the midst of a would-be
contemplative life. One form this worry took for him—a worry
heightened by the fact that he was getting near the time to take
his solemn (or final) vows—was a query as to whether the Trappist
Order was really the order for him. There was an activism about
Trappist contemplation that was troubling and that seemed to be far
from the solitude and quiet prayer that felt most important to him.

The Cistercian life is energetic. There are tides of vitality running through the whole community that generate energy even in people who are lazy. And here at Gethsemani we are at the same time Cistercians and Americans. It is in some respects a dangerous combination. Our energy runs away with us. We go out to work like a college football team taking the field. . . . If we want something, we easily persuade ourselves that what we want is God's will just as long as it turns out to be difficult to obtain. What is easy is my own will: what is hard is God's will. And because we make fetishes out of difficulties we sometimes work ourselves into the most fantastically stupid situations, and use ourselves up not for God but for ourselves. We think we have done great things because we are worn out. If we have rushed into the fields or into the woods and done a great deal of damage, we are satisfied. [14]

It is clear that the romanticized view of the monastic life is beginning to yield to a more critical insight, and no amount of obedience can blind Merton's sharp intelligence and psychological acuteness.

He kept asking himself a question that had been at the back of his mind ever since he had joined the Cistercians and before—would he be happier in an order such as the Carthusians, where the hours of work and public prayer would be much less, and the opportunity for private prayer, and perhaps, more important, for solitude, would be much greater? Sociable as Merton was, he had a strongly introverted side, and possibly one of the hardest things for him was the determined "togetherness" of Cistercian life. Although they were silent, the Cistercians slept, ate, prayed, and worked together—an intolerable situation for many introverted people. Certainly many of the happiest moments in Merton's writings seemed to come when he had managed to steal off alone, to his vault or to the woods; even at Oakham and at Olean he had needed solitude.

Yet Merton had a sense of belonging at Gethsemani, of being part of its family, and whenever he confided to his superiors his longing to set off for *La Grande Chartreuse* they firmly assured him that this was a temptation arising out of "self-love" and that he should on no account pay attention to it. If he wanted to "pack up and run off to the Charterhouse I should treat that desire like any other movement of disordered appetite." [14]

So, influenced in this way, and still wanting to dedicate himself to God as a monk, Merton began to prepare for solemn vows. He was to take them exactly three years after simple vows, on the Feast of St. Joseph. He prepared himself for it by reading the *Cautions and Counsels* of St. John of the Cross and, in the Cistercian tradition, by making his will. Just before he started on the eight-day retreat that preceded the taking of the vows, he took the significant step of "renouncing" the clothes he had brought to Gethsemani with him. The wardrobe keeper left his suitcase in his dormitory cell—a suitcase redolent of the past, with its Cuba Mail Line label and the letter "M" on it. Inside were a blue woollen sweater, four striped sports shirts, some tweeds, and a dark blue suit. The smell of the suitcase, still rich and new, brought back the past with startling vividness. "It is almost impossible to believe that was seven years ago [when he first used the suitcase]. But what is more impossible is to believe that I ever wore those clothes. I do not believe in myself as a layman at all. I was definitely never meant to be one. That, at least, is good to know." [14]

The day of solemn profession was a happy day. He felt a sense of union with his fellow monks, that he inescapably belonged to this family, this band of brothers. The day frankly gave him pleasure, "a deep and warm realization that I was immersed in my community."

At around this time, he was working on *Seeds of Contemplation* [15], his first attempt at writing a book of spiritual advice. It is a fascinating book for a student of Merton because it contains both ideas that are literally seeds, in that they later found growth and flowering in his thinking, and other ideas that he later repudiated either explicitly or implicitly. In an introduction, Merton acknowledged his debt to Pascal and to St. John of the Cross. Both in his style—that of aphorisms and disconnected thoughts—and in his views on contemplative prayer, he was indebted to these masters, especially to St. John. With what may seem an excessive humility, Merton remarks that he hopes the book "does not contain a line that is new to Catholic tradition or a single word that would perplex an orthodox theologian."

The heart of the book—and central to Merton's whole approach—is that a religious person must turn away from self-will and obsession with their own appetites, and seek only to know and to do the will of God and to find joy in that. "The only true joy is to escape from the prison of our own selfhood . . . and enter by love into union with the Life Who dwells and sings within the essence of every creature and in the core of our minds." If one had to express Merton's thinking over a lifetime, and had only a sentence in which to do it, perhaps that sentence would come as near as any. He goes on to speak of an idea central to his religious understanding—that human beings, or forms in nature, are more like God the more completely they are simply and naturally themselves, and that their true identity is known only to God. "A tree gives glory to God first of all by being a tree. . . . The more a tree is like itself, the more it is like Him. . . . No two created beings are exactly alike. And their individuality is no imperfection. On the contrary: the perfection of each created thing is not merely in its conformity to an abstract type but in its own individual identity with itself. This particular tree will give glory to God by spreading out its roots in the earth and raising its branches into the air and the light in a way that no other tree before or after it ever did or will do." Sanctity, Merton rather unusually goes on to suggest, consists in something or someone being itself, or himself or herself, even if it is "only" a tree or a flower or an animal. For human beings, though, it is more difficult, because there is choice. "We can be ourselves or not, as we please. But the problem is this: since God alone possesses the secret of my identity, he alone can make me who I am or rather, He alone can make me who I will be when I at last fully begin to be." [15]

The problem for humans, in Merton's view, is the "false self" that we take on, or rather perhaps are born with (original sin), turning away from the fullness of God's will to the refusal of our own existence and our own being. "All sin starts from the assumption that my false self, the self that exists only in my own egocentric desires, is the fundamental reality of life to which everything else in the universe is ordered. Thus I use up my life trying to accumulate pleasures and experiences and power and honor and knowledge and love, to clothe this false self and construct its nothingness into something objectively real." [15]

This attempt, he suggests, simply objectifies those who make it, filling them with a terrifying hollowness and sense of emptiness from which they then try to escape by intensifying their futile struggles. The only "way out" is to turn away from ourselves toward God, because in God is the only identity we will ever have. "There is only one problem on which all my existence, my peace and my happiness depend: to discover myself in discovering God. If I find

Him, I will find myself; and if I find my true self, I will find Him."
But discovering God, he goes on to say, is not totally within our
power. "God utters me like a word containing a partial thought of
Himself. A word will never be able to comprehend the voice that
utters it." It is God who has to discover Himself within the contemplative soul. But we have to prepare ourselves by warring against
the sloth and pride that get in the way—especially pride. "In order
to become myself I must cease to be what I always thought I wanted
to be, and in order to find myself I must go out of myself, and in
order to live I have to die." The "going out" and the death itself, is
the action of love, and this can come only by God's grace. "I who am
without love cannot become love unless Love identifies me with
Himself. But if He sends His own Love, Himself, to act and love in
me and in all that I do then I shall be transformed. I shall discover
who I am and I shall possess my true identity by losing myself in
Him." It is no good trying to find God by "escaping" from the
world—"stuffing yourself inside your own mind and closing the
door like a turtle." Rather, there is a movement outward to identify
with others: "And we shall love one another and God with the same
Love with which He loves us and Himself." [15]

At this stage of his life, however, Merton still sees virtue in
running hard from many aspects of the modern world. There is a
strong sense of "us" and "them" as he looks at the spiritual person as
opposed to the worldly, perhaps not unlike the way he and his father
viewed poor Pop on his ill-fated visit to France all those years before.

> Do everything you can to avoid the amusements and the noise and the
> business of men. Keep as far away as you can from the places where
> they gather to cheat and insult one another, to exploit one another, to
> laugh at one another, or to mock one another with their false gestures
> of friendship. Do not read their newspapers—newspapers are a
> penance, not a diversion. Be glad if you can keep beyond the reach
> of their radios. Do not bother with their unearthly songs or their
> intolerable concerns for the way their bodies look and feel.
>
> Do not smoke their cigarettes or drink the things they drink or share
> their preoccupation with different kinds of food. Do not complicate
> your life by looking at the pictures in their magazines. [15]

If the priggishness of this is alarming, it is perhaps also a
reminder of how much Merton must have missed many aspects of
the modern world—the newspapers for which he had enjoyed

writing, the jazz he had loved, the friendships and beer with the boys, and all the small but consoling pleasures of everyday life. Yet, as is clear from the depth and authority of the earlier chapters of *Seeds of Contemplation*, the absence of distraction in Merton's life had deepened and quietened him to the point where he thought with profundity, but with a rare clarity and authority, about the religious basis of life. There is a real continuity with his earlier thinking as student and teacher, and it is obvious that he has reflected deeply on his own experience, but the years at Gethsemani have transmuted random ideas, together with callow priggishness and crude theories of expiation, into the gold of original writing and theological freshness of mind. For the first time in his writing, not excluding *The Seven Storey Mountain*, we feel the chemistry of his immensely powerful intelligence, rejecting some of the sentimentalities of second-rate theology but working instead on the Church Fathers and finding material there which could act as a catalyst on his thinking. For whatever reasons, good or bad, conscious or unconscious, that Merton had chosen the harsh experiment of life at Gethsemani, it was beginning to pay off in terms of liberating his mind, although some of his superiors would have worried if they had guessed at this point how far that liberation was to go. There were, however, no problems about the publication of *Seeds of Contemplation*. It received the imprimatur from Cardinal Spellman, then Archbishop of New York, and from another prelate, and was published in 1949.

References

1. Thomas Merton. *The Seven Storey Mountain*. New York: Harcourt Brace, 1948; London: SPCK, 1990. Also published abridged as *Elected Silence* (London: Burns & Oates, 1949).
2. Thomas Merton. *Exile Ends in Glory*. Milwaukee: Bruce, 1948.
3. From Introduction to *God is My Life: the Story of our Lady of Gethsemani*. Photographs by Shirley Burden; introduction by Thomas Merton. New York: Reynal and Company, 1960.
4. Thomas Merton. *The Waters of Siloe*. New York: Harcourt Brace, 1953; London: Sheldon Press, 1976. Also published as *Waters of Silence*. London: Hollis and Carter, 1950.

5. Thomas Merton. *God Is My Life.* West Caldwell, N.J.: Reynal, 1960.
6. Thomas Merton. *Thirty Poems.* New York: New Directions, 1944.
7. Thomas Merton. *What Are These Wounds?* Milwaukee: Bruce, 1950.
8. Thomas Merton. *Cistercian Contemplatives.* Bardstown, Ky.: Abbey of Our Lady of Gethsemani (Trappist), 1968.
9. Thomas Merton. *What Is Contemplation?* Notre Dame, Ind.: Holy Cross, 1968.
10. Thomas Merton (Trans.). St. John Eudes, *The Kingdom of Jesus.* New York: Kenedy, 1966.
11. Thomas Merton (Trans.). J. B. Chautard, *The Soul of the Apostolate.* Bardstown, Ky.: Abbey of Our Lady of Gethsemani (Trappist), 1966.
12. Thomas Merton (Trans.). St. Bernard of Clairvaux, *The Spirit of Simplicity.* Bardstown, Ky.: Abbey of Our Lady of Gethsemani (Trappist), 1948.
13. Thomas Merton. *A Thomas Merton Reader*, ed. Thomas P. McDonnell. New York: Doubleday, 1962.
14. Thomas Merton. *The Sign of Jonas.* New York: Harcourt Brace, 1948; London: Sheldon Press, 1976.
15. Thomas Merton. *Seeds of Contemplation.* New York: New Directions, 1949; London: Greenwood Press, 1983.

10

THE MOUNT OF PURGATORY

Into the middle of willed silence and asceticism and penance, *The Seven Storey Mountain* burst like a bomb; the landscape was never quite the same again.

"I am just about finishing a straight autobiography called *The Seven Storey Mountain*," Merton wrote to Mark Van Doren on September 19, 1946, "a title which is literally, physically accurate. . . . It will run some seven hundred pages long." [I] The title was taken from the mountain of Purgatory in Dante's *Divine Comedy*.

In Advent, Dom Frederic broke the custom about letters and handed him a letter from Naomi Burton saying how much she liked the book. She had no doubt of its finding a publisher and proposed to begin with Robert Giroux of Harcourt Brace.

Giroux remembers, as a young executive editor, recommending the book warmly to Mr. Brace (who had not read it). Giroux had, in the past, rejected Merton's three novels, sensing in them Merton's inability to make the kind of literary resolution that a novel needs, but he had little doubt about this new book, although equally no prophetic insight about how astonishingly it eventually would sell. Meanwhile he did a little mild editing, with Merton's cooperation, excising the repetitions and *longueurs*, and in February 1947, just when Merton had made his will renouncing all earthly things, the contract was signed between Merton and Harcourt Brace, making all royalties over to the monastery. The book had been fairly heavily edited at the suggestion of Merton's superiors, who were worried about the frankness with which he described his former life; an action that accorded with the proprieties of the time but that left a curious imbalance in the book, hinting at terrible sins that never seemed to add up to more than seeing a few girls and getting drunk now and then. In April, one of the Censors of the Order objected to the publication of the book, not on theological grounds but with the suggestion that it was "unripe for publication." Woundingly, he explained this by saying that Merton was incapable of writing an autobiography "with his present literary equipment," and he advised him to take a correspondence course in English grammar.

Merton seemed faintly amused by this and said he now enjoyed thinking of himself as a "misunderstood author," but at his Abbot's insistence he sent back a three-page defence, pointing out Harcourt Brace's enthusiasm for the project, and at this the Censor subsided, more easily than his successors were to do on later occasions. But Merton submissively did more work on the book, "toning it down," fearful, as a result of the things the Censor had said, of the moral harm he might do to casual readers—"young girls in boarding schools, whom the censors are afraid to scandalize." [2] The "weaker brethren" had overruled the sensibilities of the author.

Meanwhile his other literary enterprises were flourishing. Bruce Publishing Company of Milwaukee had accepted *Exile Ends in Glory*, and Merton was feeling his usual ambivalence about literary success. "At first I felt pleasure at the thought that the book was going to be printed. But the pleasure soon ended up in a dead, heavy feeling inside me." [2]

Merton was working at intervals on *The Waters of Siloe*, often interrupted by other writing and by the claims of the harvest, but slowly the book proceeded. He was also correcting page proofs for his book of poetry *Figures for an Apocalypse* [3] and feeling disgusted with it. And he was working on the souvenir publication for the centenary of Gethsemani in 1948. [4]

In the spring of 1948, he sent *The Waters of Siloe* off to Naomi Burton and to the Censor at Our Lady of the Valley. In July, *Exile Ends in Glory* arrived from the publisher, and to Merton's embarrassment it was the book selected to be read over meals in the refectory. He manages a certain wry detachment. "When the reader gives the stuff a peculiar interpretation I feel that the book is still getting better treatment than it deserves. There are parts of it that make my stomach turn somersaults. . . . Where did I get all that pious rhetoric? That was the way I thought a monk was supposed to write, just after I had made simple profession." [2] Also in July, Dom Frederic sent for Merton and handed him the first copy of *The Seven Storey Mountain* with a loving pleasure in his achievement that Merton was to remember and treasure after Dom Frederic's death.

Even now, before publication, Harcourt Brace had begun to

suspect the book might be a success. Their original plans for the book had been to print 5,000 copies, but the prepublication orders for the book had been so good that already they had changed that to 12,000. And now three Catholic book clubs had placed orders for it, an unprecedented response to any book. The book was published on October 4, 1948, priced at $3. It carried warm recommendations from Graham Greene, Evelyn Waugh, and Clare Booth Luce.

And now began one of those publishing phenomena that puzzle even the most experienced. Without much in the way of promotion or reviews, without the book even appearing in the *New York Times* best-seller list—they claimed they did not include religious books—the book began to sell and sell. On one day alone, 5,000 copies were ordered, and the book had a higher weekly rate of sale than any other book Harcourt Brace had published—Lytton Strachey's *Elizabeth and Essex* was the nearest contender. This original clothbound edition of *The Seven Storey Mountain* sold 600,000 copies.

What was the secret of its extraordinary success, in a country with its fair share of anti-Catholic prejudice and despite the fact that in many places the book falls into a style of blatant preaching?

Merton had set out to tell the story of his conversion; because he wrote so well and because the story itself followed an ancient and fascinating pattern—that of the rake who reforms (and is equally fascinating both in his former wickedness and in his new-found goodness), he could hardly fail to attract readers. In addition to that long and absorbing account of his childhood and adolescence (with the deep pathos of which Merton himself was largely unconscious), is the parallel fascination that he can tell us at first hand, and with the eye of the writer, about what it was like to live a medieval life in twentieth-century America. Many readers must have been totally ignorant of such a way of life or supposed that it had ceased in the Middle Ages, and now here was Merton (the first of many writers who were to do so) telling us about the clothes and the diet, the work and the penances, the prayer and the innermost thoughts and feelings of a twentieth-century Trappist. Perhaps it was not only the medieval aspect of the Trappists that fascinated people, but also a buried awareness of a sadomasochistic element in some of the attitudes to penance, humiliations, and self-punishment, an element that Merton himself seemed to demonstrate in his early writings, although it faded with his growing self-awareness in the 1950s.

What also appealed, of course, especially to his Catholic audience, was the note of heroism, of idealism, of reckless self-sacrifice for a cause. In the postwar exhaustion, and the gloom of the Cold War, Merton's passionate faith made an instant appeal by its very extremism, and many of the young were profoundly influenced by his example, some of them following him into Gethsemani itself. But apart from Merton's book, the contemplative monasteries were steadily filling up with recruits, many of them war veterans, so the book, like all best-sellers, had met a hunger that was already seeking sustenance.

There is a real puzzle about the book: how could either Merton's superiors, or Merton himself, feel that it was really within the tradition of spiritual writing to which the Cistercians were accustomed? A few years later, the heads of the Order, in France, objected to the publication of the journal *The Sign of Jonas*. But this was to strain at a gnat after swallowing a camel, for *The Seven Storey Mountain* had created a new tradition of writing within the Order that made a mere journal seem very mild indeed. So far as Merton's immediate superior, Dom Frederic Dunne was concerned, we may guess that the book was permitted partly because of his affection and concern for Merton, so painfully constricted as a writer by the peculiar circumstances of his life, and partly because of his longing for "edifying" literature that would stimulate the faithful and influence the nonbeliever. He could not, of course, guess how immense the stimulus and influence was to be—and might have drawn back if he had; he was to die before publication date, although not before taking pleasure in seeing the new book.

As far as Merton himself was concerned, we can detect once again his real ambivalence about success as a writer—longing for it and fearing it. There was enough of Pop's shrewd instinct for commercial success in Merton for him to have hit on a formula that his readers could not resist, and enough of his parents' puritan "art for art's sake" fastidiousness (quite apart from the monastic requirement to become "nothing") for him to feel wretchedly miserable about it at times. "As things turned out," Merton wrote, "it [*The Seven Storey Mountain*] became quite popular. I thought it would, but I did not like to admit it, because that might possibly be pride." [2]

He knew that he was in a new situation. "The reason why I do not quite understand what it means for an obscure Trappist to become 'an author' is that the thing has almost never happened before. . . . When a man becomes 'an author' in the world outside, he adapts himself comfortably to the situation by imitating the other authors he meets at parties. An author in a Trappist monastery is like a duck in a chicken coop. And he would give anything in the world to be a chicken instead of a duck." [2]

He coped with this new situation at first by trying to treat his famous book as if it was the work of somebody else. He the famous author? No, no. He was a humble monk with no work but to pray. Yet he was too shrewd, and had too much self-knowledge, not to perceive the pride buried in this attitude. He *was*, at least with part of him, thrilled at his fame and success; it was just that he had taken up a lifestyle that made that kind of delight seem inappropriate.

But he could scarcely forget it, as the fan mail began to roll in in vast quantities. There was a tremendous irony in this, as Merton noted. A monk's letters were all read and then handed back to him if appropriate. But the monk who had the job of "screening" Merton's mail did not have the time to do it and so gave the task to Merton to do himself! He found it rather painful, both the discovery of how deeply he had moved his readers, and the knowledge of the responsibility he had thereby incurred toward them. There were also abusive and anti-Catholic letters. Robert Giroux remembers from the mail that reached him how unpleasant some of these letters were, some of them assuming that Merton was making thousands of dollars from his writing, others asking why that so-and-so Trappist did not shut up. Even practising Catholics could be very bitter about the book, perhaps recognizing a deep authenticity that made them feel threatened or exposed.

Worst of all, Merton now had the job of answering all the letters, some seven to ten of them a day. It was the usual Trappist practice to write about eight short letters a year, four of them to one's own family, and now, on top of all his other duties, Merton had this extra burden of letters. He tried to cope with it by having a card printed expressing his thanks and appreciation. This was not really a success, because his readers obviously needed individual help and attention.

An odd feature of Merton's fame was that here and there people would claim to *be* him, a fact that over the years was to give rise to many rumours that he had left the monastery. Robert Giroux remembers being rung up by the police in Chicago, who said that they had picked up a man claiming to be Thomas Merton and how could they check his identity? Giroux suggested that they ask him who his literary agent was, a device that successfully proved the man a fraud.

Not surprisingly, Merton's writing aroused interest in *him*, as well as in the Cistercian life. Evelyn Waugh, who was to edit *The Seven Storey Mountain* for publication in England, visited the Abbey. Clare Booth Luce sent records as a present, and other well-known people with Catholic interests at heart also seemed to adopt Merton to some degree. It was tempting to use their generosity to supply books or other materials that poverty denied, and Merton must have done his share of this, for he was told by a confessor to ask his Superiors before asking other people for things he needed. More happily, he also developed literary friendship by correspondence with Sister Thérèse Lentfoehr, a poet herself, whose work he had reviewed, and with others who had come to know him through his autobiography.

One of the interesting effects of publication, one well known to writers, was that the act of writing his thoughts down seemed to set him free to change his thinking. Early in 1949 he was beginning to have serious doubts about some of the things he had said in *The Seven Storey Mountain*, not about his basic beliefs, but about a peculiar bias he noted in himself. "My complaints about the world in *Seven Storey Mountain* are perhaps a weakness," he notes. "Not that there isn't plenty to complain about, but my reaction is too natural. It is impure. The world I am sore at on paper is perhaps a figment of my own imagination. The business is a psychological game I have been playing since I was ten." [2] As so often, Merton's honesty and insight about himself is devastating.

In later years, he became uncomfortable and embarrassed about the book, not wanting to disclaim all memory of it—as he did with *Exile Ends in Glory* or *What Are These Wounds?*—yet uneasy about some of its emphases, and more than a little resentful of the way it had fixed him in a certain mould in the public mind, out of which readers were then unwilling to let him grow. Writing an introduction to *A Thomas Merton Reader* in the 1960s, an anthology of his work in which extracts from *The Seven Storey Mountain* are included, he said how much happier he was with writing done much later in his life. These later writings "to me at least . . . represent a successful attempt to escape the limitations that I inevitably created for myself with *The Seven Storey Mountain*, a refusal to be content with the artificial public image which this autobiography created." [5]

The artificiality consisted in part, of the projection of his own bitterness on to the world, as described earlier, and in part, of his own romanticism about the religious life, which his readers picked up from him and adopted all too readily. Those who are not exposed to the rigours and monotonies of religious life all too easily grow romantic about it. The book unconsciously exploits this weakness, which was one of the reasons for its success. People enjoy thinking about others leading lives of heroism, and the triumphalist mood of Catholicism at the time, which resoundingly echoed both in Gethsemani and in Merton himself, suppressed doubt—doubts about whether the life was necessarily heroic for everyone (might not some people actually enjoy it? If they enjoyed it, ought they to be enjoying it?), doubts about whether some of the sacrifices—of a balanced diet, of adequate sleep, of privacy, of modest liberty, of cool clothes in summer—were necessary or useful.

In *The Seven Storey Mountain*, Merton had not begun to ask those questions. They are important at this stage only *in absentia*, in his total refusal, in his wish to "give all," to ask the questions or to think the criticisms that common sense seemed to demand. Indeed, throwing common sense overboard seemed to be part of the attraction for him, part of the action of throwing himself on God's help and mercy, of not "taking thought for the morrow."

So, for nearly the whole of his autobiography, he sees and describes Gethsemani in the most glowing colours. The most glowing colour of all is white, the colour of purity. The monks wear white, and most of the walls are whitewashed; white seems to symbolize for Merton putting away the darkness and sin of the world and embracing an utter cleanliness. The monastery is not only white but clean, as in his glimpse of it when he is led upstairs, late at night, for his first night's sleep in the place. "The place smelled frighteningly clean: old and clean, an ancient house, polished and swept and repainted and repainted over and over, year after year." [6]

The people too are better, cleaner, holier than anyone else. "Outside in the world were holy men who were holy in the sense that they went about with portraits of all the possible situations in which they could show their love of God displayed about them: and they were always conscious of these possibilities. But these other hidden men had come so close to God in their hiddenness that they no longer saw anyone but Him. . . . They were in Him. They had dwindled down to nothing and had been transformed into Him by the pure and absolute humility of their hearts. And the love of Christ overflowing in those clean hearts made them children and made them eternal. Old men with limbs like the roots of trees had the eyes of children." [6] The time would come when Merton would ask hard questions about the "childlikeness" of some religious, but for the time being everyone in the monastery was better than everyone outside.

Merton, in his guilt about the past, longed to identify with all this purity and innocence, to be as white, as pure, as clean, as childlike as any, and so fit to approach the love from which he felt excluded. Much in *The Seven Storey Mountain* illustrates Merton's self-contempt at this period—the rueful, and sometimes very painful, descriptions of mistakes and faults, reproofs and penances, and more painful than any of these his own merciless self-observation of his own weakness and self-dramatization. "Il faut goûter les humiliations ["You must savour humiliations"]!" a confessor had often advised Merton. He did "savour" them in *The Seven Storey Mountain*, dutifully recounting many of the miseries and supposed miseries of Trappist life, from the straw-covered boards he slept on to the intolerable hours in choir. It was a few years yet before he began to wonder about the covert satisfactions and, in some matters, the sheer absurdity of the suffering.

One of the things, apart from his need to project the "good" and deny the "bad" side of himself, which made it hard for him to be ordinarily critical of the life he described, was the extraordinary wave, washing all around him, of enthusiasm for the contemplative life, on the crest of which his book had sailed to commercial success.

"America," he wrote, "is discovering the contemplative life" [6], and it certainly looked that way, with the tremendous boom in vocations that had filled Gethsemani to bursting point in a very few years, and caused religious houses to spring up like mushrooms. A few years later, in the 1960s, America's interest in contemplation had moved away from the Church to an interest in meditation, Eastern gurus, psychedelic drugs, yoga, and making love, not war. Perhaps what Merton and others were witnessing in the Trappist houses were the first stirrings of that longing for a less active and less commercial life. At the time, however, it looked as if the revolution would take the form of a return to a quasi-medieval

Christianity, with many retiring to monasteries as their criticism of "the world."

Merton ended *The Seven Storey Mountain* with his romanticism, idealism, and vision of the future still largely intact. There was, however, a hint and more than a hint, that his attempt to escape "at a stroke" from the conflict he had known in "the world," to lose his "shadow" in his passionate identification with the pure and the clean and the lovely, to win acceptance by total abandonment and submission, had not worked for him as he had hoped. Despite much happiness and security in the life, he was still troubled. "There was this shadow, this double, this writer who had followed me into the cloister. . . . He rides my shoulders, sometimes, like the old man of the sea. I cannot lose him. He still wears the name of Thomas Merton. Is it the name of an enemy? . . . Maybe in the end he will kill me, he will drink my blood. Nobody seems to understand that one of us has got to die. Sometimes I am mortally afraid." [6]

Troubled and confused as he was, Merton held fast to his overriding purpose in coming to the monastery, the attempt to reach and love God, believing that in the comparative solitude of silence, liturgy, and withdrawal from family life and the life of his friends, he would be freer to do so. He began to catch a terrifying glimpse of what real solitude would entail, a glimpse that made the loneliness he had known most of his life, and the loneliness of life within the walls of Gethsemani, appear as nothing. In a last meditation, in which he imagined God speaking to him of his vocation, he said,

> When you have been praised a little and loved a little I will take away all your gifts and all your love and all your praise and you will be utterly forgotten and abandoned and you will be nothing, a dead thing, a rejection. And in that day you shall begin to possess the solitude you have so long desired. And your solitude will bear immense fruit in the souls of men you will never see on earth.
>
> Do not ask when it will be or where it will be or how it will be: On a mountain or in a prison, in a desert or in a concentration camp or in a hospital or at Gethsemani. It does not matter. So do not ask me, because I am not going to tell you. You will not know until you are in it.
>
> But you shall taste the true solitude of My anguish and My poverty and I shall lead you into the high places of my joy and you shall die in Me and find all things in My mercy which has created you for this end

and brought you from Prades to Bermuda to St. Antonin to Oakham to London to Cambridge to Rome to New York to Columbia to Corpus Christi to St. Bonaventure to the Cistercian Abbey of the poor men who labour in Gethsemani: "That you may become the brother of God and learn to know the Christ of the burnt men." [6]

Reading this brave attempt to utter the very essence of his vocation, we may feel that Merton was describing two things at once, the past and the future; his earliest experiences of the world, with his traumatic loss of love and his abandonment in the nightmare of St. Antonin, and his vision of what the coming years would bring him. He was recognizing the inner pattern of his life. Believing it to be God's will he gave himself to the pattern joyfully and with grace.

References

1. Thomas Merton. Letter to Mark Van Doren. September 19, 1946. TMSC.
2. Thomas Merton. *The Sign of Jonas.* New York: Harcourt Brace, 1948; London: Sheldon Press 1976.
3. Thomas Merton. *Figures for an Apocalypse.* New York: New Directions, 1968.
4. Anonymous (Thomas Merton). *Gethsemani Magnificat.* Louisville: Abbey of Our Lady of Gethsemani (Trappist), 1949.
5. Thomas Merton. *A Thomas Merton Reader,* ed. Thomas P. McDonnell. New York: Doubleday, 1962.
6. Thomas Merton. *The Seven Storey Mountain.* New York: Harcourt Brace 1948; London: SPCK, 1990. Also published abridged as *Elected Silence* (London: Burns & Oates, 1949).

11

HIS SOLITUDE IS HIS BEING

❦

The success of *The Seven Storey Mountain* did not mean that Merton had more liberty to exercise his talents as a writer. He was permitted only two hours a day in which to write, and this included dealing with proofs, contracts, photographs, and correspondence and even reading manuscripts that he was asked or ordered to look at. He was also still required to work at things like *Gethsemani Magnificat*, a brochure of the monastic life planned for the Abbey's forthcoming centenary. [1]

In August 1948, shortly before the publication of *The Seven Storey Mountain*, Dom Frederic Dunne died, and Dom James Fox became Abbot. Abbots were elected by the professed monks in an elaborate ceremony of voting on paper. A candidate had to be at least thirty-five years old, solemnly professed, and of at least ten years in profession counting from the first vows made.

"The Abbot," say the *Regulations of the Order of Cistercians of the Strict Observance*, "shall never lose sight of the fact that he holds the place of Christ in the monastery, and that he ought to do what Christ would do, if He were there visibly and in person." Also, "he shall look on it as his most essential obligation to watch that the Rule be observed with all possible perfection. St. Bernard expresses almost the same thoughts, when he says that in receiving the profession of his religious, the Abbot binds himself, first of all to procure for them all the helps which they need to enable them to observe the vows which their lips have pronounced; and secondly, to use, in order to lead them to this end, all the means, whether of gentleness or of severity, by which he can maintain them in the fulfilment of their duty." [2]

Once the election of a new Abbot had been announced, and he had been installed, the religious came before him one by one, placed their hands in his and said, "Reverende Pater, ego promitto tibi obedientiam secundum Regulam sancti Benedicti usque ad mortem."* It is difficult to imagine a more absolute form of power.

Dom James Fox was a Bostonian of Irish descent who been educated at Harvard and had been a naval officer. He saw the faith in almost devastatingly simple terms. He had a favourite motto—"All for Jesus, through Mary, with a smile." He had this made into a rubber stamp and printed on all his correspondence, translated into French for the benefit of the French Trappists: "Tout pour Jesus, par Marie, toujours avec un sourire."

The introduction to *Gethsemani Magnificat*, the centenary brochure, catches some of Dom James's enthusiastic spirit, a spirit that had no use for, and indeed no understanding of, shades of feeling, but was only at home with totalities of dedication and sacrifice and heroism. Writing of the remarkable boom in Trappist vocations, he describes how the very severity of the life appeals to "red-blooded American boys."

> Gethsemani alone has seventy novices. Many of these boys have distinguished themselves in the Air Force, Paratroopers, Navy and Marines of World War II. During 1941–45 they were ready to give their all for their God and Country in the natural order; now at Gethsemani they are giving all for God and Country in the supernatural order, because it will be powerhouses of prayer and penance such as Gethsemani which will be the prime bulwarks of defense of our beloved Homeland and American way of life against the rising tides of atheism and terrorism. . . .
>
> At Gethsemani, boys give—not fifty per cent, seventy per cent, ninety per cent, nor even ninety-five per cent—but one hundred per cent for God and Country. The spirit of Gethsemani may be summed up in its favorite expression—"All for Jesus—through Mary—with a smile." [1]

Many years later, Dom James contributed an essay about Merton to a book about him written by his friends and colleagues. He wrote it from the point of view of an aging man writing about his spiritual son, but, oddly, he dwelt on the penances and hurts of Merton in the Trappist life. He describes "the renowned author" of *The Seven Storey Mountain* "begging his dinner" or kissing the feet of some 270 monks; "I could not help remarking inwardly:

* "Reverend Father, I promise you obedience according to the rule of St. Benedict, even unto death."

'How powerful is the Grace of Jesus.'" [3] He notes the occasion on which a Visitor (a higher superior from Europe) decided that monks at Gethsemani should no longer be free to walk in the local woods but should remain within the enclosure. Since Merton acted as French interpreter, he was present at this conversation. "I looked at Fr. Louis," says Fox. "His face flushed red and big tears filled his eyes. He quivered a bit, but never said a word. He remained silent, seemingly crushed. To think that that one 'exercise' which he loved so much . . . was to be denied him!" [3]

Admittedly, Dom James chose to release Merton from this particular misery by making him a kind of fire ranger with access to the woods to guard against fire, but his fascination at Merton writhing under the almost intolerable restrictions of his life is somehow disturbing. Not surprisingly, there were to be many conflicts between them in Fox's long years as Abbot.

Merton's major concern in 1948, however, was preparing himself for ordination. He had undergone the minor stages of ordination— exorcist and acolyte—and had been ordained subdeacon. As sub-deacon, he felt he was "pretty small potatoes," keeping in the background at the altar and "running errands for the deacon," caring for the vessels and the linen, reading the epistle, singing certain parts of the Mass. In the long Latin Masses of the monastery, the task was complicated; he wrote down on little yellow cards the rules for the things subdeacons do in different kinds of masses and tried to put all else out of his mind.

His first experience of acting as subdeacon was at Midnight Mass at Christmas, and he was delighted by it. He made one or two minor mistakes, but "I felt as if I had been wearing a maniple and tunic all my life, and it seemed to me as if I had grown up in the sanctuary and never done anything else but minister at the altar . . . as if I belonged there and always had belonged there. . . . As I stood there with the paten in front of my face, the only unfamiliar thing was that my thumb got tired." [4]

Gradually, over a period of months, he learned more and more of the ceremonies connected with the priesthood and with monastic life, watching his brothers more closely now that he was so soon to follow in their footsteps, enjoying learning this very special new skill and bringing to it a total love and devotion.

On St. Joseph's Day in March 1949, he and another future priest were ordained deacons "in albs so starched that they rustled like canvas and stuck out all round us like hoop skirts." [4] He found the experience "dazzling" and kneeling after it in prayer felt that he ought to give up being a poet. He shared this idea with Abbot Fox, who agreed that he might, so he tore up notes he had written for new poems. When he first took part in Mass after this, he was deeply awed at the thought of picking up the Host. "I was afraid the whole Church might come down on my head, because of what I used to be." [4] But he was enormously happy, so happy that he almost laughed out loud. With his usual deep devotion to Mary, he felt now that she had taken possession of his heart. "Lady, I am your deacon, your own special and personal deacon." [4]

He began to learn how to say Mass—the gestures to make with his hands, the genuflections, the kissing of the altar—first with a priest to tell him what to do, then practising alone. He found it difficult. "It is all right up to the 'consecration' and would be all right after it too, if you did not have to be so careful about your fingers. Your thumb and forefinger of each hand, are only for picking up and breaking the Host. You use the other fingers on everything else. But I find myself uncovering the chalice, taking off the paten with those forefingers and thumbs, and touching the Host and purifying the paten with all the other fingers. In fact, the moment you have 'consecrated,' everything gets in the way. Then the dry host is hard to swallow, too." [4]

Ordination was scheduled for Ascension Day, May 26, and two weeks before it he was so excited he felt he could not live that long. He kept saying to himself, "I shall say Mass—I shall say Mass." [4]

The day arrived, and the weather was cloudlessly sunny. Many of Merton's friends—Lax, Rice, Freedgood, Walsh, Giroux, and Laughlin—came down. There were three days of celebration—ordination, anointing, ordination Mass, then a low Mass, and finally a Solemn Mass. In the intervals of the profoundly moving ceremonies, there was time to sit out under the trees and talk to friends he had not talked to for years. It was a moving reunion in itself, made richer by the fact that in his ordination he had completed a journey, or the first stage of a journey, and was supremely happy about it. "My priestly ordination was, I felt, the one great secret for which I had been born." [4] He remembered how, all those years before, in Perry Street, he had felt that becoming a priest was a matter of life and death, and of how he had longed to be thought acceptable to become one. And now, miraculously, the thing had happened.

Life, however, had not become a bed of roses. As Merton laconically said in the introduction to *A Thomas Merton Reader*, "After ordination, there was . . . a brief period of poor health and nervous exhaustion. I was almost incapable of writing for at least a year and a half after I became a priest." [5]

His journal, *The Sign of Jonas*, charting his progress almost day by day, revealed much more the extent and feel of the crisis.

> When the summer of my ordination ended, I found myself face to face with a mystery that was beginning to manifest itself in the depths of my soul and to move me with terror. Do not ask me what it was. I might apologize for it and call it "suffering." The word is not adequate because it suggests physical pain. That is not at all what I mean. It is true that something had begun to affect my health—but whatever happened to my health was only, it seems to me, an effect of this unthinkable thing that had developed in the depths of my being. And again: I have no way of explaining what it was. It was a sort of slow, submarine earthquake which produced strange commotions on the visible, psychological surfaces of my life. I was summoned to battle with joy and fear, knowing in every case that the sense of battle was misleading, that my apparent antagonist was only an illusion, and that the whole commotion was simply the effect of something that had already erupted, without my knowing it, in the hidden volcano. [4]

Before we try to think about what the "unthinkable" may have been, we must go back a little to note the signs and portents that preceded the earthquake and the volcano. Back in 1947, there had been the misery of insomnia, already mentioned, a particularly painful problem in a setting where the hours of sleep were short and strictly prescribed. He did not mention it again in *The Sign of Jonas* but later references in his journals suggest this was to be a lifelong problem. In 1949, he fainted at Mass. It was a hot day and that may have been the reason, or it may have been a warning sign of a growing psychological disturbance, for within a couple of months the church, particularly the Mass, had become the focus of an agonizing set of irrational anxieties. "This morning, consecrating the Precious Blood, I became so overwhelmed that I had doubts . . . whether I had actually said all the words properly and whether the consecration were valid." [4]

The memory of his faint undermined his confidence in a terrifying way. "As soon as I stand in front of the open book at the Gospel-stand to sing the Gospel, the memory of the time I passed out in the middle of the Gospel last July comes over me and I can't breathe and my legs turn into jelly, and it is all I can do to look at the book and keep an ordered series of noises coming out of me. This morning I thought I was going to collapse for sure. A big wave of darkness came up from inside me somewhere, but I shook my head and it went away for a bit. Hope I can finish out the week." [4]

Then, two days later: "The other night I woke up at midnight and began to worry over whether I would be able to get through the Gospel at High Mass. By Chapter the next morning I was so worn out thinking about it and making all kinds of resolutions that I had to ask Father to let me off being deacon for the rest of the week. . . . Dom Gildas, who is celebrant, upbraided me in sign language. But it was a great relief." [4]

Giving in to his neurosis afforded temporary relief but made him feel weak and ashamed. "Working in the woods in the afternoon, I felt lonely and small and humiliated—chopping down dead trees with a feeling that perhaps I was not even a real person anymore." [4]

The superficial reasons for Merton's collapse of nerve are not far to seek. He had been a priest for just over a year, and it still took a great deal of concentration to get him through the rituals and ceremonies accurately and gracefully. In addition, he was physically very tired, something he referred to again and again. "I feel knocked out" (April 1947), "washed out" (November 1947), "I have never been so busy in my life" (August 1948), "In the last two months I do not seem to have done anything but write business letters and run around in circles" (September 1948), "I have fallen into the great indignity I have written against—I am a contemplative who is ready to collapse from overwork." [4]

There were no holidays at Gethsemani, no chance to escape the conflicts for a bit by going to a different place, or having a night out with friends, or even a long chatter with his brethren; always the same formidable routine of liturgy, silence, and manual work. The idea of any sort of leisure, or a chance to do nothing, seemed to be deeply inimical to the spirit of the monastery. Merton ruefully reported a conversation with Dom Frederic that began with his own comment about the holiness of a brother who had just died. The Reverend Father saw fit to improve the occasion. "Brother was always working," he said. "Brother did not even know how to be idle. If you sent him out to take care of the cows in the pasture, he still found plenty to do. He brought in buckets of blackberries. He did not know how to be idle." Merton felt himself rebuked for his own longings for idleness. "I came out of Reverend Father's room feeling like a man who has missed his train." [4]

A difficulty was that Merton, unlike Brother Gregory, needed mental space to allow his creativity to work within him, as yeast needs space to ferment in the dough. "It is not much fun," he remarked, "to live the spiritual life with the spiritual equipment of an artist." [4]

There seemed to be a sort of double bind at work. The monastery, which existed to promote contemplation, kept you so busy and overtired that there did not seem to be very much left over, even for God, even, sometimes to say prayers. "On the Feast when we are supposed to contemplate the mystery of the Blessed Sacrament," Merton wrote, perhaps a little querulously, at Corpus Christi, "there is absolutely no time for any such thing as contemplation. You are lucky if you can get a minute to kneel down before the tabernacle and say a Hail Mary." [4] Merton felt guilty about his extreme busyness, feeling that he had somehow stolen the time from God. He knew that some of his furious writing and reading was an escape from something within, or at the very least, a helpless response to tension, and perhaps he remembered the boy of his Columbia days, fainting on the Long Island Railroad when the multiplication of activities became too much for him. It was ironic and wounding to repeat that collapse in a contemplative monastery.

His writing was not going well. Apart from the journal he was keeping under obedience, chores such as the Gethsemani centenary brochure (that "scourge of God" as he called it); earlier books that he was proofreading and correcting; correspondence with his publishers, agent, and public; manuscripts he was reading to oblige others—all to be accomplished in two hours a day—he was trying to write a very ambitious new book, his first purely theological work, in which he hoped to achieve "a great synthesis on the interior life drawn from Scripture and the Fathers of the Church."

Perhaps the sheer ambition of the project paralyzed him, or perhaps it was his growing exhaustion and his preparation for the priesthood. He suffered the most terrifying complaint that can plague a writer or artist—a "block" that made any progress impossible. He would painfully write fifty pages and then tear them up, or riffle through his innumerable pages of notes in an ever-growing despair of finding a path through the jungle. He wrote and rewrote, and then found that the result would not do at all. "I only lose the freshness of the original and am just as prolix over again, but in a different and duller way." [4] He told himself that he must pull himself together and crack the problem of the book, but time-wasting chores still made inroads into his working hours. "There is a monk at Aiguebelle who wants a map of North America with all our monasteries and all those of the Common Observance marked on it." [4]

Of course, even in the worst times there were good moments, periods of joy and exaltation, and delight, and simple happiness. Sometimes these seemed to emerge from the very centre of his exhaustion and frustration—in the middle of sickness or torturing boredom, he felt lifted on to another plane of feeling, something that manual work in particular often achieved for him. Sometimes, with the contemplative's acute awareness of the seasons and the different moods of the day, and of the natural world, he was moved by the great natural beauty of Gethsemani and its surroundings. "It was utterly beautiful out there in the snow this afternoon," he said. "Everything was blue. Plenty of snow in the branches of the cedars but it was melting fast in the sun. Before Vespers the shoulders of the hills were brown." [4] And "Before dawn. Red Mars hangs like a tiny artificial fruit from the topmost branch of a bare tree." [4] Sometimes it was the quietness and the imagery of the Trappist life itself that brought him happiness: "It was a comfort to me to look at the crucifix and presently . . . a shaft of sunlight broke through a window and fell like gold on the head and arms of Christ on the crucifix and it was quiet and beautiful in the sanctuary with no one moving and light falling on the crucifix." [4] Or, looking at Fra Angelico's "Annunciation," "Mother, make me as sincere as the picture. All the way down into my soul, sincere, sincere. . . . She is here, and she has filled the room with something that is uniquely her own." Sometimes, although rarely, religious exaltation seemed to take him over. "Love sails me around the house. I walk two steps on the ground and four steps in the air. It is love. It is consolation. . . . I love God. Love carries me all around. I don't want to do anything but love. And when the bell rings it is like pulling teeth to make myself shift because of that love, secret love, hidden love, obscure love, down inside me and outside me. . . . But, O love, why can't you leave me alone?—which is a rhetorical question meaning: for heaven's sake don't. . . . I am all dried up with desire and I can only think of one thing—staying in the fire that burns me." [4]

Yet the depression and the disquieting neurotic symptoms remained, causing him acute distress, the "Feeling of fear, dejection, non-existence," as he put it. Sometimes the feelings of religious exaltation alternated terrifyingly with dryness, or fear, or self-hatred. He describes a period of utter dryness reaching a crest, like a wave, and going over into "the awful battle with joy." "My soul was cringing and doubling up and subconsciously getting ready for the next tidal wave. At the moment all I had left in my heart was an abyss of self-hatred—waiting for the next appalling sea." [4]

Some of the depression seemed to come from the monotony of the life, the lack of the stimulus or affirmation that comes from contact with ideas and with people. Unable to speak, except to their Superiors, the monks could do little to comfort and reassure one another. Merton spoke feelingly of the lack of encouragement in their lives, a lack that made it easy to slide into the "acedia"* that is the traditional problem of monks. He found that his mind filled with schemes and ideas and enterprises, and that much of his intense activity was a kind of defence against the "nothingness" of the life; his mind played with the idea of going away from Gethsemani, usually into other, more congenial orders, such as the Carthusians. Using the imagery of Jonah trapped miserably in the whale, he said that "stability," the vow to remain where he was, was for himself "the belly of the whale."

Much of his attraction to other communities stemmed from his longing for privacy. The Trappists ate, slept, prayed, and worked together, and for Merton the perpetual togetherness became at times a kind of torture. He was perpetually hunting for places in the enclosure where he could sit and pray or reflect by himself, but this was made more and more difficult by the overcrowding in the monastery as its popularity grew. "Today Reverend Father gave official and general permission for the first time for the professed to go out into the orchard and around the wagon shed and out behind the old horsebarn in their intervals—or rather between None and

---

* Acedia or "accidie" is generally regarded as a form of depression and restlessness affecting particularly monks and hermits, who are said to be liable to it owing to the outward monotony of their lives.

Vespers on Sunday. Our garden and the cemetery are intolerably
crowded and it is hard to get extricated from the other monks." [4]

On the rare occasions when he could spend a long period by
himself, and especially if this involved physical rest, his old high
spirits returned. It was as if solitude were a form of essential
nutrition for him. He usually only got the chance to enjoy it
when illness took him into the infirmary. "As soon as I get into a
cell by myself I am a different person! Prayer becomes what it ought
to be. . . . All afternoon I sat on the bed rediscovering the meaning
of contemplation—rediscovering God, rediscovering myself—and
the office, and Scriptures and everything. It has been one of the most
wonderful days I have ever known in my life. . . . I know that is the
way I ought to be *living*: with my mind and senses silent, contact
with the world of business and war and community troubles
severed—not solicitous for anything high or low or far or near." [4]

At one point Merton tried to share his deep unhappiness about
the lack of solitude with Dom James, and confided his strong
attraction to the Carthusians. Dom James replied that he didn't
see "why things can't be fixed up right here." Before he would allow
him to be ordained subdeacon, he also made Merton formally
declare that he was not going to leave and join the Carthusians.

The place where his unhappiness about "togetherness" was most
acute was in choir. He spoke again and again, though usually fairly
obscurely, of his distress during the long hours in the church made
up of offices, much augmented at that time by additional devotions.
It is not precisely clear just *what* he minded so much; boredom, lack
of physical movement, the repetition of words that seemed often
meaningless, tiredness, cold in winter, and in summer the sort of
heat that made the sweat run down a man's ribs, and turned the
church into a "boiling tunnel." "As soon as I get to choir I am
overwhelmed by distractions. No sense of the presence of God. No
sense of anything except difffculty and struggle and pain. . . .
Dom Gildas thinks I ought to be detached from the pleasures of
other ways of prayer. I am content to sacrifice those pleasures and go
to choir, but I cannot honestly maintain that it is much fun." [4]

The Vicar General, over on a visit from France, was reasonably
sympathetic. "He advised me not to worry about suffering in
choir—told me how the cantors suffer at Solesmes! He said I
should think of Jesus going up to Jerusalem with all the pilgrims
roaring psalms out of their dusty throats." [4]

Perhaps some of Merton's suffering at Gethsemani at this period came simply from a heightened sensibility to art, music, and all forms of aesthetic enjoyment. He occasionally mentioned with pain the badness of sculpture, holy pictures, hymns, and books read in refectory that are admired by most of the rest of his brethren; and being dressed in hideous lace "finery" to celebrate mass on the Feast of St. Louis filled him with humiliation. "He was a sophisticated man," a friend of Merton's remarked to me, "with a deep knowledge of European culture. He knew about food, wine, literature, painting. The people at Gethsemani knew nothing of any of these— compared to him they were peasants—and they were incapable of understanding him."

Merton, it must be said, made no complaint of that kind. The complaints he did make, as just quoted, did not occupy a large part of his journals. Rather, his attitude was one of enthusiastic response to his brothers, to the small events of the monastery, to the authors he read, and to the wonder of the natural landscape around him. He had no reservations about living the life to the full, even when it became too hard for him. Even in the darkest moments his humour never deserted him, and he could enjoy, for example, the Chapter of Faults in which someone "proclaimed" the "duck brothers" because the Gethsemani ducks quacked in the night and kept people awake. He could also enjoy the prospect of 200 monks suddenly issued with shaving equipment (hitherto they had been communally shaved by a monk barber once a week) because a visiting French Superior was so appalled at their week-old beards.

So he struggled on with his boredom in choir, his longing for privacy and solitude, his writing block, his letters, his multitudinous writing chores, his manual work, his insomnia, his depression, his neurotic symptoms, and his occasional glimpses of religious joy. Perhaps it might all have stayed like that, but for the fact that, like the last straw on the camel's back, he was given yet another job, and, for him, a very exacting one.

In November 1949, he began an introductory conference in theology for the Scholastics (students for the priesthood) that took an hour and a half a week, and he also began to give an "orientation" course for the novices. Like the born teacher he was, he took trouble over organizing the material. With the exception of Gilson, he could find no textbook he wanted to follow, and preferred to map out his own approach, which meant intensive preparation. From here on, the burden became more and more intolerable and the neurotic symptoms much worse. "Teaching wears me out," he said, but in fact it was teaching, carefully and lovingly performed, on top of so much else, that was wearing him down.

Perhaps because his depression was too strong for him, or because he had so little opportunity of sharing his dilemma with others, he tended to see his exhaustion as almost entirely his own fault, "a sin and the punishment of sin," the inevitable outcome of his incurable activism.

But the trouble was partly his own volatile response to situations and ideas, and partly the monastery's tendency to flog a willing horse. Beneath his interminable struggles, Merton must have felt intolerably trapped between his own temperament and the endless demands of life at Gethsemani. A usual accompaniment of such feelings is anger. But Merton was in a situation where anger—least of all against his superiors whom he was suposed to love and reverence as Christ himself—was not an acceptable emotion to feel. The only way left open to express how intolerable a life without rest had become was to collapse, both publicly in church and privately in illness.

However, he had found an unexpected ally in the shape of a Dominican writer named Sertillanges. Sertillanges had written a book called *La Vie Intellectuelle* and Merton felt at once that it might cheer him up. "It has on me the effect that Dale Carnegie's advice might have on a despondent salesman." [4] What fascinated Merton was that Sertillanges—a spiritual writer—advocated care for one's health and body in a way that was unthinkable at Gethsemani. He advocated moderate manual work and a careful diet, and said such things as "Find out what you need in the way of food and sleep and make this the object of a firm resolution." [4] Sertillanges also recommended care and consideration for those who have been working hard. "The man who comes away from his work is like one who has been wounded. He needs to be cared for in a calm atmosphere: do not treat him with violence! Help him to relax. Give him some encouragement! Show some interest in the things he does."

All this seemed such a long way away from Merton's loneliness and exhaustion and perpetual harrassment that he felt all he could do was laugh about it. Neither De Rancé nor St. John of the Cross would have seen the spiritual life like that. Merton wrestled with the sheer common sense of Sertillanges, on the one hand, and his loyalty to his brothers, on the other. "It is all *true*. The monks in the Common Observance know that. But it is not our vocation, I suppose. You'd go crazy trying to practice that here." [4]

Meanwhile the food was poor, his sleep scanty, his work was going badly, and there seemed no encouragement in sight. He described the "acedia" that assailed him as a "dead rot . . . that eats out your substance with discouragement and fear." [4]

Finally, in February 1950 he came down with flu, which made him feel as if his head were full of glue. For some weeks, it came and went, until by the end of March he became rather worse. He was not alone. That winter one flu epidemic after another had hit the monastery.

"The infirmary is full. In the dormitory, there is a lot of noise, to which I contribute by my unsuccessful efforts to breathe. The terrible thing about sickness is that you tend to think you are sick. Your thoughts are narrowed down to your own little rag of a body." [4] He still struggled up to get to all the offices he could— there was a general request from the Abbot that people will attend if their temperature is not over 101°F. He took penicillin, spent what time he could in bed, but never entirely threw off infection. In September, he went to St. Joseph's Infirmary in Louisville with acute sinusitis. In October, he was sent back to Gethsemani with orders to rest, but in November he was back again for an operation on his nose. With his usual intense response to new people and situations, he enjoyed it all, even the operation. "The most interesting thing about it all is that you are surrounded by people, mostly women, in white gauze masks and caps. This is delightful." [4] There were other Trappists in the hospital (nuns who nursed in the hospital at this period remember that there were always a number of the Gethsemani Trappists as inmates, requiring rest and nutrition).

It was not only Merton's nose that needed care. Both his stomach and chest x-rays showed abnormalities, which the hospital decided to treat in the first place by rest. It was the first real rest he had enjoyed in nearly ten years. He said Mass for the sisters at the infirmary and did a little writing on a new book called *Bread in the Wilderness* [5], but mainly he slept and read.

When he got back to the monastery at the beginning of December, it was to hear a retreat preacher rebuking the monks for idleness. "If you are worn out you are just getting off to a good start." After all the doctors and nurses telling him to rest, Merton rather enjoyed that.

Physically he felt restored, and he set to work on the theology book that had caused him such distress. In his new vigorous state, he finished it in two months. It was later published as *The Ascent to Truth*. [6]

While ill, Merton discovered *Walden*, and quotes a significant passage from Thoreau. "I went to the woods because I wished to live deliberately, to front only the essential facts of life, and see if I could not learn what it had to teach and not, when I came to die, discover that I had not lived." It was perhaps for a similar reason that Merton had joined the Trappists.

His illness had left other legacies, among them the extraordinary pleasures of some sights in Louisville, particularly a junk wagon that figured magically in his dreams "like something very precious once seen in the Orient." "The bells of the mule were ringing. The brass discs glittered in the sun. The green boards held themselves together by miracle in their marvellous disorder." Yet with all the beauty and interest of the world he still retreated from it. "I see the whole world like smoke and I am not part of it. There is nothing on this earth that does not give me a pain." [4]

Now that health had returned, and all the psychological problems that beset him the previous year no longer troubled him, he was aware that a very profound change had taken place in him during that last difficult winter. In the midst of his exhaustion, irrational fears, *acedia* and physical wretchedness, he began, very gradually, to be aware that his basic problem was all about solitude. In the acute loneliness of life without close relationships and with very few diversions there was no escape from the encounter with the terrible emptiness within, and Merton, so busy, so sociable, so given to diversions in his youth, had started to learn that the way out of loneliness is solitude; that is, a completely different perspective on being alone. "Solitude is not found so much by looking outside the boundaries of your dwelling, as by staying within. Solitude is not something you must hope for in the future. Rather, it is a deepening of the present, and unless you look for it in the present you will never find it." [4] In solitude, Merton said, he could find love and reverence for others. Above all, in solitude he could find God, who can only be found in solitude, because "His solitude is His being." [4]

This recognition of solitude was perhaps the most important discovery Merton was to make at Gethsemani—a kind of pivot on which the rest of his life turned. "The peace I had found," he wrote later, "the solitude of the winter of 1950, deepened and developed in me beyond measure." [4] It was as if he had passed a place from which there was no going back, but which had made him free of a whole new country.

References

1. Anonymous (Thomas Merton). *Gethsemani Magnificat*. Louisville: Abbey of Our Lady of Gethsemani (Trappist), 1949.
2. *Regulations of the Order of the Cistercians of the Strict Observance*. Dublin: General Chapter of the Order of Cistercians of the Strict Observance, 1926.
3. Brother Patrick Hart (Ed.). *Thomas Merton, Monk*. London: Hodder & Stoughton, 1974.
4. Thomas Merton. *The Sign of Jonas*. New York: Harcourt Brace, 1953; London: Sheldon Press, 1976.
5. Thomas Merton. *A Thomas Merton Reader*, ed. Thomas P. McDonnell. New York: Doubleday, 1962.
6. Thomas Merton. *Bread in the Wilderness*. New York: New Directions, 1953; Tunbridge Wells, Kent: Burns & Oates, 1976.
7. Thomas Merton. *The Ascent to Truth*. New York: Harcourt Brace, 1951; Tunbridge Wells, Kent: Burns & Oates, 1976. Originally called "The Cloud and the Fire."

12

THE WORLD AND
THE CLOISTER

❧

Early in 1950 Merton sent Naomi Burton part of his journal, *The Sign of Jonas*, and she was heart-warmingly enthusiastic. "You know, it is exciting to read something that knocks sparks out of the tired old brain. Makes it all seem very worth while. I am, irrationally, so proud of you and so grateful for you." [1]

Naomi Burton and Merton had an important, and perhaps unusual, relationship for author and literary agent. She could be uncompromisingly tough with him, as any good agent must be with an author from time to time, but she showed a brisk, no-nonsense kind of love for him that was deeply feminine and that over the years grew into a strong and mutual friendship. She had known him in the old Perry Street days, when he longed to be a successful author and she found him a "sad kid." She frankly thought it a pity when he joined the Trappists; in fact, she described herself as "infuriated." "I imagined that this author of so much promise was now lost forever behind a high stone wall of silence. It seemed particularly sad because he had so passionately wanted to be published and had never appeared to doubt for one minute that he was destined to be a successful author." [2]

Their acquaintance lapsed—it was assumed Merton would not need an agent where he was going, and he rarely wrote letters in any case—but then in April 1947 they started writing to each other again, about "Journal of My Escape from the Nazis" (published later as *My Argument with the Gestapo*). Naomi Burton had always had her doubts about this book, and time had not changed her opinion. "Do you really think it is a good idea to publish *Journal of My Escape from the Nazis?* It is a long time since I read it and if you like, I will look at it again but I remember it as very typical of the boy you used to be and I wonder if publishing it would do you any good, either as a person or from a different point of view." [3]

Naomi Burton, of course, handled *The Seven Storey Mountain* and in the year of its publication paid her first visit to Gethsemani. She later remembered with some embarrassment that, assuming Gethsemani was quite near to Louisville, she had taken a Yellow Cab in the city, a sight that had caused some surprise when she got out into the countryside, and absolute amazement at Gethsemani itself, where she received some good-natured teasing about the manner of her arrival. Merton did not mention this visit in his journal, and only laconically referred to later visits, in marked contrast to the way he wrote about Jay Laughlin's visits, recounting just what the two of them did and the enjoyable conversations about books that took place. Did Merton think he should not enjoy the company of women, in much the same way as at this time he thought he should not look at pictures or advertisements suggesting secular life? He claimed they "made him ill." Did the company of women also upset him?

Naomi Burton made it clear that she enjoyed seeing him, however that up till then she had felt he was in a "glass case." She was not above giving him a rebuke for his sentimentality and "jauntiness.'

By the spring of 1950, the sales of *The Seven Storey Mountain* and *The Waters of Siloe* had suddenly begun to drop rather alarmingly in America (*Elected Silence*, the abridged version of *The Seven Storey Mountain*, was still selling splendidly in England), probably because of the publication of *What Are These Wounds?*, which, with its heavy piety of Merton's earliest days as a monk, was distancing readers. Merton both hoped and feared that the end of his career as an author had come, but Naomi Burton would have none of it: "Shouldn't worry about being finished as a writer if I were you, because you couldn't be." [4]

At this stage she did not share his Catholic convictions (she was to become a Catholic a few years later), but was asked at times to enter into moral and other dilemmas that few literary agents are asked to face. "I do have to smile a bit," she wrote a few years later, "when people assume that being the agent for one Trappist must be child's play." [5]) An example of the peculiar difficulties of her job came when Harcourt Brace, with whom Merton had recently signed a contract for four books, suggested making him their "sole property," thus cutting out New Directions. Merton and Dom James were not happy about this because of their loyalty to Jay (James) Laughlin, the founder of New Directions and Merton's first publisher, but Merton had scruples about working for New Directions, scruples that show him in an almost unbearably priggish light. Laughlin at the time was publishing such authors as Henry Miller, D. H. Lawrence, and others whom bourgeois susceptibilities found distressing. Merton wrote to Naomi Burton, "It [the decision] involves a moral question which would confront me if I were found to be actively cooperating in the production of books by other people, Jay's protégés, who write what might be considered as morally undesirable material. I know that it is all "art" but it might accidentally have a bad effect, some of it. I would not be concerned in the least with the character of this material, except for the very important fact that Jay uses the profits of my stuff to publish these other books. This is a question that has to be decided by me. It is a matter of conscience. If in actual fact I am actively cooperating in the publication of morally undesirable books and if there is no just cause to excuse this cooperation, then I have to pull out—or Jay has to drop half his authors."

The postscript takes an even more priggish tone. "I was a little sore that Jay had to advertise *Seeds* as another *Imitation of Christ*. But at least he can't afford to plaster me all over the papers. I realize that it is business. But it seems to me that I am going to get some of those ads and that publicity fried out of me in purgatory, unless I do something about it now. May God help me, and have mercy on me." [6]

Naomi Burton could have written back suggesting he had a bad case of swelled head, or spiritual self-importance, but she returned a short, but devastating, response. "If there are books on Jay's list that you might wish had not been published then it seems to me that by the same token these very authors might wish Jay did not publish your books." [7] She could cut him down to size without malice.

Her usual complaint against Merton was that he would answer business letters himself, without sending them on or consulting her, and that he had a nasty way of giving verbal undertakings to publishers (Jay particularly) without dutifully consulting his agent. It is odd that Merton, so drilled to obedience in the life of the monastery, could be so headstrong in business matters—perhaps he needed to feel he could break out in this direction, or perhaps it was the highhandedness people sometimes complain of in religious, as if they feel they are exempt from the conventions and customs that govern the rest of humanity. But it was frustrating at times for both his agent and his publishers. "You never really trust me to work

pause and from which he could review his life, and the question, never really resolved, of his attitude to the world outside the monastery, returned to haunt him. He tended alternately to scorn the world, in the traditional manner of monks (although he had done so long before he came to the monastery), and then to be deeply moved by its beauty and pathos.

His first glimpse of the outside world for seven years came at the time of Dom James's election as Abbot. (In those days, the monks went outside the enclosure for almost nothing except serious illness that demanded a stay in hospital. Even the dentist came to them.) The French Vicar General, Dom Gabriel, came to Gethsemani to preside over the election, and because Dom Gabriel did not speak English Merton was appointed to act as interpreter. They drove into Louisville on "an errand of charity."

> We drove into town with Senator Dawson, a neighbor of the monastery, and all the while I wondered how I would react at meeting once again, face to face, the wicked world. Perhaps the things I had resented about the world when I left it were defects of my own that I had projected upon it. Now, on the contrary, I found that everything stirred me with a deep and mute sense of compassion. . . . I went through the city, realizing for the first time in my life how good are all the people in the world and how much value they have in the sight of God. After that I returned to the peaceful routine of monastic life—I had only left it for six hours. [11]

This reflective comment, written as part of the introduction to *The Sign of Jonas*, contrasts rather strikingly with the nonchalant entry in his journal at the time. "Going into Louisville the other day I wasn't struck by anything in particular. Although I felt completely alienated from everything in the world and all its activity I did not necessarily feel out of sympathy with the people who were walking around." [11] He enjoyed seeing the country— the corn and the woods and hills, and realized he had forgotten what it looked like. But "Louisville was boring. Anyway, the whole thing was a matter of obedience." [11]

His next trip to Louisville came early in 1949 when, perhaps rather significantly, he was applying for American citizenship. He had applied once before but allowed his application to lapse in his early years at Gethsemani. Gradually the idea had returned to him that he would like to apply again. The visit was not in itself a success. "Louisville was dull as usual," and the group who went (another Father in pursuit of citizenship, one going to the hospital, and the Abbot) went without food all day. The day was largely spent hanging around waiting for Reverend Father to complete his business. They waited two hours in the cathedral praying and then spent a long time in the street outside a shop in Louisville where Reverend Father was buying tractor parts. There Merton noticed a woman shivering in rags (it was January) and suddenly felt guilty about the relative comfort of his own life. "People are starving to death and freezing and here I sit with a silver spoon in my mouth and write books and everybody sends me fan-mail telling me how wonderful I am for giving up so *much*." [11]

The peculiar irony of his situation came home to him even more clearly during the centenary celebrations when radio reporters and Fox Movietone News recorded and filmed the monks singing. Merton, with a mixture of enjoyment, amusement, and horror, took part in a press conference, in which "I, a solitary cloistered contemplative, assured some four score nuns and other people that I was neither allowed to speak nor to sign autographs and that I could only speak with reporters. Then they made me bless them and their rosaries and let me go, and I stumbled away with the cameras going clickety-click on every side. O beata solitudo!" [11]

His objection to the world was its noise and clamour, and he considered at this time that Christians ought to give up television, radio, and the movies, and try to make their homes places of real quiet. With an optimism only a celibate could manage, he suggested that they should even train their children not to cry: "Children are naturally quiet." But he had a more profound suggestion about what Christians should do: "Maybe even form small agrarian communities in the country. . . . Provide people with places where they can go to be quiet—relax minds and hearts in the presence of God. . . . Reading rooms, hermitages. Retreat houses without a constant ballyhoo of noisy 'exercises.'" [11] In this he was prophetic in sensing the real need people would discover in the 1960s and 1970s for places in which to be quiet, and the growth of the "hermit" movement within the religious life, even before he had seriously begun to consider this possibility for himself. Yet there is something disquieting about Merton's tone of voice whenever he speaks of the world at this time. Is it superiority in feeling he has chosen something better? Or a repressed longing for much that he has given up?

Merton himself senses that there is something "phony" in his attitude to "the world," and tries hard to work out what it is. But what obstructs his thinking is that he *has* to believe the monastery is a perfect solution, and cannot admit that it suits him in some ways and causes him great suffering in others. Writing about "Journal of My Escape from the Nazis," he says,

> One of the problems of the book was my personal relation to the world and to the last war. When I wrote it I thought it a very supernatural solution. . . . The false solution went like this: the whole world, of which the war is a characteristic expression, is evil. It has therefore first to be ridiculed, then spat upon, and at last formally rejected with a curse.
>
> Actually, I have come to the monastery to find my place in the world, and if I fail to find this place in the world I will be wasting my time in the monastery.
>
> It would be a grave sin for me to be on my knees in the monastery, flagellated, penanced, though not now as thin as I ought to be, and spend my time cursing the world without distinguishing what is good in it from what is bad.
>
> Wars are evil but the people involved in them are good, and I can do nothing whatever for my own salvation or for the glory of God if I merely withdraw from the mess people are in and make an exhibition of myself and write a big book saying "Look! I am different!" To do this is to die. Because any man who pretends to be either an angel or a statue must die the death. The immobility of that *Journal of My Escape* was a confession of my own nonentity, and this was the result of a psychological withdrawal. . . .
>
> Coming to the monastery has been for me exactly the right kind of withdrawal. It has given me perspective. It has taught me how to live. And now I owe everyone else in the world a share of that life. My first duty is to start, for the first time, to live as a member of a human race which is no more (and no less) ridiculous than I am myself. [11]

Yet the same man who preached himself this sermon against "psychological withdrawal" was refusing to look at pictures or advertisements and encouraging even those who were not monks to utterly reject radio, television, and the movies. He was, with part of himself, insisting that Louisville is "boring," not because of any intrinsic lack of worth (he would say the same of any other town), but on the principle that anything made by men must be boring and worthy of rejection. Yet after his stay in the hospital, which included some walks in the neighbouring streets and visits to convents to say mass, his journal was full of the small delights of Louisville, conversations overheard, climatic effects, pleasant minutiae observed in the world of men, and whatever he may have said to the contrary, it is obvious that the visit gave his mind nutrition it craved. When he went to Louisville to become an American citizen at last, in June 1951, it is clear he enjoyed every moment of it—the setting out, shaved and in a black suit with a Roman collar, the riot of flowers along the ditches and over the fences, the crowds at the Federal Building, the fascinating variety of men and women—from Russia, and Italy, and Germany, and Lebanon, and Finland, and Iceland— and the Daughters of the American Revolution, who were surprised at his erstwhile communist connections but presented them all with American flags. Altogether it had been a good day.

If he was beginning to question the need for a total rejection of the world, he was also, from time to time, critical of other strands in his thinking that the monastery tended to reinforce but that some obstinate part of him continued to question. "There is a hunger for humiliation that is nothing else but a hunger for admiration turned inside out. It is a sincere desire to be despised, and it is, perhaps, a desire cherished by those who might be saints. But is it not a desire to be admired by angels? And is it not a desire to be admired by angels only? And is it not a desire to despise what men admire? And do we not often despise what men admire in revenge for having to do without it?" [11]

Merton was moving a long way from the simplicity of Dom Gildas' advice—"Il faut goûter les humiliations"—perceiving contradictions and conflicts that never entered his old confessor's head. If it was not easy to be a monk with the equipment of an artist, it was not easy to be one with the sharp intelligence that Merton possessed. Very gradually, he was allowing himself to be critical of monastic life and values, not to adopt the "all or nothing" approach that had been so typical of him in this, as in other, areas of his life. He continued to love it deeply and to find spiritual nourishment in its routines. The exhaustion and neurotic problems had retreated after his long rest in hospital, and he threw himself back into the life with his old enthusiasm.

One of his constant and never-ending pleasures was the reading of the Scriptures, which resonated in Merton's deep religious imagination, filling his mind with their archetypal images. In the absence of much other reading and other imagery, the experience was particularly rich. Merton feasted on the scriptures and on the Church Fathers.

> I enter into this gay, windy month [it was March] with my mind full of the Book of Josue. Its battle scenes are like the Bayeux tapestry. The books of the Old Testament become to us as signs of the zodiac and Josue (somewhere near the spring equinox) stands at the opposite side of heaven from Job (where all the sky is sailing down to darkness). Here is a book for spring. The sap is rising in the trees and the children of God are winning all their battles. . . . Morning after morning I try to study the sixth chapter of St. John and it is too great. I cannot study it. I simply sit still and try to breathe. . . . Elias was a man like us. Andrew, Peter, James and John were men like unto us. And like them we bring our infirmities to Christ in order that His strength may be glorified in the transformation of our weakness. Day after day the outward man crumbles and breaks down and the inward man, the Man of Heaven, is born and grows in wisdom and knowledge before the eyes of men—who cannot recognize Him. Neither can we recognize ourselves in the image of Him which is formed in us because we do not yet have eyes with which to see Him. And yet we suspect His presence in the mystery which is not revealed to the wise and prudent. We feel His eyes upon us as we sit under the fig tree and our souls momentarily spring to life at the touch of His hidden finger. [11]

Reading the book of Job, Merton records a recurrent feeling that one day he will have to stop reading it and start living it.

Certainly the Scriptures gave him much more pleasure than most of the books read aloud in the refectory. Throughout his monastic life, he often referred to these with exasperation—sometimes they were badly written, sometimes he flatly disagreed with the ideas, sometimes they seemed to touch deeper feelings (he records as a novice having been irritated by "the breasts of the Spouse" when they read St. Bernard's commentary on the Song of Solomon). Apart from the books themselves and their individual faults and failings, there was a sense of being captive to other people's taste that he found disagreeable.

Perhaps this was akin to his problem with prayer. Prayer in a church surrounded by his brethren seemed to make him feel stifled, crushed, claustrophobically trapped in a situation that he was powerless to change. But prayer in the woods or on the hillside or in the car on the way to Louisville or alone in the church was a deep and tranquil experience, one that had grown in him to an often wordless stillness.

He continued with the routine of manual work. Because of his writing, he worked shorter hours than many of the others, but even so he often seemed to be attempting work that was too heavy for him. He described "breaking rock with a sledgehammer" and being "upset" by the experience. And it was taken for granted that he would always stop work on whatever he was writing and help with harvesting, clearing trees, or planting vegetables, or whatever work was required. The monastery was just beginning to acquire machinery to help with the work—Merton ruefully reported the noise of a machine called a Traxcavator they had begun to use—but there was still much toil that the monks undertook themselves.

Later, however, he was put to a much more congenial task as a kind of forest ranger, responsible for the woods that surrounded Gethsemani. He threw himself into it with his usual zest. "I suddenly found out all about the trees." [11] In the autumn he went through the woods with a pot of paint, marking the trees to be cut down, a nice, lonely job that he thoroughly enjoyed. Then, the next spring, he was in charge of the gigantic task of replacing them with seedlings. He found immense joy in looking at the countryside from some of these lonely stretches of wood and hillside and in reciting prayers there. In one such isolated place, he found himself entertaining the guilty fantasy of becoming a hermit.

At Merton's suggestion, one of the woods close to the enclosure came to be considered an extension of the enclosure, for the special use of the Scholastics, and Merton spent much time praying there, a source of real delight to him.

On Trinity Sunday, 1951, Merton was named Master of Scholastics, a new post at Gethsemani, brought about by the vast size of the novitiate, which made the old informal methods of instruction unsatisfactory. He had enjoyed his teaching work and found he learned more theology this way than during his own studies, but now he found that in addition to enjoying teaching he also enjoyed the time spent talking to his students one by one about their spiritual and other problems. "It is much more interesting than writing a book, besides being less fatiguing." [11] It filled him with a great desire to keep the Rule as well as possible so that what he taught about it should have real authority.

It also gave him a good sense of being what he described as a "family man." After ordination, he had suffered from the fact that a priest in a contemplative order, unlike a secular priest, had no one to care for, but now suddenly he had all his students to care for, and care for them he did, although he says that sometimes it was like the blind leading the blind. "Half my spiritual children have colds and some of them are depressed and one just changed over to the laybrothers, which was a good thing, while two of them are trying to kill themselves with overwork, being cantors and directing the choir even during the psalmody of the little hours. I understand their anguish which, five years ago, was my own anguish. But I do not approve of their exhaustion." [11] He took them out to work, or to pray, in the woods up on the knobs, and he learned from his association with them, and from the mutual love and respect.

> The more I get to know my scholastics the more reverence I have for their individuality and the more I meet them in my own solitude. The best of them, and the ones to whom I feel closest, are also the most solitary and at the same time the most charitable. . . . Now that I know them better, I can see something of the depths of solitude which are in every human person. . . . The young ones, I admit, do not have half the problems I used to have when I was a scholastic. Their calmness will finally silence all that remains of my own turbulence. They come to me with intelligent questions, or sometimes with an even more intelligent absence of questions. They refresh me with their simplicity. Very spontaneously, they come to share my love of anything I may have discovered. . . . But they ignore my persistent interest in theological complications. [11]

The Scholastics themselves felt enriched by their new teacher. In their private talks with him once a week—and he gave about an hour each every week to some forty students—he gently uncovered difficulties and problems in a way that none of them ever forgot. In some cases he was confessor to the students as well and combined this with the hour of direction. "Most of what he did was direct you in your reading and in living the life. The life was all set up so the only option you had was in your attitudes to it."

Merton did not say very much in these sessions—as one of his old students says, "He expected you to offer everything." This did not always go down well—many of them would much have preferred to be questioned—but they found that Merton acted as a catalyst in their lives and that in these sessions they often found out surprising things about themselves. Sometimes, in a desperate wish to evade the deeper issues they would find themselves chattering about books they had read, and one Father remembers Merton becoming exasperated when he did this: "Books, books, books, all you ever talk about is books!" The student felt it was unfair, but said that he was more careful after that.

Merton's great emphasis was on authenticity and honesty. "He was very hard on any form of dishonesty, whether conscious or unconscious, and it was mostly unconscious because we were trying to be as good as we could be. He wouldn't let you do things because they might be expected of you, or because they were the pious thing to do. I didn't believe everything he said at first—I resisted him—and then I discovered that when I did things his way I was more myself. He had a way of showing you how to do this thing authentically, and this was one of his chief charms. There were a lot of pressures on *him* to be the person people wanted him to be, and he refused to be it."

Another monk, whose health broke down during his studies for the priesthood, remembers Merton's unfailing sympathy and support, and his visits to him in hospital. The monk suffered from torturing scruples, and in deep depression accused himself of cowardice.

"Sure, you run away," Merton told him, "but then you run right back in there again."

In his depression, the student valued the lightness and humour with which the two of them discussed painful aspects of the spiritual life. He told Merton about the misery of distractions in prayer.

"You mean you get a lot of mental movies?" Merton enquired.

"Yeah, I win the Academy Award every year." And the two of them laughed together.

One student who later came to admire Merton's spiritual teaching very much remembers attending his first Conferences. "I didn't like the way the others all sat on the edges of their seats and ate up every word, and I said to myself, 'I will *not* be this man's disciple.' I felt you should only be a disciple of the Lord. And then when I got to know him better I found that that was exactly what he insisted on himself. He didn't want any disciples." The same man feels that his whole understanding of the monastic life was shaped by Merton's teaching and example.

"There are many interpretations of the monastic ascesis. He was certainly giving me an interpretation that was a lot more congenial than I had had up to that point, and it made sense to me, and I think helped me to live it in a healthier manner."

This time at Gethsemani was one of the happiest for Merton. Work he loved, the company of young people, freedom to wander in the woods. "I live in the trees. I mark them with paint and the woods cultivate me with their silences, and all day long even in choir and at Mass I seem to be in the forest: but my children themselves are like trees, and they flourish all around me like the things that grow in the Bible." [11] Something good and rich and satisfying seemed to be coming through his life of sacrifice, transforming the pain and making it fruitful.

References

1. Naomi Burton. Letter to Thomas Merton. March 31, 1950. TMSC.
2. Naomi Burton. "A Note on the Author and This Book." In Thomas Merton, *My Argument with the Gestapo*. New York: Doubleday, 1969.
3. Naomi Burton. Letter to Thomas Merton. April 9, 1947. TMSC.
4. Naomi Burton. Letter to Thomas Merton. May 5, 1950. TMSC.
5. Naomi Burton. Letter to Thomas Merton. April 15, 1955. TMSC.
6. Thomas Merton. Letter to Naomi Burton, January 27, 1951. TMSC.
7. Naomi Burton. Letter to Thomas Merton. February 15, 1951. TMSC.
8. Thomas Merton. Letter to Naomi Burton, April 2, 1956.
9. Robert Lax. Letter to Thomas Merton. From Lourdes, 1949. TMSC.
10. Thomas Merton. Letter to Catherine Doherty (Baroness de Hueck). February 14, 1949. TMSC.
11. Thomas Merton. *The Sign of Jonas*. New York: Harcourt Brace, 1953; London: Sheldon Press, 1976.

13

THE ASCENT TO TRUTH

𐰭

If Merton was experiencing a sense of release in his life at Gethsemani, he was also experiencing it in his writing. "The Cloud and the Fire," which had cost him such agonizing anxiety during his period of "writer's block," came easily and well after eighteen months of rest, and emerged as *The Ascent to Truth*. [1] There is a slight air of ambition about the book—ambition in the sense that every successful author seems to have a book in his mind that is the one he *really* wants to write. It is usually an ambitious project, and it rarely succeeds as well as the book that first brought success.

Merton's book is ambitious in the sense that it is an attempt to suggest a way of contemplative prayer that will speak to the modern world but, since he used the notoriously difficult method outlined by St. John of the Cross, it was unlikely, even in the spiritual euphoria of postwar America, that too many people would follow him into this difficult field. Apart from one or two fairly natural attempts to use modern imagery to make his meaning clear—the motion of an aeroplane, the skill of an ice-hockey player, the strange effect of being in a stationary train when the train standing beside it begins to move—he makes no concessions to his readers. (This is perhaps the height of ambition in a writer— to write exactly as he or she wants to write, without concessions.) Merton gave his intelligence full rein, as he struggled to make sense (for his own use as well as the readers we feel) of this great school of contemplative prayer. Sometimes he reverted to a slightly irritating tendency to be improving, with exhortations to the reader to be mindful of authority and not trust their own ideas too much, but the energy and enthusiasm of his own thinking were so much bolder and livelier than that of most people, that he could scarcely be seen as an example of timidity.

In one place, he made a statement—on the subject of the silencing of Catholic thinkers (in this case about science)—that is important in view of some of his later struggles. He defended the churchmen who rejected the hypothesis of Galileo on the grounds that the Church cannot always keep up with the latest thinking. "The Church has a perfect right to demand submission of her children when she asks them to remain silent on a subject which is, perhaps, as yet incomprehensible to an unscientific hierarchy. The bishops are under no obligation to keep pace with the latest developments of physics, but they do have an obligation to preserve the deposit of revealed Truth according to whatever light God has given them." [1]

The answer is, apparently, patience. "The Catholic scientist, or philosopher, or theologian is well aware that he may have to be patient, at sometime or other in his life, and withhold a favorite theory of his own merely in order to avoid upsetting an ecclesiastical superior. He knows well enough that the Church is the custodian of Truth and that, if his theory be true, it will be recognized at last." [1]

The purpose of *The Ascent to Truth* was to define the nature of contemplative experience, to show the kind of ascesis necessary to achieve it, and to give a "brief sketch" of mature contemplation. No wonder the book had cost Merton so much effort.

Merton began with an attack on the "diversions" that Pascal so much deplored, the pursuit of joys without substance, instead of the pursuit of union with God. When the world is treated as an end in itself, the world becomes an illusion. Men and women escape into all kinds of unbelief, atheism, or an excessive love of "creatures" when what they should be doing instead is striving for the "detachment" that will bring them to God. Detachment, Merton said, is difficult because of "passion," which we enjoy in itself too much to renounce, and even reason, which might save us from this fate, is pressed into the service of passion. The answer is St. John's passage about desiring to have nothing, to be nothing, and to know nothing. What the contemplative must strive for is "nada"—nothing.

St. John, Merton suggested, was not preaching a kind of Manicheeism, but was, rather, saying that the only way to love and enjoy "creatures" is to detach ourselves from them. The Christian contemplative does not consider the world an "illusion," like some Oriental teachers, but that it only has meaning for people when they turn away from it toward God.

Rather surprisingly, and perhaps too vehemently, Merton refuted any suggestion that the artist and the mystic have anything important in common. If a man is both these things, said Merton, "his art and his mysticism must always remain two essentially different things." [1]

The ways to God are the ways of "affirmation" and "denial." Unlike some spiritual writers, Merton did not think there is a choice between one and the other. "We have to take both. We must affirm and deny at the same time. We have to start with a concept of God, but we have simultaneously to know that it is quite inadequate as a description of him. Corresponding with these are the *via negationis* or *negativa*, the way of unknowing on the one hand, and the *via amoris*, the way of love on the other." [1]

At this point in his argument, Merton suddenly gave a severe little lecture, which surely was aimed more at himself than at his reader, who was scarcely likely to fall into the error he described, or at least less likely than Merton himself: "Like Job's friends, you set yourself up as a theological advocate of God. You justify His ways to men not according to what He is, but according to what your system says He ought to be. In the end, you find yourself apologizing to the world for God and demonstrating that, after all, He is not to be blamed for being what He is because it can be shown that He generally acts like a just, prudent, and benevolent man." [1] Quite so.

But on the next page Merton, sounding not unlike one of Job's friends, had a prim little attack on "modernism," attacking those who do not wholeheartedly accept the doctrines of religious institutions but insist on experiencing for themselves.

Merton moved on to speak of the experience of Christian contemplation and did so with the deepest feeling:

> Christian contemplation is precipitated by crisis within crisis and anguish within anguish. It is born of spiritual conflict. It is a victory that suddenly appears in the hour of defeat. It is the providential solution of problems that seem to have no solution. It is the reconciliation of enemies that seem to be irreconcilable. It is a vision in which Love, mounting into the darkness which no reasoning can penetrate, unites in one bond all the loose strands that intelligence alone cannot connect together, and with this cord draws the whole being of man into a Divine Union, the effects of which will some day overflow into the world outside him. [1]

Speaking of the ascesis that precedes and is part of all this, Merton attacked the split that can arise as will turns against the body. He noted that "the ones who punish themselves furiously for two or three years and then lose their morale, fall into despair, become hypochondriacs, obsessed with every fancied need of their flesh and of their spirit." [1]

While feeling that theology is vitally important for a mystic, Merton also felt that mysticism is important to the theologian and that theologians who are also mystics ʌ ʌ "beam in" to the truth as by a kind of supernatural radar.

What the would-be contemplative should be aiming at is "a rigorous spiritual training in self-denial and in the practice of virtue." There is another kind of ascesis that consists of a "mystical" or passive purification, which takes place without the contemplative's initiative, but both these ways, both the active and the passive, are necessary, Merton felt. So the soul moves on into the Night of the Senses, in which the senses are no longer able to register what is happening, and the Prayer of Quiet, in which man's mind is purified, simplified, and reduced to unity, and on, in almost complete darkness (so much is the soul dazzled by God's glory) into the loving knowledge of God, the illuminative flame of God's presence.

Merton wrote *The Ascent to Truth* from a background of wide reading about contemplative prayer, with a thorough knowledge not only of St. John of the Cross, but also of St. Thomas, together with Jacques Maritain's work on St. Thomas. Because the book was conceived as an academic work, Merton did not feel it appropriate to speak often of his own experience, so that it is never altogether clear when he was speaking of what he knew at first hand and of what he knew from authorities on prayer. Yet here and there, there is an air of conviction that is unmistakable, as Merton, with his whole ardent soul, tried to tell us how he saw the life of a religious man. "The whole work of our sanctification . . . can be summed up as the perfect obedience of our whole being to the will of God. . . . The deep secret of the mystery of faith lies in the fact that it is a 'baptism' in the death and sacrifice of Christ. We can only give ourselves to God when Christ, by His grace, 'dies' and rises again spiritually within us." [1]

Simultaneously with *The Ascent to Truth*, Merton was working on *Bread in the Wilderness* (1953). In fact, he wrote some of the early chapters during his hospital stay in Louisville. It attempts something much simpler, a look at the role of the Psalms in Christian worship, but behind that, remembering Merton's boredom and exasperation with the offices in choir (largely based on the

Psalms) we can see him searching for a way to make the long hours endurable and even fruitful. The painful question behind the book is "What *is* the point?" of the *opus dei*, as it is called, the "work of God" that the contemplative monk performs by reciting the Psalms hour after hour in church.

Merton began by trying to define the work of the monk, something he did many more times before the end of his life. "Monks have no other occupation in life than the search for God." [2] But, given that this is so, what is the particular point of the obligation of reciting the Divine Office? The idea is that it should unite the monk with God, but how was it to do this?

Were the Psalms intended as techniques of contemplation, which "when properly manipulated, will lead us into some special psychological state"? Merton did not think so. The recitation of the Psalms, Merton thought, is not meant to induce a psychologically receptive state, but rather to hold certain theological truths continually before the minds of those praying. This idea of "understanding" has not always been the way that the Divine Office has been expounded to novices. Merton spoke with feeling of the theory that "the Office is to be accepted merely as a form of penance . . . that monastic choirs were invented only as a test of humility, abnegation and dogged endurance." [2]

Merton struggled bravely to assert the necessity of "vocal" prayer, as opposed to a silent contemplation, quoting St. Teresa and Gregory of Nyssa as his authorities, and attacking the heretical Quietists and Illuminists who thought that the Divine Office was a real obstacle to contemplative prayer. From so much that he had already said in his journals, we may guess that he was trying to convince himself more vigorously than his readers, many of whom would never question the value of the Divine Office.

Having argued to his own satisfaction that vocal prayer in this form is necessary, Merton then went on to ask what the praying monk is supposed to do in his mind with the material presented to him by the Psalms, sometimes frankly bloody and full of warlike aggression, sometimes rather prosaic and sensible, sometimes reaching sublime mystical heights. One traditional way of approaching the Psalms and indeed Scripture in general is to do it "mystically," to find buried within the outer husk of the "letter," a kernel of spiritual truth. Merton rejected this method in favour of two other approaches: one, the literal, simply listening to what the words say; the other the "typical" or symbolic sense, in which the words open a far deeper level of spiritual understanding. There are immense difficulties about this latter approach, particularly the difficulty of "overspiritualizing" a passage of the Bible so that it becomes unrecognizable as what the writer originally intended, but Merton saw the Scriptures both as a way of spiritual growth in themselves and as becoming more and more accessible to those who are spiritually growing. Following the apostles, he saw the Scriptures as expounding God's plan for man, a plan "only fully understood by those in whom it is fulfilled."

Merton took two Biblical "types" as of particular significance to the Christian soul. The first is the Jewish Exodus, which began with the Jewish firstborn being spared because the blood of the paschal lamb was placed on the lintel of the door. The other is the *pascha Christi*, the "passion of Christ." Merton wrote with deep feeling of the Exodus experience as being part of the psychological experience of every religious person—"a journey, nourished by miraculous food, through the blighted heart of a land without vegetation" and it is from this image that the title of the book *Bread in the Wilderness* was taken, the Psalms themselves being the manna that sustains spiritual life. As we grow in faith, Merton said, "the mystery of Exodus and the *pascha Christi* tend to become more and more a matter of experience in our lives." The importance of this is not the experience in itself, but that we are becoming part of a reality, "God Himself in us." And this experience is part of something much larger, the whole redemptive plan of God working through His creation.

In discussing the poetic and symbolic value of the Psalms, Merton made a statement that is interesting in view of his later concern with nature as part of the "measure" of life. He was moving, perhaps because of the simplicity of life at Gethsemani, toward a new interest in and understanding of, natural life.

Creation had been given to man as a clean window through which the light of God could shine into men's souls. Sun and moon, night and day, rain, the sea, the crops, the flowering tree, all these things were transparent. They spoke to man not of themselves only but of Him who made them. Nature was symbolic. But the progressive degradation of man after the fall led the Gentiles further and further from this truth. Nature became opaque. The nations were no longer able to penetrate the meaning of the world they lived in. Instead of seeing the sun a witness to the power of God, they thought the sun was god. The whole universe became an enclosed system of myths. The meaning and the worth of creatures invested them with an illusory divinity.

Men still sensed that there was something to be venerated in the reality, in the peculiarity of living and growing things, but they no longer knew what that reality was. They became incapable of seeing that the goodness of the creature is only a vestige of God. Darkness settled upon the translucent universe. Men became afraid. Beings had a meaning which men could no longer understand. They became afraid of trees, of the sun, of the sea. These things had to be approached with superstitious rites. It began to seem that the mystery of their meaning, which had become hidden, was now a power that had to be placated and, if possible, controlled by magic incantations.

Thus the beautiful living things which were all about us on this earth and which were the windows of heaven to every man, became infected with original sin. [2]

This passage has the minatory tone of the preacher and reveals that Merton was not well read in anthropology or psychology, but it is interesting because it reveals that he was already struggling with humankind's relationship to the natural world, with the whole complex subject of myth and symbol, and of our projection of inner fears on the world around us. Cut off at this point from intellectual sources that might have fed him, Merton's mind was moving vigorously away from the monastery, and the special problems of a contemplative monk, to the problems peculiar to all human beings. Having moved inward to establish his stability and life of prayer at the monastery and to reach the goal of ordination, he was now slowly turning back toward the world he had excluded. It is not surprising that the symbol he selected, the story of Exodus, is a story of journey.

References

1. Thomas Merton. *The Ascent to Truth*. New York: Harcourt Brace, 1951; Tunbridge Wells, Kent: Burns and Oates, 1976. Originally called "The Cloud and the Fire."
2. Thomas Merton. *Bread in the Wilderness*. New York: New Directions, 1953; Tunbridge Wells, Kent: Burns and Oates, 1976.

14

LIKE OTHER MEN

❦

During his work as Master of Scholastics in the early 1950s, Merton's longing for solitude grew more intense. He worked in an old tool shed, where he was badly disturbed by the noise of farm machinery, or in the archive vault, for the brief time allowed for writing each day, but the busyness of life as teacher, spiritual adviser, choir monk, and manual worker left him little privacy, and he slept at night in the common dormitory. (He had been amused at Sertillanges' advice that if a writer or intellectual had a good idea in the night he should at once rise and write it down; even apart from difficulties of noise and light, the brief Cistercian night left little opportunity for such inspirations.) As usual Merton's conflict between life as a writer and as a monastic was acute.

The continued overcrowding of the cloister—the numbers were approaching 270—did not help.

Imagine that we now have one hundred and fifty novices at Gethsemani. This is fantastic. Many of them are sleeping in a tent in the *preau* [yard]. The nucleus of seniors is a small, bewildered group of men who remember the iron rule of Dom Edmond Obrecht [Dom Frederic Dunne's predecessor] and have given up trying to comprehend what has happened to Gethsemani. The house has a very vital and enthusiastic (in the good sense) and youthful air like the camp of an army preparing for a gay, easy and victorious war. Those of us who have been sobered by a few years of the life find ourselves in turns comforted and depressed by the multitude of our young companions of two and three months' standing: comforted by their fervor and joy and simplicity, and depressed by the sheer weight of numbers. The cloister is as crowded as a Paris street. On the whole, when the house is completely full of men who are happy because they have not yet had a chance to suffer anything (although they believe themselves willing) the effect is a little disquieting. One feels more solidly rooted in God in a community of veterans, even though many of them may be morose. [1]

He felt under continual tension and began increasingly to think that he was not called to the communal conventual life but to something far less structured, which, while keeping him away from the distractions of "the world," would allow him more liberty for private prayer and contemplation. It was not that he sought more freedom for writing at this stage—he was still of half a mind to give up writing altogether—but he felt he needed to be alone more, to explore the "solitude" that, ever since his ordination and perhaps before, he had felt was "the way" for him. Dom James' earlier indication that he would be able to "arrange things" in such a way that Merton would be content at Gethsemani had not been followed through.

Inevitably, Merton's mind turned back to his old dreams of being a hermit. Although in the main the Cistercians were a cenobitic community, eremites were not entirely outside the tradition. Even in De Rancé's time there had been the occasional hermit, but in any case it was not so unusual for those who felt themselves summoned to the hermit vocation to transfer to a more eremitical life. One monk who had been a novice with Merton at Gethsemani had transferred to the Carthusians, and the most famous example was Charles de Foucauld, who left a Cistercian monastery for the solitude of the Sahara.

Early in 1955, Merton reached a crisis. Ever since his ordination, he had been feeling increasingly hemmed in by the multitude of restrictions that hedged his life around, of which the lack of solitude and privacy was only the chief and most irksome to him. The greater strictness over enclosure (even though he escaped from it by way of his work on the tree plantations) was a symbol of an increasingly rigorous control of the monks and of their separation from the outside world, which reduced them to helpless dependence. News from outside was filtered to them by the Abbot. Sometimes they heard of events only very much later (it was nearly a year before they learned of the dropping of the atom bomb on Hiroshima), sometimes not at all, and sometimes with the Abbot's particular political bias.

Merton had suffered a peculiarly galling episode early in the 1950s, when, *The Sign of Jonas* having been passed by the Order's Censors, and a contract agreed with Harcourt Brace, Dom James went to a meeting of the Order in France and came back with the news that the Superiors of the Order would not allow the book to be published. The first Robert Giroux knew of this was a telephone call from Dom James to Harcourt Brace in New York, saying that he was sorry but the book could not be published. Giroux objected that the book was already in galley proofs, and Dom James said that of course the Abbey would reimburse the publishers.

Merton in the past had defended Catholic attitudes to censorship and had felt that it was not unreasonable to expect writers and thinkers to show a little "patience" about getting controversial work published, but perhaps nothing but this incident could have brought home to him how unreasonable authority could be. The French superiors who had blocked publication did not read English and so could not find out first-hand what he was saying. The objection, very possibly put into the Abbot General's mind by younger monks who had not liked Merton's popular success with *The Seven Storey Mountain*, was that *The Sign of Jonas* was not "in the tradition." Yet *The Sign of Jonas* was a journal, and St. Bernard of Clairvaux, the most famous of all Cistercians, had written a journal.

Robert Giroux ingeniously solved this delicate publishing problem by getting Jacques Maritain to write to the Abbot General in French, telling him how highly he thought of both book and author, and under his gentle persuasion the book was published. But it left a scar on Merton—there would be worse scars from censorship to follow—and may have influenced his desire to leave the Trappists.

One of his chief *confidants* about his wish to leave was Dom Jean Leclerq, a Benedictine monk, a frequent visitor to Gethsemani, and a great advocate of the eremitic life. They had corresponded in a desultory way throughout the early 1950s, Merton writing to him in a slightly ponderous style about books and spiritual interests. On April 27, 1955, Merton suddenly wrote to Dom Jean in quite a different style. The letter was in French—all the preceding letters were in English—and Merton remarked, in the letter, in a rather baffling way, that he had done this so that Dom James will also be able to read the letter. Since Dom James' French may not have been very good, it was perhaps a way of sidestepping the censorship a little, while letting Dom James know that the writer knew that the letter would be censored. But somehow the act of writing in another language released Merton, and he poured out his heart in the letter—the heart of a man who could continue no longer in his present situation. The crisis had been precipitated by the official Visitor, who had strongly condemned the "mentalité érémitique" he found at Gethsemani, and had condemned Merton in particular for not being "dans la moule" (in the mould) expected of a Trappist.

Merton's wistful hopes of the eremitical life or even of some sort of compromise (Dom James's promise "pour arranger les choses") were cruelly dashed, and in desperation he had decided that the only thing to do was to apply for a "transitus" (an official permission to move) to the Camaldolese, an Italian order of contemplatives in which the brothers, while living in a monastery, spend their lives almost entirely alone. Merton wanted Dom Jean to tell him about the Camaldolese house at Frascati, whether they would accept him and whether he would be happy there.

But he knew what a struggle he would have to put up to be allowed to go there, even though a friend of his (Mark Van Doren?) had offered to pay his fare. Merton wrote, knowing full well that Dom James would see this letter, "Je crois que mon Père Abbé cherchera a me retenir à tout prix ["I believe that Father Abbot intends to keep me here at all costs"]." [2] However, he had determined to write to the Congregation of Religious in Rome for permission to move.

As Merton had anticipated, Dom James read the letter, and, instead of sending it on, debated mentally for three weeks what to do with it. Merton had meanwhile written to Rome, so the situation was a delicate one. Dom James was determined to keep this famous son at Gethsemani, Merton equally determined to leave; only diplomacy could save the day. Unknown to Merton, Dom James wrote two letters, one to Dom Jean and one to Archbishop Montini of Milan (later Pope Paul VI), who was a member of the Secretary of State office in the Vatican and who corresponded with both Dom James and Merton.

The letter to Dom Jean is dated May 18, 1955.

Good Father Louis wrote you a letter towards the end of April. From the very nature of the case, I delayed the sending of it to you because I wanted to include a note from myself also.

You will see that Father Louis, when he wrote this letter was quite a bit disturbed emotionally. Sometimes his emotions get the better of his good judgment.

However, I am sending his letter to you just as he wrote it. However, I would ask you in your answer to use the greatest caution and prudence.

We add also, dear Dom Jean, that at the present moment Father has regained much of peace of soul. We are arranging with our Most Reverend General that Father Louis can have charge of our woods, of which we have six hundred hectares and which is really a full-time job. Thus he will be able to remain a full-fledged member of the community and yet have ample opportunities for silence and solitude within the Rule.

To me the whole problem is that God has one plan of life for Father Louis and good Father Louis is trying to follow another one, different from what God has planned for him. The result is, of course, terrific conflict.

But the final solution is for good Father Louis to try more and more to conform his will to God's Will, than to try to make God conform His will to that of Father Louis.

As yet of course Father is so obsessed with his own plan that he cannot quite see, or at least is not yet quite docile enough to accept God's Will. But I think in the end his spirit of Faith and increased spirit of obedience and humility will finally triumph.

. . . Tout pour Jesus—par Marie—avec sourire. [3]

Meanwhile, far from becoming more docile, Merton had written to Rome asking for permission to move to the Camaldolese, unaware that a letter from Dom James to Montini had also gone on its way. Dom James wrote to Archbishop Montini, on May 16, 1955, in the following terms:

We are writing to you in regard to our Father Louis, who is known to the world as Thomas Merton.

. . . Good Father Louis, as you know, is really a genius in writing books. He is very dynamic and bubbling over with energy, and has a very expansive imagination. He is writing you a letter concerning his vocational difficulties.

I thought it would be to the purpose for me to write also, so you have as complete a picture as possible.

Father Louis came to Gethsemani in 1941, some fourteen years ago. He made his solemn vows some eight years ago, and was ordained here six years ago. He has been troubled by vocational difficulties for the last several years. For a while he thought he should join the Carthusians. More recently he has changed his desires, and wishes to join the Camaldolese. In all this matter we keep before us that the question is what is God's will? Not what is Father Louis' will, or what is my will, or what is anybody else's will. God does not send a telegram; we have to form our judgement by various external and interior indices that we can perceive.

My thoughts fall into two divisions. First the thoughts about Father Louis in himself; secondly in regard to Father Louis in his relations with others.

Father Louis in himself, as we have said, he is very dynamic, more extrovert than introvert. He spends most of his free time in reading and writing books. I provided a small cabin for him within our enclosure, in some woods, primarily in order that he might be able to pray and be alone with God. He uses most of that time for typewriting his manuscripts.

The "following of Christ" says "Inspirations come from God, but not all inspirations come from God." Father Louis gives great importance to the fact that he has had the urges and inclinations and desire for a more solitary life for many years, and they still persist.

If you will allow me to be personal, I myself had terrific inclinations and attractions and urging to leave Gethsemani for the Carthusians. These have persisted, not for ten years, as with Father Louis, but for some twenty years. And yet I know that it is not God's will for me to follow these urges, even though they remain very vivid in my soul. It becomes more and more clear to me that what God wants is the immolation of my desire and will to his spoken will, no matter how I feel about it.

In my heart, Your Excellency, I think that if God had followed your desires and inclinations, you would never have accepted to become an Archbishop of Milan; but you immolated your inclinations and ideals to God's sovereign Will.

Good Father Louis was not born in a Catholic family, but came into the church when he was twenty-three or twenty-four years old. He is inclined to give much weight to subjective feelings.

Anyone who resists God's will cannot have peace with himself, or with his companions. This is the fault not of our companions, or the externals of our life. The fault is in our interior, namely, a lack of submission, keeping up the effort, no doubt unconsciously and without any positive deliberate effort, to make God conform to our will, rather than for us to conform to His will.

As regards to his relations with others, Fr. Louis does not realize that he is a public figure in our community and in the great world outside, both Catholic and non-Catholic.

In our community, he is the Master of Students, of whom he has had at various times some forty under his charge. He is very well liked by everyone of the students. They look upon him as an oracle of spirituality and lean heavily upon him for their guidance in the spiritual life. If he ever were to leave here, it would be a source of great scandal to our young professed and would betray them into the spirit of instability and change. I can hardly picture what the results of his change would be.

Concerning his relations with the outside world, both Catholic and non-Catholic, good Father Louis does not realize that he is a public figure of tremendous importance.

In my travels, I hear comments on how much confidence priests and religious place in Father Louis and his writings. Here again there would be tremendous scandal to know that he is really quite restless and unsure of himself after having spent some fourteen years in one monastery.

His influence as a writer would be destroyed in a marked degree, as indeed, some of his friends have written to him when he broached the question of changing Orders. They would not distinguish between a higher Order and a lower Order, so to speak; they would just know that he was unstable.

For example, a certain Father Barnabas Mary, C.P. of Chicago, wrote to me about Father Louis when he asked him about changing Orders. Father Barnabas is a very wonderful religious, and is a recognized theologian. He wrote that if Father should leave his present order, it would cause tremendous scandal among the reading public, both Catholic and non Catholic.

Father Barnabas wrote Father Louis directly as follows:

1. It would be an encouragement to all people in religious life who are "itching" for change.
2. It would cut vocations to your Trappist way of life, since your change would be a frank confession that you have not found there the prospect you have held out to others.
3. It will lessen the influence you have exerted, and the good you can do. Many will say, "I told you so" and will point to your change as a proof that your writing has not come from conviction but from emotion.
4. It will make many good religious uneasy in their way of life. Most nuns, and many male religious, do not reason; and so they will conclude, "If Thomas Merton could not find union with God at Gethsemani, how can I expect to find it in my way of life."
5. Practical people will make capital of this in decrying contemplation; and, once more in many quarters, contemplation will again become suspect. Superiors will ban Thomas Merton the way they have banned St. Teresa and St. John of the Cross: "They put too many crazy ideas in people's heads." . . .

Your Excellency, before God I say to you, and I am ready to meet this decision on the Last Judgement, that I cannot see the finger of God in Father Louis's desire for change. I am in no way afraid of taking the entire responsibility for this decision myself. I do not fear any criticism in any way. . . .

All for Jesus—thru Mary—with a smile. [4]

For Dom James, the issue appears simple. For Merton to leave Gethsemani would cause scandal and would reflect unfavourably on the monastery, so Merton must "submit." He does not seriously consider Merton's suggestion on its own merits; he is convinced Merton is wrong and that it is for him to "conform." Merton's serious objections to the Trappist life can be taken care of by putting him in charge of the woods.

Unaware that his cause had been undermined at Rome, Merton continued to dream of the Camaldolese. He was not entirely without supporters, even apart from Dom Jean. In a letter to Dom Jean, dated June 3, 1955, he mentioned getting a letter dated May 26 (presumably a fairly prompt reply to the desperate letter sent by Merton in April but not sent by Dom James till May 18), and said he wished he had received it sooner. But he wants to tell Dom Jean how both his director at Gethsemani and a Carthusian father he knows had given him positive encouragement, and even the Abbot General sees no reason why he shouldn't move "if it is the will of God." [5] However, "Father Abbot is very much opposed," and the two of them are "earnestly trying to reach the final solution." Dom James, obviously feeling pushed by the situation, had suggested that Merton might become a hermit there in their own forest. "If this permission were ever granted it would solve all my problems, I think. The forest here is very lonely and quiet and covers about a thousand acres, and there is much woodland adjoining it. It is as wild as any country that would be found in the Ardennes or the Vosges, perhaps wilder." [5]

By the beginning of August, Merton had still not heard from Rome, but the Camaldolese house at Frascati had written to say that they would be glad for him to come and make a "trial" of the life. But Dom James and the other superiors seemed to be coming round to the idea of Merton becoming a hermit on the spot. In a kind of inspiration, Dom James had approached the State Forestry Department, who were building a fire lookout tower on the top of one of the local hills and suggested Merton as lookout man. "It will be an austere and primitive kind of hermitage, if I ever get to live in it." [6] Nobody in the Order seems to have been against the idea, at least as an experiment.

Another decision seemed to be at hand. "I have stopped writing, and that is a big relief. I intend to renounce it for good, if I can live in solitude. I realize that I have perhaps suffered more than I knew from this 'writing career.' Writing is deep in my nature, and I cannot deceive myself that it will be very easy for me to do without it. . . . But the whole business tends to corrupt the purity of one's spirit of faith . . . for as long as one imagines himself to be accomplishing something he tends to become rich in his own eyes. But we must be poor, and live by God alone." [6]

It is obvious how painful the long struggle had been for him, a struggle that still continued. "There are never lacking souls who tell everyone who tries to be a hermit that the solitary life is a temptation of the devil. I know I must have the faith to go forward in spite of this accidental opposition . . . yet all the same it is not easy for me. Pray that I may learn to follow Christ." [6]

On August 20th, Archbishop Montini wrote to Merton a kind and considerate letter addressed rather poignantly from an old Camaldolese foundation at Brescia, now bereft of monks but with its chapel intact and a view of the mountains. He spoke with insight and compassion about Merton's longings for solitude, but doubted that a move to the Camaldolese would provide what he sought, partly because the Order itself was in a state of change and uncertainty and great material difficulty, partly because he felt Merton's work was so fruitful where he already was and that his Superior probably had a clearer judgment of the situation than Merton had himself.

Admitting that the final question was what God was guiding Merton to do, the Archbishop nevertheless felt that quite a good way to know this was by submission to the Abbot and to other spiritual masters. And, if this seemed difficult and distasteful, then Merton needed to remember that the growth of the soul had more to do with interior dispositions than with outward circumstances; nobody got precisely the conditions of life they longed for. All in all the Archbishop felt that Gethsemani offered Merton the solitude and silence he needed in order to grow and that his work there would continue to flourish.

Although there is something gentle and good about this letter, and it expresses a heartwarming admiration for Merton's work, it cannot have left Merton with much hope that he would achieve the change he longed for.

By the end of September, the longed-for decision had not been made, although Dom James was now at Citeaux and conferring with the higher Superiors. Merton was feeling the kind of emotional exhaustion that can follow prolonged uncertainty and anxiety.

As far as I know, my Superiors must have decided by now what is to become of me. . . . As time goes on, I begin to think that it is not going to be easy for me to get a real permission to lead the eremitical life here, still less to leave and go to Frascati. By now I think I can say that I have become more or less indifferent. If God wants me to be a solitary, I will be His kind of solitary, no matter what may be the exterior conditions that may be imposed on me. Of this I am certain, and I am beginning to find that as time goes on I do become, inevitably, more and more of a solitary, and that the very moves which are supposed to destroy my tending to solitude have the effect of making me interiorly—and even exteriorly—more of a hermit. Why, then, should I worry much about what is to be done? [6]

The Cistercian Superiors discussed Merton's case at Citeaux, and came up with an answer that sounds very like a punishment, an answer set out by Dom James in a letter to Dom Jean. Sure of the support of the higher Superiors, Dom James now attacked Merton's scheme much more openly and adopted a tone that assumed Dom Jean also held his point of view.

What you say about Father Louis himself is quite true. Too much of an extrovert. I wonder, as you yourself, can he actually give up writing completely?

It is strange, dear Dom Jean, our Most Reverend General, whom perhaps you know, Dom Gabriel Sortais, wrote Father and he also wrote me practically the same conditions, that Father Louis should first give up all writing for five years, that he has worked himself into a great brain fever, and he is blaming everyone else and his surroundings for his lack of peace—which is common to neurotics.

Let him first live the Trappist Life as it is written, giving up all contacts with editors and writers for five years, and then see how he is.

Also, Father Louis may say that the Abbot General feels if it is the will of God, he has no objections against his leaving our Order. However then, Father means, providing he tries to live the life for five years, which is a very important condition.

The more I think of it, Dom Jean, the more I seem to see in Father Louis just a lot of poetical fancy and imaginings, a love of adventure.

He never struck me as being destined for the eremitical life, and I feel, in conscience, that if he were to leave here, for Camaldoli, for example, he would not stay there very long either. Some new wild idea would hit him and off he would go. He would become a roamer, a gypsy.

Yet because of his reputation as a writer and his most skillful use of words, he could convince almost anyone who does not know him. [7]

After fourteen years of patient effort at Gethsemani, Merton was seen by his Abbot and described to others as a harebrained neurotic, with perhaps a touch of the con man about him. Dom James was clearly very angry at the nuisance Merton had caused.

Despite his brave struggle to attain the kind of life he needed, Merton had seriously damaged his position in the monastery by antagonizing his Abbot, and his hopes of the eremitical life had receded further than ever. He would only be permitted to leave the Order after five years of silence, and although he had such serious doubts about continuing as a writer, there was a cruelty in the ban that had no relevance to the issue under discussion and had therefore a suggestion of spite about it. He had achieved nothing.

Towards the end of 1955, the Novice Master at Gethsemani was elected Abbot at a sister house, and acting on an impulse Merton went to Dom James and suggested himself as Novice Master. As a successful Master of Scholastics, he must have been an obvious choice, but it is interesting, in view of the contempt with which Dom James had written about Merton to Dom Jean, that the Abbot agreed with such alacrity to give Merton the third highest position in the monastery. It must have seemed a very welcome solution to a year of conflict.

The job, of course, would be very hard work, and poles away from the solitude Merton craved. It would probably not allow Merton time for writing, but for both external and internal reasons he wanted to give that up anyway. It did mean that he would sleep alone, in a tiny room built over the stairs, and that he would spend most of his time in the novitiate, which itself was a quiet place.

Merton wrote Dom Jean a ruefully sad letter on December 3, 1955. Dom Jean (perhaps to express solidarity with Merton) had written to ask if he could join him in writing a book about the Psalms, and Merton wrote to explain that he was now Master of Novices, and that

> Father Abbot desires me to devote my full time to the souls of my charges. He will not allow me to consider your kind invitation to join you in your project on the psalms, although I want to express my gratitude to you for asking me. . . . I shall cease to be a writer at least as long as I am in charge of the novices. The prospect does not trouble me. I care very little what I do now, so long as it is the will of God.
>
> Will He some day bring me after all to perfect solitude? I do not know. One thing is sure, I have made as much effort in that direction as

one can make without going beyond the limits of obedience. My only task now is to remain quiet, abandoned, and in the hands of God. I have found a surprising amount of interior solitude among my novices, and even a certain exterior solitude which I had not expected. This is, after all, the quietest and most secluded corner of the monastery. So I am grateful to God for fulfilling many of my desires when seeming to deny them. I know that I am closer to Him, and that all my struggles this year formed part of His plan. I am at peace in His will. Thank you for your part in the affair. If you see Dom Maurizio, will you also thank him for all his kindness and for the invitation which, alas, I was unable to accept?

. . . Let us remain united in the Holy Spirit, and await the coming of the Lord with our lamps burning in the night of this world." [8]

It is a dignified letter, from a man who had been humiliated and who, despite pain, was facing the future with as much courage as he could muster.

The old release of writing was now taken from him, partly by his own wish, partly as a condition for achieving the solitude he longed for, and this renunciation had been enforced by the exacting job he had undertaken.

By the middle of 1955, Merton had published ten full-length books on various aspects of spirituality, including his biography and journal. There were also two other books, *The Living Bread* [9] and *The Silent Life* [10] in the pipeline, and a number of pamphlets, articles, and translations published and unpublished. It represented a very large body of work for a man with so little time for writing, a professional output achieved in an amateur's working hours.

Of the books of the early 1950s, *No Man Is an Island*, the only one published in the year of crisis, 1955, is perhaps the most significant pointing to the new Merton struggling to escape, phoenixlike, from the ashes of his old illusion and romanticism about the monastic life, and to learn something new about the universal problem of being a man:

> No matter how ruined man and his world may seem to be, and no matter how terrible man's despair may become, as long as he continues to be a man his very humanity continues to tell him that life has a meaning. That, indeed, is one reason why man tends to rebel against himself. If he could without effort see what the meaning of life is, and if he could fulfil his ultimate purpose without trouble, he would never question the fact that life is well worth living. Or if he saw at once that life had no purpose and no meaning, the question would never arise. In

either case, man would not be capable of finding himself so much of a problem.

Our life, as individual persons and as members of a perplexed and struggling race, provokes us with the evidence that it must have meaning. Part of the meaning still escapes us. Yet our purpose in life is to discover this meaning, and live according to it. We have, therefore, something to live for. The process of living, of growing up, and becoming a person, is precisely the gradually increasing awareness of what that something is. [11]

Merton had also published six books of poetry, the last of them *The Tears of the Blind Lions* in 1949. The poems can give sudden, haunting images of monastic life, intimate insights that it would be much harder to capture in a prose study, or even a journal, as in "The Reader":

Lord, when the clock strikes

Telling the time with cold tin
And I sit hooded in this lectern

Waiting for the monks to come,
I see the red cheeses, and bowls
All smile with milk in ranks upon their tables.

Light fills my proper globe
(I have won light to read by
With a little, tinkling chain)

And the monks come down the cloister
With robes as voluble as water.
I do not see them but I hear their waves. [12]

The heaviness of an August afternoon, just before a thunderstorm, as the monks work in the fields, is also conveyed.

The deaf-and-dumb fields, waiting to be shaved of hay
Suffer the hours like an unexpected sea
While locusts fry their music in the sycamores. [12]

Merton's poems are full of a shining ardour and wonder in life, but they lack the precision and care that would make a full imprint on the reader's mind. The mixing of metaphors in the last quotation, for instance, in which the fields that have been likened to a deaf-mute, yet suddenly turn into an ocean, weakens and disperses the meaning.

Robert Giroux remembers asking T. S. Eliot his opinion of Merton's poetry and receiving the stern reply that he ought to take much more care and publish much less. Robert Lowell had made a similar comment in an early review, and when the big *Collected Poems* [13] came out after Merton's death, others were to endorse this opinion. One reviewer wondered if the truth was not that Merton was a *prose* writer, lacking the special quality of exactness that makes the poet.

To those interested in Merton's life, however, the poems often reveal emotions that might be difficult for him to express elsewhere; compared to his prose work, they were obscure to his superiors, almost as if written in an incomprehensible code. It seems likely that even during the period of the ban on his writing he was still working in this way—poems, in any case, have the advantage that they can be worked on at odd moments between other demands—and the following poem in *Strange Islands* says much about his state of mind at this very difficult stage of his monastic life.

> This afternoon, let me
> Be a sad person. Am I not
> Permitted (like other men)
> To be sick of myself?
>
> Am I not allowed to be hollow,
> Or fall in the hole
> Or break my bones (within me)
> In the trap set by my own
> Lie to myself? O my friend,
> I too must sin and sin.
>
> I too must hurt other people and
> (Since I am no exception)
> I must be hated by them.
>
> Do not forbid me, therefore,
> To taste the same bitter poison,
> And drink the gall that love
> (Love most of all) so easily becomes.
>
> Do not forbid me (once again) to be
> Angry, bitter, disillusioned,
> Wishing I could die.

While life and death
Are killing one another in my flesh,
Leave me in peace. I can enjoy,
Even as other men, this agony.

Only (whoever you may be)
Pray for my soul. Speak my name
To Him, for in my bitterness
I hardly speak to Him: and He
While He is busy killing me
Refuses to listen. [14]

References

1. Thomas Merton. Letter to Dom Jean Leclercq. October 9, 1950. TMSC.
2. Thomas Merton. Letter to Dom Jean Leclercq. April 27, 1955. TMSC.
3. Dom James Fox. Letter to Dom Jean Leclercq. May 18, 1955. TMSC.
4. Dom James Fox. Letter to Cardinal Archbishop Giovanni Montini. May 16, 1955. TMSC.
5. Thomas Merton. Letter to Dom Jean Leclercq. June 3, 1955. TMSC.
6. Thomas Merton. Letter to Dom Jean Leclercq. August 11, 1955. TMSC.
7. Dom James Fox. Letter to Dom Jean Leclercq. June 13, 1955. TMSC.
8. Thomas Merton. Letter to Dom Jean Leclercq. December 3, 1955. TMSC.
9. Thomas Merton. *The Living Bread*. New York: Farrar, Straus, & Cudahy, 1956; Tunbridge Wells, Kent: Burns & Oates, 1976.
10. Thomas Merton. *The Silent Life*. New York: Farrar, Straus, & Cudahy, 1952.
11. Thomas Merton. *No Man Is an Island*. New York: Harcourt Brace, 1955; Tunbridge Wells, Kent: Burns & Oates, 1976.
12. Thomas Merton. *The Tears of the Blind Lions*. New York: New Directions, 1969.
13. Thomas Merton. *The Collected Poems of Thomas Merton*. New York: New Directions, 1977.
14. Thomas Merton. *The Strange Islands*. New York: New Directions, 1957.

15

"ONCE MY MERRY FRIEND"

❦

When Merton became Novice Master in 1955, a number of the novices arriving at Gethsemani had been attracted to monastic life by *The Seven Storey Mountain*. Even those who had were not attracted for this reason had certainly read the book.

The present Abbot, Dom Timothy Kelly, remembers how, coming on a first visit to Gethsemani to see if they would allow him to try his vocation, he was called on at the guest house by a monk who introduced himself as the Master of the Novices. In the course of their conversation, the would-be monk was asked what he had read about religious life; he mentioned Merton's works and those of another Trappist. "What did he think of them?" he was asked. "Rather exaggerated," he replied. "It doesn't do to believe everything you read," the Novice Master agreed with a deadpan expression, and only much later did the candidate discover he had been talking to Thomas Merton. Neither of them ever referred to the incident again.

A monk who entered as a lay brother in 1954 ("I couldn't sing or read Latin, so that pretty well fixed that I should be a lay-brother") had become a monk directly as a result of Merton's influence. A Kansas University graduate, an employee of the Ford Foundation with great ambitions for the future, he was looking for a wife when, at twenty-nine, he read *The Seven Storey Mountain* and decided that Trappist life was the life for him. As a lay brother, he was not in Merton's novitiate, and it was months, in that silent world, before he could even work out which monk Merton was. He had expected him to be tall and handsome and was mildly disappointed when at last, by reading his Latin name by his place in refectory, he discovered who Merton was. So rigid was the silence in those days that the two of them never held an actual conversation (in words as opposed to sign language) until 1967.

Another Father remembers how, when he entered Gethsemani at the age of eighteen, expecting to find Merton serious and mystical-looking, he discovered a teacher who seemed boyish and light-hearted. "The first time I saw him he was bouncing down the cloister making all the signs we weren't supposed to make, and which he bawled us out for making. We were all going into the church and he was going in the opposite direction which I suppose was a part of the joke. He never wanted you to take him too seriously."

He remembers Merton as an extraordinarily lovable man. "Everybody loved him. Some of the monks might think some of his ideas were wild, but he was much loved. You couldn't look up to him as an elder except in his spiritual teaching and his direction."

The feeling of mutual love between master and pupils comes out very strongly in the many tapes of Merton giving "Conferences" or lectures to the novitiate. The audience are appreciative, laughing warmly at his jokes, rising quickly to allusions, occasionally interrupting intelligently. He has a racy and informal style, often using slang, yet revealing deep academic knowledge of his subjects, knowing how to manipulate local jokes or events to make an idea stick, using secular experiences to drive home spiritual truths. And drive them home he did. More than one Father remembers Merton using human love experiences to illustrate spiritual experiences. One of them remembers him warning them about being too analytical about experiences in prayer. "When you're making love to a girl you don't spend your time analyzing the color of her hair!"

Merton's Conferences very often began with some reference that grounded what he was going to say to the world outside—an election, a letter from a friend bringing up a political point, some happening that was raising blood pressure inside the monastery—and he would then go on to integrate such things into the subject he was discussing—the mystical life, asceticism, the Blessed Virgin Mary, St. John's Gospel, martyrdom, the Early Fathers, Pseudo-Dionysius, St. Gregory of Nyssa, St. Maximus, St. Augustine, Eckhart and Tauler, the Spanish mystics, the problems of direction, the spiritual direction of contemplatives, modern psychology as it affected the training and understanding of monasticism, and much else.

Threaded through these subjects, each with its enormous background of reading, was an incidental wisdom that was there for the novice to accept or ignore as he wished. Merton was generous with his own painfully acquired insights, and he had a courageous way of getting to the root of any particular problem. "You're perfectly happy. You don't think so, but you are. You'll look back in twenty years and say 'Weren't those the days?'" [1] And "Most of the problems of the Church start with Charlemagne." [1] Merton said, "Why do you get temptations when you go to bed? You're yielding yourself to semi-consciousness and unconsciousness, and your will doesn't work as normal. To some degree you are helpless. You are giving over control to somebody else, it might as well be God. . . . The problem for monks is thoughts. Don't let them grow. The problem for seculars may be action. . . . The will isn't too wonderful. You need knowledge. Will can be wrongly applied. What is needed is understanding. You must have both *understanding* and will." [1] Of monasticism, he said, "There's a lot of external obedience but not a lot of internal obedience. . . . In addition to obedience we have to think. . . . If we are griping about anything, we are griping about poverty right there." [1]

The voice was youthful and brisk. He was very fond of inserting the word *see*: "See, there was this fellow who thought that . . . see," and part of the fascination of his lecturing style was his burning wish that his audience should see what he saw. In the middle of a lecture on the role of learning in the contemplative life—"There's no contemplative life without learning. . . . Not everybody in the monastery has to be learned, but some people in the monastery have to be learned" [1]—he digressed into the details of a "horrendous" restaurant he had heard about at Omaha—"I won't tell you what they serve there, it's that bad" and an awful meal he once had on an airplane. Then he was back to the importance of sharing the good things of the mind—"I'm not preaching anything, see"—threw in an aside that went down well with his audience, "We're always struggling with a certain amount of frustration here," and came up with yet another example: "This poor dope, see, he didn't have any science, he wasn't educated." [1]

Merton's manner was deceptively light and easy to listen to; and only toward the end of each lecture did he gather up the diverse threads, and his audience discover, to their pleasure and surprise, that they actually knew something about Origen, or Evagrius, or the Cistercian Fathers.

In the middle of his usual plea for authenticity, that the novices should be who they are and no one else, Merton suddenly digressed into asking how many of them that morning noticed that the night-blooming cactus had flowered. "The most beautiful flower I ever saw in my life—great white flowers. It blooms in the dark—the most spiritual type of flower I ever saw. Deserts are full of these darned things and nobody ever sees them but the rattlesnakes." [1]

On the Feast of St. Louis, the day that had been such an ordeal when his brethren made him wear "finery" to celebrate Mass, he was moved to audible tears at all the cards and notes the novices had sent him. "I get overwhelmed with sensible consolations every year on the Feast of St. Louis. Why don't you do it everyday?" [1]

A monk who came to Gethsemani, already simply professed in another Order, but, as a junior, permitted to attend Merton's Conferences, remembers the shock of seeing him at work in the Conference hall:

> I had expected somebody a bit emaciated, austere, ascetic, rather severe, the "ideal" monk . . . and here was Merton freely making jokes, very much at ease with the group, very responsive to them. I was always astonished how he seemed to know what we were thinking, what our doubts and questions were, and how he would qualify what he said so he seemed to be speaking right to you. He was able to talk about something quite different from what he had originally planned if it began to seem important—his digressions were often the best part. This jovial man, kind of chubby, who could laugh about all kinds of things, some of them which in other circles would have been thought very improper, and yet he was a prophet.
>
> His jolliness bothered me and I remember saying to my Junior Master that Merton didn't seem to me to be very ascetic, and he replied that he thought he was the most ascetic man in the monastery. He meant partly because his health wasn't good—he had lived through a very strict regime at the monastery and come through it very humanly, but also intellectually if he took something up he would pursue it as far as he possibly could, till he really did the subject justice. He really disciplined himself in his study and in the use of his time. What was very important to me was the depth of his reading in the Fathers of the Church—not just one or two of them, but a very wide knowledge. Anyone who exposes themselves to that knows a lot about what it means to be a Christian—it is so simple in one way, but also very complex.

Merton saw each of the novices for private conversation once a week. One of his novices remembers that it "started out pretty cool." "He might ask you how things were going at work, or something fairly external, and then somewhere along the line he would say 'Well, how're you getting along then?' and then you could start talking about yourself. He was hard on anything that seemed affected, or 'flim-flam' about spirituality, but the attitude was usually friendly and casual. You felt uplifted, spiritually invigorated."

A monk who was a novice at seventeen remembers how well Merton understood the adolescent outlook. "You think you're old, and you also think you may be better than other people. There were times when I can remember him explicitly making adjustments to my youth, but I think he related to me primarily as a spiritual being—I had a spiritual life and he recognized that. There is a certain kind of adulthood in that, and he saw that, and I always felt appreciated on that level. Whatever else he may have thought about other levels, somehow there was this real, deep respect."

An older monk felt himself, at these encounters, placed against the whole backdrop of Christianity and found it reassuring. "What kind of person was I in this situation? I felt that he had sized me up, that he knew where I was, and what direction I ought to be going in. He just hinted at a couple of things—he wasn't dominating—but I sensed he knew what was going on in me."

One Father remembers how oppressed he was in his early days at Gethsemani by the silence, the loneliness, the absence of women, and how in despair he confided all this to Merton. "He entered into it so completely that I felt wholly understood. It helped, but it also made me aware that I wouldn't have been able to keep up a close relationship with him all the time. His understanding of me was too complete."

Merton had a device that is differently remembered by different members of the monastery of "bouncing off" criticism on various fellow monks, or off the life of the monastery itself.

> He would say "This is an awfully artificial life we're leading here" and you were supposed to take that as a warning not to play those kind of games yourself. Another way of doing things was to criticize a third party. He would say how so-and-so used to come to choir and he would get this loathing for the man standing next to him in choir. He'd say, "That's just narcissism, see. What he's doing is just looking down his nose at the other guy. Comparing himself to the other person. Don't do what he's doing." It was a very nice way of letting *me* know that that's what I was doing.

It had its dangers, because if you were too immature you started projecting it all on these other guys, whereas his real message was aimed at you. Sometimes the device worked; sometimes it didn't and people tended to project their problems on other people and think "We're not like that. We're spiritually enlightened."

He did enjoy doing it; he was very good at criticism, very good at seeing through people. Some of the old-timers in the monastery were overly religious; that was something to gripe about and he would do it.

A further danger of this kind of criticism was that novices who had heard Merton's blistering comments on a third party became very frightened of incurring his criticism themselves. One man, who at one stage was Merton's Under Master of Novices, found himself inhibited in his job by his fear of Merton's judgement. In other ways he liked working with him—Merton would always be loyal to him both with the novices and with higher authority, but he feared Merton's insights. He also found the speed of Merton's mind difficult to deal with. Merton would change his mind about something concerning the novices and forget to tell him because by then his thoughts had passed on elsewhere.

Inside the monastery, Merton was establishing himself as a very good Novice Master—intellectually, spiritually, psychologically, and humanly, equal, and more than equal, to his task—and much loved, more than he was perhaps able to appreciate, in and out of the novitiate. How would an outsider have seen him? In January 1956, Mark and Dorothy Van Doren came to Gethsemani on a visit, and afterward Mark sent Merton a letter and a poem describing the experience. Mark could not be described as objective—he had retained a deep love for Merton over the years, a love that included a penetrating insight into what Merton was trying to do with his life. It is clear from Mark's letter that Merton was still in pain over the rejection of his idea about living as a hermit, that he shared this pain with Mark, and that they corresponded about it afterward. Mark sends the poem shyly, as an attempt to reassure Merton in his sadness.

Dear Tom,
This is your poem if you want it. . . . I hesitated to impose it on you at Christmas. I hesitated anyway, yet here it is as a kind of answer to your recent letter. I thought you might not mind knowing how you *looked* down there, and I assume still do. Such things as *looks* can be important facts, not discoverable except through others. I am

terribly interested in what you tell me about your wrestling over solitude again. I don't pretend to understand it all, but with your suffering I have, believe me, the fullest and tenderest sympathy. And I can doubt that you are washed literally of everything. You couldn't be, and I dare to say, shouldn't be. For instance, of your created person. Which is why I send the poem—to show that someone saw that person.

Love, Mark. [2]

This letter was scribbled in at the bottom of a sheet of paper on which Mark had typed a poem called "Once in Kentucky."

In our fat times a monk:
I had not thought to see one;
Nor, even with my own poor lean concerns,
Ever to be one.

No. But in Kentucky,
Midway of sweet hills,
When housewives swept their porches, and March light
Lapped windowsills.

He, once my merry friend,
Came to the stone door,
And the only difference in his smiling was,
It sorrowed more.

No change in him, except
His merriment was graver.
As if he knew now where it started from;
And what the flavor.

He tasted it, the joy,
Then gave it all to me:
As much, I mean, as I could carry home
To this country,

To this country whose laughter
Is a fat thing, and dies.
I step across its body and consider,
Still, those eyes. [2]

Much later Mark Van Doren described the circumstances of that visit. The Van Dorens were visiting Hodgenville, Lincoln's birthplace, which is only a few miles away from Gethsemani, and Merton had permission to receive them, although it was Lent.

> When Merton came, grinning, to shake our hands and make us welcome, I was stupid enough to be startled because he had altered in no respect from the mirthful student I once knew. Thirteen years had passed, and of course he looked a little older; but as we sat and talked I could see no important difference in him, and once I interrupted a reminiscence of his by laughing. "Tom," I said, "you haven't changed at all." "Why should I? Here," he said, "our duty is to be more ourselves, not less." It was a searching remark and I stood happily corrected. Then he conducted me through the monastery while Dorothy waited among the books and pictures in the visitors' quarters. He showed me the church, the refectory, the classrooms where he instructed novices, and the library whose books and manuscripts he had in charge. Later he proposed that all three of us drive to inspect the new tobacco barn that the monks had built out of oak trees cut on the premises. After lunch, which we had by ourselves in a guest house overlooking the roofs of Gethsemani, we came back to meet another man, a lay brother who had known Carl in New York—and who in his time had been a figure among the theatres of Broadway: he had even written dialogue for Beatrice Lillie, who only a few weeks ago was here to see him.
>
> When we left at last, Merton took us to the car and sent special messages to Krutch and Thurber, whom he knew I liked. . . . My final thought as I looked back and waved was about how wrong anyone would be who considered him a prisoner in that place. He seemed a happy man if I ever saw one: serene and certain, grave and smiling, utterly serious and utterly free. The poem, "Once in Kentucky," which I eventually wrote and sent him was acknowledged by the statement, made of course in another world than mine, that it is always interesting to learn what one looks like from the outside. [3]

Robert Lax also responded to Merton's need for love and encouragement with wonderful letters that never referred to Merton's troubles except obliquely, but were full of jokes, allusions, gossip about old friends, and loving concern. At Christmas, he wrote,

> ho Merton,
>
> from the middle of the storm i salute you.
> dying, we praise thee.
> from under the rocks we garble our words at thee.
> Merry Christmas.

Iucille is undone.
gorbuduc is take in the wash.
anaheim swings on sticks up rivington street.
little may is more diminutive than ever, and you
can imagine how diminutive *that* would be.

as to the game-warden (miss naomi burton) she'll have more plovers to
her covey, I'll warrant, than grouse in the heather or grackle in the
wold.

the sheriff of nottingham (you remember) or rather the sheriff of
nottingham's horse has had dick whittington's mouser muzzled.

in any case, Merry Christmas.

Iittle Dorritt is al bemused, etc.

reinhardt (a very airdrome of the graces) would send thee a picture, a
very small picture (block on block) of verticals and horizontals cross-
ing. . . .

. karl stern was here a couple of days ago, a nice, nice fellow who
thinks of you all the time. he would like to write you, even post-cards
and he wonders if he could.

he is like someone we might have gone to villanova with.

N—— and G—— are all divorced; he on the island; she in boston
with the children. he is very, very sad; and she very far from trium-
phant.

(a constant desire to defeat himself, was
she felt, what finally defeated him). reinhardt is wonderful.
really think he likes you, rice, etc. better than anybody, and is
always news of the aungels.

i am wishing i could see you again for the mere delight of it; perhaps in
spring, perhaps in summer, perhaps in the following fall.

madame lubienska tells the following after-dinner speech:

a man goes to his confessor and says:
i can't love God.
and the confessor says:
all right, then, let Him
love you.

of course it's much better in russian.

all the world sends Merry Christmas, rings bells, says prayers. sing
with us, then, from thy comparative solitudes.

Lv,

Lax. [4]

Despite the love and encouragement of his friends and the
success of his work with the novices, Merton was still not really
out of crisis. Partly, perhaps, in the need to understand more about
the psychology of his novices, but also in an attempt to resolve his
own depression, he began to take an interest in psychology. He
gave himself a Rorschach test, and decided that what he needed was
analysis, developments that Naomi Burton commented on forth-
rightly, yet with an underlying sympathy in a letter of May 1956.
"My personal opinion is that you need analysis, and your dreams
interpreted, like you need a hole in the head. You have become
involved in it all because of the ban on writing. It's another way of
writing, of self-expression, isn't it?" Later in that letter she commented, "You dream of journeys you are not allowed to take." [5]
    Merton had written to the psychoanalyst Gregory Zilboorg
asking for advice about reading, and also, it would appear, for
some light on his problems. About Freud, Dr. Zilboorg wrote,

> The reading of Freud is not very useful when one's self is in a state of
> being disconcerted by the problems of which you and I are talking.
> Freud takes too much for granted and it would seem that only someone
> with a background of having been analyzed can read the writings with
> real benefit. *The Psychopathology of Everyday Life* is good reading. Then
> the *Three Contributions*. After that I would leave Freud alone and turn to
> the *Collected Papers of Abraham*. You are right—Fenichel is heavy,
> literal and dull—not very imaginative. After *Abraham* I would read
> Anna Freud's *The Ego and Its Defences*. Then we could talk again. [6]

Zilboorg mentions to Merton that he holds courses in psychiatry
for religious in Collegeville, Minnesota, and that other Cistercians
come to them. "Last year we had three Trappists in Collegeville
taking the course. They came from your daughter house in Georgia."
Zilboorg mentions the possibility of his coming to Gethsemani in an
attempt to persuade Dom James to allow Merton to go. [6]
    Perhaps from fear of losing Merton altogether, Dom James did
let Merton go to Collegeville, where he stayed at St. John's Abbey,
the Benedictine house, and attended workshops, by Zilboorg and

others, on psychiatry and pastoral care. Merton knew himself to be in crisis. Without either solitude or writing to ease his tensions, and with a workload as heavy as it had ever been, he teetered on the edge of breakdown. But he still tried to "submit" to what his superiors demanded of him. "I grow closer to the state," he wrote to Dom Jean, "in which nothing at all is written. I have not attempted anything like a book since I became novice master. But with the inveterate itch of the writer I have turned some novitiate conference into a pamphlet. Of this too, I shall soon be cured."[7] Perhaps only Mark Van Doren and Naomi Burton, among his immediate friends, knew something of his inner suffering.

There is a photograph of Merton with Zilboorg and others at the Collegeville Conference, looking overweight, and clutching a bottle of beer. A naturally photogenic man, extraordinarily vivid in so many pictures of him, in this one he looks distant, abstracted, maybe sad.

His encounters with Zilboorg at Collegeville were not happy. Zilboorg was a fashionable psychoanalyst, who had made a name for himself as a skilful analyst of well known writers and artists and others. He was a Jew who had recently converted to Catholicism; it may or may not be fair to guess that like many recent converts he was idealistic about his adopted religion, and particularly idealistic about the monastic life. Certainly he seemed to bring a particular sort of bias to the whole discussion.

Whether or not this was the case, at his first private meeting with Merton he launched into an extraordinary personal attack of a kind unusual in a profession one of whose principal techniques is silence and listening. He had disliked an article that Merton had sent him and was adamant that he must not publish it—he was also critical of Merton's conversation with a third party he had over-heard at dinner—and he now informed him that he was neurotic, narcissistic, possibly megalomaniac, hung up on fame and publicity, a "gadfly to his superiors", a man determined to get his own way, and one who used words as a "substitute for reality", whose interest in being a hermit was bogus, and who was incapable of loving.

It is almost impossible to imagine a more devastating set of statements, the more so since there were small half truths in among the huge assertions. Not surprisingly Merton was very upset and crept away to the lake to write it all down in a rather bravely humble spirit, though while the onslaught was going on he caught himself muttering "Stalin, Stalin!" inside himself. (Zilboorg did have a physical resemblance to Stalin.) Zilboorg's conversion seemed to have had a strange effect on his analytical method.

But Merton was always perversely capable of getting enthusiastic about direct criticism of him, and, once over the first shock, he rallied and decided that every word must be true. He wrote to Naomi Burton the next day giving wholesale credence to Zilboorg's sweeping views, and saying that they had cured him of the desire to be a hermit.

So things might have remained if the next day Zilboorg had not behaved in a way that even Merton could not tolerate, or pretend was within the limits of a professional relationship. Zilboorg invited Dom James, who had just arrived at the Conference, to sit in on a meeting with Merton and then, incredibly, began freely to discuss the issues that he and Merton had spoken about privately. Merton began audibly to mutter "Stalin!" Then, humiliatingly, he began to cry, of grief, or rage, or both, but Zilboorg in no way spared him, asserting according to Michael Mott, "You want a hermitage in Times Square with a large sign over it saying 'Hermit'."

Not surprisingly, although Zilboorg seemed to have long-term plans for Merton to go to New York and embark on an analysis, their relationship ended right there. Robert Giroux, who was Zilboorg's publisher, had noted earlier that Zilboorg seemed to have an alarming number of preconceptions about Merton before he ever met him.

Merton struggled on unaided with his psychological problems and with his physical problems too. His health in general was poor, and during 1957 he went into hospital to be operated on for haemorrhoids. Lax had also been in hospital, with bad arthritis, and he wrote Merton one of his cheering letters from Olean House, where he was recuperating with Benjy and Gladio.

Ho, ho,

I had to larf when I seen you was at the Flageolet Memorial Hospital. It certainly is the year of the wood-mouse what with you and me and Monsignor Ed Coogan all laid up with our feet in the air. And no place to go.

I too was king of the sitz baths for about a month at the Corps. The tub I sat in was a furnished pail, furnished, that is, by the laundry-nuns who in a fit of self-abnegation gave up all their travaux for at least 3 weeks while I languished, read novels, ate Milky Ways. (However, I must tell you, dear gossip, I never went under the knife). . . .

I visited only yesterday (on my way to the unbenders) a few of the old haunts: river, Swatt's groceries, Lippert's and the mined road to Healey's. Then over the hill to the Bradford General Hosp.

Someone told Rice I was running around with arthritis and he says: you have to watch out for those Greek girls. . . . Am glad you had a dream about him, sorry you forgot it. What would have happened if St. John the Apocalyse didn't remember his dreams? Must close now as the entire household slumbers. Nothing so disturbing to a profound but uneven snore as the scratch-scratch scratching of an underwater pencil. . . .

                    and so I am

                              most exceedingly yours,

enclosures will fly after   Bishop Milligan [8]

Dom Jean was another faithful friend. Merton had heard of how a monk in the Benedictine order had recently been allowed to become a hermit and wrote longingly about it to him. "I was overwhelmed and edified by Dom Winandy's retirement to solitude. Clearly your order is much more clearsighted than ours. You have the flexibility which we so sadly, so miserably, lack. I am afraid there is a rigidity endemic in the very structure of the Cistercian Order which in the end will stifle all serious development in the right direction. True, it also prevents development in the wrong direction. At least a negative advantage. . . . May I ask your prayers for a new hope of mine—that perhaps some day we may make a foundation in the Andes, and that I may be sent there if God wills. Again, if we were only a little more flexible, we could do it tomorrow. However, the Lord is bringing us good postulants from Latin America and I am sure the project will one day mature." [9]

It is interesting to speculate on what Dom James must have thought when he read this letter, as he almost certainly did. Merton might be "submitting" but he was showing an independence of thought he had never revealed before, and a willingness to criticize.

Moreover, the postulants coming from Latin America were filling his mind with new dreams. An indication of a deep change in Merton's attitude was given in *Basic Principles of Monastic Spirituality* (the Conferences to the novices he had mentioned to Dom Jean). [10] His old love of the monastic life was as much in evidence as ever, but something new was mixed with it. The loneliness of his suffering and his sense of injustice had matured the trusting, childlike Merton who was prepared to accept anything his superiors did as right. Nothing was blindly accepted any more. He was now asking what the monastic life is supposed to achieve and whether life as lived at Gethsemani helps or hinders it.

In one sense, he felt the monastic life is what it always was. "It is a life totally abandoned to the Holy Spirit, a life of humility, obedience, solitude, silence, prayer, in which to renounce our own desires and our own ways in order to live in the liberty of the sons of God."[10] That is the general answer, but the individual monk must ask himself what he is doing in the monastery, not just at the beginning, but again and again during his life there. "Not that it is a question whose answer we have known but tend to forget. It is question which confronts us with a new meaning and a new urgency, as we go on in life." [10]

In the main, Merton saw the answer in the area of "a search for God and not a mission to accomplish this or that work for souls." Part of this seeking is in contemplating the Word in nature, in the hills, fields, flowers, birds and animals, the sky and the trees. "Hence in the monastic life, our senses are *educated* and elevated rather than destroyed." Part of the seeking is in the movement toward virginity, or wholeness. "The first step is the total acceptance of all the parts of our being—body and soul, mind and instinct, emotions and will, in order to give all to God in the harmony of a balanced and spiritualized personality." [10]

But the monastic life does not always help those who live it toward that precious wholeness. "Some souls full of good will and generosity embrace the monastic life, only to find their good will dissipated in futilities and in routine." [10]

Yet it was not that Merton believed in rebellion for its own sake; on the contrary, he had a deep awareness of the need for the soul to submit itself to the will of God. Writing with his usual deep feeling when he mentioned the Mother of God, he said that it is in her that the monk finds his perfect model.

The whole monastic life is lived in and with Mary the Virgin Mother who has given us the Word Incarnate. She is the model and the summary of all monastic spirituality, and the fathers could call her the "rule of monks"—Maria regula monachorum. . . . In such a life, we are completely conformed to the Virgin Mother of God, who by the perfect simplicity of her faith received into her Immaculate Heart the full light of the Word. . . . Hence to live "in the spirit" is in effect to live in and by Mary, the Bride of the Holy Spirit. Life in the Spirit is a life which she herself has obtained for us and given to us as Mediatrix of all grace. The movements of our life in the Spirit are directed by her motherly heart. To acknowledge Mary perfectly as our Queen is then to abandon ourselves entirely to the action of the Holy Spirit, who comes to us through her. If Mary becomes our Queen and our "Rule," the inspirations of the Holy Spirit will tend more and more to reproduce in our lives the virginal detachment and the pure love of God which led Mary to submit her whole being entirely to the will of God . . . we will give ourselves as she did. [10]

Merton had always had a deep devotion to the Virgin, but now there seemed to be a widening of his perception about the feminine in religion and in life. He had become friends with Victor Hammer, a Catholic artist and book designer, and Hammer had written to ask about Hagia Sophia, the "Wisdom" aspect of God. Merton replied in a letter of deep conviction and feeling:

The first thing to be said of course is that Hagia Sophia is God Himself. God is not only Father but a Mother. He is both at the same time, and it is the "feminine aspect" or Feminine principle in the divinity that is the Hagia Sophia. But of course as soon as you say this the whole thing becomes misleading: a division of an "abstract" divinity into two abstract principles. Nevertheless, to ignore this distinction is to lose touch with the fullness of God. This is a very ancient intuition of reality which goes back to the oldest Oriental thought. . . . For the "masculine-feminine" relationship is basic in all reality—simply because all reality mirrors the reality of God.

In its most primitive aspect, Hagia Sophia is the dark, nameless *Ousia* (substance) of the Father, the Son and the Holy Ghost, the incomprehensible, "primordial" darkness which is infinite light. The Three Divine Persons each at the same time are Sophia and manifest her. But where the Sophia of your picture comes in, is this: the wisdom of God, "reaching from end to end mightily" is also the Tao, the nameless pivot of all being and nature, the center and meaning of all, that which is the smallest and poorest and most humble of all: the "feminine child" playing before God the Creator in His universe, "playing before him at all times, playing in the world" (Proverbs 8). . . . This feminine principle in the universe is the inexhaustible source of creative realizations of the Father's glory in the world and is in fact the manifestation of His glory. Pushing it further, Sophia in ourselves is the *mercy* of God, the tenderness which by infinitely mysterious power of pardon turns the darkness of our sins into the light of God's love.

Hence, Sophia is the feminine, dark, yielding, tender counterpart of the power, justice, creative dynamism of the Father. [11]

That the feminine occupied Merton a great deal at this stage of his life is apparent in many of his dreams. One such dream he described in a letter to Boris Pasternak, inspired by Pasternak's own description of Lara, the anima figure of *Dr. Zhivago*:

One night I dreamt that I was sitting with a very young Jewish girl of fourteen or fifteen, and that she suddenly manifested a very deep and pure affection for me and embraced me so that I was moved to the depths of my soul. I learned that her name was "Proverb," which I thought very simple and beautiful. And also I thought "She is of the race of Saint Anne." I spoke to her of her name, and she did not seem to be proud of it, because it seemed that other young girls mocked her for it. But I told her that it was a very beautiful name, and there the dream ended. A few days later when I happened to be in a nearby city, which is very rare for us, I was walking alone in the crowded street and suddenly saw that everybody was Proverb and that in all of them shone her extraordinary beauty and purity and shyness, even though they did not know who they were and were perhaps ashamed of their names— because they were mocked on account of them. And they did not know their real identity as the Child so dear to God who, from the beginning, was playing in His sight all days, playing in the world.

Thus you are initiated into the scandalous secret of a monk who is in love with a girl, and a Jew at that! One cannot expect much from monks these days. The heroic asceticism of the past is no more. [1]

The mention of the "yin-yang" complement of reality in the letter to Victor Hammer reveals that Merton was already exploring Eastern religion and was trying to see how the languages of different religions contradicted or complemented one another. According to Edward Rice, Merton had already been studying for some years the work of Patanjali, the Hindu writer, and toward the end of the 1950s he started a correspondence about Zen with D. T. Suzuki.

He was still thinking a good deal about becoming a hermit, trying desperately to batten down his longings for solitude in his extremely busy life. When he heard news from Dom Jean of Dom Winandy, the hermit in Martinique, in May 1959, he sent a longing reply. "I hope he will pray for me. . . . I naturally keep a certain desire for solitude in my heart and cannot help but hope that some day it will be realized. But I no longer have any thought or desire of transferring to another Order. I believe that to move from one institution to another is simply futile. I do not believe that there is any institutional solution for me. I can hope, however, that perhaps I might get permission to live alone, in the shadow of this monastery, if my Superiors will ever permit it." [13]

In the course of that summer, however, his longings for solitude and his exhaustion grew more intense, and he felt himself near to breakdown. He consulted Jean Daniélou (later Cardinal Daniélou) who suggested, mildly enough, that it might help Merton to get away from the monastery occasionally for a change of scene and ideas. As before, in a time of near desperation, Merton wrote to Dom Jean, and Dom Jean sent a sympathetic reply. This never reached Merton, however, since Dom James, on reading it, decided to return it to the writer: "I deemed it better not to give it to him as you had written it." [14] Dom Jean had offended by referring to Merton's "vocation as hermit," and Dom James would prefer him not to refer to this in future—if he wished to continue corresponding with Father Louis, perhaps he would be kind enough to rewrite his letter?

Deprived of confidants about his problems within the monastic framework, Merton went to consult Dr. James Wygal, the psychiatrist in Louisville whom he used for novices who needed psychological help. Wygal's verdict was, as he wrote later to Daniélou, reassuring:

> I have consulted the psychiatrist in Louisville who tells me that I am not neurotic and that my problem here in the monastery is quite a natural reaction to the situation. He feels, as you did last year, that it would help me to get away from the monastery now and again and renew my perspective. He also suggested the possibility of my withdrawing to the mountains of Kentucky to found a small annex to my own monastery for the purposes I had originally, remarking that since

the "glory" of this would redound on the monastery there might be less objection to it. I have not given the matter much thought because I don't think the proposal would be well received and at any rate I am not prepared to make it at this time as I have no plan, and do not feel like making one. I shall just continue with things as they are, for they are passable, and the work I am doing is clearly God's will. . . .

One thing, though; I wish some day I could get away on a really useful trip—something that would contribute to my monastic education and life. For instance to Mt. Athos for the millenary celebration. Or perhaps to Oxford for the International Patristic Conference, or something like that. I would prefer it to be a monastic journey, especially in the east . . . but I do not dare to suggest such a thing. Later the man in Louisville is going to suggest this himself to Father Abbot. I shall not try to push my own ideas. [15]

Wygal confirms that this was his view of Merton's situation, that Merton struck him as one of the least neurotic personalities he had known, with an exceptional capacity to relate to others, and that he felt him gravely underestimated and misunderstood by his Abbot. (It is worth mentioning that Wygal is a Catholic and is basically sympathetic to the ideals of the monastic life.)

But either from fear of losing Merton, or concern that news of his plight was spreading to other houses and to Rome itself, Dom James at last made a grudging move to give Merton a little of the solitude he craved. The Abbey had, largely through Merton's instigation, begun a series of ecumenical conversations with local, non-Catholic churches. Because these often delicate conversations could not be carried on uninterrupted, or unoverheard, in the guest house, it seemed a good idea to erect a building for the purpose, and a site was chosen on a hillside about ten minutes' walk from the Abbey. Merton was told—it is difficult to see it as much more than a bone thrown to a whining dog—that he might use this building when it was not in use, not to live there, but for prayer or for writing and reading. He persisted in seeing it as a hermitage. In December 1960, he wrote to Dom Jean,

My personal problems seem to be working themselves out in a way. A very fine little hermitage has been built in a nice site, it is for the purpose of "rencontres" and conversations with protestant ministers and professors, but it also serves for solitude and I have at least a limited permission to use it part time. This is to a great extent a hopeful solution and I find that if I can have at least *some* real solitude and silence it makes a tremendous difference. It can at least help to stave off the kind of crisis that arose in 1959 when I felt it was necessary to change my situation and go elsewhere. As long as this solution exists, this can be avoided. [16]

References

1. Thomas Merton. Tapes. TMSC.
2. Mark Van Doren. Letter to Thomas Merton. December 1, 1956. TMSC.
3. Mark Van Doren. "A Note (and Poem) by Mark Van Doren on Thomas Merton." *Voyages* 1(1).
4. Robert Lax. Letter to Thomas Merton. Noel 1956. TMSC.
5. Naomi Burton. Letter to Thomas Merton. May 12, 1956. TMSC.
6. Gregory Zilboorg. Letter to Thomas Merton. June 6, 1956. TMSC.
7. Thomas Merton. Letter to Dom Jean Leclercq. Late 1955. TMSC.
8. Robert Lax. Letter to Thomas Merton. Thanksgiving Day, 1957. TMSC.
9. Thomas Merton. Letter to Dom Jean Leclercq. November 13, 1957. TMSC.
10. Thomas Merton. *Basic Principles of Monastic Spirituality*. Bardstown, Ky.: Abbey of Our Lady of Gethsemani (Trappist), 1957.
11. Thomas Merton. Letter to Victor Hammer. May 14, 1959. TMSC. Published in *Boris Pasternak—Thomas Merton. Six Letters* (Lexington: King Library Press, 1973), pp. 11-12.
12. Thomas Merton. Letter to Boris Pasternak. October 23, 1958. TMSC.
13. Thomas Merton. Letter to Dom Jean Leclercq. May 22, 1959. TMSC.
14. Dom James Fox. Letter to Dom Jean Leclercq. November 9, 1959. TMSC.
15. Thomas Merton. Letter to Cardinal Jean Daniélou. April 21, 1960. TMSC.
16. Thomas Merton. Letter to Dom Jean Leclercq. December 1960. TMSC.

16

UNCLE LOUIE

❦

At the beginning of the 1960s, Merton was still Novice Master, was retiring whenever he could do so to the ecumenical meeting-house in the woods, but was taking his expected part in the life of the monastery. His determination not to write any more books had in a sense been honoured—he had undertaken no major work—but all the same writing had crept up on him, and to the outside world it must have seemed as if Merton was writing as usual. *The Secular Journal* had appeared, and a selection of his poems, and short essays about the Nativity, and about a Chinese parable. There was also a photographic essay about life at Gethsemani, with photographs by Shirley Burden, and a short text by Merton. In 1960, six books appeared by him, none written as a book, but each a collection of essays, the weightiest of them being *Disputed Questions* [1]. There was also *The Wisdom of the Desert* [2], a set of translations by Merton of stories about the Alexandrian Fathers, with a perceptive introduction.

What must have been becoming obvious to Merton and even to his Superiors was that he could not *not* write. Place a ban on writing books, and essays, introductions, lectures, and translations flowed from his pen, many of them much more readable than his major works, full of sudden unexpected insights, like his lectures. It is interesting that, without the pressing need for money that often pushes writers into print, Merton felt a need to write so continually; Robert Giroux suggests that it was a release from tension, one without which Merton simply could not survive. It happened almost by itself, whatever resolutions he made, or strictures were laid on him. Merton wrote,

> If the monastic life is a life of hardship and sacrifice, I would say that for me most of the hardship has come in connection with writing. It is possible to doubt whether I have become a monk (a doubt I have to live with), but it is not possible to doubt that I am a writer, that I was born one and will most probably die as one. Disconcerting, disedifying as it

is, this seems to be my lot and my vocation. . . . I have also had to accept the fact that my life is almost totally paradoxical. I have also had to learn gradually to get along without apologising for the fact, even to myself. . . . It is in the paradox itself, the paradox which was and still is a source of insecurity, that I have come to find the greatest security. I have become convinced that the very contradictions in my life are in some ways signs of God's mercy to me: if only because someone so complicated and so prone to confusion and self-defeat could hardly survive for long without special mercy. [3]

This is a humble and honest statement and is extraordinarily revealing of Merton's innermost self. Whatever else he was or wasn't, whatever else he could or couldn't do, he was a writer; that was his fundamental vocation.

At around this time a curious link grew up between him and another born writer, Flannery O'Connor, which worked by proxy through their mutual friend Robert Giroux. Giroux writes that "over the years I came to see how much the two had in common—a highly developed sense of comedy, deep faith, great intelligence. The aura of aloneness surrounding each of them was not an accident. It was their metier, in which they refined and deepened their very different talents in a short span of time. . . . Finally they were both as American as can be." [4]

Each of them was intensely curious about the other, prompting Robert Giroux to tell anecdotes and give details. He told Flannery about Merton's life at Gethsemani, with its silence and structure, and of how, when he gave Merton a recording of Edith Sitwell reading *Façade*, he played it over and over, laughing so much that the tears ran down his cheeks. He told Merton on the other hand (in response to close questioning) about Flannery's home at Milledgeville in Georgia, with its collection of peacocks, and at Merton's request he took a presentation copy of one of his books to give to Flannery.

Merton's gifts as a teacher were as great as his gifts as a writer. As Novice Master, he was now widely known as "Uncle Louie," a "character" who was a tremendous influence on the young men under his care. The young monks were now beginning to go to Rome for some of their studies, which produced a very different atmosphere around the monastery from the old, closed world. Merton wrote asking them questions about their courses and the conversations they were having, keeping them in touch with developments at Gethsemani, and revealing the kind of comradely concern that made him so loved: "Be good, keep your feet dry, your eyes open, your heart at peace and your soul in the joy of Christ." [5] He mentions, in November 1962, the possible amalgamation of the two novitiates, the novitiates for lay brothers and for choir monks. "It would be a logical time to fire me, and I would be delighted. However, we will see what comes. I think it is going to be a pretty delicate operation and it will have to be done slowly and carefully and without false optimism and easy clichés, or celebrations of Sunday school euphoria." [5] Letters came back for Merton telling him of the latest developments in the Catholic world, of the process of change beginning that was to lead into the Vatican II council and beyond. Merton began to talk to his students about politics—partly to offer a radical point of view in contrast to the conservatism of the Abbot's political viewpoint—and about art.

During the "suffering" years of the 1950s, and in particular during the great conflict about going to the Camaldolese, Merton had changed enormously. He was no longer dutiful, no longer worried about being a "good monk" or even a "good Catholic," and no longer "pious" in the old priggish sense. He was now sharp and sometimes bitter—his old, blind trust of authority had gone for good—he thought and questioned with enormous vigour. Part of his questioning was about the structure of life within the monastery itself. He was becoming fierce in his increasing condemnation of mechanization within the monastery. The Abbot was using the considerable business expertise of some of his monks to modernize the methods by which the farm was run, and to establish a thriving business in cheese and fruitcake. Merton attacked the boredom and lifelessness of the work many of the monks were now obliged to do, and also the intolerable noise of the new farm machinery, which broke the old contemplative peace.

Merton was critical, too, of what he called the "overcontrol" of the monks. He saw novices give up and leave the monastery not, it seemed to him, because they were unsuited to the contemplative life, but because they sensed an unreality in the way life was being lived at Gethsemani. "The old ones are convinced that it is a matter of tightening up discipline and centralizing. . . . This is tragic because the young ones, I see it more and more, are getting into a frightful state of frustration and despair precisely at being constantly organized and marshalled this way and that and told to close their eyes and obey, that this is the only possible way to be a monk. They know it isn't." [6]

He had begun to see that enormous changes were afoot in the Church itself and that everything previously accepted would be called into question, the structure of the Trappist Order no less than the rest. But this awareness of change coincided for him with an extraordinary inner development. It was as if the physical and intellectual restrictions of twenty years had allowed him to build tremendous reserves of mental energy. For many of those years he had read little but the Scriptures, the Fathers, and books of spiritual advice. And now, quite swiftly, his old appetite for literature was returning. He began to read on the most extraordinary scale. Novels, for a start. William Faulkner, George Orwell, Henry Miller, Albert Camus, Julien Green, Flannery O'Connor, André Malraux. Then he was reading Sartre, C. G. Jung, Simone Weil, and Gabriel Marcel, Bertolt Brecht, Lewis Mumford, Christopher Dawson, Hannah Arendt, Gandhi. There was poetry—particularly the Latin American poets, but also St. John Perse, W. H. Auden, Zbigniew Herbert, and many more. There were theologians, too, who would not have figured on earlier reading lists—Karl Barth, Dietrich Bonhoeffer, J. A. T. Robinson, and many more. Altogether it was an astonishingly rich diet after the austerities of his recent intellectual nourishment. He was now no longer concerned with proprieties, nor whether the writers were "good Catholics" (although a few of them were), but with whether they had something to tell him about the contemporary world. He seemed to have an intense hunger for knowledge about the world outside, and in pursuit of this he read furiously—poetry and politics, psychology and sociology, anthropology and environmental studies, philosophy and religion. His religious reading was no longer that of the "good Catholic"—he was interested in Protestant writing and Jewish writing, Buddhist writing and Hindu writing—what mattered to him was that the writers he read should have something important to say about the contemporary world and its dilemmas. He was preparing for himself a kind of springboard from which to launch a series of explorations into the problems of the world of the 1960s—the problems of war, of nuclear weapons, of racial conflict, of environmental pollution. These, not the specifically Catholic and religious issues that had occupied him in the 1940s and 1950s, now seemed to him to be what mattered most, although he was deeply interested also in Catholic and monastic renewal. He began to turn outward, to correspond with writers and thinkers and men of action who were deeply engaged in current problems, and paradoxically, to see his own growing solitude as an act of solidarity with them. It was as if he had abandoned all interest in the *persona* of the monk; his concern was, for much of the time, focused on the world, the world he had so much despised, in an attempt to look with clarity at its problems.

This extraordinary release of energy not surprisingly felt threatening to his superiors, who somehow sensed that Merton had escaped, had passed from beyond their control. While they kept him physically at Gethsemani, under the strictest discipline, they had paradoxically managed to release him, more by accident than intention; they must often have wished they had assented to his original wish to transfer to the Camaldolese. As it was, his very retirement in the 1960s caused people to beat a path to his retreat. It sometimes seemed as if all the world was corresponding with him, sending him books and articles, beating on the doors in remote Kentucky and asking to be allowed to talk to him. Rules about receiving gifts, visitors, letters, were continually having to be changed, stretched, adapted, to cope with the extraordinary phenomenon of Thomas Merton. And the new ideas that flowed through Merton's head flowed straight into the heads of the novices, and often, through Merton's Sunday Conferences in Chapter, into the heads of other monks. Thus the former Harvard business graduate, who was in the process of reorganizing the cheese and fruitcake business with model efficiency, found himself forced by Merton's attitudes to question not only the work he was doing at the Abbey and all the principles on which business life is based, but also, ultimately, everything he as a good Catholic believed about religion and society, a questioning that was to get him into deep water when later he was sent to South America and saw the desperate poverty there. Not only was Merton a disturbance, but he *believed* in disturbance: "See, if Dan Berrigan or Dan Walsh comes down here and says something that disturbs you, see that's good."

There was a considerable inner cost of this intensive thinking and questioning. Dom John Eudes Bamberger has described Merton as having four times the psychic energy of most ordinary men but suggests that his psychic energy exhausted his physical frame. Twice before in Merton's life, as we have seen, he came near to physical collapse as a result of his voracious interest in life. It may have been just this awareness of a tendency to live with a destructive vigour that drove him first to the relative seclusion of

Gethsemani, and then to the further seclusion (imperfect as it was) of the hermit life, but even so his body paid a heavy price for the adventures of his mind and spirit. From the early 1960s onward, he suffered from a series of minor and major complaints, some of which caused him considerable distress.

A major cause of distress was his stomach and bowel, parts of the body notoriously sensitive to emotional upset. Part of his trouble was that he was allergic to lactic acid and therefore should not have been eating dairy products or anything made with milk; but this problem was not diagnosed until 1967, by which time he had endured years of digestive troubles. In the early 1960s, too, colitis was diagnosed, a distressing complaint about which Merton says little to his friends. Novices of the period remember that Merton never celebrated Mass for the community, although he did so for the novices in their chapel, and their understanding was that this was because of the problem of colitis. This suggests that Merton had never quite overcome his old panic sensations about performing rituals in the church and that attempts to do so now brought on attacks of colitis.

He was also troubled by a damaged vertebra in his neck—the result of an old school injury caused by playing rugby—and this gave him increasing pain during the 1960s. Sinus trouble bothered him, too.

The friends closest to Merton were aware that he had become much more irascible in this period, less inclined to put up with fools gladly, particularly any fools on his own doorstep. At times he became mildly paranoid in his conviction that letters were being kept from him, manoeuvres were going on behind his back, a sad decline from the total trust of his early years as a monk. Naomi Burton, with her loving common sense and her capacity to stand up to Merton, showed particular skill in responding to this aspect of him, both in her visits and in her letters.

"The fault in this case," writes Merton about a lost letter, "rests then on the absolutely absurd, crackpot and infantile system of mail censorship and distribution that we have in this monastery. Only last week an important letter from Ed Rice got 'lost.' No one seems to know about it. Four or five times in the years I have been here, most urgent and important letters have somehow failed to reach me. These are just times that I *know* about. How many others? It is not usually real malice, sometimes just carelessness, sometimes pure arbitrary fantasy. You understand this." [7]

"Now Tom," Naomi Burton wrote in reply, "don't start flying

into a fury with everyone around the Abbey because they haven't mailed something to me. If you worked in a large office, you would find that this is a daily occurrence and one simply has to accept it and never get into the frame of mind where one thinks it's all being done for personal reasons against oneself. Don't ask me why it takes, for instance, somebody six days to run off eighty-five copies of a mimeographed letter, but that's just happened to me, and I would be stark staring crazy by now if I took it personally." [8]

She also advocated a calmer approach both to conflicts within the Abbey and to ones outside, advice that indicates the stage of nervous exasperation that Merton had reached:

> Try to be calm however hard it is. And remember that white hot communiqués are better left to cool near an open window over night if not longer. And learn to say no gracefully and often. Most of all, work at a journal that will tell your most passionate convictions written from the heart and not the top of your head, about the predicament of the world today. It is important and you can reach so many people. You need to reach those people and not just the ones who already agree with you anyway. Do you see that? And when you get frustrated, think about this which just struck me. Is it wholly sensible to feel so passionately that the Church must change, that sluggish Catholics must awake and take stands and so on . . . but then for you to feel so irritated by alfalfa pellets and industry? Because aren't the monks really adjusting rather well to the 20th century and would it really make more sense for them to grind corn by hand and not use mechanical devices? [9]

That Merton's ire was not only unleashed on his fellow monks, or mechanized monastic life, or on sluggish fellow Catholics, is revealed by her last sentence, which shows that close friends could also bear the brunt of his unhappiness: "Don't get mad at me again because I can't take that at this point."

Her ability to care about his problems, survive his rage, and still tell him what she thought, led to a new closeness between them. His letters become much more revealing, and between then and the end of his life he shared his griefs and his illnesses, his problems and his doubts, his joys and his triumphs, quite openly with her. In 1963, he suffered protracted pain in his left shoulder—it turned out to be bursitis. "It is possible I may have to go to the hospital for a checkup in a few weeks. Have lately had a bad shoulder and it seems to affect my whole left arm which is in a torpor almost constantly. Maybe some strange disease. I will die a martyr to fallout smugly saying 'I told you so you beasts.' Ah what a lovely prospect." He added a postscript: "Fr. Abbot as you probably know is away. Maybe he has had a secret meeting with you about how to handle me. It is just the kind of thing he would like, and just the kind of thing that ties my guts in knots of utter despair." [10] Later he wrote, "My arm and shoulder are quite bad. A half hour in choir or typing or anything like that makes me feel like hell on earth. Toothache just isn't comparable to this. Heat pads and aspirin don't do anything for it. . . . Death, where is thy sting? Rhetorical question." [11] And five months later: "If at times my letters sound a bit incoherent and mad it is usually because my arm is bad, I am rushed, and can't see perfectly straight. This is not at all unusual, and becomes more usual every day. I am in my dotage." [12]

He began to open up to her a different kind of pain from the pain in his shoulder. He had written some articles against war and had proposed to include them in a book he was editing, discussing the terrible threat of nuclear war (see next chapter). To his horror, the Cistercian censors had forbidden him to write about war, a move that he saw as dictated by political prejudice rather than religious conviction.

"I can't say exactly that it constitutes a temptation against my 'vocation' but it certainly raises some pretty profound questions indeed. I know, one must just take it on the chin and shut up etc. etc. But with all the attention that has been drawn to the obedience of an Eichmann and now even the question of Pius XII, the props given by the conventional arguments don't offer much support. One is faced with the very harrowing idea that in obeying one is really doing wrong and offending God . . . it certainly wrings all the last drops of alacrity out of one's obedience and one's zest for the religious life. It is a bit weird to foresee that one may have to end his life in something that may have turned out to be the most monumental mistake." [13]

A few days after that letter, he wrote again, trying once more to tell her what was "wrong" with him, and this time he reached the nub of his difficulty with the religious life:

I know exactly what the thing is. I am always grumbling about solitude and this is one of the forms it takes in my own life: a progressive alienation from people with whom I ought normally to live in perfect understanding and agreement. Having to get along without too much support in an area where no one is either very sympathetic or very interested in my ideas. Above all it means having to figure things out in a somewhat lonely and insecure way and this brings out the fact that I have always been more dependent than I realized. But at the same time that being "dependent" is just totally useless and even dishonest in this kind of situation. The net result is having to face things alone before God and hope for the best, and to go on with this even though other people may not quite like it or understand it. . . . Of course the worst element in it is that I am getting in so many ways disillusioned with the Order and the Church even (that is the thing that upsets people). [14]

It needed great trust, and perhaps great loneliness, for Merton to raise such issues as these, above all the painful issue of dependence, the deep emptiness and need of one who has not been securely loved as a child. But there were lighter moments in their correspondence. For instance, "Best Christmas wishes to you and Ned. I suppose Maine will be deep in snow. Yesterday I was up to my neck in robins. Really. Scores of them, clouds of them, all around my cottage up there, the most obstreperous chirping and hopping around, thought they were in Miami yet. Sick of robins." [15]

Naomi Burton was not the only friend of whom he was making good use. The extraordinary inner change of the late 1950s that had turned him outward facing the problems of the world instead of inward to the concerns of the monastery, had also the effect of releasing energy for affection and for many relationships outside the monastery. One of them was with the psychiatrist James Wygal ("Jim," to Merton) whom he had consulted about his own problems and on other occasions about the problems of his novices. Now, on his frequent visits to Louisville for hospital tests and treatment, Merton would telephone Jim and they would lunch together, beginning, Wygal remembers, with generous helpings of "Planter's Punch." Merton liked to use these occasions to "sound off about the Abbot," but apart from that their talk ranged over many things, most of them nothing to do with monasticism at all.

Apart from these blessed escapes from the claustrophobia of monastic life, Merton had a constant stream of visitors, to which the Abbot assented, when he did assent, under protest. In addition to Merton's old friends—Ed Rice, Seymour Freedgood, the Van Dorens, Bob Giroux, Jay Laughlin, Naomi Burton, the Hammers—there were new ones, some of them from distant countries. There was Donald Allchin, an Anglican clergyman from England; Miguel Greenberg, a young poet from the Argentine; other young people from the Catholic Worker movement; Daniel Berrigan and others deeply involved in the struggle against war; others involved in the civil rights movement; and others like Ernesto Cardenal, in the whole evolving protest in Latin America. Merton was nearly as ambivalent as his Abbot about the way in which he attracted visitors. He loved them individually, and often learned a tremendous amount from what they had to tell him, but they eroded both the little solitude left over after his long hours in choir and with the novices, and the passionate reading that had now become so much a part of his life. "It seems to me," Merton had written to Naomi Burton in September 1963, "that one of the smartest things to cut down on here is visits of visiting firemen. I have seen a lot of interesting people this summer, but it cuts into everything else and I am just not that sociable anyway, so it wears me out more than anything else. I will try to do this, and don't anticipate anything but encouragement from the Superior." [16]

Miguel Greenberg remembers how tired Merton was when he visited him in 1964, how suffocated by the heavy burden of his work with the novices, and yet how acute in his observations about South America and how deeply interested and aware about what was going on there.

Merton was, in fact, in the ironic situation of trying to be a hermit while doing a full-time job, having large numbers of visitors, and corresponding on a gigantic scale. It was one of those paradoxes of which he had said his life was full. Usually in the afternoons he got away to the cinder-block hut on the hillside that he had adopted as his hermitage, and there he would type or sit and read. Despite the overwork, he found time to notice, be part of, the natural world, as he had never done before, and to see the everyday world with a special acuteness. "This morning, before Prime, in the early morning sky, three antiquated monoplanes flew over the monastery with much noise, followed by a great heron." [17] "As I was coming back from Dom Frederic's lake, a green heron started up from the water in the culvert under the roadway where all the blackberry bushes are, and flew up into the willows. I could see his beautiful mahogany neck, and his crest was up as he looked at me. His legs were bright yellow." [17] "More and more I appreciate the beauty and the solemnity of the 'way' up through the woods, past the barn, up the stony rise, into the grove of tall, straight oaks and hickories around through the pines, swinging to the hilltop and the clearing that looks out over the valley." [17]

"Sunrise: hidden by pines and cedars to the east: I saw the red flame of the kingly sun glaring through the black trees, not like dawn but like a forest fire. Then the sun became distinguished as a person and he shone silently and with solemn power through the branches, and the whole world was silent and calm.

It is essential to experience all the times and moods of one good place." [17] "Heavy snowflakes flying in all directions. But when there is no wind they descend so slowly that they seem determined not to land on the ground. When in fact they do touch the ground they vanish completely. Then the pale sun comes out for a moment, shines uncertainly on the grass, the wheel, the pale pine logs, the rusty field, the fence, the valley." [17]

"A cat running in the windy dark through the light cast by the novitiate windows." [17] "There was a small white colt, running beautifully up the hill, and down, and around again, with a long smooth stride and with the ease of flight. Yet in the middle of it he would break into rough, delightful cavorting, hurling himself sideways at the wind and the hill, and instantly sliding back into the smooth canter." [17]

"How high the corn is this summer! What joy there is in seeing the tall crests nod ten and twelve feet above the ground, and the astounding size of the silk-bearded ears! You come down out of the novitiate, through the door in the enclosure wall, over the little bridge, and down into this paradise of tall stalks and leaves and silence. There is a sacredness about the beauty of tall maize and I understand how the Mayas must have felt about them. . . . How can we *not* love such things? . . . The completely irreligious mind is, it seems to me, the unreal mind, the tense, void, abstracted mind that does not even see the things that grow out of the earth or feel glad about them: it knows the world only through prices and figures and statistics." [17]

Work with the novices continued well. They caught some of his own intense enthusiasm for Zen and built a Zen garden in the monastery. At the end of 1963, they made a Japanese fish kite of red paper, and on January 1st they celebrated the New Year of the Dragon by flying it over the Zen garden.

Much in Merton's correspondence indicates how deeply he was questioning not so much the value of the cenobitic life as the expression of it at Gethsemani. Occasionally he sank to the kind of grumbling that is typical of any institution (Dom John Eudes Bamberger is credited with the observation that what keeps monks together is "mutual gripes"), but many of his comments indicate much deeper thinking. Speaking of a monk going through "difficulties," he wrote,

> That is one of the things I mean about the cenobitic life when it is a little off standard: instead of the good in people being encouraged it is slapped down, not through malice, but just because it is more convenient that way. . . . I think too that we suffer (not least I myself) from the disease of absolutes. Every answer has to be the right answer and, not only that, the final one. All problems have to be solved as of now. All uncertainties are intolerable. But what is life but uncertainties and a few plausible possibilities? Even the life of faith, in practice, is full of contingencies, and rightly so. That is why it is a life of faith. And its certainties are dark, not absolutely clear. Nor are they the kind we can use to produce immediate conviction in the interlocutor. . . . Actually I think a few pages in P. Placide's new Directory say the best things that have so far been said about the cenobitic life. Certainly the function of such a life is to draw out the best in everyone, not stifle it, slap it down, kick it against the wall. Perhaps our problem here is that we prefer the security that can be gained by screwing everything down tight and keeping it that way, to the risk of letting people really discover themselves. Or else we make pseudo reforms suggested by people who have long since left and not needed by the people who have stayed. . . . Actually our life is lived in such a way that it generates an unusually consistent state of resentment, and I think this is even unconsciously fostered, because when people are eaten by resentment they run to the Superior and give him information which he appreciates, and which helps him to tighten the screws some more, perpetuate the resentment, divide the monks against each other, draw them with more information to the center of the hive. . . . This is not very edifying and in the long run it is very self-defeating even for those who think they profit by it, for the ultimate target of the greatest resentment is the queen bee. [19]

One of the monks in Rome mentioned to Merton that he had heard mentioned in religious discussion something called "Mertonism," and Merton responded with rueful irony,

> If there is such a thing as "Mertonism" I suppose I am the one that ought to beware of it. The people who believe in this term evidently do not know how unwilling I would be to have anyone repeat in his own life the miseries of mine. That would be flatly a mortal sin against charity. I thought I never had done anything to obscure my lack of anything that a monk might conceive to be a desirable quality. Surely this lack is

public knowledge, and anyone who imitates me does so at his own risk. I can promise him some fine moments of naked despair. [20]

In 1964, an amazing event occurred. Except for his trip in the crisis year of 1955, and his visits to the hospital in Louisville, Merton had never been permitted to leave the monastery, although others were allowed to study elsewhere and attend Conferences. Even in 1961 when Columbia, his old university, wanted to present him with a medal, Merton had to depute Mark Van Doren to receive it for him. But then, incredibly, Dom James gave Merton permission, the only such permission he was to give to him in his reign as Abbot, to visit New York. It was an act of real mercy. The aged Suzuki, in his nineties, was visiting New York and wanted to see Merton. Not surprisingly, he did not feel able to make the long journey to Kentucky and the Abbey, so Merton was to go to New York to see him—he was not to contact friends or in any way to advertise the trip. Merton was intensely excited by the thought of the trip, thinking of the pleasures not only of seeing Suzuki himself but also of looking at the Klees at the Guggenheim, the Zen and Rajput paintings at the Metropolitan Museum. He was also quite frightened, the mere thought of New York giving him stomach spasms when he was dressed and ready to go. Nothing perhaps could reveal the inner change in Merton so clearly as his reactions to this journey. The old contempt for the world is gone forever—he brings to it now a joyful, although refined appetite.

He found himself delighted to see New York again, overjoyed to recognize the two big gas tanks at Elmhurst from the aeroplane and his own familiar Long Island. He felt as if he was going home. [18]

He stayed two nights in Butler Hall, Columbia, in a room that looked out over Long Island Sound. There was "a Black Muslim riot" in Harlem, and he could hear shooting for most of the night.

The visit to Suzuki was very successful. The old man had an ear trumpet, into which Merton spoke, and his young secretary performed the tea ceremony. Merton loved the green tea. Then Suzuki read some Chinese koans to Merton and translated them, and Merton read Fernando Pessoa to Suzuki and translated that. He felt as much at home, he reflected later, as when visiting his friends the Hammers. What happened next is told in a letter to Lax in their own private language. "In the middle they gang up on me with winks and blinks and all kinds of friendly glances and assurances and they declare with one voice 'Who is the western writer who understands best the Zen IT IS YOU they declare.' You in this connection means me. It is I in person they have elected to this slot and number of position to be one in the west. First west in Zen is now my food for thought. What did it ever get me I ask ruefully. . . . Well it did get me to a visit with Suzuki." [15] Suzuki apart he found New York thrilling, but exhausting. He celebrated Mass at Corpus Christi, the church where he had been baptized all those years before. He walked about the wet empty streets full of foreign students. He looked at books in the book-shops, feeling overwhelmed by their sheer quantity, and dined in the New Asia restaurant, where he felt overwhelmed by the quantity of food. It was good to get back to Butler Hall where he was staying, and sit on the floor in his pyjamas drinking cheap sherry "on the rocks" and looking out over Harlem. It felt like a marvellous holiday. [15]

The next day he went to a Van Gogh exhibition. "Wheels of fire, cosmic, rich, full bodied honest victories over desperation, permanent victory." [19] The Metropolitan Museum was some how a disappoint-ment—"an old station I passed through long ago," but the Columbia library delighted him because "unlike Louisville" he could find every-thing he was looking for in it. The most important things about the visit, though, were the human contacts, and his new discovery of the beauty of New York. "At noon on Wednesday I rode down in the taxi to the Guggenheim Museum through the park under tunnels of light and foliage with the driver talking about his problems, his nerves, his analysis and his divorce. . . . The people walking on Fifth Avenue were beautiful . . . a stately and grown up city, a true city, life-size. . . . Anything but soulless. New York is feminine. It is she, the city. I am faithful to her. I have not ceased to love her to the last gasp of this ball point pen . . . (Pen runs out!)." [18]

Lax was the only friend he told, presumably because obedience did not cover friends in far-away Greece. "Zip zip out and back in the jets with nobody the wiser not allowed to tell Rice or call Jubilees or Naomi Burstong or Bob Gingeroo or the N Yorker or nobody not allowed to hunt for Lilly Reilly any more either, but ate in some sly French restaurant drinking benedictines and making like tourists. All this is sober truth big secret don't ever tell anybody or I end up in the calabozo." [21]

The trip had been a wonderful experience, but it was delightful to get back to the peace of Gethsemani. "There is no party there is no riots there is only . . . fresh air and all that there is the cells and cells is best there is also the hermit cottage where I wander about and think such thoughts as befits the number one Zen of the west: that is to say not one thought of Zen." [21]

References

1. Thomas Merton. *Disputed Questions*. New York: Farrar, Straus, 1960.
2. Thomas Merton (trans. and ed.). *The Wisdom of the Desert*. New York: New Directions, 1960; London: Anderson, 1988.
3. Thomas Merton. *A Thomas Merton Reader*, ed. Thomas P. McConnel. New York: Doubleday, 1962.
4. Robert Giroux. "Introduction." In Flannery O'Connor, *The Complete Stories*. New York: Farrar, Straus, & Giroux, 1978.
5. Thomas Merton. Letter to Fr. Tarcisius Conner. November, 27, 1962. TMSC.
6. Thomas Merton. Letter to Fr. Illtud Evans. August 3, 1964. TMSC.
7. Thomas Merton. Letter to Naomi Burton. August 22, 1963. TMSC.
8. Naomi Burton. Letter to Thomas Merton. August 30, 1963. TMSC.
9. Naomi Burton. Letter to Thomas Merton. May 25, 1963. TMSC.
10. Thomas Merton. Letter to Naomi Burton. September 5, 1963. TMSC.
11. Thomas Merton. Letter to Naomi Burton. September 10, 1963. TMSC.
12. Thomas Merton. Letter to Naomi Burton. February 17, 1964. TMSC.
13. Thomas Merton. Letter to Naomi Burton. March 3, 1964. TMSC.
14. Thomas Merton. Letter to Naomi Burton. March 13, 1964. TMSC.
15. Thomas Merton. Letter to Naomi Burton. December 23, 1964. TMSC.
16. Thomas Merton. Letter to Naomi Burton. September 5, 1963. TMSC.
17. Thomas Merton. *Conjectures of a Guilty Bystander*. New York: Doubleday, 1966.
18. Thomas Merton. "Vow of Conversation." Unpublished journal, dated 1964–1965. TMSC.
19. Thomas Merton. Letter to Fr. Chrysogonus Waddell. January 4, 1964. TMSC.
20. Thomas Merton. Letter to Fr. Chrysogonus Waddell. January 26, 1963. TMSC.
21. Thomas Merton. Letter to Robert Lax. July 10, 1964.

17

"TO CHOOSE THE WORLD"

❦

For Merton, the 1960s were a period of growing involvement with the sin and suffering of the world, in contrast to those early years at Gethsemani in which he had seen his task as one of total detachment *from* the world. In conversation with the writer James Thomas Baker, Merton implied that life at Gethsemani had made any involvement almost impossible:

> Merton explained to this writer . . . that for the first few years of his monastic life the rules were so strict that the monks had little time for thoughts of the world, spending all their time in worship, physical labor, and trying to stay healthy. They never went outside the enclosure walls, and received almost no news from the outside world. . . . They prayed constantly in an unheated chapel in below freezing weather, sometimes got as little as three hours sleep a night, and were not provided with a sufficiently nourishing diet. Merton's own body reacted negatively to these harsh conditions, and he became ill with a respiratory disease that was at first incorrectly diagnosed as tuberculosis. [1]

There was much truth in this account but in fact, by the early 1960s, when Merton embarked on a deeper involvement with the world there was still little change at Gethsemani; what was different was that he had ceased to collude with the world-denying strain in monasticism. Writing of the process of change in himself in 1966, Merton mocked what he felt had been his delusion. "Due to a book I wrote thirty years ago, I have myself become a sort of stereotype of the world-denying contemplative—the man who spurned New York, spat on Chicago, and tromped on Louisville, heading for the woods with Thoreau in one pocket, St. John of the Cross in another, and holding the Bible open at the Apocalypse." [2] In the same article, he formally rejected the follies of this former self and outlined his new way of thinking. (As John Eudes Bamberger has pointed out, Merton was never the least embarrassed about changing his point of view. One week, says Dom John, he would come out with some huge assertion such as "Rilke is the most fantastic poet of this century." This would be followed within three, or maybe four, weeks by "Of course, you can't put much stock in Rilke's approach to things. He was awfully limited when it came to. . . ." [3] But Merton's attitude to the "the world" was more deeply pondered than his attitude to Rilke, having produced one of the central conflicts of his monastic life.)

The "new" Merton took pleasure in seeing and saying that he was part of the modern world. "I *am* the world just as you are! Where am I going to look for the world first of all if not in myself?" [2] The old problem, he felt, came from the Carolingian view of the world and of Christian society. In this view, Christian society was a world-denying society in the midst of the world, and monks were the professional world deniers within that society. The world was radically evil and doomed to hell, and although this world was potentially saved by the cross of Christ it was marking time until such time that everyone could hear the message of salvation. Meanwhile, men and women must strictly discipline themselves and one another because they were basically evil. "They cannot be left to their own freedom or even God's loving grace. They have to have their freedom taken away from them because it is their greatest peril. They have to be told at every step what to do, and it is better if what they are told to do is displeasing to their corrupt natures, for this will keep them out of further subtle forms of mischief." [2]

Merton cannot accept this view, one that had been such a painful feature of his life at Gethsemani. He felt that, on the contrary, the Christian commitment was "to *choose* the world." "To *choose* the world is not merely a pious admission that the world is acceptable because it comes from the hand of God. . . . To choose the world is to choose to do the work I am capable of doing, in collaboration with my brother, to make the world better, more free, more just, more livable, more human. Rejection of the world and 'contempt for the world' is in fact not a choice but the evasion of choice." [2]

Given this new compulsion to "choose the world," where did Merton turn? Perhaps most important of all because it was the most painful, the most terrifying, the most intractable, the most potentially destructive of all human problems, to the problem of war. In the 1960s, the full horror of the H-bomb and the various refinements of the nuclear weapon designed since 1945 were still percolating through people's minds, and the implications were so terrifying to contemplate that they were finding all sorts of ways, practical, and psychological, to defend themselves against it. There were elaborate plans for shelters and early warning systems; there were incredibly optimistic speculations, such as those of Herman Kahn, a spokesman for civil defence, about the kind of society that might survive a full nuclear attack; there was a great deal of projection in the form of paranoid suspicion about "Reds"; and, finally, there was a temptation simply to shut the whole conflict off, to leave it to "those in authority" and eat, drink, and be merry, ignoring, as the citizens of Pompeii had once ignored, the light rain of ash and the distant rumblings that presaged ultimate disaster. There was, as Merton noted, a Christian form of this withdrawal into an ivory tower, which was to prate of "just war" in a situation where any war could be nothing less than genocide.

Merton's own attempt to grapple with the terrible facts of nuclear war began with a long meditation he wrote about Hiroshima in 1961: *Original Child Bomb.*

1. In the year 1945 an Original Child was born. The name Original Child was given to it by the Japanese people, who recognized that it was the first of its kind.
2. On April 12th, 1945, Mr. Harry Truman became the President of the United States, which was then fighting the Second World War. . . . About one hour after Mr. Truman became President, his aides told him about a new bomb. . . .
3. President Truman formed a committee of men to tell him if this bomb would work. . . . It was decided Hiroshima was the most appropriate target, as it had not yet been bombed at all. Lucky Hiroshima! What others had experienced over a period of four years would happen to Hiroshima in a single day! Much time would be saved, and time is money!

When they bombed Hiroshima they would put the following out of business: The Ube Nitrogen Fertilizer Company; the Ube Soda Company; The Nippon Motor Oil Company; the Sumitoma Chemical Company; the Sumitoma Aluminium Company; and most of the inhabitants. [4]

The deliberately ironic style of the writing may nowadays seem too flip to carry the weight of the tragedy and to be less than fair to the appalling complexity of choice that modern war imposes on statesmen, but Merton had begun, with his special courage and asceticism, on a kind of penance infinitely more exacting than anything the Trappists in their wildest moments had ever dreamed up, the penance of getting to know the nightmare cruelty of the modern world, not this time from any unconscious masochistic motive, but in order to begin on the heartbreaking task of trying to evolve a new pattern. During the 1960s, in article after article (in *Jubilee, The Catholic Worker, Peace News, Blackfriars, Ramparts, Commonweal, Saturday Review, Peace,* and *Fellowship*), and in book after book, Merton was to work patiently away on the infinitely depressing and discouraging shadow side of the modern world, nourishing his thinking with the widest possible reading about politics and philosophy, about psychology and sociology. He read and wrote, not, as he had done as a young man, with a vast superiority toward the sins and follies of the world but painfully, as one who knows himself to have colluded in every error he writes about. He is no longer the righteous youth of *The Seven Storey Mountain* but the "guilty bystander," looking on such themes as authority and submission to authority in the horrible mirrors of Adolf Eichmann and Auschwitz, and recognizing what a ubiquitous problem they reflect, one not unknown even in a contemplative monastery.

On February 9, 1962, Merton published an article in *Commonweal* called "Nuclear War and Christian Responsibility." This was, in the main, an attack on the weakness or laziness of Christian response to the fact of nuclear war. "Silence, passivity or outright belligerence seem to be characteristic official and unofficial Christian reactions to the H-bomb." [5] Merton's contention was that Christians could not go along with the way both East and West treated nuclear weapons as a "rational option," that the genocide automatically involved in any nuclear war was "a moral evil so great that it cannot be justified even for the best of ends, even to defend the highest and most sacrosanct values." [5]

Later in 1963, this essay appeared in a remarkable book that Merton edited, called *Breakthrough to Peace* (1963), with other contributions from Erich Fromm, Lewis Mumford, Herbert Butterfield, Norman Cousins, and others. The book was subtitled *Twelve Views on the Threat of Thermonuclear Extermination,* and one of its main purposes was to attack the "nuclear realists" who seemed so complacently to accept nuclear war as one of the inescapable facts of modern life and who urged adjustment to it rather than a serious attempt to outlaw it. In his introduction, Merton says the object of the book is "to break through barriers and open up rational perspectives. . . . It is vitally important to create a general climate of rationality, and to preserve a broad, tolerant, watchful and humanist outlook on the whole of life, precisely in order that rash and absurd assumptions may not have too free a circulation in our society." [6]

One of these rash assumptions, as Erich Fromm and Michael Maccoby make clear in the book, was that the problems of survivors (in the United States) of a nuclear attack had been, in Herman Kahn's words "grossly exaggerated." The assumption was that, given fallout shelters to protect people in rural areas from the immediate effects of radiation it would be possible to rebuild society. Fromm and Maccoby believed that the inevitable effects of widespread hunger, disease, despair over the shattering of society, grief, and guilt (about those killed or deliberately excluded from the safety of the shelter) would make recuperation problematic.

Merton's own concern was primarily with the "normality" of nuclear war and with the psychological problems that seemed to lend a bias toward moral failure in the area of achieving peace. "What remains to be explored by the Christian is the area that is least considered, which also happens to be the area that most needs to be examined and is perhaps the one place where something can be done.

"By what are our policies of hatred and destructiveness dictated? What seems to drive us inexorably on to the fate which we all dread and seek to avoid?" [6]

He believed that the Christian's first duty was to acquire a deep knowledge of the weapons themselves, of the political situation, of the outlook of friend and enemy alike.

> We must try to remember that the enemy is as human as we are, and not an animal or a devil. Finally, we must be reminded of the way we ourselves tend to operate, the significance of the secret forces that rise up within us and dictate fatal decisions of prejudice and hate. We must be reminded of objective moral standards, and of the wisdom which goes into every judgment, every choice, every political act that deserves to be called civilized. We cannot think this way unless we shake off our passive irresponsibility, renounce our fatalistic submission to economic and social forces, and give up the unquestioning belief in machines and processes which characterizes the mass mind. History is ours to make; now above all we must try to recover our freedom, our moral autonomy, our capacity to control the forces that make for life and death in our society. [6]

In the United States of the early 1960s, it was not very popular to suggest that the enemy was "as human as we are" nor to invite readers to look deeply into their own prejudices and aggressions. Merton's strongly worded comments—which went beyond the usual kinds of woolly advice to Christians about "prayerful consideration," to the real nitty-gritty of the problem—were inevitably bound to arouse anger and irritation both from those outside the Church who are always enraged when Christians try to act on their beliefs and those inside who prefer to use their beliefs as a defence against the horrors of the world. But, more seriously for his future work, Merton's writing about peace aroused unfavourable comment inside the Trappist Order, and when, in 1963, he was collecting his essays for a book called *Seeds of Destruction* [7] he was forbidden to include any that touched upon the subject of peace. Ironically, it was the year of Pope John's encyclical *Pacem in Terris*, which was in itself a piece of writing that went far beyond the usual empty utterances of pontiffs and archbishops, and which tried, as Merton was trying, to reach the roots of the terrible problem that was tearing the world apart. But Merton was told that he did not know enough about the problems he was writing about and that the task should be left to others who did. As it happened, many of his essays about peace had already been mimeographed and sent out to friends, who prepared to give them a wider circulation. Even at home Merton was not silent, as he shared the ideas about peace that had begun to fill his thoughts with clergy who came for ecumenical meetings at Gethsemani. But the ban on publication hurt deeply and made him wonder, as we saw in his letter to Naomi Burton, whether he might not be committing one of the great sins of the age, like Eichmann, that of acquiescing silently in wickedness with the excuse that authority had ordered him to do so.

Within the ecumenical meetings at Gethsemani in 1963, he outlined his thinking about the Christian's duty in the face of nuclear war. No clear and definite solutions were in sight, but much work needed to be done in learning about and readjusting to the "essentially new, tragically critical situation in which the entire human race finds itself." The Christian's duty, "where the very existence of man and the continuation of life itself" were at stake, was "to strive in every way to preserve and protect His creation. Our duty is to help save humanity for which Christ died. We cannot condemn man, or disregard his plight, and allege loyalty to abstract beliefs as an excuse, still less as a reason for policies based on hatred and destructiveness. To 'kill Commies for Christ' is to admit that one has lost all sense of the meaning of the gospel of Christ." [8]

Christians had been taking it for granted that the nuclear threat was a Christian solution to the problem of communism, thereby "actually aligning themselves with pragmatists for whom the moral issue is totally irrelevant." They were supporting "overkill" as enthusiastically as everyone else, and if anything, with their fear of atheism, adding to the dangerous tensions between East and West.

No easy answer occurred to Merton—"We are very poor in ideas and insights"—but he drew up a list of possible approaches to the problem, recognizing that fanatical nationalism and racism often appealed to "moral principles" to buttress their wilder actions. All fanatical and bellicose solutions had to be ruled out. But the conventional "pacifist" solution also would not do: it was too individualistic, and it took too little account of the fears that a sweeping policy of "unilateral disarmament" would arouse. Any disarmament could only be a very gradual process. A purely "spiritual" approach to the problem was totally inadequate—an evasion of responsibility—and the old theory of the "just war," although not totally rejected by Merton in itself, took no account of modern problems of escalation and radiation and had begun to seem simply irrelevant.

Merton's tentative solution, tried out on the visiting Catholic and Protestant clergy, and deeply influenced by the writing and example of Gandhi, was to work toward "nonviolent methods of defense." The mass media, the military, the politicians, the industrialists all seemed to Merton to be "sold on military defense and the arms race," therefore making it difficult for populations to examine or believe in alternatives. Those who wanted peace were up against both this fact and the difficulty of getting people to face the moral evil of a nuclear war.

What was needed was a transformation in people's attitude to life, so that to destroy it became impossibly repugnant. A much deeper reciprocity was needed, a dialogue between opposites, a social justice *within* societies, including the United States, so that the deep causes of war—boredom, frustration, despair—could be attacked at the root. The more immediate task was to look at opportunities for nonviolent defence.

In 1964, Merton was holding a retreat with Dan Berrigan at Gethsemani on "spiritual roots of protest," in which they looked at what the individual man might do in a technological society largely shaped by the mass media. Interior life, asceticism, contemplation, intercessory prayer, above all personal renewal, seemed to them the only weapons strong enough to stand against the dehumanization of man and the crude mass thinking that followed it.

In 1965, Merton was writing that he saw war as "an avoidable tragedy" and that the problem of solving international conflict without massive violence had become "the number one problem of our time." "The human race today is like an alcoholic who knows that drink will destroy him and yet always has 'good reasons' why he must continue drinking. Such is man in his fatal addiction to war. He is not really capable of seeing a constructive alternative to war." [9]

Also in 1965 Merton wrote a letter to *Commonweal* about the Vietnam War:

> I would like to question the reasonableness of the rather common idea that any opposition to the Vietnam war is "pacifism." In fact, it seems that nowadays people are more and more tending to qualify *any* idea of abstaining from force in *any* international conflict as "pacifism" (with the implication of course that it is also the "pacifism of the weak"). It is my considered opinion that, quite apart from moral considerations, the Vietnam war is taking on the aspect of folly, brutality and massive stupidity that characterizes the blindness of the power politicians and leads eventually to its own ruin—along with that of the nation, perhaps! It is my considered opinion that quite apart from questions of conscience, power politicians in their right minds would devise some other way of handling the Vietnam situation to better advantage for their own national interest. It is obvious to the world that the "escalation" of the guerilla war (in which technological power has been made to look ridiculous by the fierce and dedicated resistance of a few half-starved men with holes in their pants) is an expedient for putting the conflict on a plane where the American war-machine can function in the style to which it is accustomed. [10]

Merton sent a copy of this letter to Senator Cooper, saying that he would not have voted for President Johnson had he known the line he was going to take on Vietnam.

Merton had managed to burst out of the straightjacket of enclosure and to overcome his Order's determination to silence him on the peace issue. Some of the young monks from Gethsemani had gone to Rome to study, and in a letter to one of them Merton remarked that the moral theologian Fr. Bernard Häring has been visiting Gethsemani, has encouraged Merton in his stand, and has promised to take the matter up with the Vicar General. But Merton has heard that the Vicar General "was strongly in favor of that absolutely appalling French deterrent system, which has no purpose whatever except to threaten cities even when, if a missile attack came . . . there would be only five minutes in which to mount a whole reply. All this is entirely at the mercy of computers in one center, and the chances of accident are fantastic. The element of human choice involved seems to be almost minimal. It is just a giant robot affair that, given the right stimulus, will start sending bombs over twenty or thirty big cities. . . . And a monk should wind himself up in his cocoon? . . . Should he consider that leaving the world absolves him from all responsibility in these matters? Can he safely leave it to others, when others have been either silent or obsequiously favorable to a solution that looks like an abdication of Christian responsibility?" [11]

Merton's interest in the peace question very quickly became public knowledge, not only in Catholic circles, and many who shared his views wrote to him or came to see him. After his death it was said that the "Catholic peace movement in America may have lost its most impressive and influential spokesman." To say this is not to deny or diminish the contributions others—Dorothy Day, Paul Hanly Furfey, the Berrigans, to mention an obvious few— have made, some over a much longer period of time. It was through Merton and his works, however, that Catholic peace teachings and traditions won a far wider audience. What he had to say carried an aura of unchallenged "respectability," due partly to the intensely spiritual character of his best-known works and partly to the image and associations stirred in the general Catholic reading public by his identification as a Trappist priest. [12]

While Merton gave himself so passionately to a study of war and peace, he was also acutely aware of other social problems, some of which were intimately linked to it. In the United States of the early 1960s, racial integration was a burning issue, one about which Merton had cared even in the old days at Columbia when he had visited Harlem to listen to jazz and to work with the baroness and had been appalled by the conditions under which urban blacks were obliged to live. Now he linked himself publicly by his writings with the struggle of the blacks in the South, bitterly regretted that he was not able to march on Selma, and arranged for money to go from an exhibition of his calligraphies to pay for the education of a black student at Spalding College in Louisville.

Another growing concern of his was the plight of the Latin American poor. The two years in which the poet Ernesto Cardenal had been a novice under Merton had aroused Merton's interest in South American problems that grew steadily, and was fed by the stream of Latin American visitors that called to see Merton. Cardenal had returned to Nicaragua to found his own community at Solentiname but the two corresponded, and Merton seriously considered going to South America. At one point he asked to go to Chile, a request rejected by Dom James, and he also had dreams of going to Nicaragua or the Argentine. Miguel Greenberg, to whom he wrote the following letter, thinks Merton was too vulnerable, too sensitive for the brutalities of South American societies, that he had not trained in a hard-enough school to face the loss and death of so many friends, which those who fought for new regimes had to endure. But Merton's joyful contact with so many of the poets and young men who were working for new societies, and his determination that North Americans, and particularly Catholics, should ask the hard questions about what was happening in Latin America, were seen and appreciated by many.

Merton wrote to Miguel Greenberg in May 1963,

> The whole question of inter-American contacts and exchange is of the greatest importance. It is important for Latin America but it is even more important for North America, because unless the US finally gets in touch with the reality of American life in its broadest and most relevant sense, there is going to be a lot of trouble for everybody. It is of the greatest importance, then, that the cultural vitality of the Latin American countries should be known and recognized here. It is a great misfortune that the technological blindness of the "advanced" countries should gradually be spreading everywhere, without necessarily bringing any real benefits, and communicating mostly the severe disadvantages of our state. . . . The problem is the dehumanization of man, the alienation of man. The Marxists could have developed this concept, which is found in Marx, but they have not been able to. On the contrary, the world today seems to be in a maniacal competition between giant powers, each one striving to show it can do more than the others in brutalizing, stupefying and dehumanizing man, in the name of humanism, freedom and progress. [13]

Merton goes on to speak of his great affection for Ernesto Cardenal, "one of the most significant voices of the two Americas," and of his concern and hope for friends in Nicaragua, striving, in the teeth of great opposition, for change. "I wish I had more time and more leisure to communicate with everyone, but the limitations of my vocation do impose restraints which I cannot always ignore! However, do believe me in deep union and agreement with the forces of life and hope that are struggling for the renewal of the true cultural and spiritual vitality of the 'new world' which is sometimes so tired, so old and so shabby. It is what pretends to be most 'new' that is often the oldest and weariest thing of all. But the forces of life must win." [13]

With Ernesto Cardenal himself, Merton kept up a close and affectionate correspondence, much of it based on discussion of the work of the young South American poets who were struggling, often at great personal cost, to bring a new social consciousness to birth in their countries.

> The world is full of great criminals with enormous power, and they are in a death struggle with each other. It is a huge gang battle, of supremely well armed and well organized gangsters, using well meaning lawyers and policemen and clergymen as their front, controlling papers, means of communication, and enrolling everybody in their armies. What can come of it? Surely not peace. There will be repeated crises, like the last one in which intellectuals fled from the US to Australia and in which the students of Oxford drank up all the old wine in the Union Club because they thought there would not be any more time for drinking anything. The cataclysm will come without giving anyone time to drink up what is left. It will not be planned by the cleverness of men. And we must pray and be joyful and simple because we do not after all understand most of it. Behind it are good meanings which escape us. But let us avoid false optimism, and approved gestures. But seek truth. [14]

Merton's own truth seeking had taken the form of a long journey by way of monastic vows and priesthood, all of it aimed at a special form of detachment. In the early years, it had seemed as if the detachment was in itself a sort of reproof to the world, a showing it a better way, free of desire for money, or fame, or success, of sexual relationships, or possessions. In those early days, there had been a priggishness, a self-righteousness, a kind of willed *persona* of the "good monk," which Merton had gradually abandoned. What was left, what had been implicit in his monastic life from the beginning, was a longing for union with God. Because of this he had survived the bitter disappointment and loneliness of the 1950s, the disillusion with Gethsemani, the pain of an "authority" that misunderstood him and his work and would not even allow him to comment on such a fundamental subject as war. And then, in the loss of his old *persona*; in his discovery of a new identity, not self-willed; in the intense struggle toward union; he had stumbled on new truths about "the world." "If I have written about interracial justice, or thermonuclear weapons, it is because these issues are terribly relevant to one great truth: that man is called to live as a son of God. Man must respond to this call to live in peace with all his brothers in the One Christ." [15]

It is necessary at this point to understand more of how Merton saw the contemplative life. It is unlikely that, in this later stage of his life, he saw it "holding up America" as he had seen it more romantically on his first visit to Gethsemani, rather like an engine holding up an aeroplane by its forward propulsion. Rather he had come to see the monk as one who, because he was spared many of the mundane worries that occupy those forced to earn livings and bring up families, was free to explore other, crucial, areas of human experience, on behalf of the whole of society. "It seems to me that if a monk is permitted to be detached from these struggles over particular interests, it is only in order that he may give more thought to the interests of all, to the whole question . . . the reconciliation of all men with one another in Christ. . . . A contemplative will, then, concern himself with the same problems as other people, but he will try to get to the spiritual and metaphysical roots of these problems—not by analysis but by simplicity." [16]

The very nakedness of the monk, both intellectually and in worldly terms—he is "nothing" in the world's terms, a "marginal" man—gives him a special sort of freedom, a freedom to move out of "alienation," to become quite simply, happy. Men have lost happiness because they have forgotten how to experience their spiritual selves and therefore cannot be whole, or free. The Jesuit John Higgins wrote

It is this estrangement from himself, from society and from God, that has resulted in modern man's apparent incapacity for any kind of spiritual experience. . . . Merton boldly emphasizes that men cannot live together if they do not love one another, and they cannot love one another as brothers if they do not love God their Common Father. Thus man's love for his fellow man must come from his communion with God in prayer. For, in prayer man becomes aware of his inner or real self, and, in so doing, realizes that he cannot live merely for himself but must live for others; above all, he must live for God—in Him and with Him. [17]

Nothing, Merton felt, could restore modern man, lost in technology, in depersonalizing societies, in fierce activism, except a new contemplative vision. "We find ourselves living in a society of men who have discovered their own nonentity where they least expected to—in the midst of power and technological achievement." [18] Identity could only be found in contemplation, and in this the monk and the Christian were the signs of hope in the world.

But for them, as Merton well recognized, this was no easy task. Their tendency was always to be trapped and imprisoned by the "false self." "Everyone of us is shadowed by a false self. This is the man I want myself to be but who cannot exist, because God does not know anything about him. And to be unknown to God is altogether too much privacy. My false and private self is the one who wants to exist outside the reach of God's will and God's love—outside of reality and outside of life. And such a self cannot help but be an illusion." [19]

The task of the religious person is rather, a self-emptying—a quieting and ordering of their life by prayer and self-denial and goodness so that God can take possession of them. To this end, the exterior self, the empirical ego, the fascination with ourselves as objects of reflection, must go, and a terrifying emptiness must be faced, an utter aloneness in order to reach the next stage. This is a passing out of the self, a surrender of the private little bubble of being, and only at this point of complete emptiness and nakedness is the soul free to be filled with the presence of God.

> A real "transformation of consciousness" occurs in the individual subject from an awareness of his false self, or empirical ego, to the true self or person. Now the individual is no longer conscious of himself as an isolated ego, but sees himself in his inmost ground of being as dependent on Another or as being formed through relationships, particularly his relationship with God. By forgetting himself both as subject and as an object of reflection, man finds his real self hidden with Christ in God. And so, as his self-consciousness changes, the individual is transformed; his self is no longer its own center; it is now centered on God. [20]

In arriving at this, his mature belief about prayer, about union with God, and about the relation of the monk, and to a lesser extent, every Christian with the world, Merton had drawn ideas not only from his own Catholic and Christian tradition—from such authorities as St. Benedict and St. Bernard of Clairvaux, from St.

Gregory of Nyssa, St. Augustine, St. John of the Cross, and others who had struggled with the nature of the spiritual journey—but also from Zen. Zen teaching was similarly occupied with a particular kind of transformation, or unself-consciousness—the moment when the ego is perceived to be an illusion, a cramp of the personality that is unwisely taken to be the personality itself, and can be escaped from in a single bound of "enlightenment." Taoism, too, with its perception of the human will as a deadly weapon constantly interfering with and subverting the divine harmony, led Merton more deeply toward the kind of transformation he had written about so many years before when studying St. John of the Cross. So he wrote to the young poet Greenberg in 1964,

> What you say is right. *Fluencia* [flowing] is the right way. What stops fluencia is the wrong kind of ignorance and the wrong kind of ignorance is the conviction that we can know exactly what is going on. Those who have too many programs and answers are absolutely blind and their ignorance leads them to destruction. Those who know that they do not know, are able at least to see something of what is in front of their nose. They can see a shadow of it, anyway. And they can move with the light and the shadow and keep from getting immediate sunstroke. So we must all move, even with motionless movement, even if we do not see clearly. A few little flames, yes. You can't grasp them, but anyway look at them obliquely. To look too directly at anything is to see something else because we force it to submit to the impertinence of our preconceptions. After a while, though, everything will speak to us if we let it and do not demand that it say what we dictate.
>
> Total corruption. Everything is corrupt and corruption spreads from one structure to the other, although they all have more than enough. The only incorrupt things are silence, not knowing, not going, not waiting, etc., mostly not saying. You are right that as soon as one has finished saying something it is no longer true. Herakleitos.* Love is all right as long as statements are not made and as long as it does not itself become a program, because then it is another tyranny. . . .
>
> The monk is a bird who flies very fast without knowing where he is going. And always arrives where he went, in peace, without knowing where he comes from. [21]

What was growing in Merton was a sense of the monk as a man who was free, part of the *fluencia*, the flowing, able to belong everywhere, to

---

* Herakleitos or Heraclitus, a philosopher who lived around 500 B.C., claimed that there is nothing permanent except change.

give himself where this was needed, just because he had abandoned the vested interests that are an inescapable part of the life of those who beget children, engage in commercial enterprise, or become pillars of society. The monk was free to observe, to comment, to take part, or just to "be" in the world in the classic Oriental tradition of "wu-wei" (without action), just because he was, by choice, nothing. "My monastery is not a home," Merton wrote in the preface to the Japanese edition of *The Seven Storey Mountain*. "It is not a place where I am rooted and established on the earth. It is not an environment in which I become aware of myself as an individual, but rather a place in which I disappear from the world as an object of interest in order to be everywhere in it by hiddenness and compassion. To exist everywhere I have to be a No one." We may contrast this with Merton's earliest writings at Gethsemani when he felt he had found a home. But for the lifelong orphan this turned out to be illusory, not just an impossible achievement, but perhaps an undesirable one, an intolerable limitation, because it would cut him off from all who were similarly orphaned and uprooted.

Merton's fear, at this stage of his life, was not of any kind of wicked "Them" who persecuted the defenceless—he had become too clearly aware of the guilt of the ordinary bystander to be able to continue to project in that way—but rather was a fear of the "dehumanized" person who did what he or she did for "good," logical reasons, or simply obeyed orders. He thought and wrote at length about Adolf Eichmann, a man, not psychotic, who was responsible for the torture and death of thousands, and Merton observed that it was the sane people we had now to fear most. He wrote a similar piece about Auschwitz, quoting the calm, business-like exchange of letters between the manufacturers of the gas chambers and their Nazi clients, instancing the "sensible" rules of the camp that harnessed efficiency to lunatic ends. Merton quoted the tragic instance of a child so tiny that it needed to be carried into the gas chamber, confidentially asking the guard who carried it about the "birdie" on his cap. [22] "In his [Merton's] writings," wrote Gordon Zahn, the sociologist, "Auschwitz and Hiroshima fuse into a common proof of the dehumanization of man which he saw as the critical challenge that this generation must face." [12]

The problem for all was to regain some lost perspective before it was gone for good, a perspective that would make it impossible to project so much evil on to an enemy or a racial minority that any outrage might then be committed. For Merton, the problem went far back behind the follies of individual statesmen, or the fears and obsessions of nations, to the loss of a contemplative stance, a sense of "measure." Without some such measure, the sense of the unimportance of the ego in comparison to the true centre on which it should rightly be focused, there was a total disharmony in individuals and societies, a loss of all true happiness, and a corresponding attempt to fill the void in ways that were destructive and suicidal.

Merton's way to tackle the problems of the world—problems of which he was aware in acute and agonizing detail—was the most radical one he could devise. In a United States that teemed with conflict over integration, the Vietnam War, nuclear weapons, and much else, Merton turned away from marching and making speeches (although he continued to write articles and was a sponsor of Pax Christi—an international Catholic peace movement—and of the Catholic Peace Fellowship) and set himself instead to do two things. One was to be totally informed about the conflicts of the modern world—and it is immediately obvious how widely he had read the reports of the Eichmann trial, the material about the Nazi death camps, information about Hiroshima, as well as news reports affecting more recent events. The other was quite simply to try to be, within the simplest framework of life he could find, that of the hermit, the "human" man, a man who had attemped to recover "measure," to be happy in the special sense of one who is attempting to live not just in and for the ego, but with his gaze directed beyond himself. There were, he would have been the first to say, other ways of trying to save the world, but this was his way. "The hermit life is no joke at all," he was to write to Dorothy Day in 1967, "but in it one gradually comes face to face with the awful need of self-emptying and even of a kind of annihilation so that God may be all, and also the apparent impossibility of it. And of course the total folly of trying to find ways of doing it oneself. The great comfort is in the goodness and sweetness and nearness of all God has made, and the created 'isness' which makes Him first of all present in us, speaking us." [23]

References

1. James Thomas Baker. "The Social Catalyst." *Continuum* 7(2), Summer 1969.
2. Thomas Merton. "Is the World a Problem?" *Commonweal* 84.
3. Dom John Eudes Bamberger. *Continuum* 7(2), Summer 1966.
4. Thomas Merton. *Original Child Bomb*. New York: New Directions, 1962.
5. Thomas Merton. "Nuclear War and Christian Responsibility." *Commonweal*. February 9, 1962.
6. Thomas Merton (Ed.). *Breakthrough to Peace*. New York: New Directions, 1963.
7. Thomas Merton. *Seeds of Destruction*. New York: Farrar, Straus, 1966.
8. Thomas Merton. "Christianity and Defense in the Nuclear Age: Notes for Conference to an Ecumenical Group." 1963. TMSC.
9. Thomas Merton. "Peace and Protest." November 1965.
10. Thomas Merton. Letter to *Commonweal*. May 8, 1965. TMSC.
11. Thomas Merton. Letter to Fr. Chrysogonus Waddell. January 4, 1964. TMSC.
12. Gordon Zahn. "The Peacemaker." *Continuum*, Summer 1969.
13. Thomas Merton. Letter to Miguel Greenberg. May 5, 1963. TMSC.
14. Thomas Merton. Letter to Ernesto Cardenal. November 17, 1962. TMSC.
15. Thomas Merton. Statement made concerning collection in Bellarmine College Library, Thomas Merton Studies Center [TMSC]. Santa Barbara: Unicorn Press, 1971.
16. Thomas Merton. *Faith and Violence*. Notre Dame, 1969.
17. John S. Higgins. *Merton's Theology of Prayer*. Spencer, Mass.: Cistercian Publications, 1971.
18. Thomas Merton. *The Living Bread*. New York: Farrar, Straus, 1952; Tunbridge Wells, Kent: Burns & Oates, 1976.
19. Thomas Merton. *New Seeds of Contemplation*. New York: New Directions, 1961.
20. Brother Patrick Hart. "The Contemplative Vision of Thomas Merton." Offprint from *Cistercian Studies*, 1978.
21. Thomas Merton. Letter to Miguel Greenberg. May 11, 1964. TMSC.
22. Thomas Merton. *On Peace*. London: Mowbrays, 1976.
23. Thomas Merton. Letter to Dorothy Day. August 18, 1967. TMSC.

18

THE LONELY ONE

᛭

As the 1960s wore on, Merton was moving steadily toward the restructuring of his monastic life. It was as if the fantasy he had woven around his cinder-block building in the woods had come true in the minds of other people as well as himself, and it was becoming less and less a kind of outpost of the monastery, where it was proper to converse with the "separated brethren" (although the Baptists and Episcopalians and Jews continued to come) and more and more the hermitage of Merton's dreams. Merton's sheer persistence in asserting that he needed time alone, coupled with the enormously heavy work-load he had carried for years at the monastery and the kind of insouciance in the face of authority with which he had survived the "terrible" years of the 1950s, somehow made it inevitable.

> I received permission to take some time in solitude up at the hermitage [Merton wrote to Dom Jean in June 1963] and so far I have had six full days up there, with more to come. Not allowed to sleep there, or say Mass there, but what I have had so far is a great godsend. It has certainly settled any doubts I may have had about the need for real solitude in my own life. Though I realize that I am not the ideal of an absolute hermit, since my solitude is partly that of an intellectual and poet, still it is a very real inclination for solitude and when I have continuous solitude for a more or less extended period, it means a great deal and is certainly the best remedy for the tensions and pressures that I generate when I am with the community. It is indeed the only really satisfactory remedy that I have been able to find. Distractions and "recreations" with visitors and active retreat work etc. do absolutely nothing to help. Also this little bit of solitude helps me to appreciate the real values that do exist in the common life, though they certainly manage to get hidden when I get too much of them. I hope to take more time in retreat later in the summer or the early fall. And perhaps get a day at a time, more frequently. [1]

Before very long, Merton was not only having "retreat" periods at the hermitage, and going down there to read or write on most afternoons, but spending one whole day a week there. He had also obtained permission to sleep there; he found to his pleasure that he began to sleep well for the first time in years. A whole new life was gently, very gently, beginning for him, a new routine, a new, and somewhat frightening exploration of unknown areas within him, yet also a return to something of the joy and hope he had felt when he first came to Gethsemani all those years before. The winter of 1964 brought back the memory of that other winter when he had first arrived. He remembered something of the cold and mystery and wonder of those first days at Gethsemani twenty-three years before, and thought how much he and the monastery had changed since then. [2]

It was partly that life at the hermitage gave some of the closeness to nature and the exposure to reality that the sophisticated young New Yorker had once experienced with all his senses freshly attuned to monastic life. Sleeping at the hermitage altered Merton's sense of time—it made him aware of the phases of the moon (sometimes he needed a flashlight to go down to the monastery for the night office, sometimes not), it made him aware, as people had been for centuries, of the shortness of the winter day and the difficulty of reading or writing by lamplight. It brought an acute knowledge of the reality of cold— using the outside "jakes" in winter was, as Merton wrote to a friend, "a grievous shock." It brought an awareness of trees and birds and insects and deer. Any grievousness was far outweighed by his pleasure in his new way of living. Among other things it was good to experience the cold, not by glancing at the thermometer, but by piling on the clothes and cutting logs for the fire.

Part of the pleasure lay in doing the ordinary chores that are familiar to those outside institutional life. He enjoyed collecting pine cones to light the fire, sawing, sweeping, making hot drinks over the fire. He enjoyed washing in the warm water left over from making the coffee, and then walking down to Mass in frost and moonlight. Above all, he enjoyed the lack of stress and tension, the absence of the old desperate search for quietness and solitude. [2] Nevertheless, prolonged periods of solitude and silence were still really impossible for him, since he was Novice Master with a heavy teaching load, and the slow, careful business of spiritual direction was very much part of his duties. This, of course, was in addition to the long hours in choir, his large correspondence, and all the work associated with his own writing.

Partly because new plans were afoot for reorganizing the novitiate, but also perhaps because Merton's health was deteriorating rather seriously, he was promised release from his duties as Novice Master in the near future. During the whole of 1963 and 1964, he was plagued by the misery of his bursitis and, intermittently, by colitis. He had a bad back pain, deriving either from the damaged vertebra in his neck or another displaced disk lower down in his back that was not discovered until a year or two later. His aches and pains involved a number of hospital stays and visits, and he complained to Seymour Freedgood at the beginning of 1964 about a hospital stay "because the pixies have chewed a piece out of one of my vertebrae." [3] When the pain was at its worst, he was excused night office and used to spend the time on a traction machine trying to get some relief from the ache of neck and shoulder.

Later on in 1964, the skin on his hands became so inflamed that he thought his work in the woods had given him a case of "poison ivy," and his friends and others were generous with advice about how to cure this painful and (to a writer) disabling condition. Naomi Burton recommended yellow laundry soap and "Rhulicream." "I ordered some yellow laundry soap," Merton told her, "through the 'channels' we have here, but I know how they look at such orders in the 'channel.' They just decide you are slightly nuts and forget it. I also ordered through other channels some Rhulicream. The other channels have not yet channelled, though it is nearly two weeks. . . . Fortunately Dan Walsh went into town and got me some and it works all right. The only trouble is that I have it so bad it is now in my system and I can't seem to get it out." [4]

Not all his brothers were indifferent to his sufferings. "A novice just came in with an invention of his, a poison ivy medicine made from a herb 'that the Indians used.' That is all I need." [4] But, despite Rhulicream, Indian medicine, and yellow laundry soap, Merton's skin worsened, particularly on his hands, and though soon he was under a specialist's care and having ointment, pills, and serum shots, there was no sign of improvement. On February 24, he wrote (and he rarely complained in his private journals about his physical health, bad as it often was at this period of his life) that his skin was so badly cracked that it hurt to work or even to tie his shoes, and he had to wear gloves to make his bed. It was not until later in 1965 that the cause was traced to an allergy caused by a particular wave of sunlight, a condition easily cured by wearing thermal gloves out of doors when the trouble appeared.

The year 1965 was not happy in any case, as far as his health was concerned. In March, a sapling sprang back and wounded the cornea of his eye when he was working in the woods, and for a while he had to wear a black patch. In April, he suffered a prolonged bout of diarrhoea and vomiting, the cause of which was quickly traced to a staphylococcus in the spring water that ran behind the hermitage. (Until this spring was discovered, it was necessary to carry drinking water down from the monastery—a tedious chore—and Merton was delighted to believe a local farmer who assured him, erroneously, that this water was the purest in the area.) Merton wrote to Naomi Burton,

> As to the bother I was having with the stomach, I finally went to the hospital for those very unpleasant tests and they found that I had a bug, which antibiotics appear to be controlling. I have a strict diet which I obviously cannot keep to except in the sense that I let them give me what they like in our so called "diet kitchen" and then try to work out an approximation for myself, which sometimes means not getting much to eat but I can stand to eat less, and don't worry, I am still surviving, besides which if the worst comes to the worst I eat something that is not on the diet like Chow Mein. This because I happen to have two cans of it in the place where I am living in the woods and it goes nicely with rice which I can cook and which I am encouraged to eat a lot of. So much for that, the things of the flesh and of the fleshpots. [5]

Naomi Burton wrote a sisterly rebuke on the subject of dieting on chow mein and received a repentant reply. "You are, of course, perfectly right about canned Chow Mein. Perish the thought. Tonight, the menu is Cream of Wheat. Not tasty, of course, but so healthy, so simple, so frugal, etc. etc. In the monastery one of the brothers made some 'grape juice' and a bottle of it exploded. All are now very eager to get some. I won't offer to send you some, there might be a disaster on the airways." [6]

Then, in August, he went back to hospital for tests for ulcers. He had come to have a deep dread of these tests. Over the years, he had become increasingly sensitive to physical examination and found any kind of probing excruciatingly painful, but on this occasion they found no ulcers, only inflammation of the intestines. Perhaps, however, it was this hospital stay, combined with Merton's patient but interminable pleas for solitude that made it possible for him finally to give up his work as Novice Master in August 1965 and hand the job over to Fr. Baldwin.

For all his ill health in the previous two years, however, he had accomplished an amazing amount of work, reading, and general participation in the life of the monastery and the world. He had continued to read with his immense voracity—he seemed to be particularly interested in Protestant theologians around this time. He was taking a close interest in Anglicanism, an enthusiasm fed by his friendship with Donald Allchin of Pusey House in Oxford. With advice from Fr. Allchin, he was reading a good deal of Anglican history, as well as some seventeenth-century Anglican divines, and modern Anglican writers such as Thornton and Stranks. "It seems to me that the best of Anglicanism is unexcelled," he wrote, "but that there are few who have the refinement of spirit to see and embrace the best, and so many who fall off into the dreariest rationalism. For my part I will try to cling to the best and be as English a Catholic as one in my position can be. I do think it is terribly important for Roman Catholics now plunging into vernacular to have some sense of the Anglican tradition." [7]

At just this time, when he was reading so much about Anglicanism, and perhaps remembering the Anglican services and some of the beautiful Anglican churches of his English boyhood, he had a dream that he suspected of having some relevance to Anglicanism: He dreamed that a distinguished woman Latinist came to talk to the novices about St. Bernard, only instead of talking to them she sang in Latin. The novices giggled and were restless and Merton was distressed at their reaction. In the middle of all this, the late Abbot, Dom Frederic, entered, the singing stopped and everyone stood up. Merton suddenly realized that he had violated the cloister by bringing in a woman and apologized in an undertone. The Abbot asked where she came from, and Merton replied, "Harvard," in a loud whisper that he knew she overheard. At this point the scene changed, and the novices were all in an elevator going down from the top of the building. Merton escorted the Latinist down by the stairs instead, but by now her clothes were torn and dirty, she was puzzled and sad and silent, and her Latin seemed to have deserted her. [2]

What, Merton wondered, could this dream be about? Was it about the Church, or about liturgical revival, or about Anglicanism? Did the central figure of the dream represent a secret Anglican anima of his own?

In October 1964, Merton held a one-man exhibition of abstract drawings in Louisville, all calligraphies he had done on Japanese paper sent by Ad Reinhardt. He worried a little about the pain this might cause to his friend Victor Hammer, who disliked abstract art. He said it made him feel like saying to Victor that if he knew Merton had a mistress he would be sad but he would understand. The drawings might seem to his friend to represent a similar apostasy, or a worse one, but he hoped he might look kindly upon them as a human folly, as a vice that Merton might charitably be permitted. [2]

The monastery itself was seething with ideas and experiments, some of them brought about by the Vatican II Council, some by the heady ideas of young monks who returned from studying in Rome, some ardently fomented by Merton himself. Dom James was having a difficult time keeping a grip on the situation, and one brother memorably described him as a man trying to keep hold of the papers on his desk when a furious wind was blowing through an open window behind him.

One change occurred while Merton was in hospital having his ulcer tests: a number of the monks reverted to the Christian names with which they had entered Gethsemani, while at the same time the practice of wearing the monastic "crown" was abandoned. Merton wrote ruefully to Robert Lax about this not very inspiring piece of *aggiornamento* ("bringing up to date"). "Here everybody change the name, but when the names was changed I was in the bathyscaph and became overlooked, so I came back with the same name. Here is change the haircut for *aggiornamento*. They got me and cut my hair when I was not looking I was in a brown study when they cut my hair and after I come out it was no more crown. This is what they have done around here in lieu of *aggiornamento*. As to the taking away the whips not a bit of it man, still the same old whips, just change the haircut in the name of *aggiornamento*." [8]

There were innumerable other changes either happening or about to happen, apart from name changing and hair cutting. Merton found it exasperating that, as with the hair cutting, monastic renewal seemed to have less to do with getting at the roots of the sicknesses and distresses that ruined contemplative life and more with tinkering on the surface with things that mattered very little. "One of the Fathers and several brothers worked out a whole elaborate new system of signs," Merton wrote to Dom Jean, "as complex as anything since Ulric of Cluny, and even going so far as to include signs that in a rudimentary way attempt to conjugate verbs!!! . . . The next thing will be subjunctives, imperatives, pluperfects and God knows what else. The author of this genial scheme . . . is determined that this will go through and be accepted for the entire order, even though one assures him that the very existence of sign language is now brought into question." [9] (It was later abandoned altogether.)

The old system had divided the monks into fathers and brothers—the fathers, the choir monks, spending more of their time in choir, being the singers and Latinists, and, historically, the scholars of the monastery, and the brothers spending less time in choir but more on other kinds of labour around the place. The root of this lay in a past in which a fair proportion of any monastic community were "gentlemen" with an educated background, and the rest were of humbler origin, some perhaps not even able to read or write. This state of affairs had gradually been changing for years, and part of the process of monastic renewal was to see how to remove the snobbish element in this ancient practice and how to join the two groups into one homogeneous community. Endless discussion about this took place at Gethsemani in the early 1960s, and in this Merton was, or felt himself to be, an odd man out. He visualized the "brothers" as living a more flexible life within the community, able perhaps to pursue careers, but at least able to follow bents that the very rigid hours of the choir monks made impossible. He was, in any case, in favour of a more flexible life for all within the community, a real consideration of the different needs of individuals rather than a determined effort to fit everyone into "the mould," sometimes, as in his own case, at a tremendous emotional cost. It seemed to him that the community, and in particular the Abbot, were threatened by the concept of change and that the threat drove them to further rigidity, which was beginning to be costly in terms of a satisfactory monastic community—already the great postwar boom in vocations was beginning to fade, and numbers were seriously dropping off.

The "changes" seemed to Merton precisely to lack the "authenticity" that he had preached so assiduously, to be merely token bows in the direction of a changing Church and world, empty gestures because the need for a real change of heart and mind was too terrifying to contemplate.

Merton wrote to Dom Jean,

> Unless we have a real reorientation a lot of our younger vocations are going to end in despair and we will not get any new ones. The handwriting is on the wall here: the more desire to get the monastic life well organized, and the effort to centralize everything in the monastery by reducing the brothers to complete conformity with the choir (under the pretext of giving them something, when one is taking away their real vocation and the relative flexibility and liberty which it allows them) is an illusion, and when the monks who have ingenuously given their heart to this idea find out that they have been "had" there will be considerable trouble. What we need most of all is the ability to grow and make some creative adaptation to situations that *cannot be defined in advance.* The great danger now seems to be that people are making rigid provisions in the light of situations that have always existed and may not continue to exist much longer. [9]

One of the big debates in monastic communities was about the vernacular liturgy. Was this desirable only for lay congregations, or should monastic communities adopt it as well? Merton wrote movingly of his own feelings about the Latin liturgy:

> I think that in the long run there will have to be readings in the vernacular, but I wonder if there are not quite a few complexities to consider. There is first of all the matter of Gregorian chant. Whatever may be my evil reputation among chant people, I am really deeply in love with the chant. I think it is certainly the greatest religious music we have available to us. I also like the Latin office, myself, and am so far demented as to love the Vulgate Psalter. I know that I may have to give this up for the good of others, eventually. But at the same time I think we ought to recognize that something valuable and great in itself cannot be discarded thoughtlessly. I certainly think that it will not be easy to replace by something objectively half as good, though of course for the benefit of those concerned there will be immense advantages. I also hope that the enthusiasm for readings (good) will not end with interminable ones, and offices that go on until 5 A.M. each day. I think that we must not add anything without proportionately subtracting something elsewhere, or else we will end up with the old business we tried to get away from a few years back. One trouble with the innate activism of so many in this order is that really they don't want intervals and lectio, they want things to be planned for them, they want entertainment and passivity (although they mightily like to plan new forms of this). [10]

Merton went on to complain about "the useless and trivial and often incomprehensible changes that have been made one on top of another in the last few years. Some of them will go out of effect even before they go into it, I believe." [10]

What has begun to be noticeable in Merton's letters is an exasperation both with the Order as a whole and with members of his own monastery in particular that borders at times on bitterness, and sometimes breaks out especially strongly when he writes to his closest friends. Thus, writing to Lax in April 1965, in the first delight of his freedom to use the hermitage he reveals, however lightheartedly, a sense of alienation that comes as a bit of a shock. "Yes it is true I sleep in the woods, I eat in the woods, I come down to the monastery only to say an occasional fie upon the commandant and to subvert the troops. . . . In my house in the woods I resist war. I resist everything. That is why the hermit life is called the pièce de resistance." [11] Physically moving out of the monastery had made Merton aware of a growing gap between himself and his brethren.

This intense irritation was later to surface in letters to other friends, in particular the Catholic theologian Rosemary Radford Ruether and Dom Jean LeClercq, and in conversation with Ed Rice (much of it appears in Rice's book *The Man in the Sycamore Tree*). In Merton's private journal, the irritation appears and is wrestled with, more in terms of a deep and painful psychological battle that Merton and Dom James seemed to be waging between them than in the general exasperation of the letters. Particular incidents aroused Merton's anger, often simultaneously bringing on stomach troubles and other physical ills.

One particularly painful incident occurred in October 1964 when a meeting of Abbots and Novice Masters of the Order took place at Gethsemani. While the meeting was being arranged there was a good deal of discussion about where it would be, until Dom James, according to Merton, advanced the information that it would have to be held at Gethsemani if Merton was to attend, because he was not on any account to leave the place. That Merton felt humiliated by this is obvious from his description of the event to Dom Jean:

> The Abbots' meeting was lively and I think everyone was satisfied or at least glad that the meeting took place. It was also profitable to have the novice masters involved, and I think it is really most important for the novice masters in our Order to get around and get experience of

other houses. Unfortunately it seems that my Father Abbot refuses to let me travel and even insisted that the only way a novice master's meeting could be held with me in it was for it to be held *here*. It is even likely that he opposed another meeting, since it would involve me travelling to another monastery. In general the other Abbots think this quite amusing. I must admit that it seems to me quite odd, and I can't say I am flattered to have my Abbot give the impression that he does not trust me. However, if I don't travel to other monasteries of the Order, I can manage to survive the blow, I think. [12]

One of the good things that came out of the meeting from Merton's point of view was that, instead of dismissing the hermit life as totally out of the cenobitic tradition, as had tended to happen in previous discussions in the Order, the Abbots began to consider "the extension into solitude as a normal and legitimate prolongation of what begins in the cenobium, and temporary solitude as a dimension of the *cenobitic* life itself," something that had certainly been Merton's own experience.

In a sense, the humiliation was repeated a few months later when Merton was invited to a very important ecumenical meeting at Collegeville; it was a subject close to his heart, and one at which many contemporaries of his own standing would be present. It seemed a rare and ideal opportunity for him to glean knowledge and exchange ideas.

Writing about the invitation in *Vow of Conversation*, Merton said that he felt it was the sort for which any other Superior would have granted permission, but that in his case it had been refused. It was not that he had set his heart on going, although he felt it would have done him good, but he would have learned a great deal, and had an opportunity to contribute to the Church's dialogue. What hurt him most was that he felt it was not really possible to discuss the issue rationally with the Abbot, since when Merton tried to do so he became emotional and looked both pained and obstinate, as if Merton was trying to steal something from him. Merton's impression was that he felt threatened and that his response to this was to resolve that Merton should not "get away with it." [2]

There was a reason given for the refusal—that it was not the Trappists' vocation to travel and attend meetings, but this did not seem to make sense in view of the fact that at least one other brother was travelling extensively in Europe and attending all kinds of functions. Merton felt his invitation to Collegeville was somehow a threat to Dom James' personal prestige. [2]

The problem was, how to accept the situation without resentment, and Merton felt he did not know how to begin to do it; in fact, it filled him with anger and distracted him from proper preoccupations. He wondered whether what the vow of obedience came down to was submitting yourself to another man's prejudices and fetishes. All the same, he had made the vow and felt he must keep it, yet knew he must seek to find a kind of submission that was true to his own feelings and understanding. He felt there were several wrong kinds of submission available to those living under a vow of obedience, that it was not enough to believe that any kind of submission would do. But it was hard to find a kind of submission that he could willingly accept. [2]

So now, at the beginning of 1965, Merton was once again in a state of crisis over his religious vocation, not in the sense of being tempted to give it up or to change his location, but of how to live his vow of obedience honestly in a situation where the reasons given for refusals seemed arbitrary. There was, as members of his brethren have since noted, something oddly compulsive about the way Merton and Dom James "got across" one another. Other monks, not only the much-travelled Father C., came and went on proper occasions, and although everyone shared at times the "mutual gripes" common to those under authority, few seemed to suffer as Merton did. Dom James, too, seemed to feel the pain of their disagreement. The two seemed sometimes to be colluding in some disastrous compulsion *à deux* that both hated and that neither could break out of, a condition not unknown in religious communities. In his early days at Gethsemani, Merton had needed, had almost revelled in, the utter dependence and submission by the vow of obedience. Now he had all but outgrown it, felt the deep resentment and sense of impotence it imposed on him, but could not quite break free.

Within a few days of the disagreement about the ecumenical meeting, Dom James preached a long and impassioned sermon in Chapter on vanity, ambition, and using one's gift for one's own glory.

Merton noted, in *A Vow of Conversation*, that the Abbot seemed to be in a very emotional state, with his voice trembling and his breathing not quite under control. He had no doubt the sermon was aimed at him and sat in burning but helpless resentment, humiliated not only by what was being said but also by the fact that he minded so deeply.

He could not stop thinking about it all day, yet the more he tried to argue himself out of minding and tell himself that it was trivial, the more he *did* mind and he found himself lying awake at night (something that rarely happened at the hermitage) fuming about it.

Finally he wrote to the Abbot saying he was sorry if he had offended him, but that his sermon had made him miserable and that he did not think it was fair to suggest that his work was only motivated by vanity and ambition.

Dom James's reply was that the sermon had had nothing to do with Merton, that he had no wish to hurt him and was most concerned for him. Merton wondered if he (Merton) had been the victim of his own illusion, whether he had been throwing the sort of childish tantrum that he ought to be beyond, but in his heart he did not really believe his Superior's reply. [2]

The depth of emotion involved, the furious exchange of appeals and denials, the agonized and obsessive reflection, has something of the air of a quarrel between long-standing lovers, the lovers in this case being not Merton and Dom James, but Merton and the way of life he had once romanticized and idealized into a travesty of itself. If Dom James had difficulty in accepting Merton realistically, then so, for many years, had Merton had difficulty in seeing the religious life for what it was: not a collection of saints nor a home in which he could enjoy the safe dependence of which he had been deprived as a child, but a family of very ordinary and fallible beings, not all of them capable even of recognizing his genius, but trying, for a mixture of good and bad reasons, to make a way of life within the walls of the Abbey.

Apart from this exceedingly painful relationship between him and the Abbot, there was much that was good and joyful in his life. Most important of all was his happiness with the hermitage, which he was gradually turning into a home, with bookshelves, a table, a few simple chairs, and a bed. It is difficult not to read a frustrated home-making instinct into the pleasure with which he arranged his things. On the wall, he hung the name plate that had once hung over his cell in the dormitory "N. Maria Ludovicus." He returned there at every opportunity. Thus, after the meeting with the abbots, an exhausting occasion, he recalled getting back to the hermitage about nightfall and relishing the deep silence. He said Compline with a candle burning in front of the icon of the Virgin and felt a wonderful sense of peace and rightness, something he rarely had in the Community. Then he slept deeply and well, although there were hunters and their dogs making a noise in the woods, and he woke up in time to say Lauds, quietly and slowly, sitting on the floor. [2]

Life was slowly getting more livable, on a practical level, at the hermitage. In October 1964, he was delighted to find a kerosene lamp awaiting him in a paper bag on his desk after Mass, and took it down to the hermitage eager to try it. He found that it filled the hermitage at night with a primitive and mysterious light, but that it was difficult to read by and smoked a lot. The contemplative in Merton thought that was good—it forced him to sit and meditate more—but the scholar found life easier down at the novitiate where he could read with uninterrupted ease. A couple of months later, when winter had really set in, he acquired a Coleman lamp and stove that filled him with delight. "Beautiful lamp: It burns white gas and sings viciously but gives out a splendid green light in which I read Philoxenos, a sixth century Syrian hermit. . . . Meanwhile, what does my Coleman lantern tell me? (Coleman's philosophy is printed on the cardboard box which I have (guiltily) not shellacked as I was supposed to, and which I tossed in the woodshed behind the hickory chunks.) Coleman says that the light is good, and has a reason: *'Stretches days to give more hours of fun.'*" [13]

Merton was not sold on Coleman's philosophy, which contradicted his idea of how days should be lived and of fun in general. His fun was peculiar, as he admitted, since he liked nothing better than listening to the rain on the roof and being generally alone and at peace with himself.

> I came up here from the monastery last night, sloshing through the cornfield, said Vespers, and put some oatmeal on the Coleman stove for supper. It boiled over while I was listening to the rain and toasting a piece of bread at the log fire. The night became very dark. The rain surrounded the whole cabin with its enormous virginal myth, a whole world of meaning, of secrecy, of silence, of rumor. . . . What a thing it is to sit absolutely alone, in the forest at night, cherished by this wonderful, unintelligible, perfectly innocent speech, the most comforting speech in the world, the talk that rain makes by itself all over the ridges. . . . As long as it talks I am going to listen. But I am also going to sleep, because here in this wilderness I have learned how to sleep again. [13]

This is the talk of a man who had learned, or was learning fast, about happiness. The hermitage was full of small joys and delights, and his senses seemed more acutely attuned to them—the gentle whistle of a blue bird, pigeons engaged in some "love-play" on the roof, saying the Psalms surrounded by pine trees, the bristles in his nose freezing in the cold, being aware that "you are one man in this snow where there has been no one else but one cat," the myrtle warblers "playing and diving for insects in the low pine branches over my head," the "whiskers of frost on the dead corn stalks," the arrival of a flashlight from Sears—"a hard bright pole of light probing deep into the wet forest," the pleasure of trying to take photographs of old tree roots.

Although he usually ate at the monastery, he was acquiring a few domestic arts, learning to cook rice properly, making potato soup out of a packet of dried powder, getting together a little supper for himself of soup, toast, and chopped pear and banana.

Strikingly, he continued to dream of the feminine, in ancient, archetypal forms, very reminiscent of "Proverb," the girl in the dream recounted earlier. This time, however, she came to him in the form of a Chinese princess, accompanied by her "brothers," he was delighted by her freshness and youth and truthfulness, on the one hand, and by her complete understanding of him and love for him, on the other. [2]

Perhaps even more moving were his dreams of a mother, a black mother, a woman of ugliness and severity yet of great warmth. The two of them embraced and danced together and he felt her deep love for him and his own intense gratitude. [2] This orphan was finding his home, the place where he belonged.

As with any growth, there were deep fears associated with the changes in his life. He might yearn for solitude but he also knew that there were dangers attached to it, that it threw him back on his own resources in a way that aroused anxiety, depression, and many other emotions. Even while he still worked in the novitiate, he observed that loneliness made it easy to fall apart. Talking to himself in the hermitage, singing, sometimes dancing he observed his own weakness in isolation, a dizziness that was potentially dangerous. [2] Seeking for an image to describe the loss of his old identity that he felt when left completely alone, it seemed to him to be like the loss of skin from his hands in his allergy, to be replaced by a new skin that both was and was not part of the "old" person. The following day he wrote that in the hermitage he would have to pray or go to seed, and the prayer would have to be a very genuine kind of prayer. Solitude induced its own inescapable pressure, so that the hermit prayed passionately to be shown how to pray. [2]

In a way Merton was still playing in his imagination with the idea of being a hermit, getting himself ready for what he imagined the real problems of loneliness would be. He knew that a certain sense of order was important—not just the order of mass and office, but the little chores of every day, the cooking and the washing up and the living with a certain cleanliness and self-discipline—a necessity he was to describe very movingly in his essay "The Cell." [14]

All through 1965 he was mentally preparing himself for his new life. He wrote to Naomi Burton in August 1965,

> At the end of this month I am out of my novice job and permanently in the hermitage. I am of course very glad, and also I see that it will not be any big joke either. The more I get into it, the more I see that the business of being solitary admits of absolutely no nonsense at all, and when I see how totally full of nonsense I am, I can see that I could wreck myself at it. Yet I really think God asks me to take this risk, and I want to do this. So please pray hard, really. I am an awful fool, and I know it, but if I can just be obedient and cooperative for once in my life, this can be a very good thing for me, incomparable in fact. [15]

A few days later he wrote to her,

> I am really very hopeful for the future, even though my system is acting up furiously at times. That is the way it has to be, and I am glad it is so.
> One thing is very clear to me: this going into solitude is really what I must do. I know, if one can ever be said to know, that this comes from God and that I must obey him. Of course my mad stomach tells me that He has lured me out there to destroy me. But of course I don't "believe" such a thing. And in the long run what is happening is the kind of acceptance where one says: "Look, if you want to destroy me, that's fine, because I would rather be destroyed by you and to please you than to have everything else in the world and not be pleasing to you." And the funny thing about this is that I absolutely mean it, and I can't think of anything else in the world that makes sense or calls for two seconds of interest, compared to this. Of course I would like to go out and be a hermit in grand style, but I realize that I will probably be a pretty damn silly one, but I don't care, I'll make the best of it. I can, with God's grace, and if it's absurd, well, classify it as existentialism and forget about it. But I think, in my stubborn head, that it is the real fulfilment of my monastic vocation. Also, however, I am aware that since there is much lacking in me, the lack is going to make itself felt. [15]

Some of those who knew Merton best had their doubts about him as a hermit. "Perhaps the worst thing that could happen to you," Naomi Burton had written with her usual blend of honesty and tact in response to his earlier letter about going into the hermitage, "in one sense would be your own realization that it wasn't the right thing for you. That would be a terribly hard admission and take a lot of guts to accept." [16]

This argument was to be put to Merton again, as we shall see, by others who understood him well, and it was a well-founded one. Merton had a profoundly social side and needed other people, not to mention books, ideas, and the conflict of social intercourse. If he also had a profoundly solitary, "poetic" and contemplative side, as he did, was it right or necessary, to feed this at the expense of his more extrovert side? Or could it be that what he most needed was a long "recuperative" period away from the activism of teaching and writing and that, given the peculiar circumstances of cenobitic life, and his own tendency to write for anyone who asked him, and to attract visitors, as well as to play a vociferous part in the ongoing debates within the monastery, this extreme step offered the only legitimate release?

There are different ways of considering this period of his life. Dom John Eudes Bamberger pointed out, with a certain dryness, that at no point in his life did Merton become a complete hermit—"It turned out that, even though Bardstown is somewhat remote from the American mainline of foreign visitors, there was a steady stream of persons of multifarious interests coming to speak with him from all over the world. He counted among his friends Vietnamese Buddhists, Hindu monks, Japanese Zen masters, Sufi mystics, professors of religion and mysticism from Jerusalem's University, French philosophers, artists and poets from Europe, South America and the States, Arabic scholars, Mexican sociologists and many others." [17] Some of these were merely correspondents; others actually turned up on the doorstep, with and without appointments, having travelled thousands of miles to see him; and although it is true that many of the famous medieval hermits also enjoyed vast numbers of visitors it is also true that at no point was Merton a hermit in the desolate sense usually conjured up by that word.

Dom John Eudes feels that this established exactly the right "balance" for him, a balance that presumably saved him from some kind of nervous collapse.

In spite of his deep, unvarying, and intense attraction to solitude Fr.

Louis was one of the most sociable of men, who had an absolute need for human society. Not a compulsive need, by any means. I do not mean that he could not dominate this need, still less that it was leading him around by the nose. Only that when he was most himself, and in order to be most himself, he would require, with considerable regularity, to meet with people with whom he could be simply present. As intense as his longing for solitude and silence was—and this was a very real, urgent necessity for him—it had always struck me that in an out and out battle, if it ever came to that, his social instinct would easily win the day. As victor in such a battle, however, he would have never reconciled himself to the ensuing pace, for life without solitude would have been unendurable. And I suppose that is why, in fact, a pitched battle never developed. The entrenched, semiconscious conflict between these two needs never developed. The conflict remained, active and intense, till the end. [17]

The wisdom of this assessment is undeniable, yet we may also perhaps detect other strands in Merton's attraction to the hermit life. One, which echoes something that can be found time after time in his writing, from *The Sign of Jonas* onward, is that Merton was seeking something he believed could only be found in solitude. It could be described in many ways, but in Merton's writing it was usually called "identity." The "lonely one" went out into the desert and there found himself stripped of all the comforting affirmations of friends and society and social contacts. Like Jacob, he wrestled with an angel, the angel of his own identity. Without the social props, would the "lonely one" have found anyone there, anything more than a miserable decline into anxiety, paranoia, depression, hallucination? Merton's own writing had often asserted that the "lonely one," passing through his ordeal by isolation, discovered a new identity, who he was in God's purpose, his own true name— but it was one thing to write this, another to put it to the test. It demanded a real "leap of faith." When Dom James permitted Merton to forsake the novitiate in August 1965 and make his permanent home in the hermitage, he was, wittingly or unwittingly, giving leave for this experiment to take place.

Dom James was probably conscious of what he was doing, at least to a large extent—not just because of Merton, but because of deep and mysterious changes in the tides of the Church in and around Vatican II; the idea of the hermit was capturing the imagination of more and more people. Cistercian abbots were looking with increasing favour on the idea as a development for monks who had lived the cenobitic life for a long time and were seeking a new spiritual environment and development, and Dom James himself had been captured by the new enthusiasm. A friend of the Abbey had willed some land to the monastery some eight miles away, and Dom James (who later did, in fact, become a hermit on that site) was envisaging a small community of hermits there, living near to one another, possibly in trailers, but leading separate lives.

Merton responded to that idea with a good deal of distaste. Predictably, he disliked the idea of "trailers," for a start. "Do you get the picture?" he asked Dom Jean ironically. "Bright modern little machines for living with all possible comforts etc. etc. Not only do I find myself incapable of accepting it, but my friends think it is very funny." [18] Merton was clearly also horrified at the thought of finding himself back in a group, even if the group consisted only of four or five like-minded people. Further, he feared the problem of "overcontrol," which he had, in a sense, run away from at the Abbey. "I am very much afraid that this 'colony' will turn out to be over-organized and that in the end we will end up there with Dom James running it like a little abbey and everyone under his thumb not able to move or breathe without doing so in the way that he would like. I know he is my Abbot, but I am very much afraid that I have never honestly been able to deal with him as with a 'spiritual father' and it would be impossible for me to do so sincerely." [18]

This letter is perhaps even more revealing than Merton intended, although it says nothing that he was not later to repeat to other friends. In some very deep sense, he had discovered that he could not tolerate being "part of a group" any more than his hands could tolerate a particular wave of sunlight. Both physically and psychologically he had separated himself from his brothers and could not endure the prospect of rejoining them. Nor could he, in the deepest sense, any longer live out the vow of obedience to his Abbot, however painstakingly he kept the vow on the surface. Whatever Dom James's feeling of goodwill toward Merton or lack of it, Merton had distanced himself from his Superior and was no longer to be won over by a generous concession to his own point of view. It was almost as if, except in the most formal sense, Merton had ceased to be part of the Order altogether.

References

1. Thomas Merton. Letter to Dom Jean Leclercq. June 10, 1963. TMSC.
2. Thomas Merton. *Vow of Conversation*. London: Marshall Pickering, 1988.
3. Thomas Merton. Letter to Seymour Freedgood. January 2, 1964. TMSC.
4. Thomas Merton. Letter to Naomi Burton. September 16, 1964. TMSC.
5. Thomas Merton. Letter to Naomi Burton. June 15, 1965. TMSC.
6. Thomas Merton. Letter to Naomi Burton. July 6, 1965. TMSC.
7. Thornas Merton. Letter to Rev. D. M. Allchin. April 25, 1964. TMSC.
8. Thomas Merton. Letter to Robert Lax. July 17, 1965. TMSC.
9. Thomas Merton. Letter to Dom Jean Leclercq. August 2, 1964. TMSC.
10. Thomas Merton. Letter to Fr. Chrysogonus Waddell. January 4, 1964. TMSC.
11. Thomas Merton. Letter to Robert Lax. April 28, 1965. TMSC.
12. Thomas Merton Letter to Dom Jean Leclercq. October 22, 1964.
13. Thomas Merton. *Raids on the Unspeakable*. New York: New Directions, 1964.
14. Thomas Merton. *Contemplation in a World of Action*. New York: Doubleday, 1971.
15. Thomas Merton. Letter to Naomi Burton. August 9, 1965. TMSC.
16. Naomi Burton. Letter to Thomas Merton. August 12, 1965. TMSC.
17. Dom John Eudes Bamberger. *Continuum* 7(2), Summer 1969.
18. Thomas Merton. Letter to Dom Jean Leclercq. May 11, 1965. TMSC.

19

"MONSIEUR WIND, WHAT'S HE SAY?"

❦

The early months of living as a hermit, although preceded rather inauspiciously by the hospital tests for ulcers, were a good and fruitful time.

Merton wrote to Dom Jean in September.

> It is working out very well. I go down once a day for Mass and dinner, the rest of the time I am here alone, and later I hope to be alone all the time. For the time being it is difficult to get Fr. Abbot to allow me to say Mass here.
>
> For the first time in twenty-five years I feel that I am leading a really "monastic" life. All that I had hoped to find in solitude is really here and more. At the same time I can see that one cannot trifle with solitude as one can with the common life. It requires great energy and attention. . . . But in any case it is good to have this silence and peace and to be able to get down to the *unum necessarium*. [1]

Fantasizing about solitude in the days before he retired to the hermitage, he had experienced real fear. It seemed to him that solitude could wreck him if he desired it for the wrong reasons and he was not at all sure that he might not be overcome by the loneliness it imposed on him. Sometimes solitude seemed to him like a stern mother, who would take "no nonsense," and he was afraid that, because of his "nonsense" she would reject him. But he longed not to be rejected, to learn enough about prayer to survive his loneliness, and to achieve what he thought the eremitic life was all about; that is, learning "to be" in the most ordinary human way. Ordinariness consisted in getting on with the tasks of everyday life, feeling hunger and fatigue, heat and cold, getting up and going to bed, preparing food and drink, defrosting the refrigerator, reading, meditating, working, and praying. These, as for his forebears, were proper ways for a man to occupy himself until he died. [2]

The reality when it came was as good as he hoped. His thankfulness was an almost tangible thing, in which he felt his whole body relaxing, even his gut relaxed and at peace. It felt good to go for days without speaking to anyone except his Mass server and an occasional brother.

Electricity had come to the hermitage. One of the brothers had wired up the lighting and the cooking stove that awaited its arrival, and for all his dislike of technology Merton loved it, particularly being able to see to read better at night. One afternoon the foreman came and set up the meter, and Merton pressed the switch and knew the blessing of light had arrived. He took particular pleasure in the fact that a Mexican mask he had on the wall showed up well, and also the ink on the scroll Suzuki had given him. He celebrated this technological marvel by cooking his supper on the stove. He found that being able to get up and put on an electric heater made it easier to start praying, as he did not have to lay and light a fire.

Another pleasure of the electricity was the refrigerator, which kept him awake the first two nights with its little noises. He was not sure whether having a refrigerator was an infringement of poverty, but reflected that even the poorest local farmers had refrigerators and usually television too.

Much of his new lightheartedness spilled over into his other relationships, and as always, into his "nonsense" correspondence with Lax. "Well now I got to take Rex for a run round the clock, and fire off the steam engines, and lay open the thermostats to dry out in the weather, and fly a kite and put out the cat and bathe the canary and punish the children and sell the estate and wheel Uncle Ray back into his closet." [3] The delightful cares of the householder were descending on Merton.

But in 1965 there were more important matters afoot than being a hermit. In April of that year, Merton had mourned the feeling of being the only priest in the country, it seemed, who had not actually marched at Selma. In February, he had written to President Johnson, the kind of hopeless letter written to a politician to protest against intolerable policy, in this case the Vietnam War. He had struggled in his mind over the birth control controversy that was rocking the Church at the time, feeling a great respect for the lonely stand of Archbishop Roberts who supported the use of contraceptives, and being driven by his example to reexamine the whole subject of "natural law."

In September 1965, he joined in a fast for peace organized by women who believed in nonviolence. Knowing of the fast only by hearsay, he got the dates wrong. "Obviously I did not go ten days without food," he wrote humorously to Dom Jean. "I am not that ascetic. I took a week on ordinary Lenten fast as we have it here." [4]

He was deeply distressed when a young member of the Catholic Peace Movement, Roger Laporte, burned himself alive as a form of protest. Merton came close to resigning from the several peace groups, fearing a particular kind of hysteria that seemed to him to be taking over, supporting the wholesale burning of draft cards and encouraging the "kids" to see themselves as totally at enmity with "the system." Nevertheless, he continued to support his old friend Dorothy Day of the Catholic Worker movement and to write steadily for her newspaper, even though she and her workers were by now very much at odds with authority. "If there were no *Catholic Worker* and such forms of witness," he wrote to Dorothy Day in December 1965, "I would never have joined the Catholic Church." [5] Members of the Catholic Worker movement used to visit Merton at Gethsemani, and according to Lax, said that Merton "was the hippest of cats—that it was a real trip, man, and everyone was grooving. Now they are all in jail." [6]

Dan Berrigan, Merton's priest friend, was in trouble because he had encouraged the young to burn their draft cards; his Superior had "silenced" him. Catherine Doherty corresponded angrily with Merton about this "silencing," but found him unexpectedly sympathetic to the Superior, believing his action to be a strategy to prevent higher superiors from taking more damaging action. But he "anguished" deeply, to use his own word, about the political chaos and about many Catholics' complacent adherence to the status quo of war and racial injustice.

There were happier moments. Merton enjoyed and was amused by his friends' pleasure in taking photographs of him when they came to stay. He had filled out over the years and somehow managed to look entirely unmonklike. "Thanks for the contact sheets of pictures of the irascible and stupid looking old man," he wrote to Ed Rice. "Now like an ape, now like Picasso, now like God knows, Hilaire Belloc maybe. . . . I know I missed my vocation: in some of them I am distinctly an investigator for the

NKVD." [7] He was particularly glad to have some copies to send to aunts in England and New Zealand with whom he had now established contact. One of them had knitted a sweater, and he wanted a picture of himself wearing it to send to her.

Merton's face also resembled that of Henry Miller, something Miller himself had first remarked on. Miller had loved Merton's *Wisdom of the Desert* and *Original Child Bomb* and had sent messages to Merton via Jay Laughlin that had led to a correspondence of some years. Merton wrote to Miller, "Yes, I have often thought of the resemblance between our faces. I had not associated Genet with it, not knowing what he looks like. I suppose the person I most resemble, usually, is Picasso. That's what everybody says. Still I think it is a distinction to look like Picasso, Henry Miller and Genet all at once. Pretty comprehensive. It seems to imply some kind of responsibility." [8]

Miller and Merton also discussed the worrying problem of writers of being deluged with letters from unknown people and of finding time, or knowing how, to respond to them, or of being plagued with guilt if they didn't respond to them. Merton was a formidable letter writer—thousands of his letters exist, to all kinds of people, known and unknown—but he shows an interesting detachment in his comments to Miller about the problem. "People going down for the third time think a letter will keep them afloat. But often what they are going down in is itself an illusion, and the letter itself will be to them an illusion. Sometimes I answer sometimes I can't and I mean not to worry about it. There is a destiny involved there too. But there is no question that we spend our lives battling with mountains of crap and this is no mean exercise." [8]

But Merton could show the deepest compassion to friends or other correspondents going through periods of anguish, not least the kinds of anguish, such as divorce or business difficulties, that might at first sight seem farthest from his own experience. The following is part of a letter to one of his closest friends, who was approaching divorce:

> Listen man, about the anguish. There are things you can intelligently do about it. Not easy, no hopeful slogans, no crap. Angst is a big mess, can't help being horrible. What is angst anyway it is the result of truth and life getting fouled and bottled up through fictions, obstacles, social forms, plain crap, and personal errors. So what burns you is

good but it is working against you in such a way that it is against you instead of for you.

First big thing is not to get so damned attached to the angst that all you are able to do is tread the mill and keep it going round and round. Get off treadmill if you can.

There is very serious reason why the life of the Catholic Kirk should induce all forms of neurosis and anxiety and everything else right up the line. The way the Christian faith is lived is so schizophrenic that it is a wonder one can be at the same time Christian and sane. I mean to say a Christian according to the pattern and the approved forms. You think I got fun here? Man, you think more. You think I got no angst? Man, think again. I got angst up to the eyes. [9]

Several paragraphs of practical advice and suggestion followed. Then Merton concluded,

God is in you, crucified in you, through stupidity of people including your own. This ought to be enough for anybody, your troubles are his more than yours, you should worry. But O.K., you worry. It is possible to worry less. He is God. You got enough native good sense and grace to tell the true from the false. Wheat and cockle, growing together. . . . God will take care of the cockle and meanwhile get some angel to lift the stone, out of the way so you can be a little more easy. I pray for angel to lift stone, you pray too, everything O.K. one of these days (maybe after the end of the world). Joy in Christ. [19]

He could suit his style to his correspondent, but what most of his letters to people in trouble had in common was his capacity to put himself alongside the pain, to speak not from some spiritual vantage point where the fight seemed to be over, but to stress his own failure to make a success of the very problem that perplexed them. He wrote gently to a woman whose husband had left her and who complained bitterly of her loneliness. He said that there is no fully satisfactory answer—loneliness and death are part of the human condition, and this must sooner or later be accepted.

I know from my own experience that the loneliness and the confrontation with death only become intolerable when I have unconsciously argued myself into a position in which I am in fact refusing to accept them and insisting that there is some other way. But there is no other way. . . . I wonder if you are not doing what so many of us do: acting on the assumption that one ought not to be lonely and that one ought not to be travelling towards death, in fact that one ought not to be tempted to faithlessness and despair. This is unrealistic. It is also universal. But all of us Christians, since we know that we must live by faith and hope in Christ, assume that our formal commitment to Christ must be tested by its capacity to exempt us forever from any further anguish and danger of despair. But it does not do this. Quite the contrary. The Christian is one who knows that without the constant help of grace he cannot help but despair. And he knows that no amount of agitation and struggle on his own part can exempt him from this temptation. But once we have the gift of accepting our existential situation, everything is likely to come along with it. [10]

He said that, of course, having chosen the life he has he has more reason to expect loneliness than those who live in "the world," although he is not very good at dealing with it. But both of them are almost incredibly lucky compared to many of the world's most wretched people. "Neither one of us has yet been beaten to death with chains like the negroes in Mississippi. . . . Have courage and do not expect too much of men. The more you fix your hope and love on God the more He will tend to resolve these other conflicts. Yet do not expect a perfect solution." [10]

Quite apart from angst and loneliness, Merton had, as usual, his share of physical troubles. The pain caused by the damaged vertebra in his neck had been growing worse for several years, and in the end the only solution was a complicated and unpleasant operation in March 1966. "It is off with me to the old hospital, to the lazaerto, to the krankhaus," he wrote Lax. "Carry me off to the hospital, I cry. But without enthusiasm. The back is in a crick. The neck has refused. The vertebra has crumped. The spine has diverged. The head has rolled off. . . . I am off to the hospital to have the neck removed. I will return with eyes in the back of my neck." [11]

The operation actually involved removing bone from the hip and using it to fuse two vertebrae. He rarely mentioned this fairly daunting operation except to joke about it, save to his Aunt Gwyn in England. "I hate to have them getting into my central nervous system. It knocks you out for a bit, and is unpleasant. I still feel numb in one of my legs as a result. But still, one has to put up with this sort of thing." [12]

To Ed Rice he remarked not long after the operation that he was suffering from bursitis, a sprained ankle, and another displaced disc, but that the real problem was his digestion. "The food problem is beyond reason. For a while I solved it by not eating but now I am hungry again. Lost 20 lbs. but have got back about 10 I guess." [13]

One bonus of his convalescence, however, was that he was given permission to use a phonograph, and he discovered the records of Bob Dylan. He was rapturous about "The Times They Are A-Changing" and "Highway 61," described Dylan's work, rather mysteriously, as "baroque," and begged Rice to send him more Dylan records, which he got official permission to receive. Jokingly Merton suggested Rice send a barrel of LSD along with the records: "I am going to be the teen culture king of Trappist Nebraska."

He also enjoyed the songs of Joan Baez, who visited him once at Gethsemani, and he told the visiting Anglican Donald Allchin that one of the nice things about being a hermit was that you could sing out loud while you cooked your breakfast. What did he sing, Fr. Allchin inquired. A favourite, Merton admitted, was "Silver Dagger," one of Joan Baez's hits, a folk song with rather alarming incestuous overtones:

> Don't sing love songs,
> You'll wake my mother,
> She's sleeping here right by my side,
> And in her right hand a silver dagger,
> She says that I can't be your bride.

A later line goes "I'll sleep alone all of my life."

Another, much more devastating, effect of his hospital stay, was that he fell in love with a young nurse, to whom Mott gives the concealing initial "S". S., according to Mott, was dark, slim, grey-eyed and pretty, of Irish descent, but reminiscent of the girl "Proverb" in Merton's dream. Of course, the sort of attraction that so often exists between a male patient, in the regression of convalescence, and his nurse, is a well-known phenomenon. It was heightened in this case not just by her beauty, but by a deep sense of rapport between the two of them. A Catholic, S. had read and enjoyed some of Merton's work, and was very ready to enter into and discuss the ideas behind it. They found they liked similar jokes, loved Peanuts cartoons, relished conversation and teasing.

To his total surprise, by the time he left the hospital Merton found he thought continually about S. He knew that she was engaged to a boy in Chicago, which, together with a considerable age difference, maybe made him feel safer, but he encouraged S. to write to him in an envelope marked "Conscience Matter", which meant that the letter would not be censored, and on the hospital visits that succeeded his operation he arranged to meet her, and, on one occasion, arranged for Jim Wygal to pay for their meal. Then began a period of letting some of his closest friends in on the secret, in order to persuade them to arrange meetings that included S. Ping Ferry described to me taking Merton for a car ride only to have him stop at the first telephone and beg for change to call S. The friends took up various positions from loving sympathy to feeling they were being used for an end that worried them. The most forthright was Jim Wygal, who told Merton he was in danger of destroying himself. S. herself felt caught in the situation—she loved Merton in return—but also distressed and anxious about it.

Merton was now trapped painfully in obsession, endlessly scheming how to talk to S. on the telephone or in person, fantasising at times about marriage, yet also striving to pursue the life of monk and hermit as if nothing had happened. It is impossible not to feel sympathy for the overwhelming sexual and emotional love and longing for a woman after all the years of abstinence. It is possible too to see this develop-ment in his life as a kind of fulfilment of the dreams of the feminine that had been haunting him—it is not strange at all that he found an actual woman in whom these dreams were realized. His psychological growth depended on coming to terms with the feminine.

But his circumstances made the working out of his feelings almost intolerably difficult. His vows, his reputation, the surveil-lance of Dom James, but above all his deep inner commitment to monastic and eremitic life, warred against the new vision S. represented, her love for him, and of his for her. There was no doubt that he was on a collision course.

There was the doubtful honesty of his using friends and hospital visits to "cover" his meetings and conversations with S., or asking her to write "Conscience Matter" on her letters; it revealed the appalling inner split between the life he had so publicly chosen and his tremendous longing for love.

He resolved the conflict in a somewhat "unconscious" way, seeing S. in ever more indiscreet circumstances and making a series of telephone calls to S. from the Abbey itself, which sooner or later were bound to be overheard by a monk supervising the switch-board. When they were, the monk concerned promptly reported Merton to Dom James. Another monk passed the information to

Merton, who then, perhaps relieved, went to the Abbot to face the music. Dom James was gentler and kinder than Merton had expected, though he inevitably told him it must all stop. There began a series of farewells to S., by telephone and in person. S. herself took the action of taking a job away from Louisville, and in August she left—there had been five months of pain and joy for Merton and now it was over. He was left with an agonizing loneliness, a new awareness that he was able to love and be loved, but perhaps also the discovery of how totally he was given, body and soul, to his life of monk and hermit, and the fact that he would "sleep alone all his life" as the song had said. Only now he had a different understanding of himself and the world to weave into that knowledge. He suffered for the pain he had caused S.

On September 12, he made a permanent commitment, although not a vow, to live as a hermit. "Here I sit in the big silences and nothing speaks but the gas heater which clucks and chunks but gives out the big heat," Merton wrote to Lax in November, "for because of the burse and the bump I no longer chop the log or fell the pine. I just sit here looking at the snow and wishing hard for some whiskey but there is none. I live a flawed existence. I am utterly without rapport.

"Also was here Maritain, very fine, very noble, back from the old days when there used to be people." [14]

Merton was working on a book called *Mystics and Zen Masters* [15] and in September his *Conjectures of a Guilty Bystander* [16] came out, the journal that perhaps brought home to many readers that Merton had warmed and matured over the years and that despite his passionate enjoyment of Zen and Chuang-Tzu, of Gandhi and of Eastern thought in general, his native language was still Catholic Christianity, although the vocabulary was no longer that of the young monk of quarter-century before. "Copies of Subjunctive of the guilty bartender have reached my overburdened desk," Merton wrote Naomi Burton on September 18. "This young bartender shows promise but has awfully strange ideas. I will recommend it to my friends." [17]

In that autumn of 1966 a very important correspondence began between Merton and the Catholic theologian Rosemary Radford Ruether. In August, she had sent him her book *The Church Against Itself* [18], and Merton had sent a rather stiff reply, which concluded, "I would be happy if you would send along anything that you think would be good for me to read. I depend to a great extent on the light and love of my friends who keep me informed, notified, alerted, etc." [19]

This was the beginning of a long and very searching intellectual discussion between them, which went on nearly up until the time of his death. Rosemary Ruether challenged many of his easier assumptions and also confronted him on the question of his reasons for staying at Gethsemani with a directness that none of his friends attempted. What was also important, as becomes clear in his correspondence, is that she was a woman who was his intellectual equal, on whom he projected, at least for a time, the "severe, cerebral" image he had carried with him from his childhood memories of his mother.

In their earliest letters, they discussed the Augustinian theology of sexuality. She urged him to read Bonhoeffer's *Act and Being*, and Merton commented on the necessity of love between man and woman depending on "a true acceptance of createdness." [20] The Augustinian ecstasy that was a perfection of giving, *caritas*, recognized this createdness; the common travesty of "love," which was fusion, narcissim, did not, but worked on the level of *cupiditas*. Merton confessed to not having read much of Teilhard de Chardin, whom Ruether quotes, partly since anything he wrote about Teilhard would get censored by the Order, and partly because he did not enjoy Teilhard's work enough.

There was a mild, but interested reply from Rosemary Ruether in which she basically agreed with Merton but puzzled about his lack of anger where she felt he ought to be angry. "I think your perspective is much like mine, although with a little more touch of melancholia where I tend to be angry: also without the agonizing which I have done over modern Bible exegesis which makes it so difficult to make the kind of statement about 'what the Church teaches' which still comes easily to you. It is precisely this agony which I seem to share with so few other Catholics (except perhaps Küng who struggles with this too). . . . They take for granted things which for me are not only questionable but insupportable." [21]

Suddenly the correspondence between them took a different turn, as if Merton had suddenly found someone he had been looking for and knew it was safe to go further. The change began in January 1967, when he read a discussion about women in the Church in *Commonweal*:

It happens that you, a woman, are for some reason a theologian I trust.
Almost the only one. And I do think I need the help of a theologian.
Do you think you could help me once in a while? I do not intend to be
very demanding on your time, but I would like to feel that I can resort
to you for suggestions and advice. Not so much for my work, as just to
help me think. I have no great project in mind. I just need help in two
areas where I have serious trouble and where I have simply been
avoiding a confrontation. The Bible and the Church.

To begin with the Church: I have no problem about "leaving" or
anything. My problem with "authority" is just the usual one and I can
survive it. But the real Church. I am simply browned off with and
afraid of Catholics. All Catholics from Ottaviani to du Bay, all down
the damn line. There are a few Catholics I can stand with equanimity
when I forget they are Catholics and remember they are just my
friends, like Dan Berrigan and Ed Rice and Sister Mary Luke and a
lot of people like that. I love the monks but they might as well be in
China. I love all the nice well meaning people who go to Mass and
want things to get better and soon, but I understand Zen Buddhists
better than I do them and the Zens understand me better. But this is
awful because where is the Church and where am I in the Church? You
are a person who might have an idea of the Church that might help me
and that I might trust. . . . Is the Church a community of people who
love each other or a big dog fight where you do your religious business,
seeking meanwhile your friends somewhere else. . . . I do wonder at
times if the Church is real at all. I believe it, you know. But I wonder if
I am nuts to do so. Am I part of a great big hoax? I don't explain
myself as well as I would like to: there is a real sense of and confidence
in an underlying reality the presence of Christ in the world which I
don't doubt for an instant. But is that presence where we are all saying
it is? We are all pointing (in various directions) and my dreadful
feeling is that we are all pointing wrong. Could you point some place
for me, maybe? [22]

Were these the questions that Merton had come out into the
wilderness to ask? Silence, loneliness, the absence of the corsetlike
structure of Offices and Chapter (although Merton continued with
the Offices alone) made inevitable an examination of the whole
purpose on which his life had been based. Rosemary Ruether
immediately realized the importance of what was being revealed:
"I was profoundly moved by your last letter. I have had a feeling in
reading your words previously that you were holding back; that
though you were treating profound ideas, you were doing it with
the surface depth of your being. In this letter, I felt some swirl of

deeper troubled waters, that I had sensed were being held back, but I didn't expect to see them surface. I thought that the 'Catholic' structure would keep them under." [23]

She goes on to give her view of the Church as a "necessary but secondary structure serving as the temporal vehicle for a tradition about a certain reality . . . but the reality is not only or even primarily happening there." She defines the "Bible problem" as "part and parcel of our wrong definition of God's incarnation. God's incarnation is not magical new nature—this is the heresy which was condemned as monophutism (sic). . . . Incarnation whether Jesus, the Bible, the Church, the Eucharist—this is man's word about God's word. . . . But this happens really within or rather *as* words, persons, gestures, 'stuff' that itself remains quite human; fallible, stumbling, imperfect, full of error and sin." [23]

Commenting on a remark of Merton's that "he had no trouble with his vocation," Ruether said,

> Maybe you should be having some trouble with your vocation. I love the monastic life dearly (I am a Third Order Benedictine) but today it is no longer the eschatological sign and witness in the Church. For those who wish to be at the "kingdom" frontier of history, it is the steaming ghetto of the big city, not the countryside, that is the place of the radical overcoming of this world, the place where one renews creation, disposes of oneself and does hand to hand combat with the demons. I don't see how anyone who is stuck in the old moribund (once eschatological) structures and is at the same time alive to the times cannot be having some trouble with his vocation. But perhaps for you more important: mere more reading and thinking about Word and Church will not help. I think you will have to find some new way of having Word and Church happening *for you*. Perhaps you have gone as far as you can go in the hermitage direction, you are running out of fat from previously accumulated community contact, and need renewal in a period of service. I may be wrong . . . but that is what I saw rising between the lines, a cry of help for community "I have no trouble with my vocation," the hermit doth protest too much. Withdrawal and solitude is not a life vocation, it is part of a larger rhythm of life. [23]

In his response, Merton moved away from the theological difficulties he had presented at first ("I am not enough of a theologian to be really bothered by theological problems") and got down to the discussion of his hermit vocation that Rosemary Ruether had initiated.

I always tend to assume that everyone knows I had a monumental struggle with monasticism as it now is and still disagree violently with most of the party line policies. I am a notorious maverick in the Order and my Abbot considers me a dangerous subject always ready to run off with a woman or something, so I am under constant surveillance. If I am allowed to live in a hermitage it is theoretically because this will keep me more under wraps than otherwise. So when I say I "have no problem with my vocation" I just mean that I am not for the moment standing over the Abbot with a smoking gun in my hand. . . . In other words I have the usual *agonia* with my vocation but now after twenty-five years I am in a position where I am practically laicized and de-institutionalized, and living like all the other old bats who live alone in the hills in this part of the country and I feel like a human being again. My hermit life is expressly a *lay* life. I never wear the habit except when at the monastery and I try to be as much on my own as I can and like the people around in the country. Also I try as best I can to keep up valid and living contacts with my friends who are in the thick of things and everyone knows where my real "community" is. I honestly believe that is the right place for me (woods, not Gethsemani) in so far as it is the right battleground. But from my experience I would myself be leading a less honest and more faked life if I were back in the cities. This is no reflection on anyone else. In staying here I am not just being here for myself but for my friends, my Church, and all those I am one with. Also if there is one thing I am sure of too it is my need to fight out in my own heart whatever sort of fight for honesty I have to wage and for fidelity to God. I am not by any means turning my back on other people, I am as open as the situation (of overcontrol) permits and want to make this more open as time goes on. Lots of people would like me to get out and join them in this or that, but I just don't see that I could do it without getting into some absurd role and having to act a dumb part or justify some nonsense or other that I don't really believe in. I know I firmly disbelieve all the favorite clichés about monasticism and community knows it too. I can't say where and when my life is eschatological, because as far as I can see I am a tramp and not much else. But this kind of tramp is what I am supposed to be. This kind of place is where I am finally reduced to my nothingness and have to depend on God. Outside I would be much more able to depend on talk. [24]

Rosemary Ruether replied warmly, relieved not to have hurt him by opening up parts of Merton that he himself was not yet ready to examine. She discussed the danger not only of the "theology of the big city" but also of the false ecstasies of woods, silence, and apparently communing with God, because all too often she discovered "I have been communing with nothing but myself." For her the alternative was what she called "prophetic community," the real struggle of encounter with others with all their pain and our own. "Only theology bred in the crucible of experience is any good." [25]

She shared with Merton just how little of the old comfortable "Catholic Christ" had been left to her as a result of the crucible of experience and of the kind of faith she had built on that:

> The agony of plain history has dismantled the Catholic Christ for me bit by bit until finally the last fragment of it is gone, and I am relieved. Jesus was a Jewish eschatological prophet filled with visions of the kingdom of God, increasingly convinced that he was God's instrument to announce the crucial hour, he and his disciples went up to Jerusalem to see the great glory, and he got strung up like a common criminal and his followers cut the scene like rabbits. What then to do? Admit you were just wrong, or quixotically reaffirm the vision in a new form. Turn the denouement itself into salvation. Something like that. All very human, and yet revelation, the start of a seminal idea that continually lights up reality in new ways. But basically this salvation is not some magic figure in the past, but the disclosure situation here and now for me the Christological structure of creation: of which Jesus of Nazareth is historically the foundational kairos, but which we encounter not by encountering that one but this one right here before me. [25]

She urged Merton to read two Protestant theologians, Martin Dibelius and Krister Stendahl—"plain New Testament historians"—not Rudolf Bultmann and those who are trying to create a new theology. She said that the point of being a Christian in the city was to try to humanize modern technology and modern society, and more or less told Merton he was escaping all this. "Let us admit at the outset that I am radically out of sympathy with the monastic project, not merely in its fallen state, but also in its original and most intrinsic self-understanding. This being the case I despair of being able to say anything useful to you. All monasticism rests on a mistaken confusion of creation with this world, and so they suppose by withdrawing in some symbolic fashion from creation they are leaving the world. But creation is precisely not the world but its antithesis, and so what they do is essentially the opposite of salvation. They withdraw from creation into the desert taking 'this world' with them and then they dwell apart from creation, but in a newly erected kingdom of the prince of this world. . . .

You have not withdrawn from this world into heaven, you have withdrawn from creation into hell." [26]

Merton responded to all this attack with a deeply hurt and angry response. In addition to the attack in her letter, he had just had a visit from a friend who had told him how "out of touch" all the monks were, and suddenly he had had enough. Anyone would think, he said, that he was living in a sixth-century virgin forest with wolves prowling at the door.

> This is not sub-human nature out here, it is farm country and farmers are people with the same crucial twentieth century problems as everybody else. Also tree planting and reforestation are not simply sentimental gestures in a region that has been ravaged by the coal and lumber companies. . . .
>
> And while we are on that, another thing. I wonder if you realize that you (at least from your letters) are a very academic, cerebral, abstract type. You talk about God's good creation, the goodness of the body, and all that, but I wonder if you have any realization at all of the fact that by working the land a person is deeply and sensually involved with matter. I return to the point I made in my last letter and which you dismissed as romanticism. It is not romanticism at all, my friend. It is something you city people need very badly indeed. And for all their gnosticism, monks (at least in the West where manual work has been held in honour) have had this sensual contact with matter and have not in fact despised matter at all except in theory. Hence I would say that in my life the cultivation and expansion of the senses, and sensual awareness of things and people, and sensual response, are probably a whole lot more important than they are in yours. [27]

He challenged her suggestion that the Christian in the city is necessarily any more effective than the Christian in the country—can she stop the war in Vietnam any more than he can?

> Certainly the demons down here are small time. But it is by confronting them that a monk has to open the way to his own kind of involvement in the big time struggle . . . to be effectively iconoclastic in the modern world. I am personally keenly aware that if I merely threw up the sponge down here and went out to engage in something ostensibly more effective, it would be a real betrayal. . . . I am in the most uncomfortable and unenviable position of waiting without any justification, without a convincing explanation, and without any assurance except that it seems to be what God wants of me and that this kind of desperation is what it means for me to be without idols—I

hope. I don't expect anyone on earth to congratulate me on this, but it seems to be what I have to do. But I do think, given a more favorable situation, the monastic life can play a very helpful part in the worldly struggle precisely because of the different perspectives which it has and should preserve. What is needed is for the doors to open and for people to get around more and learn a little. [27]

He said that for her being a monk seemed to mean being an artificial kind of man, whereas for him it meant being "mere man," not dressed in a role as a banker, doctor, politician or whatever. And he came to what was perhaps the nub of his whole life and hope: "What would seem to me to be the beginning of the resolution of all alienation and the preparation for a real return without masks and without defenses into the world, as mere man. . . . Your critical mind will chop it down to size but I think there is some thing valid there." [29]

Although in her reply Rosemary Ruether addressed Merton for the first time as "Dear Thomas" instead of "Dear Father Merton" or "Dear Thomas Merton," she came back with a fairly fierce reply, beginning "I am really kind of disappointed in you. Do you realize how defensive you are, how you are forever proving, proving how good your life is, etc. You really won't hear the kind of balance I am trying to establish in my letters, but immediately distort it into your own caricature." [28] She suggested that he was not listening to how deeply they were, in fact, in agreement and that this was because of some conflict of his own: "I again get the impression that you are in some period of crisis whose implication you are fighting off with loud arguments." She did not know what crisis, but said it must be met by a real development in him, a new level of perception, or a regression.

I think your subconscious is sensing the need for a change and your superconscious is fighting it off, and this is why you manifest a great deal of defensiveness towards monasticism in particular when the discussion veers on something that touches your present "rightness."

P.S. Sorry you find me so abstract. If I weren't a woman would it have occurred to you to accuse me of being cerebral? Interesting resentment there. . . . I wouldn't mention the resentment bit if it wasn't so absolutely predictable. I am just as fleshly as you, baby, and I am also just as much "thinking" animal as you. [28]

Never in his life at Gethsemani had Merton been spoken to like

that. Apart from the kind of "bat and ball" struggle he had with
Dom James, in which move and countermove were almost as
predictable as in the case of an old married couple, he was
accustomed to altogether more politeness. His old friends might
be teasing, but they were unvaryingly kind. His women friends
were mostly Catholic women, many of them nuns, and they had
been brought up in the old tradition of absolute courtesy, if not
adulation, toward priests. One or two were perhaps more than a
little in love with him, although at the distance his life prescribed.
Most of his readers, with the exception of the crudely anti-Catholic,
deeply admired him.

And now here was a woman and a Catholic, a better theologian
than himself, flatly arguing with him and contradicting him,
questioning the validity of his vocation and refusing all attempts
to charm her out of her cool dismissal of his motives. Merton
might, I suppose, have been very angry indeed. In fact, he was
fascinated and delighted.

Yes, he said honestly in reply, he *was* in a crisis, and he *was* much
too defensive, and he became frightened of her being so cerebral
"probably because I resented my mother's intellectuality." Yes, he
did need to get out of the place and move around a bit, only his
Abbot wouldn't let him and refused even to discuss it.

Thank God, he said, for having found in her someone he could
really talk to at last, who had been the catalyst he desperately
needed to pull him out of his artificiality. "You will have to be
my confessor for a while: will you please? I think you have already
implicitly taken on the job anyhow." [29]

From here on a new and very important friendship began
(entirely by correspondence. An arrangement for Rosemary
Ruether in August 1967 to visit Gethsemani fell through at the
last minute). To her, Merton confessed his deep fears of his life as
monk and hermit being a lie and yet the conviction that he was
right to stay where he was, that some vital conflict that was being
worked out in that place and on that spot, that getting out would
be for him a giving in to a temptation "to be part of a real groovy
worldly in-group," whereas the exile, humiliation, and desperation
that he was experiencing were his way of living out his vocation.

Their correspondence gradually opened up. She confided that her
real Christian life had begun to take place in an Episcopal parish
despite her Roman Catholic allegiance. He continued to justify

himself, and she continued to point out that, if he needed to justify, something was wrong. He complained about the Abbot, whose refusal to let him out made him feel "castrated." She could not understand why he put up with it, and suspected his motives. "People aren't swallowing that shit any more. . . . The most Christian thing you could do for that chap is to tell him to go to hell." [30]

She listened, questioned, and continued to insist that he needed change and also that he somehow needed to be more integrated into the outside world. She parodied his response: "Come on in, the water's fine. No, sorry, for some reason I prefer my tree top." [31]

As time went on, the tone became less earnest and more teasing. "You are really a shocking and dissolute fellow." Merton replied, "Ah yes, I have become very wicked. This is due in great part to my hanging around with these women theologians. What a downfall. Let others be warned in time. Young priests can never be too careful. Tsk. Tsk." [32]

References

1. Thomas Merton. Letter to Dom Jean Leclercq. September 18, 1965. TMSC.
2. Thomas Merton. "Vow of Conversation." Unpublished journal, dated 1964–1965. TMSC.
3. Thomas Merton. Letter to Robert Lax. April 2, 1965. TMSC.
4. Thomas Merton. Letter to Dom Jean Leclercq. November 13, 1965. TMSC.
5. Thomas Merton. Letter to Dorothy Day. December 29, 1965. TMSC.
6. Robert Lax. Letter to Thomas Merton. Undated. TMSC.
7. Thomas Merton. Letter to Edward Rice. January 27, 1966. TMSC.
8. Thomas Merton. Letter to Henry Miller. August 16, 1964. TMSC.
9. Thomas Merton. Letter to a friend. February 6, 1966. TMSC.
10. Thomas Merton. Letter to a woman correspondent. Undated (around 1966). TMSC.
11. Thomas Merton. Letter to Robert Lax. March 10, 1966. TMSC.
12. Thomas Merton. Letter to Aunt Gwyn (Gwyneth Trier). September 8, 1966. TMSC.
13. Thomas Merton. Letter to Edward Rice. July 20, 1966. TMSC.

14. Thomas Merton. Letter to Robert Lax. November 4, 1966. TMSC.
15. Thomas Merton. *Mystics and Zen Masters*. New York: Farrar, Straus, 1967.
16. Thomas Merton. *Conjectures of a Guilty Bystander*. New York: Doubleday, 1966.
17. Thomas Merton. Letter to Naomi Burton. September 18, 1966. TMSC.
18. Rosemary Radford Ruether. *The Church Against Itself.* New York: Herder & Herder, 1967; London: Sheed & Ward Ltd, 1967.
19. Thomas Merton. Letter to Rosemary Ruether. August 18, 1966. TMSC.
20. Thomas Merton. Letter to Rosemary Ruether. September 21, 1966. TMSC.
21. Rosemary Ruether. Letter to Thomas Merton. October 10, 1966. TMSC.
22. Thomas Merton. Letter to Rosemary Ruether. January 29, 1962. TMSC.
23. Rosemary Ruether. Letter to Thomas Merton. February 5, 1962. TMSC.
24. Thomas Merton. Letter to Rosemary Ruether. February 14, 1967. TMSC.
25. Rosemary Ruether. Letter to Thomas Merton. February 17, 1967. TMSC.
26. Rosemary Ruether. Letter to Thomas Merton. March 12, 1967. TMSC.
27. Thomas Merton. Letter to Rosemary Ruether, March 19, 1967. TMSC.
28. Rosemary Ruether. Letter to Thomas Merton. March 21, 1967. TMSC.
29. Thomas Merton. Letter to Rosemary Ruether. March 24, 1967. TMSC.
30. Rosemary Ruether. Letter to Thomas Merton. August 4, 1967. TMSC.
31. Rosemary Ruether. Letter to Thomas Merton. September 16, 1967. TMSC.
32. Thomas Merton. Letter to Rosemary Ruether. December 31, 1967. TMSC.

20

A NATIVE OF CASA

Merton continued to draw much from life in the quiet of the hermitage. He brooded a good deal on his past life, remembering school, his Cambridge days, girls he had loved in the past, and in particular his aunts, with whom he had developed a correspondence he much enjoyed. Aunt Kit, although in her seventies, came over to see him from New Zealand. To Aunt Gwyn, he confessed that Iris Bennett, the wife of Tom Bennett his old guardian, had been in the country and had written to him, but that he rather funked a meeting, feeling her old disapproval of his youthful misdemeanours. He liked to have snapshots of his relatives and sent photographs of himself, always in his "working clothes"—now his habitual dress, old jeans and denim jacket.

His pleasure in the life of the woods around him deepened. He particularly loved the deer and received a lot of pleasure in watching them through field glasses. "The woods here are where I belong," he wrote to Miguel Greenberg, the Argentinian poet. "The deer were out the other night and I was looking at them (in the evening light) with field glasses, looking right into their big brown eyes. They could see me just as clearly as I could see them and they did not run away." [1] He was haunted by the soft red colour of the does, with its almost burning intensity. Watching the deer in movement, he felt he caught something of what the primitive cave painters saw, something that could never be captured in a photograph but that filled him with awe. He thought that this essential "deerness" was a form of the *muntu* or spirit that primitives regarded as sacred, and he felt that in perceiving it he had learned something not only about the essence of the deer but also about the essence of himself. [2]

As he came to and passed his fiftieth birthday, he felt a deep change taking place in himself. He also spoke occasionally, both in his writing and to his friends, of a presentiment of an early death.

To Miguel Greenberg, he said that he was experiencing a kind of shedding. "Now I am in my fiftieth skin and trying to get it off like a tight bathing suit, too wet, too sticky, and irritating in the extreme. . . . As I get older [he remarked incidentally] I find it harder to keep my head above the flood of books and papers and letters and things that are all around me." [3]

There were a great many of those. Brother Dunstan was helping him with the interminable floods of letters and the other paraphernalia of a writer's life. Merton's solitude was complicated and interrupted again and again, by the many people who came to visit him, about whom Merton was impossibly ambivalent. He longed to see them, drew a great deal from their company, but then regretted the lost time. "He would be all for going on a day's picnic," Brother Patrick Hart remembers, "but then when it was over, well, there was another day shot to pieces!"

Yet he needed friends and outside contacts, exactly as Dom John Eudes has noted, in almost equal proportion to needing silence and solitude. There were the old friends, enormously precious to him— Lax and Rice and Jay and Naomi and Bob Giroux and Mark Van Doren. There was a friend called Ping Ferry, and the Hammers and new young poets who lived in Lexington and Louisville.

One newer, but precious friend was Mrs. Frank O'Callaghan, usually known as "Tommie" who, with her husband Frank and large family of young children, would bring a picnic to share with Merton in the Gethsemani woods or would entertain him at home on his visits to Louisville to the doctor. Jim Wygal, too, continued to be a close and important friend. Listening to Tommie speak of Merton, it is tempting to see him fitting into that family group as one more child in her lively brood, to see Merton filling in one more place in his lost childhood, of finding a mother, if not in the "severe" mould he remembered, at least a firm, brisk, and practical woman who treated Merton with no more and no less ceremony than she treated any other guest, but simply as "one of the family."

A different kind of friend was John Howard Griffin, whose book *Black Like Me*, about the effects of racial prejudice in the southern states, had excited Merton's admiration. Griffin was a magnificent photographer, and under his tutelage and with the loan of an excellent camera Merton himself learned to take some fine photographs. Griffin was fascinated at the way Merton saw things with a camera—"What does he do with his eyes and his camera?" he asked, and Merton was enthralled with the loan of a Nikon complete with a 100-mm lens to take close-ups of plants, roots, and other subjects dear to Merton's heart. Merton wrote to Griffin,

> It is fabulous. What a joy of a thing to work with. . . . The camera is the most eager and helpful of all beings, all full of happy suggestions. "Try this! Do it that way!" Reminding me of things I have overlooked, and cooperating in the creation of new worlds. So simply. This is a Zen camera. As for the F.100 I tell you I'm going to blow my mind with it! It is fantastic, at least in the viewfinder. I'll wait and see what the contacts look like. [4]

Within Gethsemani, life seemed to be full of change and rumours of change. There were rumours that Dom James was going to resign, was going to become a hermit (at which Merton uncharitably said that he could see him "trying to get a nut away from a squirrel"), that Merton might become Abbot, that Merton might go to become part of the community in Chile (he did in fact volunteer). The system of mail censorship, which tended to arouse increasing resentment, at least among the younger monks, was removed for a while, then replaced. (Merton complained at its removal that he had found it a useful method of letting the Abbot know what he intended to do.)

Early in 1967 the Church had been rocked by the resignation of Fr. Charles Davis, a subject on which Merton wrote movingly. He noted that Davis's quarrel with the Church had been about authority and that he did not think "these criticisms were altogether baseless or unjust." "There have been bad days," Merton wrote, "when I might have considered doing what Fr. Davis has done. In actual fact I have never seriously considered leaving the Church, and though the question of leaving the monastic state *has* presented itself, I was not able to take it seriously for more than five or ten minutes." [5] He went on to say that this was not because he did not consider a great deal wrong both with the Church and with monasticism, but that he felt a kind of hope in both that, whatever their ghastly failures, he could not deny, especially in the light of his own failures and arrogances and mistakes.

There was still, in fact, a good deal wrong with his own situation at Gethsemani. Dom James had from the first insisted on a very precise account from Merton of how he was spending his time— meticulous details of when he was meditating, saying offices, reading, and so on—and this produced in Merton the feeling that the Abbot thought he was somehow cheating on the experiment. This feeling was heightened when rumours reached the Abbot that Merton had visited the houses of friends in Louisville, and Merton was summoned for an interview—in fact, one of several. The following day, Merton wrote Dom James a letter that reveals both pain and anger.

Will you let me make a couple of suggestions about the future of hermits around here and related topics?

First, there is the question of control by authority. I think we will all have to devise some kind of workable system so that you will not be in a position of struggling with suspicions, rumors, half-baked reports and distorted suggestions that may come to you from various sources. I noticed yesterday that you had a great deal of information that was being slanted this way and that, and your material could easily have taken a form that was completely unreal, though based apparently on "facts." This was due in part to the fact that once you get suspicious, the suspicion really works on you and you spend a lot of time trying to get to the bottom of it, mainly because you don't want anyone to put anything over on you. The point I am making is this: if you are down in your office thinking that the hermits are putting something over on you, life for the hermits will become impossible and there will be a regular detective and spy system working. Perhaps there already is, I don't know. But on that basis, how can we get anywhere? It would be a scandal itself, even though devised to prevent scandals.

Obviously, the first thing is openness on the part of the hermit himself. As regards my friend in Louisville, I admit that I have been very reticent, and I felt obliged to be so since the rights of another person and the good of a soul seemed to me to be very deeply involved. I ask you to respect that judgment of my conscience. . . . But as for my own affairs I can promise you in the future complete openness as in the past. I assure you that I will not carry on any sinister underground activities of any sort up here, and if you want to check on me and inspect the place, then I think it would be proper and practical to provide for a regular visit once in a while. This might be a routine thing for all hermits, and would keep you from having suspicions. Of course I assume you know I have a hermitage full of books (they have all passed through your office) and many of these sent to me without any choice or request of mine, are not the most edifying. . . . Also if there is something you definitely would regard as scandalous, let us know, we might not imagine it in advance. Or I might not. My imagination is unusual.

However, I would suggest that it would be a good point if ordinary monks did not visit the hermits in their hermitages. I think only superiors and officers and those who for reasons of work etc. go there, should be in the hermitage at all. I would suggest this because thinking of the situation here the chief danger seems to proceed not from women but from people of the same sex. (This has no reference to myself, I am not so inclined.)

As to the hermits themselves, my opinion would be that as long as they keep to themselves and mind their own business (and others mind theirs) a relative freedom should be allowed with ample scope for individual differences. [6]

There was a thinly veiled exasperation about this letter that bordered on rudeness—Merton feared that the fact that others were now taking up residence as hermits (Fr. Flavian in particular) would encourage a general "tightening-up" in the Abbot's rules, and it was humiliating at the age of fifty-two to be called to order like a naughty schoolboy.

At around the same time, however, another letter from Merton to Dom James indicated all too clearly the power that Dom James had over Merton and that made open defiance dangerous as well as difficult. Merton began by promising to discuss what the Abbot called his "psychological problems" with Fr. Eudes, the psychiatrist on the premises, but the letter is in the main an agonized plea to be allowed to stay at the hermitage, obviously in response to a threat that he might be moved back into the Abbey. After a long defence of his joy in the hermit life and his conviction that it is right for him, Merton ended,

> If I could not stay in the hermitage life would not be worth living and I would certainly create far more problems because I would be a burden to myself and to everyone else. As I said before, I rely very much on your prayers, but I am sure that Our Lord will show me the right way here in the hermitage. I am sorry to have caused you so much trouble.
> Filially in Our Lord.
> [P.S.] If I get too cooped up in the hermitage it is usually enough if I go for a walk to one of the lakes or climb one of the knobs. This is all I need, and I assume that it is all right to do this. [7]

In a sense, Merton was being less than honest both with Dom James and with himself in his postscript—much as he loved roaming the countryside, it was *not* enough to feed him emotionally—he needed the occasional company of Jim Wygal, Tommie, and her family, the local friends he had, and the "visiting firemen" as much as he needed food. Visitors often gave him physical freedom from the environs of Gethsemani—Jay would come and drive him to other parts of the countryside, and Donald Allchin and a friend took him on a much-enjoyed visit to Shakertown at Pleasantville. One Louisville couple close to Merton remember an urgent telephone call from him urging them to give him an evening out; they spent it in a Louisville hotel that had a black jazz band, which enthralled Merton, who struck up a long conversation with the drummer.

Two of his old friends—Ad Reinhardt and Slate—died in 1967. "Let there be no more gaps in the ranks of old chums during 68," Merton wrote to Seymour Freedgood in December 1967. "Slate, Reinhardt, all too big gaps. The mind boggles." [8] (Tragically, Freedgood, as well as Merton himself, was to die in 1968.)

Merton's stomach troubles were still a problem, and early in 1967 it was discovered, as mentioned earlier, that the problem was that he had an allergy to lactic acid. The specialist, according to Merton, was pursuing the problem now with an "almost medieval ruthlessness." "I find that probably the main trouble has been that, having an allergy to milk products, I have only given up obvious things like milk and cheese, whereas there is milk in lots of other innocent seeming stuff (bread). He has got me off all of it, which means eating strangely, but it seems to help. In addition another fungus allergy was working on top of the milk one all adding up to general unpleasantness." [9]

Naomi Burton could be amusing about Merton's innumerable ills—"you have as much trouble as a prize pitcher," she remarked in February 1967 when his elbow was giving yet more trouble, but in the winter of 1967–1968 when the food from the Gethsemani kitchen seemed inadequate for Merton's diet she got busy sending him parcels of food—Lipton's complete meals, Rice-a-roni, Keryaki, Betty Crocker mixes, and "hermit cookies," which helped sustain this particularly delicate hermit.

Toward the end of 1967, Dom James's resignation was announced, and there was a good deal of debate about his successor, some of it amusingly recorded between Merton and the monks studying in Rome who were keen to know the "form." Merton had long ago made a vow that he would never be Abbot, although there were those who wanted him to be so, and the running seemed to be between Fr. Baldwin, the current Novice Master; Fr. Flavian Burns, who had been living as a hermit for the past year; and Fr. Timothy

Kelly. Merton favored Fr. Flavian, who did become Abbot, saying that Fr. Timothy's turn would come (it did, five years later).

Fr. Flavian Burns was elected Abbot in the spring of 1968, an event that was to have important results for Merton's life and death. Fr. Flavian, an old student of Merton's, and a man with a very similar contemplative cast of mind, had great plans for change, including reducing the monks' hours of work to allow more time for contemplative prayer. But he was also much less afraid of external contacts than was his predecessor, and by no means averse to Merton making the occasional journey, although he did bind on Merton the not entirely congenial task of making his decisions for himself. Merton would come to Dom Flavian with an invitation and expect him to decide what he should do with it. "Oh no!" was the new Abbot's response. "*I'm* not going to decide. *You* are." It was no longer possible to get out of disagreeable invitations with the Abbot's blanket refusal.

Merton continued to enjoy life at the hermitage but with a new sense of freedom, of unlived possibilities, a feeling that the angel, of which he had once written in a letter to his friend, the poet Ron Seitz, had indeed lifted the stone. "We got a new broadminded Abbot," he wrote in January 1968, "so maybe it is easier for everyone to come on out and sit around the lakes, so come some time in spring and bring beautiful redhaired wife she needs fresh air. Babies also need fresh air." [11] That spring and summer the Seitzes and other friends did come and enjoy the lakes, the lakes in which once Merton, as Novice Master, had taken the unprecedented step of taking the novices swimming. And an old correspondent and poet, Sister Thérèse Lentfoehr paid her first visit to Gethsemani, brought by Tommie O'Callaghan, and they spent a day with Merton, picnicking in the woods.

Merton was by now beginning to play with the delicious idea that he might make occasional trips away from the monastery. One such was to visit the Monastery of Christ in the desert at Abiquiu, New Mexico. Unusually, he was able to give Lax a piece of worldly information gleaned from his travels: "Stay off American flight 774 out of Dallas, that's all I ask. It is a lousy flight. I ask the young lady (otherwise most sympathetic) where is all the cocktails? She reply on this line no cocktails because no competition. Therefore stay off flight 774 out of Dallas and look for one with competition." [12]

In April, the tragic news came from New Zealand that his Aunt Kit, aged seventy-nine, had died by drowning on a ferry boat called the *Wahine*, which had foundered on a trip between islands, killing a number of passengers. Merton learned this from his cousin, an Anglican Vicar at New Brighton, and replied, "She was to me very much like Aunt Maud. There was a special kind of calm about her even in her death, as I understand it." (She had been seen comforting other passengers on the lifeboat until it capsized.) "I do want to keep in touch with the family in New Zealand. Somehow I have always stayed close to my Anglican friends, notably one at Pusey House, Oxford, and many others. I think of myself very much as an English Catholic, though a Roman. Anyway all that is very much in evolution these days. . . . Though we are all so far apart and some of us have never met, still you are about all the family I have left—with Aunt Gwyn in England, and I do feel that the ties are there. I keep all of you in my prayers." [13]

References

1. Thomas Merton. Letter to Miguel Greenberg. March 11, 1966. TMSC.
2. Thomas Merton. "Vow of Conversation." Unpublished journal, dated 1964–1965. TMSC.
3. Thomas Merton. Letter to Miguel Greenberg. August 16, 1964. TMSC.
4. Thomas Merton. Letter to John Howard Griffin. March 29, 1968. TMSC.
5. Thomas Merton. Letter to friends (mimeographed). Septuagesima 1967. TMSC.
6. Thomas Merton. Letter to Dom James Fox (1). Around January 1967. TMSC.
7. Thomas Merton. Letter to Dom James Fox (2). Around January 1967. TMSC.
8. Thomas Merton. Letter to Seymour Freedgood. December 31, 1967. TMSC.
9. Thomas Merton. Letter to Naomi Burton. May 7, 1967. TMSC.
10. Thomas Merton. Letter to Dom James Fox. Around June 1967. TMSC.
11. Thomas Merton. Letter to Ron Seitz. January 29, 1968. TMSC.
12. Thomas Merton. Letter to Robert Lax. 1968. TMSC.
13. Thomas Merton. Letter to John J. Merton. April 1968. TMSC.

21

THE SHADOW AND THE DISGUISE

❦

In November 1967, Dom Jean Leclercq wrote to Merton telling him of a big meeting that was to take place at Bangkok in December 1968. It was organized by an international Benedictine group interested in monastic renewal, who invited would-be Asian monastic leaders to the Conference. In the past, Merton had assumed that any invitation of that kind was out of the question—once, when someone had thoughtlessly invited him to Tokyo to pursue his interest in Zen, Dom James had been "unutterably shocked." Even now, although change was in the wind and Merton already guessed that Dom James's successor, whoever he was to be, was likely to take a more lenient line with him, he was inclined to think he had better stay put.

In January 1968, however, when Merton mentioned the project to the new Abbot, Dom Flavian, his superior felt a certain "openness" to the idea, although he was far from certain how he would clear it with higher superiors. Merton too had begun to get excited at the idea and to think of embellishments that went far beyond Bangkok. "I do hope that I can participate in it with you," he wrote to Dom Jean, "and would love to travel out there with you via Japan. . . . It is necessary that I finally find out what is going on and attendance at these meetings is one essential way of getting some reliable information." [1]

Soon he was planning not only to go to Bangkok but also to deliver a paper in Calcutta a few weeks prior to the Bangkok meeting, to visit a number of Catholic communities, including ones in Indonesia and Hong Kong, to visit the Dalai Lama in exile at Dharamsala, and to talk with a number of lamas at Darjeeling. In 1969, he intended to go possibly to Burma and Nepal and certainly to Japan, and he hoped that before he returned to America he might get to Greece to see Robert Lax and to Wales to look up his Welsh roots and see his friend Donald Allchin and the scholar John Driver.

It was understood between him and Dom Flavian that part of the purpose of the trip was to look for sites where Gethsemani might set up future hermitages. For Merton, if not for others among his brothers who wanted to lead the hermit life, the cinder-block hut was too accessible and too well known—visitors had a way of turning up there unwanted and unannounced.

Before he finally set off on his Asian journey, Merton paid two visits to a Trappist convent, Our Lady of the Redwoods, at White-thorn, California, and made visits to Alaska with the help of the bishop. Looking back on the reports on these various sites he received from Merton as possible places for future hermitages, Dom Flavian feels that Merton was not always very practical in assessing the pros and cons. He loved the quiet of the Redwoods and felt that the great expanse of ocean was ideal for the contemplative, but overlooked the prevalence of fog along the coast (the sun was shining when he was there), and when Dom Flavian himself followed up his advice with a winter visit it was to discover that all visibility was cut off by the fog.

Merton was also puzzlingly indiscreet about his identity for someone who wanted anonymity. The sisters and priests at the convent had been advised not to mention Merton's arrival and presence to anyone, but Merton introduced himself casually to the first couple of tourists he met on the beach.

These preliminary journeys were a good preparation for that last and most special journey, for which there were many much more complicated preparations. There were the obvious ones, of course, of "shots," visas, and goodbyes to dear friends. Bellarmine College in Louisville had for several years been making a collection of Merton's papers, and Fr. Irenaeus at St. Bonaventure's College in Olean also had a collection. What was not given to these two sources needed to be sorted against some possible disaster—papers to be destroyed in the event of Merton's death, material to be returned to rightful owners, and so on. And other projects needed to be tied up, in particular *Monks Pond*, the lively magazine of poetry and articles he had recently started and to which he had persuaded many gifted friends to contribute. Brother Patrick Hart was to deal with his correspondence in his absence, acting as liaison between Merton and the monastery.

There were innumerable plans to be made in advance to facilitate his journey, details of language, food, climate, and places to stay (all the more important because the journey must be done on a monastic shoestring) that took much time. There was an enormous amount of reading, to enable Merton's talks with members of other faiths to be as fruitful as possible. In addition to all his earlier reading about Asia and its religions, he now read extensively in Asian studies, in the works of Dom Aelred Graham, Alain Daniélou, Marco Pallis, W. Y. Evans-Wentz, Amiya Chakravarty, S. B. Dasgupta, Giuseppe Tucci, T. R. V. Murti and others.

Finally, in July 1968, Merton wrote to Dom Jean:

> Thanks for your good letter about the arrangements for Bangkok. I will be glad to give the talk on Marxism and so on. Important indeed!! I've familiarized myself pretty well with Herbert Marcuse, whose ideas are so influential in the "student revolts" of the time. I must admit that I find him closer to monasticism than many theologians. Those who question the structures of contemporary society at least look to monks for a certain distance and critical perspective. Which alas is seldom found. The vocation of the monk in the modern world, especially Marxist, is not survival but prophecy. We are all busy saving our skins.
>
> Best regards always in the Lord,
> Tom.
>
> Do I talk in French or English? [2]

And so he set off from San Francisco, loaded with so many books (he had been staying with the poet Lawrence Ferlinghetti, owner of City Lights Bookstore) that he had to pay excess baggage.

> The moment of take-off was ecstatic. The dewy wing was suddenly covered with rivers of cold sweat running backward. The window wept jagged shining courses of tears. Joy. We left the ground—I with Christian mantras and a great sense of destiny, of being at last on my true way after years of waiting and wondering and fooling around.
>
> May I not come back without having settled the great affair. And found also the great compassion, mahakaruna. . . . I am going home—to the home where I have never been in this body, where I have never been in this washable suit. [3]

He promises himself a "katharsis" of the suitcases when he gets to Bangkok, a sweeping away of the accumulation of books.

He enjoyed the brief stop in Honolulu, where he boarded a plane bound for Tokyo, Hong Kong, and Bangkok. It seemed wonderfully romantic. "When the stewardess began the routine announcement in Chinese I thought I was hearing the language of Heaven." [3] The stewardess handed out newspapers and Merton got the Hong Kong Standard. He solemnly studied the stock market news and the information that the astronauts had colds, and he read the horoscopes and the comic strips with equal interest. "The utter happiness of life in a plane" he wrote "quiet, time to read. But long, long. Endless noon." [3] He slept, said prayers, read Hesse's *Siddhartha.*

He had a whisky with a young mother and her baby when the plane stopped at Tokyo, and then at Hong Kong, where there was a brief stop, he got out and walked up and down under the tail of the plane, looking at the lights of Kowloon. He did not know that this was against the rules of the airline, and it earned him a roundabout reproof that amused him somewhat: "a special announcement . . . that passengers were under no circumstances to do this!" [3] Finally, at 1 A.M. he got out into the hot tropical night of Bangkok and travelled in a rattling old bus to the Hotel Oriental.

Next morning he breakfasted on the hotel terrace enjoying the sights of the river and then took a taxi to Wat Bovoranives, one of the traditional Buddhist temples of Bangkok, where he met Phra Khantipalo, the author of books on Buddhism. Later that day he met a Buddhist abbot, and they talked at length about Theravada Buddhism and the various steps by which the disciple progressed toward *mukti* ("freedom"), with Khantipalo acting as interpreter. "What is the 'knowledge of freedom'?" Merton asked him. "When you are in Bangkok you know that you're there. Before that you only knew about Bangkok. And," the abbot added, "one must ascend all the steps, but then when there are no more steps one must make the leap. Knowledge of freedom is the knowledge, the experience, of this leap." [3]

After further brief study of Theravada Buddhism and visits to country temples and Buddhist relics Merton continued his journey to Calcutta "the big, beat-up, teeming, incredible city. People!" But the pain of the beggars was intolerable at first. "The little girl who suddenly appeared at the window of my taxi, the utterly lovely smile with which she stretched out her hand, and then the extinguishing of the light when she drew it back empty. I had no Indian money yet. She fell away from the taxi as if she were sinking in water and drowning, and I wanted to die. I couldn't get her out of my mind. Yet when you give money to one, a dozen half

kill themselves running after your cab. . . . Then there was the
woman who followed me three blocks sweetly murmuring something like 'Daddy, Daddy, I am very poor' until I finally gave her a
rupee. OK, a contest too. But she *is* very poor. And I have come
from the West, a Rich Daddy." [3] Like so many Westerners,
Merton was almost overcome by the tragedy of Calcutta, reflecting
that "Gandhiji led all these people, exemplified the sense they
might make out of the life, for a moment, and then, with him,
that sense was extinguished again." [3]

He said Mass at the Jesuit Sacred Heart church in Calcutta and got
diarrhoea from the impure tap water used, enormously enjoyed the
Indian museum, with its "footprints of Buddha" engraved with
beautiful symbols, and he went to dinner with Lois Flanagan, the
information centre director of the U.S. Consulate in Calcutta. Then,
quite by chance, he met Chogyam Trungpa Rimpoche, a Buddhist
teacher who, after the Chinese invasion of Tibet, had established a
meditation centre in Scotland (and, since Merton's time, in Color-
ado, and Vermont as well). Merton was deeply moved by Chogyam
Trungpa's spirituality and described him as "young, natural, without front or artifice, deep, awake, wise." [3] Their meeting was on
the eve of the Hindu festival of Divali (Feast of Lights) and late in the
afternoon Chogyam Trungpa, his English secretary, two Australian
girls, and a driver piled into a jeep and went off to see the market,
which was full of lights, incense, special foods, garlands, statues, and
fireworks for the festival. They bought some firecrackers.

Merton spoke at a Conference (on the monk as a "marginal
person") where he met Sufis, Jews, Jains, and the monks of
Ramakrishna (a movement that believes that God is the Mother
of the universe), visited an ashram, and the home of the painter
Jamini Roy, whose religious paintings moved him greatly. A
telegram came from the Dalai Lama's secretary saying that Merton
would be expected at Dharamsala, where the Dalai Lama had his
residence, on November 4. Merton continued to read extensively in
Buddhist and Hindu literature, and to visit spiritual teachers. Not
all of them impressed him. One of them, he said, reminded him
irresistibly of Groucho Marx. "He has great white teeth and
contempt for all competitors. Even his Kleenex is saffron!' [3]

Not surprisingly, so much travelling and so many new faces and
new impressions made Merton feel tired. "For God's sake I hope I

can get to the Himalayas and into a quiet cabin somewhere and get back to normal!" [3]

He flew on to New Delhi, deeply moved, when the clouds parted, by the sight of the Himalayas in the distance, and he was fascinated by New Delhi itself with its mixture of exotic beauty and ugliness. In preparation for meeting Tibetans he began to read Tucci's *The Theory and Practice of the Mandala*. [4] He could not feel that the mandala was likely to help his own prayer life very much, but feared it would merely complicate what seemed simple. Dr. Lokesh Chandra, the director of the International Academy of Indian Culture in New Delhi asked Merton if he would like to choose one of his prints of mandalas. "I picked one, the general pattern of which attracted me as being very lively. On close inspection I find it to be full of copulation, which is all right, but I don't quite know how one meditates on it. It might be a paradoxical way to greater purity" [3]

At the beginning of November, Merton travelled up by train and jeep to Dharamsala, immensely enjoying the beautiful Himalayan landscape and the silence of the mountains. "Yesterday as I came down the path from the mountain I heard a strange humming behind me. A Tibetan came by quietly droning a monotonous sound, a prolonged 'om.' It was something that harmonized with the mountain—an ancient syllable he had found long ago in the rock—or perhaps it had been born with him." [3]

An important contact Merton soon made at Dharamsala was Sonam Kazi, a teacher of Tantric Buddhism, who had been the Dalai Lama's interpreter for many years. He told Merton that the purpose of meditating on the mandala was "to be in control of what goes on within one instead of 'being controlled by it.'" He also suggested to Merton that he might consider finding a Tibetan guru to bring him to enlightenment. Merton wrote,

> At least he asked me if I were willing to risk it and I said why not? The question is finding the right man. I am not exactly dizzy with the idea of looking for a magic master but I would certainly like to learn something by experience and it does seem that the Tibetan Buddhists are the only ones who at present, have a really large number of people who have attained to extraordinary heights in meditation and contemplation. [3]

"What is important," Merton observed a few days later, "is not liberation from the body but liberation from the mind. We are not entangled in our own body but entangled in our own mind." He was doubtful about the value for him of very visual forms of meditation. "Are Tantrism, and meditation on the mandala, the evocations of minute visual details like the Ignatian method in some respects? And as useless for me?" [3]

While he waited to have his interview with the Dalai Lama, Merton stayed in a cottage with a view of the Himalayas. It had "a washroom with two stools. Concrete floor. A hole in the corner leading out. You empty the washbasin on the floor and the water runs out the hole." [3] Through this hole, Merton could not help reflecting uneasily, a cobra or other snake could easily come.

On November 4, Merton had his first audience with the Dalai Lama at his mountain quarters where he lived at the heart of the Tibetan refugee community. He was immediately impressed. "He is strong and alert, bigger than I expected (for some reason I thought he would be small). A very solid, energetic, generous and warm person, very capably trying to handle enormous problems." [3] At that first meeting, they talked entirely of religion and philosophy, particularly about methods of meditation. Merton found that the Dalai Lama already knew a great deal about him and his work. He advised him to get a good grasp of Madhyamika philosophy (the "middle path" school of Buddhism) and invited him to return for further conversation two days later. Merton did return on November 6, and they talked at length about *samadhi*, the condition in both Hinduism and Buddhism in which the mind becomes so absorbed in concentration that it forgets itself in ecstasy. Again, the Dalai Lama asked Merton to return to continue their conversation two days later. Later Merton thought that this last meeting was in many ways the best. The Dalai Lama showed much curiosity about Western monastic life, questioning Merton about the vows, silence, what the monks ate and drank, whether they watched movies, and how their progression in the spiritual life in fact worked. Then Merton asked a number of questions about Marxism and monasticism and found his host remarkably open-minded, in view of his own exile, sympathetic to Marxism in so far as it implied an equitable social and economic structure but inevitably critical of its attempt to suppress all forms of religion. Before they parted the Dalai Lama described Merton as a *geshe*—a "learned lama."

This relatively quiet Tibetan episode in Dharamsala with time for reading and thinking and talking to spiritual teachers had put

Merton's life at home somewhat into perspective. "I have needed the experience of this journey. Much as the hermitage has meant, I have been needing to get away from Gethsemani and it was long overdue." [3]

One advantage was the break from the interminable correspondence, since he was now seeing only the most essential letters. Another advantage was learning that other hermits did not have it so easy either:

> Even here in the mountains there are few places where one does not run into someone. Roads and paths and trails are full of people. To have real solitude one would have to get very high up and far back!
>
> For solitude, Alaska seems the very best place. But everyone I have talked to says I must also consider others and keep open to them to some extent. The rimpoches [spiritual masters] all advise against absolute solitude and stress "compassion." They seem to agree that being in solitude much of the year and coming "out" for a while would be a good solution. [3]

In the course of his travels, Merton was saddened to learn that Richard Nixon had become President of the United States, although glad that Kentucky had not voted for Wallace. "Our new president is depressing. What can one expect of him?" [3]

Merton went back to Delhi, where he photographed the eighteenth-century observatory Jantar Mantar and sent these and other photographs back to John Howard Griffin for developing. Then he returned to Calcutta, for which he began to feel a baffled respect, as if there were an inexplicable nobility in its sordidness. From there he went up to Darjeeling where he visited some Catholic colleges and studied Madhyamika, as the Dalai Lama had suggested. "The essence of the Madhyamika attitude . . . consists in not allowing oneself to be entangled in views and theories, but just to observe the nature of things without standpoints. . . . It is primarily a path of purification of the intellect. . . . It is not nihilism, which is itself a standpoint asserting that nothing is. The dialectic is rejection of all views including the nihilistic." [3]

Merton was amused at being accosted by Tibetan students on the road, asking his address and wanting to become his "pen pal." "I assure them I have more than enough pen pals already." [3]

From Darjeeling, Merton set off for the Mim Tea Estate, high up in the mountains, where a European couple had offered to let him use their bungalow for a few days' retreat. Merton had a bad sore throat that seemed to be aggravated by the coal smoke in the air, but in spite of this he stopped to visit a hermit, Chatral Rimpoche, who Merton thought the greatest rimpoche he had so far come across, deeply spiritual and impressive. They talked through an interpreter, laughing quite a lot together, discussing meditation, Christian and Buddhist doctrine, and the difficulty of achieving "perfect emptiness."

> He said he had meditated in solitude for thirty years or more and had not attained to perfect emptiness and I said I hadn't either.
> The unspoken or half-spoken message of the talk was our complete understanding of each other as people who were somehow *on the edge* of great realization and knew it and were trying somehow or other, to go out and get lost in it—and that it was a grace for us to meet one another. . . . He burst out and called me a rangjung Sangay (which apparently means a "natural Buddha"). . . . He told me, seriously, that perhaps he and I would attain to complete Buddhahood in our next lives, perhaps even in this life, and the parting note was a kind of compact that we would both do our best to make it in *this* life. . . . He was surprised at getting on so well with a Christian and at one point laughed and said, "there must be something wrong here!" [3]

When he arrived at the bungalow on the Mim Tea Estate, there was a fire in the grate and it was peaceful and quiet. The owners were out, but had left a message "Dear Father Merriton, Please make yourself at home the moment you arrive and just ask the bearer for anything you may require." Merton unpacked, gratefully drank tea, and then retired to his room and the pleasures of the fire, books, cold remedies, and a big, comfortable bed. The owners of the bungalow continued to let him enjoy his quietness over the next few days, and, feeling very tired and unwell, he read and thought and prayed. The mountain of Kanchenjunga was an almost tangible presence in the bungalow, sometimes dazzlingly beautiful, sometimes almost absurdly picturesque. "What do I care for a 28,000 foot post card when I have this bloody cold?" he enquired rhetorically. [3]

He felt an obscure shame about his journey so far. "Too much movement. Too much 'looking for' something: an answer, a vision, 'something else.' And this breeds illusion. Illusion that there *is* something else. . . . I am still not able fully to appreciate what this exposure to Asia has meant. There has been so much and yet also so little." [3]

He was a month out of Gethsemani, and he still felt no nearer to solving his problem about it. His feeling of "turbulence" the previous summer, both internal and external, made him feel he ought to find another hermitage, perhaps in the Redwoods or Alaska, yet "I do not think I ought to separate myself completely from [it]. . . . I suppose I ought eventually to end my days there. I do in many ways miss it. . . . It is my monastery." [3] Beneath this tantalizing dilemma, there seemed to be something else Merton was looking for that he found impossible to define.

When he got over his cold, Merton went back to Darjeeling and then on to Madras where he wanted to see the Seven Pagodas, the famous shrines on the seashore at Mahabalipuram. As famous as the shrines was the enormous lingam of Shiva, "which stands alone . . . black, heavy, tumescent," with the incoming tide sweeping over it. "There is no 'problem' in the black lingam," Merton remarked. "It is washed by the sea and the sea is woman: it is no void, no question. No English anguish about Mahabalipuram." [3]

After Madras, Merton flew on to Ceylon, to Colombo, and thence to Kandy with its famous palace. In Kandy, he visited a number of hermits living in caves, and he found the landscape "incomparably beautiful." But Merton's most important experience in Ceylon, and indeed on his whole Asian trip, came at Polonnaruwa. He went to visit the giant Buddhas and took a series of superb photographs of them.

> I am able to approach the Buddhas barefoot and undisturbed, my feet in wet grass, wet sand. The silence of the extraordinary faces. The great smiles. Huge and yet subtle. Filled with every possibility, questioning nothing, knowing everything, rejecting nothing, the peace not of emotional refutation . . . that has seen through every question without trying to discredit anyone or anything—*without refutation*—without establishing some other argument. For the doctrinaire, the mind that needs well established positions, such peace, such silence, can be frightening. I was knocked over with a rush of relief and thankfulness at the *obvious* clarity of the figures. . . . Looking at these figures I was suddenly, almost forcibly, jerked clean out of the habitual, half-tied vision of things, and an inner clearness, clarity, as if exploding from the rocks themselves, became evident and obvious. . . . I don't know when in my life I have ever had such a sense of beauty and spiritual validity running together in one aesthetic illumination. Surely, with Mahabalipuram and Polonnaruwa my Asian pilgrimage has come clear and purified itself. I mean, I know and have seen what I was obscurely looking for. I don't know what else remains but I have now seen and have pierced through the surface and have got beyond the shadow and the disguise. [3]

That was on December 4. Then he travelled on to Singapore and arrived in Bangkok on December 7, once again "secretly enraged and humiliated" to find his luggage was overweight. He stayed again at the Oriental Hotel, from whence he visited the Temple of the Emerald Buddha and where he wrote to Brother Patrick Hart at Gethsemani "I think of you all on this Feast Day and with Christmas approaching I feel homesick for Gethsemani." He spoke of his pleasure in the fact that he would at least be spending Christmas in a monastery (in Indonesia) and that he would be visiting the Trappist house at Hong Kong, and then concluded "No more for the moment. Best love to all. Louie." [5]

Then he set off to the Red Cross Centre to meet Dom Jean Leclercq and the other delegates. He ate at Nick's Hungarian Diner and spent the night in the cottage room assigned to him at the centre.

The next morning, December 10, he gave a talk on "Marxism and Monastic Perspectives," filmed by an Italian television company. He sat down to talk with his usual ease, humour, and informality. He spoke first of those who had suffered from communism, but said that that he had come to speak about dialogue with the Marxists, that he was influenced by the thinking of Marcuse. He noted similarities of dedication between Marxists and monks and quoted a young French Marxist he had met in California who had startled him with the proposition, "We are monks also." [3]

What interested him, Merton said in his lecture, was the man who took up a critical attitude toward the world and its structures, whether monk or Marxist—the monk (or the man who thinks of himself as a monk as the Frenchman did) is one who believes that "the claims of the world are fraudulent." Both monk and Marxist therefore want a world open to change, "the world refusal of the monk is in view of his desire for change." [3]

Merton continued at some length about the difference between the religious approach and the antireligious approach to society but tried to point the way to a new ground of agreement. "I would just point out that in Marx himself you can see something of this same desire to evolve from *cupiditas* to *caritas*, when you see the idea of Communism—which is a progress from capitalist greed (in their terms) to Communist dedication, according to Marxist formula in which Communism consists in a society where each gives according to his capacity and each receives according to his needs. Now, if you will reflect for two seconds on that definition, you will find that it is the definition of a monastic community." [3]

Merton examined Marcuse at length and then Erich Fromm, looking at the problem of Western alienation and then passed on, slightly curiously, with a message sent from one Tibetan abbot to another asking for advice in the light of communist invasion. "From now on, everybody stands on his own feet." [3]

So what Merton was preaching, he said, was not Pelagian (a doctrine that humans could save themselves by their own efforts alone), but a suggestion that Christians should not, may no longer be able to, rely on structures, but on something more deeply experienced and understood and lived out. "What is essential . . . is not embedded in buildings, is not embedded in clothing, is not necessarily embedded even in a rule. It is somewhere along the line of something deeper than a rule. It is concerned with this business of total inner transformation." Merton concluded with a great plea for openness, openness to other religions, other ways of life, but above all to the "painfulness of inner change." [3]

When he had finished speaking, he left the platform and was followed by the cameras. Giggling, he held his paper up in front of his face in mock shyness, made a face or two, and remarked, "So I will disappear and we will all go and have a coke or something" (later bowdlerized by the hands of the hagiographers into the mystical "So I will disappear").

Merton had lunch and did disappear to his room, commenting to a colleague on the way how much he was looking forward to having a siesta. In a long letter later written by the delegates at the Conference to Dom Flavian what then occurred was expressed in the following words: "Not long after he retired a shout was heard by others in his cottage, but after a preliminary check they thought they must have imagined the cry.

"He was found at the end of the meridian (afternoon rest) and when found was lying on the floor. He was on his back with the electric fan lying across his chest. The fan was still switched on, and there was a deep burn and some cuts on his right side and arm. The back of his head was also bleeding slightly." [6]

One of the nuns who was a doctor was summoned, but it was obvious he was dead. Two other doctors came, but no one was able to establish precisely the cause of death.

"It is believed he could have showered and then had a heart attack near the fan, and in falling knocked the fan over against himself; or again that being in his bare feet on a stone floor he may have received a fatal electric shock." [6] One of the monks who discovered the body himself received a shock when he attempted to remove the fan, but was probably saved from death by wearing shoes.

The police investigated the death, then the delegates washed and dressed the body in robe and scapular, and kept vigil by it all night. "In death Father Louis' face was set in a great and deep peace, and it was obvious that he had found Him Whom he had searched for so diligently." [6] In the morning, the U.S. army collected his body and took it to their hospital at Bangkok, and a week later it was flown back to Louisville (an army plane returning from Vietnam carried it as far as California).

Meanwhile at Gethsemani the first news received of Merton's death was a cable from the American Embassy at 10 A.M. on December 10. Dom Flavian summoned Brother Patrick Hart to his office and, shocked, they waited for two hours for confirmation, hoping the whole thing might turn out to be a mistake. By noon (local time), they had learned that Merton was indeed dead, electrocuted in Bangkok at 2 P.M. (Bangkok time). Dom Flavian announced the news to the community in the refectory, and Merton's old students, novices, brothers, and friends tried to take in the news that they would never see Father Louis again. "I just got up and walked out" one of his novices remembered. "I just couldn't stay there." Ironically, one of the oldest fathers in the monastery, for whom Merton had a particular affection, had come in to find a postcard from Merton awaiting him in his place at table. (Correspondence at Gethsemani was distributed at meal times.)

The body was met at Louisville by Dom Flavian and a group of monks, and taken to New Haven, where the casket was opened and the body identified. The remains of Father Louis arrived at Gethsemani early on the afternoon of December 17. Monks and friends chanted the funeral liturgy in the church, and he was buried at dusk in the monastic cemetery under a light snowfall. He had, after all, returned home in time for Christmas.

Perhaps any death brings with it both a sense of surprise and a sense of its inevitability. There are always those, and there were many after Merton's death, who feel that it somehow "had to be like that." Merton had, from time to time, both spoken and written comments that suggested that his death might come early. Some of his friends commented on the extraordinary, almost Zen-like way that death had come to him. Fewer people than one might expect noted that he died on the same day as the great Protestant theologian Karl Barth, and it was a measure of the ecumenism in Louisville, which Merton had been instrumental in promoting, that Catholics and Protestants there united in a joint memorial service for both of them.

Many years before Naomi Burton had made the suggestion, humorously, that Merton was accident-prone. "I couldn't help noticing that it's your visitors who get locked out of the church, and your server who forgets things, and your vestments that get caught in the folding chair. . . . I find your incredible adventures with nature and with publishing extremely endearing." [7] Perhaps Merton was accident-prone; perhaps, like many intellectuals, he tended to get lost in his thinking, and absent-mindedly forgot about the dangers of touching electrical equipment with wet hands; perhaps the fan was merely faulty. Perhaps, however, he had finished his life six days before at Polonnaruwa and was called to the God he had loved and served so well.

References

1. Thomas Merton. Letter to Dom Jean Leclercq. January 4, 1968. TMSC.
2. Thomas Merton. Letter to Dom Jean Leclercq, July 23, 1968. TMSC.
3. Thomas Merton. *The Asian Journal of Thomas Merton*, ed. Naomi Burton, Brother Patrick Hart, and James Laughlin. New York: New Directions, 1973.
4. Giuseppe Tucci. *The Theory and Practice of the Mandala*, trans. A. H. Broderick. London: Rider, 1967.
5. Thomas Merton. Letter to Brother Patrick Hart. December 8, 1968. TMSC.
6. Six Trappist delegates to the Bangkok Conference. Letter to Abbot Flavian Burns. December 11, 1968. TMSC.
7. Naomi Burton. Letter to Thomas Merton. April 2, 1956. TMSC.

EPILOGUE

No one could look very deeply into Thomas Merton's life without discovering that he inspired enormous love. He attracted warm friendships, was attractive to women, was respected by his brothers at Gethsemani, even when they disagreed profoundly with his ideas, and was admired and loved by the students and novices he trained. Yet at the centre of all this love was a deep loneliness that only a handful of close friends penetrated, and perhaps nobody fully comprehended it. It is impossible to say with any certainty what caused it—the early death of his mother perhaps or his conviction that she found him unsatisfactory; the tragic death of his father—but there is no doubt that he had a very profound sense of himself as orphaned and outcast (which gave him great sympathy for others who were in any way outcast), and that no amount of subsequent love and devotion could change that for him.

It was not that he did not try to break out of it. The warm male friendships of his Columbia days, the busy experimenting with girls, were each different ways of coming at the problem, but the loneliness continued and found expression in a desperate busyness and ambition, and frantic drinking, smoking, and "having a good time." Looking back many years later, Merton could see how desperately he had longed for love and how difficult he had found accepting it, even from girls who truly loved him, perhaps particularly from them. Part of him needed to "keep clear," dreaded emotional involvement, and could only interpret loving approaches from others as a kind of clinging, which no doubt it often was.

His conversion opened a new source of love to him, and, like many who learn by being deprived of human love, he learned to see human love as itself a reflection—at best a rather pale one—of the love of God. Conversion itself gave him a needed sense of being loved, lovable, and, in time, chosen for a special task—that of the priesthood. In *The Asian Journal*, he quoted a French writer to the effect that those who believed themselves to have a vocation, a call, needed to reach a stage in their development when they knew that the constraint had not been quite of the kind they originally thought, but rather an inevitable outcome of their temperament, upbringing, and the particular problems they had.

Merton's call to both the priesthood and to the Trappist Order had something of this inevitable quality. He needed badly to feel "special," chosen, loved; he needed, too, to have the security of a home, a home from which neither he, nor any of the rest of the "family" could go away, and perhaps nothing could provide this quite so certainly as an enclosed order. He needed structure of a fairly rigorous kind, quite simply to prevent his own vigorous appetites and questing mind from destroying him. Finally, and on a more neurotic level, it would seem from his autobiography and some of his subsequent writings, that he needed to punish himself, most obviously for unintentionally fathering a child and then abandoning both child and mother, less obviously for having been, throughout his life as it often seemed to him, a deeply unsatisfactory person.

So, with this accumulation of needs and aspirations he entered Gethsemani. He had a deeply romantic view of it and had a sense of the monks as "special." His first hope seemed to be that by sacrificing so much—sexual pleasure and many of the other pleasures of the senses, the company of women, a family, the company of like-minded friends, conversation, a career in the world, freedom to travel or to order his own life—some of that "specialness" might rub off on him, but already before the end of his autobiography, written very early in his monastic life, he had voiced suspicion that it had not done so. He was the same old Thomas Merton, with his innumerable schemes for success as a writer and his longing to make his mark in the world.

Yet the rigid structure of life at Gethsemani, although it often bored him extremely, did hold him together. By taking away the multiplicity of choices open to a (in many ways) privileged young man, it forced him to live the life left to him more deeply and intensely. By taking away most of the sensual delights that others take for granted, it opened him up to the sensual beauty of the natural world around him and made him observe it in detail. Of course, the neurotic conflict did not simply go away, and in 1949, probably not by chance the year of his ordination to the priesthood, it became painfully evident in his life, so evident that he was forced to take notice of it. In many ways, the monastic resolution of his problems had not worked—he felt ill, stricken with panic, was working compulsively, yet was also suffering from "writer's block." Nor was this all: he was gradually developing a bitter resentment of authority (which peeps out in many utterances in *The Sign of Jonas*), while also feeling submissive toward it. Anger, fear, dependence, and an ambivalent attitude to pain appear in his writing and obviously distress him deeply.

Throughout Merton's conflict in the late 1940s and early 1950s, Gethsemani continued in its solid medieval way to be "there," a mountain strong enough to take Merton's anger, if not able to respond very imaginatively to his needs. The truth was, perhaps, that Merton needed an order less austerely designed than the one he had, perversely, chosen, an order, say, like the Benedictines, with a strong tradition of learning and aesthetic sensibility, and much more open to what was happening in the world outside.

Merton, however, until almost the beginning of the 1960s, continued to see it as the task of the monk to evade and avoid the world, and so only the strictest order would do. His solution to his unhappiness at Gethsemani was to attempt to retire into the greater loneliness of life as a Carthusian or a Camaldolese. Gethsemani had not solved the old problem of his loneliness, but had somehow accentuated it, perhaps by making him aware of how little his brothers shared his preoccupations, either intellectual or spiritual. When Gethsemani refused to let him go, he gradually withdrew from the common life, as it were from within, at first by building a kind of separate world within the monastery with the novices, and later by living more and more alone at the hermitage. Eventually, he reached a stage when he wore his habit as little as possible, felt deeply at odds with the Abbot and many of his brothers, and tried to see himself as little different from many of the farmers and "old bats," as he put it, who lived alone up in the hills of Kentucky. The irony was that he had many contacts in his life (certainly many more than the "old bats" in the hills, who were not formally trying to be hermits), not simply by letter but through the many friends he had in Louisville and Lexington and in other parts of the United States and indeed of the world, who would

travel hundreds or thousands of miles to spend a day or two with
him.

But before the relative freedom of life as a hermit was reached he
had undergone his biggest struggle with authority (in 1955), a
struggle so sharp that it proved the initial step in disillusioning
him about authority (in all forms) and so gradually releasing him
from dependence on it and submission to it. Somehow, between
1955 and 1960 Merton became, painfully and slowly, "his own
man," no longer believing that anyone else "knew best," but
seeking and questioning for himself with a new energy. Scales
seemed to fall from his eyes, and the world and its people, which
had filled him with such revulsion, were suddenly flooded with
beauty and meaning.

In his essay "The Cell" (in *Contemplation in a World of Action*),
Merton charts what he believes is the essential route of the contemplative (and perhaps ultimately of all human beings), a route
downward through loneliness and acute boredom, to the place
where a man or a woman, deprived of diversion and the constant
affirmation of others, begins to doubt his or her identity. When the
"disciple," as Merton calls him, reaches the point in which all
illusion is stripped away, and he knows his own weakness, failure,
and despair to the full, then the way is made clear for the *akme*, "the
moment of truth," in which a new identity is discovered in God
himself. "The cell is the place where man comes to know himself
first of all that he may know God." From this rediscovered identity,
and this total awareness of dependence on God, comes a new
independence toward other human beings, a new joy in the beauty
and wonder of the world, a new compassion and insight.

As always, Merton writes of what he has experienced. At some
time between 1950 and 1960, perhaps once, but more probably
repeatedly, he underwent the pain of having all his illusions about
the religious life and much else stripped from him. Probably for such
an extremist there was no other way of finding himself—and we owe
the Trappists a debt for offering Merton such a way and owe his
unconscious a debt for so skilfully finding it. Happily, he found the
way, went faithfully through the process of loss of identity, and found
the new identity of which he wrote so well and which is evident in
almost everything he did and said in the last eight years of his life.

He liked to refer to this lonely journey as "the desert." What
Merton found in the desert, in place of his old world-hating self,

was a passionate love of the world, an intense enjoyment of nature, a deep love for other human beings, women as well as men, and a wonderful gaiety and humour.

Nothing was taken with the terrible solemnity that he had taken life in *The Seven Storey Mountain*, not monasticism, not the Abbot, not the Catholic Church. To a friend taking the hard Catholic line on birth control in the late 1960s, Merton said lightly that perhaps married couples would give up sexual intercourse for pleasure when priests got around to giving up whisky. It was a saying that would have been unimaginable earlier in his monastic life.

Perhaps some of the lightness came from his knowledge of Zen, with its method of using jokes to shock the disciple into an awareness of truth. But a similar sense of the deep humour of the human situation, particularly when overlaid with spiritual pretensions, was often evident in the Desert Fathers, whom Merton deeply loved, and in many of the saints. It was as if, at a certain point in a disciple's understanding, everything was turning inside out, and what had before seemed serious now seemed funny, what important, unimportant. What this change of perspective removed was the old need for self-punishment, and, as that disappeared, Merton again began to enjoy many things he had formerly renounced, trivial things such as beer, and pleasure in eating, and a wry amusement at advertising, and more important things such as literature, politics, and human company, more particularly the company of women and children. He was, in fact, changing direction, using the inner revolution to help him to turn outward and look again at the world he had so despised and rejected. And, with the same energy that he had once used to refuse and deny, he took up public causes and learned the careful art of showing private compassion. He plunged with extraordinary zeal into everything that made up the public consciousness of the 1960s, from presidential elections to fallout shelters, from Bob Dylan to ecumenism, from the beat poets to the renewal of the Catholic Church. He was passionately engaged, not only in public controversy, but in the minor controversies that raged at the Abbey as the monks debated such issues as factory farming, meaningful labour, and prosperity as it affected their own lifestyle.

He was not the easiest of monks to live alongside, and many observers feel a keen sympathy for Dom James Fox at having him as one of his community, although since Merton's death Dom James has written of him with affectionate sympathy. His charm, commitment, and boyish enthusiasm made him a popular figure, much more popular than he himself was able to believe at times in the hermitage when he was feeling paranoid about what "they," up at the Abbey, were doing to him. His struggles with health, none of them deadly, but a number of them very unpleasant, perhaps had something to do with this, together with his tendency to work himself to the point of exhaustion and beyond. It was as if there were so many ideas teeming from his mind that he could not be patient with the frailty of his body and worked it continually beyond its strength. Certainly the amount of reading, writing (of both papers and letters), meeting people, and thinking, in the last ten years of his life was phenomenal, particularly when we remember how strict he was about keeping the Rule, working dutifully at the prayer, meditation, and spiritual reading required of him, and adding a certain amount of yoga exercise and Zen experimentation of his own. The relative peace of the hermitage gave him the mental space he needed for so much intensive concentration; he did not have to worry about annoying others or disturbing anyone's sleep. Also, the fairly simple routines of lighting lamps and fires, of heating drinks and making simple meals, of chopping wood and washing up, gave him something to do that was mechanical but enjoyable, a change from intellectual activity.

The hermitage also brought him much closer to nature. For years he had been keenly interested in the planting and growth of trees. Now added to his absorbed study of trees and plants was an interest in birds and animals, in hills and sky, in cold, sunshine, rain, and the passage of the seasons. He saw this as a conscious struggle to return to a capacity people had lost—to feel himself part of nature, instead of its rapacious lord—and believed that this was a proper part of a monk's vocation, the discovery of "man as the measure." An important part of that discovery and of Merton's mature mellowing, was the discovery, by dreams and fantasies, and in actual friendships, of the feminine, the feminine that he had once so clumsily pursued in Cambridge and New York and was now at last ready to acknowledge as part of himself. He became at ease with women, admiring and appreciating them—it is striking how often on his journey to Asia he comments on the prettiness of the stewardesses or the tourists or passing girls in the street, with pleasure but without lust.

Yet even as he set out on that last journey, with so much of his inner journey completed, he knew that something had still eluded him and hoped very much that he would find it in the Asian religious communities. Some Christian observers have seemed to take offence at this, as if Merton might only be permitted to drink truth from a Christian source and as if all other springs might be contaminated, like the spring behind the hermitage. But Merton never thought or wrote of ceasing to be a Christian. Christianity was, quite simply, his language, and could no more be renounced than any native tongue; but this did not mean that other languages might not be loved and yield striking new insights in the old familiar phrases and ideas. In a number of the Buddhist and Hindu teachers Merton met in Asia, he found holiness and a deep knowledge of the realities of prayer, and he was humble enough to listen and to learn.

It is often said that people are born and die in ways entirely consonant with their lifelong characters, and although nothing is known of Merton's birth his death seems to confirm this theory. It had an element of surprise, of drama, of unusualness, and even, despite the overwhelming sadness of his friends and brothers, a kind of black humour about it that fitted both the boy Merton had been, and the man he had become. The Zen masters formally said goodbye to their disciples when they knew death was imminent, and one or two, deliberately and cheerfully, lit bonfires when they felt their lives were rounded and complete, and climbed on them. There is no suggestion that Merton's death was in any way deliberate, but there is a sense that, like the Zen Masters before him, his life, after Polonnaruwa, had made a perfect circle and was complete. He had "seen through the shadow and the disguise."

INDEX